October Harvest

— *first part.* —

Magnus Aurelio

Copyright © 2024 by Magnus Aurelio

Paperback: 978-1-965632-11-6
Hardcover: 978-1-965632-37-6
eBook: 978-1-965632-12-3
Library of Congress Control Number: 2024919596

All rights reserved. No part of this publication may be reproduced, distributed, or transmitted in any form or by any electronic or mechanical means, without the prior written permission of the publisher, except in the case of brief quotations embodied in critical reviews and certain other noncommercial uses permitted by copyright law.

This Book is a work of fiction. Names, characters, places, and incidents either are the product of the author's imagination or are used fictitiously. Any resemblance to actual persons, living or dead, events, or locales is entirely coincidental.

Ordering Information:

Prime Seven Media
518 Landmann St.
Tomah City, WI 54660

Printed in the United States of America

Magnus Aurelio's Volume I of Complete Poems in English

Two translations (to begin with)

A Laughing Matter

England, blessed nation,
Queen of civilization,
her saviour, redeemer and finest fruit,
blessed be thy name forever,
let's lose your example never;
let's for all eternity bask in your splendid light's circuit.
Your light is universal;
may it therefore be eternal.
Allow us to enjoy it as long as there is history,
o God, for no one but you may grant us such pleasure.
O, offer us that leisure!
After all, without England, what would the world be but misery?
Whatever England does is right
history has proved with might,
and whoever marches against England marches against life.
Let there be no more such folly;
let this life be most jolly.
Let us enjoy the world in the light of England without strife.
England, have I lauded thee enough?
Let us then relax and laugh.

A Vision

by Gustaf Fröding, Swedish poet (1860-1911),

translated by request.

Hell was open to my eyes
full of begging voices and hoarse cries
for just a drop of water.
I heard voices stutter desperately,
despairingly, in flames atrociously
shining hot in fiery slaughter.

Glances painfully erring
for vain comfort stirring
in fights of desperation, -
Faces terribly shivering,
breasts in anguish quivering
in languishment and desolation.

Then one tormented rose
resembling to the devil;
his face was like a withered rose
with traces of pride though not of evil.

A faint light crossed his eyebrows,
as if again a distant dawn was casting
a ray into his lost and weary side-rows
of some kind of newborn daybreak everlasting.
And he said: "It is ourselves
who make our torments ache,
who nourish all those flames
that make us boil and bake.
But let us make an effort and forgive ourselves
to end our selfish woes and tribulations,
and let us always strive towards the future only
and not dig our trenches turning down and backward solely
just to find old grievous sins and shames
but instead get rid of all our introverted complications."

And gradually the flames abated
vanishing around the devil's apparition;
and how splendid was the sight
of everything becoming bright,
and how the fallen angel's brows elated

in a more majestic and magnificent complexion,
and how his lips began to tremble from felicity
and broke into a smile, -
it was as if a breath went through of pure serenity
extinguishing all flames of hell and guile.

(from "New Poems", 1894.)

(Since this translation there has risen a considerable
English interest in this Swedish poet, and there is now
a collection of his poems available in English.)

She

How shall I consider her?
She is too much for earth's desire.
Every manly heart must stir
and secretly admire
her wisdom's personality
combinded with beauty's modesty
in perfect unattainable respectability,
too much for men's morose brutality.
She calls for higher education
in men's hearts. Qualification
is her absolute condition.
Without that – no inspiration.
Touch her not with your suspicion,
for her honour must have recognition.

The enigma

I love
incapable of hatred.
I give and cannot take.
I live and cannot die.
I bleed
and can't stop bleeding
but cannot bleed to death.
Panic anguish is my only illness
and my elixir of life.
I languish constantly
but enjoy it
and cannot cease therewith.
I burn
but am myself the victim of my flames
and cannot be consumed
however much the pain thereof consumes me.
What am I then more than love and suffering?
– The eternal thirst
for more love and suffering.

Enter

I waited in excitement
since I hadn't seen you for so long,
not in six months
but still associated with you constantly
by your next kin
and ever more intensively
the closer your return approached.
How often did my eyes not anxiously
seek out the entry door with all the people entering
of which at any moment
one of them would be yourself,
a living legend,
who had chosen to abstain from life's good things,
all comfort and security
to live instead with focus on the soul,
the quest of poetry of beauty,
the expression of it and its creativity,
which path of hardship had brought you to cross my own,
as if that could be of any service to you.
That remains to be found out.
It is a double Via Crucis,
since when, as we meet, at the same time
and cross each others' destinies,
they both the more stand out more clearly
as more vulnerable in their critical condition
of only thorny difficult ordeals
of trials without end.

What is love? It is all that is good.
It is neither strife nor contention,
it never hurts but only blesses,
it only gives and bereaves you nothing,
it is one-sidedly positive and constructive,
it is what builds and never destroys,
so quarrel and criticism is never out of love.
It is creativeness of life
and the very essence of life
and all that it has to live on
and therefore so brittle and delicate.
So take care and nourish your love
as life's most precious treasure,
and the fundamental generosity of love
will reward you without measure.

The wounded tiger

I cry for pain, for love and for mercy
handicapped by the cruelty of fate
with no hope for my hellish infirmity
being a decrepit old fool
good only for drinking and doting
in abject imbecility
like a dying lion without teeth.
They say a tiger turns a cannibal
and coward man-eater as he grows old
having nothing left to fall back on
except the dishonour of his misery.
But mind you: as long as he at all remains alive
he still has the right to love
and can use that right to some advantage
since no one can make love like tigers.

The important but secret meaning of your dreams

The truth is not in what you dream
but in the meaning of your dream.
The meaning is a different dimension
altogether from all facts of life;
but dreams are in the habit of specifying them,
and that's the meaning of your dreams.
Most dangerous of all is therefore to interpret them,
for the hidden meanings of your dreams
are far too subtle for interpretation.
You must therefore feel with extra sensitivity
to get at all that there's a message,
and if you at all can sense that message
you can only grasp it by your extra senses
which of course defy all explanation.

The lover

He is not ridiculous.
He only suffers.
He can not reach her,
so he can not trust her,
so he suffers the more,
being persecuted by her memory

which torments him worse
than any shrew could do.
Is he then a self-tormentor,
or is she tormenting him?
The dilemma is that both are innocent,
which makes their love the worse for both.

The problem

The problem is not that you are different,
that we are uncombinable,
that I can do nothing to further your career
nor help you in any way,
that we are both poor like pauper orphans
and too strong individualists
to ever be able to join hands
in any kind of unitedness.
No, the problem is something entirely different.
The problem is that I love you.

MAGNUS AURELIO

Obsession

Sleepless nights of persecuting phantoms
dominated by one single constant thought
and worry about the impossibility of our case
completes the Via Crucis of obsession
which seems never-ending in its fever
of a roller-coaster turbulent persistance.
But this hell is thoroughly enjoyable,
a self-tormentor's paradise and perfect dream
of beauty and enjoyment in its total pain,
as if a victim at the dentist's did enjoy it
even with some lustful and delightful relish,
as if this kind of love was the ideal consummation.
And perhaps it is, since I don't know of any other
and since this one is for real and here and now.

My love, what can I tell you more
than that my constant piety
shows thee more care than it can show
since your delicacy forbids me ostentation,
making me afraid to even touch you,
flowers being loveliest untouched
and free in meadows virginal untrodden.
Can I love you more? Yes, constantly,
as long as I can share your freedom with you
and enjoy it in its beauty,
being able thus to make it grow
and constantly increase in beauty.
Can our love be more ideal?
That is the question,
but the answer seems affirmative,
since pious constancy so far
has only made it grow
in wonderful maturity.

Crisis

Golden dreams along with tears of blood,
that is your life and destiny,
to never feel at ease and never be in safety,
always anguish on the brink of death
unfathomably in complete despair,
to rise triumphantly on wings of glory

to redeem civilization
in abounding possibilities of limitless success,
a life of contrasts, hovering above the abyss,
always to look down and partake in utter misery
to never reach the safety of a peaceful home,
although nothing would be more deserved.
Hardened thus in stalwart wisdom
you can meet with any crisis and survive,
and crying out will help you reach your destination
of the final comfort of redemption.

My twin soul

My twin soul is like myself:
never to be pinned down,
never to be explained,
never to be defined,
all truth and therefore unspeakable,
too easily touched and hurt,
as vulnerable as untouchable
and as free and sovereign of heart and soul
as the purest essence of music itself
and as delightful in its constant flight
to ever-increasing freedom and expansion
striving only for what matters to eternity.
A relationship like that makes love superfluous
since it is so obvious in its spiritual sincerity
and therefore doesn't need expression
since the mutual golden dreams
are more expressive than reality.

We children of the stars think differently
and do not associate on trivial terms.
We need not fight and quarrel mortally
but rather dwell on wings of harmony
to constantly exalt our love
to nourish it in bosoms of eternity,
thus sacrificing trivial mortality,
postponing practical prosaic problems
to the peripheric unpoetic world
that stands outside our love's dimension,
this one only being of importance
since it gives us all the beauty of the world,
which it is our responsibility
to make its beauty universal.

The wandering mind

What matters lack of concentration
as long as you are free?
What do we have a mind for
if not to make good use of it,
and what use could be better
than to constantly apply its freedom
to the constant exploration

of the greatest of all universes,
that of pure spirituality?
So let me fly about
and all around infinity,
that is my privilege
as human soul incarnated with wings
to never lose my contact with eternity.

Be my guest

Welcome to my home,
my fellow nomad
on our wayward strayings
out of life and in it
to get out of it and over it
in toilsome search for any subtsance,
although there is not much in it,
being out of bed and having none of it
in crowded rooms of junk and memories,
of memories of junk and junks of memories
to encourage claustrophobia
and continue fencing in your soul
in fears of losing this your prison.
Sorry, friend, but there is nothing I can offer you,
except my poverty and lack of everything,
but be my guest and share with me my life
of nothingness and gruesome toil for nothingness,
since that is all a nomad generously has to offer
to his fellow straying victim of this nothingness.

I cry for you and don't know why –
Maybe it is just because I don't know why –
Or maybe I just miss you even if I don't know why,
since you are always closest to my heart
and I can never do without you
nor can ever lose you,
since I always see you all around me
closer even in your absence maybe
than when I am favoured by your sight
and presence, which forbids me trespassing
the delicacy of your feelings,
since I am the last to importune in love,
love being too much of a sacred thing

to ever being risked by any falsity.
So let me never importune
and risk us falling out of tune.

The musical mind needs discipline
since the musical mind is a cosmical mind
which therefore needs order and systematization,
or else she falls out of order in disorder
which would be the end of the music.
For sustenance music therefore needs some pedantry,
like Archimedes in his thesis, "do not touch my circles,"
since those circles have to be intact
in order for the mind to work constructively.
They must therefore be untouched
like love in her most powerful virginity.

Perfect freedom combined with love –
is that a possibility?
It must be, since it's a necessity.
I could never love you unless I was free
to do so on the ground of perfect freedom,
which alone could make my love completely free.
Love is threatened only
when it is inhibited
by bounds and rules and limitations
and confined to narrow corners.
Cornered love will bring forth violent reactions,
since love cannot be restricted
without complete revolt.
So therefore our love must be completely free
in boundlessness forever
just in order to survive.

De Profundis

Why is the world and times so dark?
The unrighteous sufferings of the righteous
cry unto the relentless silence of a God
who as long as he existed has been doubted
and for only valid reasons,
since he never has lived up to his ideals:
the crooks have always dominated the establishment,
while the poor and innocent
forever have remained in poverty and innocence
without the slightest interference
of any God of righteousness
who rather constantly has proved
a silent God of cruellest indifference
insensible to human sufferings
with no heart but a hard and frozen stone.
So what can we do but suffer the insufferable
and stand up to bleak reality of godlessness
in a most natural unhuman world of cruelty
and scorn it all.

Our naked souls

As souls we stand forever naked,
we can't dress up or mask ourselves or even hide
but must be just and true just as we are
in inescapable and utter nakedness
with all our lacks and wants, our wounds and sins,
our ugliness and loads of gathered vices, –
but at the same time, our true nature is exposed
in all its naked beauty,
which stands out incapable of being hidden,
totally undressed forever to its basics,
in which beauty there is nothing we can hide
of what is true in us
which nakedness is totally reduced
to basics of eternity.

The decrepit dilettante

My love, I am sorry, but I am no good for you,
just a pathetic old invalid and maybe even a freak,
who has done nothing good in his life
and produced only failures,
like one of those parasite amateurs
who only turned out professionals
working like hell for no gain
and succeeding at nothing but wreckage.
Still, there is something in this utter mess
which was worth something in its vain effort,
a kind of idealism buried alive
under failures galore of disdained invalidity:
I did it all just for love,
even if that love only was constant in this,
that it failed, being cursed and doomed
to forever remain as alive as unlucky.

We are the mutants
who change the world
without being seen or even noticed,
since the highest responsibility is invisible
and only can be handled with the utmost care
which necessitates all handling to be clandestine.
Thus we do not interfere nor disturb
but do our work in stubborn silence

just to get it done.
If we don't do it, no one else will,
and it must be done in order for the world to stay alive
and never stop its urge for life
which is its constant recreation.

You stole my heart,
but I did not object.
I let you steal it more than willingly,
so I suggest you keep it
safe, because I think it would be safe with you,
perhaps more safe than even with myself,
since it is better out of me
than burning out inside me
just for thee;
so it is yours
to blend with yours
in harmony of love
out of our minds.

How can I reach you
when you aren't here?
How can I love you
when I cannot see you?
Must we then rely entirely on just our souls
and their vague metaphysical antennae
just to live
and let our love survive with difficulty
on the ice of our frustration
brutally reduced to basics of our soul
in the supremest narrow-mindedness
of humiliated ashes of our fire?
But from fire rise the Phoenix
and there's our hope:
to rise again from ashes
triumphantly
to once again burn out and die
in mortal glory
more resplendent for its love than all eternity.

How shall I describe you?
In my old age I have reached my dotage
and want words to say the least
since I am lost and out of definition
out of my senses and of orientation

and can only laze bemused in gaga
thinking but of you in stupefied infatuation
like an idiot lolling out of reach
lost to reality and to translation
since I stumbled into some strange alien dimension
out of this world into you.
So here we are and can do nothing
but accept the facts and sort things out
and do the best of it with lots of work;
although love is a thing
that no man ever did succeed
in working his way out of.

I can only think of you with love.
I care not much for riches and own nothing,
but my heart and feelings are a bottomless infinity
of which I generously can afford to spend forever.
But what worth can all this nothing be to you,
all abstract without sustenance,
all air and spirit, wind that blows away,
perhaps to change his way and mind tomorrow
in another wayward alien direction?
Still, the wind of warmth is now in your direction
which irrevocable fact not any human history can change
and which I stand for here and now in perfect honesty
to spite all history that dares to challenge it or change it.

The Poet's Prayer

Let our life be only beauty
and let all things non-beautious be banished.
Let our life be filled with poetry
to such degree that nothing else but poetry may rule.
Let our lives be free from conflict and contention

so that harmony and concord rule alone.
Let nothing evil ever cross our path or brains
but may only goodness come out of our lives
and spread all round to our environment
and thus make every human being better
constantly and in continuos development
for all humanity and for the world.

Ways of escape

There is always a way out.
There is always an escape,
a crack and hole in every fencing wall,
a possibility to sneak away,
a way out to development from every prison,
even for your spirit to evade and cheat your invalidity,
since every fortress has a weakness,
all that stops you is in vain,
impossibilities are lies preposterous,
and life consists of only openness,
to which old brother death himself
is but another option.

The Irish argument, (after John Bede).

Going down the bleeding heart of Ireland
the depth of history reveals innumerable wounds
like of a raped mother,
since Ireland was christened long before the English,
who for centuries were arduously compelled to seek protection
against civil wars and barbarism in most remote and isolated places
such as Lindisfarne and Iona just to survive,
while Ireland was gloriously alive and making harps
committing all their life to culture and to music.
All we could do about Britain was to pity their barbarity
as they oppressed us in the middle ages,
occupied us and turned Ireland into endless civil wars
and slaughtered us through centuries
to crown their senseless cruelty by ethnic cleansing,
planting protestantic Englishmen in Ulster,
the worst thing that England ever did to Ireland;
and so we pitied them and even more
when they went into the Great War

partaking in the massacre of humankind
and of civilization,
at which point the best thing we could do
was simply finally once and for all to leave them on their own;
and thus we still continue pitying them today
but think they should be better off without us.

Questions not to be asked from the voice of experience

What do we know except nothing?
What's the worth of all knowledge but air?
How true is my love in your absence?
What dreams can ever come true?
Reduce me to basics and truth,
and nothing remains of what in me is human,
since all that is human and live is in vain,
just a hazard connection, a random engagement,
a blow in the air of a wind without trace,
just a normal nonsensical dream
to be easily obliterated at once,
like the puff of a long ago vanished forgottenness.
Is love then no more than the vilest of self-deceits?
Why do we love if not to be deceived?
 — Your questions, my son, are not to be asked,

since the answer can but be the infinite silence of nothing.
So love while you can, and use your love well,
and at best you might get some good poetry out of it.
— No, you are wrong, old man, I must object,
your experience is false if your poetry is all you get,
for if something is poetry, then there was meaning behind it,
and then it was worth it and can't be reduced any more
to anything less than the truth of your feelings' dynamics
of more universal commotion than all supernovas together.
— And what, then, is that worth, the puff of all novas together?
— Exactly, that is what I mean:
one moment of love and the shortest of dreams
is of more vital consequence than the Big Bang.
What shall we do with our love?
Is it compatible?
Can it be brought to fruition?
Is it at all possible for this idealism
to be brought down to normality
on this base earth of mortality
and without being debased?
Can our lives be combined,
or must we be like aliens
to both the world and each other
because of the purity, quality and perfect beauty
of this our magnificent heavenly love?
The questions are answers enough to themselves.
Our love has been brought to existence
and can never more be denied it.
It is, and it lives by itself
and must simply be recognized,
tolerated, humbly sustained and supported,
and not without caution, mind you,
but without reservations enjoyed,
and adored and consistently glorified.

We are one soul together, you and I,
but that I have already told you.
How, then, shall I vary this tremendous truism,
this self-evident manifestation fact of love,
this inexhaustible resource and treasure
of the most infinite energy and power,
this fantastic marvel of two souls becoming one?
My love is inexpressible, because it is too true
to stand a definition and can therefore never be pinned down,
like all true love, that is too vulnerable

in its delicacy to be comprehensible
to anyone except its two exclusive sharers.
So shall I keep silent then about it?
That is thoroughly impossible, because,
as Jesus said himself, if human calls are silenced,
then the rocks will cry instead, and, in our case,
even mountains, continents, the sea,
the sun and moon and all the planets of the universe.

My love, what right have I to call you so?
We must be cautious not to risk disturbance
of our budding plant the precious future
of a delicate and brittle tenderness
to constitute a sensitive relationship
of some uniqueness in its frail vulnerability.
So let me whisper only and in darkness
secret messages of love, the honesty of which
be proved by its consistent silence,
that in time may speak more loudly
and more clearly than the finest music ever played on earth
to shame all noise and falseness,
rudeness and disharmony,
since we in disciplining carefully our love
will be responsible for the most absolute and true
and beautiful and purest music eve played on earth.

Poetry is not enough
to express the ways of love
how it lures us to obey
blindly the atrocious way
in which we simply are deceived
beyond our senses far astray
into the wilderness of childish play.
I can't object. I am all for it,
lead me on, you are my guide,
blind goddess, since you are the only one
to know the better proper way
of how to make the show go on
forever without any stage to play it on
and without any stuff to build it on.

Longing

My longing overtakes me
every moment when my thoughts engulf me
like a whirlstorm of nostalgia
concentrating on but one thing in the world
which is of course Yourself.
If all this monstrous pain
and languishment of longing is not love
in honesty and utter purified sincerity, –
whoever possibly could think so is not human
or is ignorant beyond repair,
because no one knew what love was
who could not see and recognize its suffering.
All love is high-strung self-inflicted torture
of the most enjoyable and sympathetic kind,
since it is only true and self-denying generosity.

How many poems must be written
in order for my love to be expressed?
I am afraid my powers will not be sufficient
to fill up those volumes of infinity.
Or shall I say, that not the finest poem
in existence will do justice to my love
since she is far more perfect than what any art can be?
Or being human, she transcends all art,
since beauty is a matter of spirituality,
which therefore matter can not form.
So let's abide by that and with respect resign
from further effort to expose our love
and its true nature, since it is too intimate
to ever be unveiled to uninitiated eyes.

Let our love be secret
so that it be kept from insight
from improper alien eyes
that would not understand its wonder,
this fantastic marvel of agreement
and this harmony of unison and mutual understanding,
so that our wee newborn babe,
so vulnerable in her freshness,

may stay uncontaminated
by the envious minds of smaller fry
who would not understand how much we love each other
although we do never meet.
So shall they never harm you
since they can't identify you,
thus our love will be safeguarded
for its growth and sacredness
in limitless perpetualness
and blessedness for all those happy few
that happen to be touched by our love.

Discretion

The language of disguise and dreams
in delicacy and in understatement
is the web of poetry
in which each poet is forever lost,
since he has too much to express
and finds that cloven tongue of ambiguity
far too applicable to ever be abandoned.
Add to this a knowledge of a higher language still
in which the inexpressible find touch and tune
of higher than a mortal note,
and we can break all records of discretion.

Sensitivity

I don't think we can hurt each other.
That is my constant premonition,
which I think and hope is true,
because the last thing that I ever wanted
was to hurt a lady or for any matter any person,
so I rather kept apart, surrounding me in music
to keep out the rotten influences of the world.
It's like a smoke screen but efficient
for the spirit which needs most protection
and the more the higher your spirituality aspires,
since all feelings true pertain entirely and solely to the soul,
which is the only lasting essence of your life
which you were given by eternity
to guard it well and use it well
for infinite construction.

In despair

You have left me alone with my ghosts
and I suffer outrageously
being alone in this dark hell of nothing
with only intolerable abstinence to make me cry
out for mercy in ravaging agony
since I thought you were my friend
and you left me with nothing.
No love has bereft me of thee
and no love can now ever restore thee.

No love is the sinner and criminal
in this outrageous iniquity,
no love at all was there ever that joined us
but only illusions, pretensions and false golden dreams
of a love that was stillborn and fraudulent,
hopeless and vain from the very beginning.
I lived in a dream I imagined of light and of truth
and find me awakened in abysmal darkness
like lost and thrown out in the emptiness of outer space.
And my love? She is lost since she found all her freedom
which bound me in chains of her loss in a night without end.
May she do what she can with her freedom.
My life's only comfort is that I was sacrificed for it.

My love is health and bliss and happiness,
but without her I am a forlorn child
in agony and darkness of a total hell
of suffering and pain and hopelessness,
since I feel abandoned and betrayed
although I know not how I am deceived,
a blind man robbed of cane and dog
and left without a human voice to hear in all eternity.
And where are you in this abysmal darkness?
Surely you must be somewhere,
or maybe lost like me,
wherefore I feel your loss like if it was my own.
My love, you are inside me still,
and I have not deserted you,
continuing our secret conversations constantly
in soul and spirit ever stirring
in the faintest whispering of constant love
which though remains the only sound that matters
dominating and resounding through the universe
in perfect harmony and silence of discretion.

We hide ourselves in art
to mask our naked souls
that stand not getting hurt
by human common baseness
so predominant among the multitude
from which we separate in horror
to protect the frail vulnerability of our ideals
that all too easily gets sullied
and pulled down in dirt by envy
and the ignorance and shortcomings
of lack of understanding
that so dominates the world,
society and humankind
in constant and atrocious tragedy.
So we protect ourselves in masks
and hide ourselves in art
to do our best to make a good performance
just to spite vulgarity and commonness
and thus make show and play
to hide reality from view
and make believe there is a better world
if nowhere else at least inside ourselves,
if only we could be convincing
in the art of this deception,
which is all the world's constructiveness.

Nostalgic trip

Take me back to hippieland,
the promised land of happiness and joy,
where all were rebels and authority was dead
with beauty reigning sunnily alone with flying colours,
spreading colourfulness everywhere,
tainting all humanity in psychedelic splendour,
drowning noise and ugliness in music and of fantasy
encouraged by intriguing spices like of drugs
which only was a brilliant explosion
of creativeness and of imagination,
promising a better world for everyone,
for all the future and for all humanity,
with shining innovative dresses
and adornments, jewellry galore
with earrings and the longest hair in history
and no limitation to expansion.
So let me dwell there in the land of nowhere
everywhere in every age,
where beauty is the queen
and fantasy is law
and pure creativeness is all religion
with no end to tolerance and universal love.

Yet another poem
out of love and from my heart
to you, my love, in spite of all
the inexpressibility of our predicament,
that we fly high above the stars
and can't return to earth
maybe forever,
maybe since of ages past,
as if we always had each other
or at least knew well each other
deeper than the depths of any faithful heart,
since hereby our souls are proved in constancy
more permanent in faith than any life;
so let us just continue soaring
high above the stars
and be content to nevermore return
to mortal triviality.

What am I to ever think that you could love me?
This old fogey past his prime
is nothing but a wretched wreck,
an invalid who never lived,
a sorry and pathetic caricature
of a fool who always and persistently deceived himself
and lost himself to vanities of ephemeral dreams,
temptations without end and without sustenance
that filled my life with nothing except losses.
How could I expect, then,
that anyone could love me?
How could anyone be asked to love a dream?
You do not love it. You just dream it.
And when the dream is over, you forget it.
Some say you should fall in love as many times as possible,
have love affairs and even some engagements sometimes
but be married just for once or never
or at least as rarely as possible;
but I was married from the start
to the idealism of beauty and of art
and ended up this parody like some odd fart,

so just forget me: I was born a hopeless case
unqualified for love and life,
a dreamer and no more himself than just a dream,
for others no more than perhaps an alien
to condescendingly at most think kindly of at times.

The difficult mission

Our difficult mission is patience
with coarseness and rudeness,
with ignorance, negligence and lack of feelings
for naturalness, for the obvious and for religion.
Our problem is that we are wise,
which is a most unbearable responsibility,
since that obliges us to teach humanity
by our examples to grow and improve
as spiritual beings into something better.
Just to be and to work is our mission,
but just as long we just keep at it
maintaining appearances and our high standard of love,
the good news is in the long run
that we cannot fail.

Niagara

Whenever something happens
that enhances and speeds up your love,
just throw yourself right into it,
abandon life and soul and everything
and let yourself be swept along the current
even if it carries down the Niagara;
for what higher meaning can you find in life
than just for once allow yourself the privilege
and joy of falling down the ultimate extinction
of yourself in a cascade of splendour
in abysmal adequate abandonment
of enthusiastic life and love
in the exhilaration of consummate beauty?
Let yourself be brought to heaven
just by falling down as long as possible
the whole path of the Milky Way
to end up in another way
triumphantly with all eternity.

How could I else than love you
when you are like my own other self
but many years more young and beautiful?
How could I else but love you
when the whole world goes against us
separating us by continents and seas
and keeping us by force away from love and pleasure
by the brutal means of labour and economy?
How could I anything but love you
when we are the same and have the same ideals,
when we share both the same conception
of true beauty, honesty and sensitivity?
How could I resist loving you
when I am man and you are woman?
It is all too obvious. We need each other.
The only problem is that we can't have each other – yet.

One love poem too much

Can there be one love poem too much?
Of course not. Never. That's precisely the problem
that love can never be enough.
That's why you ladies never can be satisfied,
since you are only made for love
and love can never be enough.
That's why we men can never quite exhaust ourselves
since we can never give enough of our love –
the more we give, the more there is for us to give,
and thus the burden grows of what we have to give
the more we give it, and we have no choice.
We have to constantly keep at it, overstressed and overloaded,
since that is the rule of love that keeps us all alive.
The only possible escape is now and then to go away.
We have to keep on loving till we die,
and that is just a temporary and ephemeral relief,
since all that love consists of is eternal continuity.

Even though I leave you far behind me
and my life with you is lost,
I can't get rid of you within my heart
nor am I willing to.
Remain, my love, although just as a relic
like the memory of some capricious glimpse
of what perhaps could have been possible;
and such a faint momentum of a passing dream
will in its revelation all the same remain
a firmer base than any solidness
of the prevailing lasting permanence of our love,
which in its very fainting flickering flame
will loom much hotter and more fierce than any fire,
just because it's all about sincerity and love.

What am I to be a lover
and a rogue at that in exile?
Who am I to make pretensions
on any lady's love
much more beautiful than me?
Who am I to nourish wishful thoughts
when it is certain that they can't be realized
beyond a reasonable doubt?
My love is totally impossible,
but the more it keeps on burning,

inflaming and consuming all my life
in a wreck of worry, chaos and pathetic tenderness,
as if impossibility
was all it needed to transcend mortality.

The more I am alone, the less I am alone,
because there's always you,
like someone to watch over me in darkness,
like someone's company that never fails,
like some continuous dream in permanence,
that constantly remains a witchcraft
as protecting talisman and guardian angel.

Let me be your guardian angel from some distance
like you are to me, so that our permanence
remain constructive, like a marriage
but without or with no mortal ties.
Thus have I expressed our strange agreement
beyond words, without control and out of order
so that nothing in the world can keep us down to earth.

Evoking thee, my love,
is to cry out like from the end of darkness
on the farthest side of the universe,
but since my cry is pure and honest as a love call

it will sound throughout the universe
and reach thy soul by means of silence
since it merely consists of honesty.
Is our love a problem? – Only if we try to realize it,
by combining practically our lives,
which although match each other
since we both so often are away.
But this our silent love call will reduce all distances
and make us one in the dimension of those golden dreams
in which the souls of beauty are at home forever.

We are the happy few, the fortunate outsiders,
the most privileged among the privileged,
since we stand outside the vulgarity of mankind
and are happily excluded from all commonness,
the common lack of wisdom, knowledge and spiritual insight,
that most vital know-how of discernment, judgement and clairvoyance,
observation of the soul behind it all,
its movements of all-powerfulness
that is life itself and its main secret.
So are we not outsiders but insiders,
initiated in the mechanisms of spirituality,
while the real outsiders are all the others,
those who follow thoughtlessly the madding crowd
to death and without even having seen the truth of life.

Let me give you all my freedom,
the freedom of my heart,
the freedom of my love,
the freedom of life itself,
although that is all that I can give you;
but nothing is more precious
for love and its continuity,
there is nothing more valuable,
since there is no love without freedom.
So let us meet in this most senseless freedom
and join hands in love therein forever,
since there is actually nothing more to it
than just outrageous freedom
without any possible limitations.

I can only think of you as my beloved,
love is all there is between us,
nothing else is needed or of any matter,
since love covers all that is of any good.

No words are needed to express it,
no presence is of any urgency,
since we so clearly love each other
through all dimensions and throughout eternity,
so why at all express it, then?
Because it is so real
and therefore needs documentation
as some kind of evidence against base incredulity
and against that time of superficial momentariness
which claims all things must end and even immortality.

Passion without end, where wilt thou lead me?
Anywhere or nowhere but to somewhere without end?
Just lead me on, and I will follow
faithfully, obediently to anywhere
as long as your constructiveness keeps shining
like a lone star in the darkest night
and like a lighthouse in the hardest storm;
and I will sail in safety through the blackest rocks
in pure obedience following your call
naïvely and uncritically like a sheep
of purest faith and a good heart,
the shepherd of my faith and love who cannot fail me;
since I know full well that love will never fail
as long as you stay faithful to your love.

I can't believe that it is real,
that you are coming home to me,
but for how long this time?
What limitation do you grant me for thy keeping?
Will you escape again out of my hands
for new adventures with your friends,
for me just foreigners and strangers?
I am bound to you in love and at your mercy,
you will lead our dance, and I will just join in,
obey thy lead, adapt myself and sing thy tune
as an accompanist to your impeccability
and listen carefully to every hint you make
so that I never may step on your toe
in the delicacy of our pas-de-deux of love.

No one knows that I love you
and perhaps not even you,
or do you feel my trembling tenderness
vibrating clandestinely in the air?

I try to capture yours, but I am captive in my own
and can not separate them from reality,
while yours are based on tender memories
of facts of words that you have spoken
and that never can be taken back;
for words of love are valid for eternity
since they because of love are truth itself
and the truest possible of truths forever.
There we are, exposed and outcast to our love
which we as artists are to form into some kind
of lasting continuity, creativeness and beauty.

Your tears convinces me of your sincerity,
for tears are evidence of pure humanity,
tears can not lie, nor grief, nor pain, nor suffering,
but is the bareness of the soul in helpless nakedness,
which must be taken care of, comforted and loved
if, for nothing else, then just for being there a living soul
of bleeding openness and vulnerable to exposure.
Take my own soul in return, for keeping
and safeguarding in your heart like I keep thine,
and let us thus exchange our lives instead of rings
and keep them safely locked up in each other
like a secret closed to human ignorance and baseness
but forever free to anyone that cares
for universal and eternal good investigation.

How much do I love you?
The amount thereof can not be specified,
since that indefinite infinity is not to be defined
by any mathematical and scientific definition,
since, as we are well aware, that love is relative,
immeasurable, undefinable and even quite untouchable,
since there is nothing more supreme and sacred than our human feelings
which are sovereign to life and paramount in all existence,
guiding human life, embracing all
and breathing and bestowing life on all things human,
gracing and endowing it with beauty.
That is my confession of my love
which concentrates on you, my lovely woman,
putting you in centre of it all.

My love, is it weakness, or is it strength?
– This magic that obliges me to love you
senselessly and mercilessly,

ruthlessly against myself and you,
which is why I have to do it with restraint
and not let any feeling show to you or anyone
in order just to keep it safe
from harm, intrusion and exposure
to unqualified, unwanted and debasing eyes.
So am I forced to love you clandestinely
for how long, and to what unendurable direction?
No one knows; so let's just keep it on,
endure its heat with patience and discretion
and face the possibility
of never seeing any end to it.

There is no importuning in true love.
All doors are open – there is nothing to break down,
true love can never be enforced,
since its existence makes all force unnecessary.
Thus is even sexuality made superfluous
when love exists as all that matters.
Only one thing you must never do in love:
desert your heart and your beloved.
If she has gained access to your heart
you must not ever lock her out from there,
since spiritual divorce is an impossibility
and worse than suicide and murder,
since it is the soul that is involved and matters.
When your soul is the performer of your art of love,
and your soul has been taken in possession by another,
there is no way out in all eternity from that engagement.
You were married long before you even met.

Is music our self-deception,
the seducer of our lives,
that led us wrong into the blind alley of self-love
as addicted slaves in selfless and blind service
to the cruel insensitive divinity of beauty?
Doubt is necessary for our love,
there is no right way unless it is doubted,
re-evaluated, criticized and tried again for life
in constant re-examination and exacting scrutiny,
so that our love can overcome all obstacles
and indefatigably purefied proceed and grow
and spite all human baseness and vulgarity
to triumph constantly forever like a Phoenix
leaving everything behind that was not beautiful enough.

My doubts are not about your character
but about our possibilities.
How can love exist and thrive
in a world denaturalized and dehumanized
where ugliness replaces beauty more and more
and music is replaced and drowned by magnified noise?
Our love then is a parenthesis,
an exception from this world of baseness,
an ideal that is not seen as real
and can not economically be accounted for,
since money in this selfish world is all.
So how can our love survive,
an alien thing in this to love so alien world?
Our hope is universal love, which always saves us all.

My love of you is total.
There is nothing more to add.
I want to share with you my all,
my soul and body,
mind and universe
and feel your soul inside my own
in a mutual coitus more advanced
with no harm done to anyone,
no humiliation and no hurting
being both completely at a level
in a brilliant consummation
of the purest highest beauty
reaching higher levels than can be imagined,
fulfilling the marvel peak of life called love.

The clown's testament

Do not laugh at me,
because I am not funny,
just a grumpy fool on his way down,
my greasy mask decaying
mingled with the putrid mucus of my running nose,
congested into some kind of sour goo
just like my failure of a life
supposed to be a pleasantness to others
but which turned to only grief and tears
for this interminably laughing caricature
of a clown, who probably quite soon
will only have his last smile left:
the final scolding deathscull grin.

Turning a leaf

How can we stand this world of cruelty
where humans nought but run each other over
caring nothing, going blindly on as parasites
with self-love as their only guide,
the greatest ignorance of all
and the only sure way to perdition?
Shall we stand by and just look on this folly,
doing nothing to direct them to salvation?
Yes, my dear, I am afraid that that is all that we can do.
If they can't help themselves, then even less can we.
All we can do is faithfully to pursue
our pious diligence and efforts to constructiveness
and work in peace as hermits if we must,
and maybe one day they will see
the better world we built for them.

The eternal conflict

The constant conflict between reality and ideals,
the eternal opponents that never can make peace,
the dreamed of and the wished for is constantly transformed
to just the brutal unwished-for and self-deceits;
beauty never can accept debasing ugliness,
which always tries to drag down beauty to its baseness;
the soul can never become body,

since the body's course tends to corrupt the soul.
This war we just have to accept
as an eternal and interminable unendurable predicament
and fight it out intrepidly until we die,
with this sole comfort: that the essence of all beauty and our soul
in contrary to all the rest can never die.

Downfall and survival

My love, how can I reach you?
You were here expected long ago,
and suddenly then your arrival was announced,
and I was all on edge like some newborn and trembling deer,
and what an orgy of tremendous feelings and of love!
And then you didn't come.
Exactly everything was perfect,
there was nothing missing in our happiness,
except that you did not appear.
And now, what other end to this most awkward business?
Failure, capital defeat, a lost quest to give up,
just another total fiasco?
No, our friendship conquers all and everything,
in friendship nothing ever can be missing,
it is solid and more pure and valuable than gold,
and this, of course, we can continue building on
whatever happens and forever.

Rape –
poor comfort to a bleeding friend

Don't ask me how it feels.
You do not feel it any more when it is over,
but you bleed forever,
and the only way to get away from how it hurts
is to repress it and to stifle it with stoicism.
That will not stop the wound from bleeding,
but it is the only way to maintain your survival:
to walk through life on razor's edges
and pretend it doesn't hurt.
There is no medicine, you can not drink that pain away,
no drugs will help, and there is no escape.
All efforts to aneasthetize the pain
will be but vanity and self-deceit.

Just bear it out, and keep the anguish buried
although the spear will pierce your heart
in constant pain of this infected wound
that will not heal but was inflicted once
to only be renewed forever and a day,
like some life sentence for the innocent.

My love, you make me desperate
by keeping out of touch,
by missing our appointments
and by seeing that ex-lover of your past,
a periodic drunkard, who has lost his touch,
whom I don't know if he still has some claim on you,
while I for certain know how you love him.

An awkward situation? Not at all.
Just so typically feminine,
so desperately out of order,
so outrageously chaotic;
but this abysmal och dwindling darkness
adds but fuel to my fire's light
and makes me love you even more,
and, naturally, with even greater desperation.

A melancholic drizzle
fills our hearts with dampness
after wholesome shower outbreaks,
like your cloudburst of despair
the other day, which rent my heart in twain.
I will not ever hurt you, only soothe you,
comfort you and love you,
wallowing in the magnificence and generosity
of your dynamic heart and soul,
the richness of which speaks out clearly
in the lovely abundance of your hair.
Let me with my decrepit life
hide out and drown in that deluvion,
glorifying in your beauty's cornucopia,
worshipping and senselessly extolling
in the jubilant unification of our souls
in boundless and ecstatic love
that spites the oceans in its overflow.

In praise of folly

Am I mad to be in love with you?
Of course, but nothing is more important
than to be in love.
There is no other wisdom
than the folly of love,
and the madder you are as a lover,
the saner your mind, the higher your wisdom,
no matter whom you are in love with,
because loving for the sake of loving
another is all that counts,
and it can never be too much,
or even enough.

Everybody loves you,
but who loves you the most?
The fervent admirer,
who has had any amount of wives?
Or the fallen lover,
who desperately tries to forget you?
The old man,
who pathetically keeps his love a secret,
since he knows he never can have you,
or myself, who never loved until now?
You were only made for love
but for a higher kind of love
than what any woman can be loved by
mortally, since your essence is more than that,
your soul lying bare like your music
like the divinity of beauty
that only can be loved by adoration
at a distance to make it safe
from ever running the risk of getting defiled.

Is exhibitionism of love a folly, vanity or just stupidity?
The problem is it can't be kept under a bushel.
Love is only true when it cries out
resoundingly to make the world reverberate
and tremble at the genuineness of higher feelings
that in power easily transcend all worldly powers.
Love is more than just an earthquake,
more than just exploding supernovas,
more than just the alteration of world history,
since it is so more subtle in its clandestine vibrations

that can only be observed and felt and recognized
by lovers who are sure of what they feel,
who therefore can control this most tremendous force of nature
and who therefore know that nothing can be greater
than the fundamental heart of life,
which is the urge to just go on, expand
and gloriously continue with your love forever.

Comfort

Let me share your tears
and shed them with my own
and thus cry out with all the misery of all humanity
to purge the world in oceans of compassion.
Let me mix my grief with thine
and thus in some way maybe neutralize it
to provide a better platform for the future
not for us alone but for all life.
No tears are ever shed in vain,
they are the true manifestation of compassion,
and there is no compassion without love.
Let us not ever set a limit to our empathy,
but let it flow in tears to overflow all oceans,
let the generosity of our grief not ever cease
but piously provide a fountain for the future and for life,
for there's no better life than that which rises from compassion.

Josef K.

I am wasted, dead and buried.
I am all used up and spent, kicked down the graveyard
into the black hole of oblivion that awaits us all,
like some old skeleton without identity,
a skull of emptiness and nonsense,
worn out, burnt out, sorted out,
refused a hearing by all terminals,
forgotten formally, buried alive
without a gravestone or a ceremony,
for my love is gone, and I am left alone
a vacuum of loneliness,
a drifting satellite astray in space
without a purpose, like a lost cause in the universe,
doomed miserably just to wander
as a zombie or a ghost through darkness,
sentenced to existence in a limbo of despair,
for there is nothing left for me
but to survive myself.

Dream of Paradise

My love is like a dream of love
but all too true to dream.
She dreams of beauty and of love
but is too pure to voice that dream.
My love is like a perfect understatement
and without exaggerations:
not a word escapes her
that lets out the truth
about the width of this reality
that is a dream but carefully
and gradually come true,
like a momentous opening of a theatre curtain
that with the greatest care reveals but faintly
more and more of an unheard of heaven
that excels all paradaisic dreams
that ever could be dreamed.

You were never lovelier
than at this present moment,
and let it last forever
and continue ever to improve.
My love, you are the incarnation
of what's best with feminism –
the charm and wisdom of its motherliness,
its grace, ethereal aestheticism and soul,
and that for me is the most precious thing
that ever came across my troubled path
of what was so far only tragedy and toil.
My love, be free of me and of my past,
and let us only live that our love may last.

My love, there is no more demanding difficult ambition
than to strictly keep to doing what is right,
especially in normal close relationships.
So far we have done well,
but it has certainly been difficult indeed.
My greatest worry has been,
ever since I found myself completely hooked by you
or by my fate, the difficulty for us to combine our lives
mundanely, practically and accordingly.
Theoretically there was never any problem,
spiritually we are perfect and can never be at odds,
but how adjust this perfect spiritual consummation,
harmony and order, unity and kinship of our souls
to any normal and material, practical convenient life?
That is our difficulty and our challenge;
and the only means of overcoming it
that I can see is patience and continued self-control
in simply waiting for our time to come,
although that wait is the most difficult of all.

You are my morning prayer
like a symphony of beauty.
You are my awakening
to a reality more beautiful than any dream.
You are like the untouchability of sensitivity
that only can be felt and loved but never known.
You are my life
without which there is only death.
You are my responsibility
that I must always strive for and live up to.
You are my best friend and my only friend
that I am constantly conversing with
and even when you are not there.
You are my love, my love, and I must love you.

The Musician

A victim to her beauty and transcendent talent?
Many geniuses of music have been this, not only Mozart,
who was only number one.
Through initiation in a world of beauty
that transcends all others
the musician has a liable propensity
to more than others be the victim of a self-deceit.
Through his harmonious outlook
and capacity to see life through the temperament of music
she unfortunately can more cruelly be deceived
and on a much profounder level,
since her bid is more than just her life but even all her soul,
and if then it is being dragged down and deceived,
for instance by an opportunist or a life-abuser,
the catastrophe must be much more severe
than if it only was material.
Through his poetical and musical temperament
the true musician can but see her fellow beings positively
since her basic attitude is pure idealism
and so idealistic that it must exclude the contrary.
Thereby we have cases such as Schubert, Schumann,
Hugo Wolf, Tchaikovsky, Mendelssohn, Bellini,
crushed by the awakening from their ideal dreams
which but consisted of the highest good
and which could but be wakened by its contrary,
by what can only be described as mortal violation.

That is the dilemma of musicians: their ideal
can not be understood by those who do not have it,
they see an additional dimension and a life of beauty
which is cruelly denied by those who do not grasp it –
from ignorance, stupidity or just indifference,
which is the most stupid thing of all.
And still, in spite of so many musicians' personal catastrophes,
they are so much more fortunate and happier than those poor devils
who can never understand what music is.

The ideal union

To be free and allowed all freedom
while at the same time bound to the beloved;
without bonds and vows and ceremony
to base the union entirely on trust;
to be able to rely on that trust
and keep the line of communication open
always, no matter the distance or on what wayward journey;
that would be something of the ideal union,
but it would need some maintenance:
especially the constant presence
in thought of both parts in each other,
manifested in regular communication
by letter, by mail or by whatever,
even by telepathy would be better than nothing;
but could such an ideal marriage of souls be made real?
That is our challenge.

You come to me in flashes
like in occasional bursts of limelight
proving you are constantly ahead of me
although I venture to keep the initiative,
and thus our intercourse becomes a race:
who shows the way? Who leads the course?
We both do for each other, and that's the miracle,
as if we both were entering each other
and were each other's personalities.
I saw in you from the beginning
something of my own and other self,
I understand your thoughts and feel them,
and this must work both ways to work at all:
you must likewise be familiar with my mind
and understand it even in our separation.

Thus we two are one and cannot part
and can't be separated even by reality,
the petty physical preposterousness
which is called the universe.

Cry, my beloved, cry out
and let the world be cleansed in thy tears,
let the dirt wash out from the sewer cities
and let mankind be purged from her crimes.
What is all mankind's wealth and riches
to a woman's tears of compassion and pity?
All might loses its right and gets lost in its vanity
when the world is washed out by the motherly tears,
the greatest force on earth, since it is so natural
and gushes forth from the purest of purities,
the flow of emotions from the heart of the soul.
A man who cannot cry is a waste and doomed
worthless, since he cannot make his emotions work,
the only human force equivalent to any force of nature.

An intimate whisper

The beauty of the wind
that blows our kisses across deserts
to spite all distances that separate us
manage to conserve the freshness
of the tender wishes of our minds
and embalm those sacred kisses
in safe envelopes of sovereign protection
against any interference of profanity
to intercept the messages of our thoughts
to halt them on this way between ourselves
to settle after wayward journeys
in our hearts to there keep warm
and safe for maintenance and custody
in vivid preservation for eternity.

MAGNUS AURELIO

Deadly tired, sorted out and all washed up
I stagger blindly through the alley
blindfolded by life, like some forgotten addict
struck by sudden total hopeless cruel amnesia
with completely lost identity as a result,
completely devastated like some ruined zombie,
but whatever happened to me?
It was just a seizure, just a normal fit,
it happens normally to anyone,
there is no person so complete and perfect
that he doesn't quite occasionally have fits,
and I am just another one of them,
a mortal nobody, who every now and then
is good for nothing else than just to go to bed.

How much may I love you?
Let me never come to close,
to avoid importuning and trespassing,
but let me hold our feelings sacred
so that they may never come to harm.
Let me not enter except by your invitation,
so that I may love you ever but with care.
Give me the sacred office to maintain our fire
but with moderation, that it may not burn too violently
nor scorch, but at the same time never to abate
but just to keep us warm enough
to draw but pleasure and enjoyment from it,
so that it may ease construction
in our sacred office of creation.

How is our union to be best described?
An ideal friendship that could not be better,
clinically free from all the lies of sex,
a pure and sane relationship of constant growth,
a fair exhange improving every day,
a paragon example of good musical communion,
a perfect philosophical platonic intercourse,
an intimate concurrence quite impossible to sully,
and what else; but are we happy?
Yes, together, but when we are not together
I am only happy when I think of you.
Is thinking then a proper substitute for company?
It could be, if it works well telepathically,
which means we can always become happier.

Is it honest of me to withold my feelings from you?
I don't know, but I did it only from consideration,
that is, at any cost I wanted to spare you, save you,
protect you from getting hurt and not risk burdening you,
because you were free, and I wanted you to remain free.
So please be free, my love, and let me love you freely,
and you won't get hurt by that freedom,
since it is the highest freedom of love
that can't be valued, fettered or brought down,
I give you my freedom that you may save your own,
and thus my love is the more free and pure and honest
for my protecting you from it.

Love's true manifestation is no sexual act,
no carnal wallowing in sleazy sauces,
no material token, ceremony or vows
but faith alone, fedelity and continuity,
all that which does not show and does not boast
but rather hides in intimacy and precaution,
piously avoiding ostentation, keeping to itself,
safeguarding faithfully all that which does not count
in worldly measures, concentrating on maintaining life,
considering but that which is of vital matter to the soul,
which is the only thing that lasts,
thus being constantly on the defensive
to protect the worthwhile preciousness of love
against all mortal trivialities that drag it down
from highest holiest religion to profane perishability.

The junkey

The self-humiliation of the lusts of alcohol
resulted in a holiday at the resort for freaks,
the local funny-house, where everyone is happy
in disgrace, appearing nuts, completely without sanity,

a dried up drunk place, where sobriety is just a fake,
since everyone, as soon as he gets out of there,
refreshed and loaded with some monetary aid of charity,
immediately vanishes to drinking bouts again,
where soon he will again be picked up like a parcel
and collected by the office of assortment
that indifferently and automatically will return him
to his only constant destination and his last definite home:
the rehabilitation clinic, where he always finds his own,
the comrades that he shares his life with
and who understand him, since they all have nothing left
than for the rest of their degraded lives
in common share their constantly increasing damage of the brain,
which is the only thing they manage to accomplish
by abandoning themselves to self destruction
through the blessings of the self-deceit
of finally one day succeeding in
the quest of drinking one's brains out to death.

The possibilities of the impossible

Our impossible love affair is celebrating triumphs.
There is nothing at all compatible in our relationship,
no ground to stand on, no economy to build on,
no mutual material interests, no family concerns,
nothing but impracticability and thin air,
and still our friendship has never had a flaw,
we are as solid as a union as the universe,
and even separated we remain together,
hopelessly tied up in the ruins of our lives.
This relationship has brought us into something
like the world of surrealism, the chaos of impossibilities,
a hippie world of no order and no structure,
the complete mess of things that can't be organized,
and yet we live, and we almost stay and stick together
although we shouldn't since everything speaks against it.
So what is our case? To spite reality, mortality and superficiality
with perhaps an impossible world of love and beauty that cannot be defined?
Well, nothing could be worse than the mess of our past,
so let's just embrace whatever mess is coming of the future.

Presentation

I was far too old even before I was born,
and that is not the worst of it.
Suicidal already as a child,
three times I failed to drown myself,
and those were only my life's first failures.
My disappointment with mankind was total at eleven,
and how do you survive an intellectual rape,
which is even worse than a sexual one,
which conclusion I could draw after the experience of both.
I lost my family into an abyss of spiritual addiction,
the brainwash, self-deceit, tomfoolery and what not
of a capitalistic buddhism made attractive by science fiction,
a philosophy they called it, which ruined their possibilities,
so I just had to work hard all my life and earn nothing for it
since I chose the wrong professions:
the service of the muses, creation, knowledge,
the love of beauty, idealism, so I had to work alone,
protected against the ignorance and madness of mankind
by isolation in a hermit's one person monastery,
and thus I carry on. Is that a happy life?
And yet people envy me for nothing,
while I just keep struggling on,
a lover who is used to never getting anything for all his love.
- But as long as the band plays on, you can stand the music.
Let's just face the music and keep it going.
At least, with music you can never get bored,
so music of the right kind would be the only therapy possibility
for the hopelessness of mankind.

"The truth is generally beyond recognition, but never quite."

The truth is never what it seems to be
but much profounder, usually well hidden,
maybe even buried deep.
The truth is not for words or definition,
since there is no justice in defining truth.
How, then, are we to reach the truth?
The truth is what we feel is true,
since feelings never lie,
and you are certain of their genuineness.
The truth speaks to you from the heart,
and if you but can listen to your heart

you certainly will know the truth;
but even from your heart and from your feelings
this evasive truth is never quite complete,
you need to constantly investigate it further,
and you must be well aware
that you will never be quite finished with it,
since the truth is nothing but a lifetime work
which never gets completed.

Finally a piece of comfort:
when your heart is full of love and friendship
of that kind which is worth while and never shallow,
you shall know that is the truth,
while enmity and hatred, self-love and enforcement,
arbitrariness, high-handedness and other blind manifestations
that ignores the contact lines with others, turning feelings negative,
are nought but passing lies and bad dreams never to take seriously,
which you will see when you awaken to the feelings of your truth.

Longing.

When, my love, shall we at last come together?
When at last may I encompass you with all my love?
My longing has no end, but my comfort is
that all our waiting must have an end,
that one day we will meet completely
and join not only hands together
but everything that can be joined.
Just to live for that moment is joy enough
for an eternity or longer,
since that joyful moment is explosive like a chain reaction
continuing forever, spreading love and joy
not only within us but all around us.
So let us be patient with our waiting
and let our longing constantly increase,
if possible to multiply the power of our love forever.

When we can not meet, at least I can remember you
in words to substitute my tenderest caresses
sending them to you like sweetest dreams and prayers,
like windhorses, to bring comfort, joy and happiness,
although they are but momentary puffs of whims and wishes,
if you will forgive my fancy and capriciousness;
but in these miniature thoughts of my best wishes

are in spite of all my truest love contained
in wished for dreams of enduring embraces
and the sought for union of our personalities
on wings of music, beauty, poetry and loveliness
to bring us far above the mundane world forever
and to keep us there for our own benefit,
which welfare we should spread around the world
and impregnate all mankind with.

On such a rainy day, any love can rain away.
The tears you shed are not enough
to wash the skies from dreary clouds,
who cover us the more horrendously
with pitiless deluges of misfortune,
turning moods into a holocaust
that frets away all clarity
and robs us of our course,
that was so clear once
but now is all confused
in shipwrecks, madness, alcoholism
and complete macabre chaos
leading us into a dance of lunacy
that threatens to confound us.

How shall we survive?
I see no end to darkness,
even truth is clouded from our sight,
my love is drowned in bottomless despair
and doubts that exile me in limbo,
and I am entangled in the web of my own folly,
paralyzed by Aphrodite, who is laughing
at my awkwardness.
I ask and pray for mercy,
that is all what I can do;
and worst of all is this,
that you are in no better state yourself,
since we are one,
and your mind is the same as mine.

All your problems are your own.
That is, whatever happens to you,
that is your own problem,
which you have to carry out alone:
you have no right to burden others with it,
only you can solve it perfectly alone,

it is your own responsibility,
and that is all.
If you can get some help from others with it,
still the problem is but yours,
and you can never trust them with it.
Solve your problems on your own,
and you will be a free man,
free to have your own integrity to share with others.

Thy torment is my own,
the tears you shed for him are my tears,
and your life that he destroyed is my life.
Like yourself, I can not bear him,
and yet must we stand him
with the wrecks he made of every person's life
that he became a part of.
Must we be dragged down into an addict's tragedy
just because once someone fell in love with him
in blindness without seeing that his life was but a waste
and devastating to whoever came into his life
of nothing but addictice self-destruction?
Pardon me, but I will not have any share in it,
and if you will, that must be without me.

Any kind of love is transcendental

Transcendental love is too serene to be approached,
too sacred to be touched and too divine to be defined.
And yet, it is but love, like any kind of love
that cries for outlet and expression
and demands response and feedback.
Monologues are tragedies while comedies are dialogues
that carry forward and increases life,
while the monologist can end up speaking but of death.
So let us speak of life together
and extol in life's abandonment
and never give up dialogue,
the mingling of our blood in pious transcendentalism
and just ignore it whether it be spiritual or real –
in love all languages of love are all the same,
and transcendental metaphysics are no better and no worse
than just the carnal touch.

Insomnia

My love is like a sunrise
that never sets again
but just keeps shining
like a soul that never sleeps
but just keeps beaming
like some constant dreaming
turning life to an explosion
of not only energy
but of all kinds of creativity
and altogether a new life
of wonder and of joy
in almost a surrealistic way.
If that is how love works,
just let me love and never die,
and never let me even sleep again.

The misguided musician

What's his skill worth
if he only drowns it in booze?
For me, those musicians are false
who abandon themselves to addiction
and thereby destroy their own music,
that gift of divinity that they were given to cultivate.
That isn't music to me
which compels the musician to paths of destruction,
which has been the destiny of most musicians
that gave themselves only to jazz and to rock.
For me, music is only music
if it is enough pure and leads but to purity
and to a higher degree of spiritual clarity
than just sobriety from common drunkenness.
Music which tempts to abuse of narcotics and liquor
is not really music but merely sound abuse,
better than which any silence would be;
for the most true and pure kind of music
is that which can only come to you in silence.

MAGNUS AURELIO

Fly away

Come with me, my love, and let us fly away
on wings of music for a lovely day
that will outlast eternity and outshine all dismay
of doubts and tragedy and matters of foul play
that bring us down from heaven's lofty lay,
the paradise of poetry, where all our freedom, pray,
shall keep us and deliver us and stay
sustaining us forever and a day,
so that at last one day we may
perhaps turn over yet another leaf to have our say
of glory, love and freedom, beauty and a ray
of truth to safeguard all to keep us gay
like in a never-ending glorious month of May
to sing the praise of Mother Nature and for aye
to keep to Music, not to ever go astray.

Intermezzo

Just another poem
while I wait for you,
a vain outsider
who believes in what they say
when people make appointments
and who faithfully
is rather soon than late
and rather punctual than runs the risk
of missing someone who might come
and waits for those who don't,
and thus I have been waiting all my life
for ladies who have never come,
for answers that were never made,
but I don't care,
for I can wait forever
for my love if she is honest –
that is all that counts,
the only definite priority,
the first and last and only true criterion of love,
that you can trust her honesty,
so that you can yourself be honest;
for honesty is all that lasts –
one word of honesty is more worth
than a load of novels full of speculations,
since the highest proof of honesty
is that it, even if it's silent,
speaks much more than words.

The background lover

The less he is seen, the more he is loving,
the less he is seen as a lover, the greater a lover he is,
forced behind the curtain by experience
which has taught him never to be open with his love,
since no one is more vulnerable than the lover,
and nothing is easier to misunderstand
than true love that manifests itself openly
for those who are not included and not intended.
Bad luck has taught him the hard way
not to interfere with ghosts of the past,
of former lovers of his loved ones,
skeletons in the wardrobes like drunkards and addicts,

whose pollution of love remain a stain and pain forever,
for no wounds go deeper than aborted love.
He is thereby content with the lover's part of a protector,
a helper and creator of safety, a reliable friend, –
and that is perhaps the highest form of love:
a constant faithfulness with no pretensions
with no reservations and no end to its sustainment.

The Caretaker

Let me love you all,
you poor lost souls,
demented vagrants gone astray,
you homeless crying doting victims
of a fate that brought you down by violation
of which you were innocent,
you poor beautiful forever errant knaves,
raped virgins that are virgins still
since you were never willing to your rape,
philosophers and hippies, new age children,
addicts that were igonrant of your addiction,
drunkards that were never really drunk,
anonymous drug addicts, alcoholics, lovers
that are saved by anonymity and therefore can remain
forever on the booze and drunk as lovers,
beautiful young victims of perpetual ecstasy,
I shall take care of you and love you all forever,
for I am the caretaker,
the Orpheus forever singing for the living dead
and for the dead that never die.

Our love works on two different levels,
that constantly keeps playing tricks with us,
which is why you are so confused,
lost in the chaos of your subconscious,
where all you have to cling to is your memories,
the dreams you had that were so brutally shattered,
but which were constructive initially,
and their constructiveness remains
in your surviving dreams that never died.
Make me nourish them and make them live again
above all in your music, but make it twain,
so that my music may accompany you

along the path of life to the incessant glory
of the continuous beauty of the finest love on earth
which also is the strangest and entirely our own.

What are you afraid of? is your question,
but I have no fears but only worries and concerns,
and I see the only threat ahead in any materialization
of the essence of our union, which is purely spiritual.
I want it to remain that way, so that it can be free
to soar in wild dimensions in extraordinary heavens
and thus keep alive and inspirational
and never lose the spirit.
So I have no fear of flying
but alone of getting down to earth
in any non-creative way
that could result in fetters.
So let me be free with you,
so that I constantly can give you all my freedom
with unheard of dreams of beauty and perpetual construction
that we never may be tired of each other
or of life.

The Trauma

There is more to it than just your alcoholic cavalier,
his messing up of his own life and yours therewith,
the bleeding wounds that can't be cured as a result
and the tremendous instability, both practical and mental,
in which you find your wrecked life as a consequence;
and in this fatefully amassing mess you meet with me,
who only formerly has had as lovéd ladies
talented artistic beauties with an alcoholic burden for a cavalier,
whom none of them were ever able to let go.

My first love had for her first love a wild drug addict,
while the father of her child became a periodic alcoholic,
making a complete mess of her life.

My second found me to escape to from a widowhood
but told me nothing of two former lovers,
both completely irresponsible and violent,
who never let her go and with whom she made constant suicide attempts.

My third had been forever marked by her beloved alcoholic husband
with a wound that had been cut around her breast
and sewn with many stitches, which had cut her soul in twain.

In each of these three cases, they would never free themselves
of all those wounds inflicted by their husbands,
which cut more deep into their souls than in their hearts,
since they could never cease to care for them.

I ask you: Was it right? Did they deserve their fates,
to suffer from their men atrociously for nothing?
No, their failure to detach themselves from all those wounds
became a self-inflicted punishment for nothing.

Love must never be a punishment but a reward.
If I can change your punishment to a reward, please let me.

Old friends are not just like old grass
which always grows under your feet to trample on,
a nice reliable green which is there to remain
and always to return after the winter's ice and snow.
No, old friends are like necessary roots,
the most important thing in life.
And therefore we depend on our grass roots,
which gives new life when we doff our shoes and stockings,
walking with our naked feet directly on the ground
in wholesome closest touch with mother nature,
our life's origin, the dust which we invariably return to,
which is constantly dressed up for us in lushness,
all that friendship which remains to grow forever
independently on how much we keep trampling on it.

My love is like the glory of a sun-flower,
continuing her beams after the sun is set
like as if never there was any sunset,
while at the same time she outshines the moon
in glory and in beauty, like as if the moon was always full
and never went away to bring the morning.
At the same time she is like a garden full of flowers
that is always flowering and never withering,
since she is beauty herself personated
gloriously invigorating the whole world
with overwhelming perfumes of the moon's own charm.
But most of all, my love is here, and she is here to stay,
like music of the purest kind that never stops to sing,
and that is the supremest glory of my love

OCTOBER HARVEST FIRST PART.

Your tears are diamonds that cry for others,
costlier as pearls than any jewels
since they are not shed for those who shed them
but for others, like heart-rending sacrifices
not so much for charity and pity
as for empathy and pure compassion with despair.
That gives them, priceless as they are,
a lustre rainbow-like in splendour

that enhances in immensity their value
since we talk here but of human values,
human dignity, integrity, nobility and admirableness
that rises from the ruins of destructive self-decay,
the alcoholic's urge to get away from his predicament,
as if to burn himself out could solve any problem.

Madame Butterfly

My heart's own melody
is full of melancholy
like a butterfly in winter
lost in random alien land

of futuristic surrealism
that can't make anyone feel at home,
and least of all a singing butterfly.
But somehow my songs keep me up and going
since they only tell of my yearning
for better worlds of more beauty,
for closer love and warmer humanity,
for everything that enhances life
and makes it more endurable
for all those alien singing butterflies
that came into this world like from another planet
to use their brittle fluttering wings
to make even the worst possible world
come around from dead end troubles just to fly.

Reflection

You are the peace of all my wars,
the harmony that made disharmony disperse,
the dream that woke me up
from the intolerable madness of reality,
the sanity which suddenly replaced my lunacy,
the beauty that cleaned up my mind from dirt,
the love aquitting my perversions,
all the joy I never really had,
some relaxation to ease up my stress
and finally above all someone I could care for
to make up for all my negligence of life,
a beam of sunlight after lifetime darkness and imprisonment,
in brief, would I not be a perfect fool
if I ignored the possibility to love you?

My offer

I love you.
What does this fact imply?
Unsurveyable consequences.
First of all practical problems
of responsibility and action.
But everything is possible,
and I believe a love relationship in our case
could be based on our mutual demand for freedom.
For creative spirits, a stable agreement

could be based on and built on thin air,
since we both are wise enough to know
that in this life there is nothing more stable
than anything writ in water.
Our mutual freedom is our major mutual urge,
and that is what I have to offer you,
the only thing I think that we could build
some lasting love on.
For me, it would be mainly work,
for you, you know already
that I always wished for you
to further your own music
in illimitable freedom and expansion.

Somnambulistic telepathy

The only truth about the matter,
our only valid and important conversation
is our mumbling in our dreams,
the things we say while we are sleeping,
like some strange kind of somnambulistic love,
where lovers walking in their sleep share one and common dream,
which is the only truth about their most remarkable reality.
They dwell together in the truth of their ideals
which no one else can share
unless they find themselves in that same dream
which only can be dreamt by honest lovers,
whose transcendency of love is such a fact
that in their dreams reality becomes a lost nonentity
since all that matters is that perfect honesty
found only in that dream they share somnambulistically
in their sleep at night, and they don't even have to sleep together.

Philosophy

When words are not enough
there will be silence more expressive
than a thousand conversations
and a million symphonies
if that silence harbours feelings
and vibrations disciplined by thought
that tends in one direction

of creativeness and love.
Vibration of creative thought
is maybe the most potent power in the universe,
and if it is well disciplined at that
there are no bounds to what it may accomplish.
Harmony and melody is one manifestation
of that discipline, which brings a breed of brooders
who with their depth of thought are carrying on their shoulders
the responsibility for universal life.

Evening Prayer

Let the most beautiful moments of our love
transform into highlights of eternity
to light the sky of our lives in constant twilight,
the most beautiful and colourful moment of truth
and of light's sensitivity during the day.
Let the stars beam the truth of these moments
throughout all the nights of our lives
to endow them with beautious dreams
and of wonder that may outlast history.
Thus is my evening prayer for you
that the blessings of these lights may never leave you
but constantly watch over you like guardian angels
ordained by me for your protection,
that your sleep may be as wholesome
as your gentlest dreams.

The uncontrollability of love
which makes everyone mad about her
is an interesting phenomenon
since no one can control it,
least of all herself, the very hub,
the heart of innocence,
who casually observes the insanity around her
and simply cannot do anything about it,
having trouble enough to keep on the defensive
to ward off the clumsiness of the rude clouts
whose madness thereby is but added to.
How can I help her, since I love her myself?
All I can do is to at least control and behave myself
and keep my love in humble faithful constancy
to spite the madding crowding turbulence of love.

The twilight of departure

The twilight of departure is a sad affair
since there is no return to what is fair.
You leave behind what you are unwilling to leave
and move to unknown destinations of incertitude,
perhaps of tribulation, certainly of trials
to never know what you one day will be returning to
after your trials after an infinity of changes
of the world and of your character,
because you'll never be the same again after a journey.

But this is the test of miracles.
There might be something left for you that hasn't changed,
and that stability is proof of continuity
that outlasts time and change and mundane troubles
and may prove that after all, in spite of all,
your love will never change.

New life

A new life begins for us more difficult,
a life of separation and of trial,
which could be a training of our spirits
to be free and stalwartly remain free
in our minds within each other's souls
in faithfulness galore without an end,
but still there are some worries:
I can not protect you any more,
we cannot see each other daily any more,
we have to brace ourselves against an alien reality
and trust completely to our dreams alone,
but that is maybe our supremest strength:
the knowledge of the power of our dreams
against which earthly powers with their strifes and wars
amount to nothing, since all life
acknowledges but one authority
which is the constancy of love.

The Travelling Companion

You go with me. I feel you by my side.
It is not strange, since we are lovers.
We don't have to see each other
since it's easier to feel each other
which we do invariably
depending on our constancy.
Thus don't I have to miss you
since I know you better in your absence
when my senses can't play jokes with me
when I can concentrate on what you are,
your presence with me being so apparent
and the more the more in soul you are.
The more I love you for your presence
even in your present absence.

One might almost say you are the best thing that has happened to me.
This is wondrous strange considering your poverty,
in view of that I never was myself a rich man
nor had anything to offer you except my poverty.
But we are two old souls that must have known each other long
before we knew each other or were even born,
like as if our reunion in this life
awakened us to find ourselves alive once more
after a loss of life for many centuries.
My Indian princess - or are you Arabian?
Anyway, you certainly are not of this world,
just as little as I am myself,
but we have found each other
and can thus create a new world.
That's a challenge irresistible,
and I would gladly try if you are with me.

Come and fly away with me
beyond the clouds to surreality
where everything is just amazing
not to say astonishing and constantly surprising,
for it is a land of marvels without end
where nothing is predictable nor as you would expect
and therefore never can be boring.
That is my land where I live and fly
on wings of beauty and of universal love
that never fails me, since I only deal with constancy.
I give you willingly my hand
to come along as my companion and accompaniment
into my everlasting world of beauty and of music
that will never cease to soothe you, worship you and love you.

Now

It's only now that counts,
this fearful moment of so ominously constant truth,
in which we make our present and the future
and create our history and take care of the past,
and nothing stands outside this momentous intriguing hour
in which universal destinies are solemnly determined
and lives and fates stand not a chance of being saved
if they can not live up to the importance of the present.
Here you have me in your favour for the present loving you,
and honestly I pray to God that it may last forever.
That, however, is not in our power for the present to decide,
but let's at least be happy for the present hour
and perhaps succeed in keeping up our happiness
so that it might spite history to outlive time.

The Call

the muse to her darling

Come into my world, my loved.
Feel yourself at home among these beauteous people
who live only for idealism and golden dreams of beauty.
We live for a better world than this one, which exists,
a surreality which must eventually replace the low one,
that of barbaric materialism and egoism,
but we must not enforce ourselves but keep to patience.

Meanwhile let us cultivate our garden and our music,
all that is constructive and beautiful that favours life.
So shall we love each other to give birth to that desired future
of our dreams, a world of artistry and grace,
of freedom of creation and expression,
of magnificence, imagination and intelligence,
a contrary world order to this mess of politics,
this madness of control, manipulation and deceit,
this havoc of ambition, egoism and greed.
I offer you the contrary, which is the easiest thing,
a world of harmony and discipline and common sense
ruled only by the liberal divinity of love.

Trust

How much can I trust you?
I trust you with my life
for you to keep and harbour in your heart
forever, if you like,
for my life is my love,
and if I can not share it with my love
it is a waste for nothing
worth no more than nothing.
So it is better that you keep it
safe, from me, so I don't waste it
on what is not love, that is,
that it is better for my love to keep it
in safe custody for her own love
than it is given up on anything that is not love.

My love is like a thousand stars

My love is like a thousand stars
each beaming and conveying different aspects of our love,
each holding its own character and colour,
varying like the wave-lights of the sea
and flickering like the sunrays in it,
each containing a profound and mesmerizing mystery
of unknown depths unfathomable
and of stories whispered forth in unintelligible dreams
that never can be told, explained, but only listened to.
And every star of different aspects of our love
has its own solar system of immeasurable compass
of more planets with more life than can be counted,
each inviting to new worlds of vast discovery,
and thus, to our love there can not be an end.

Missed

Missing you is like confessing to a crime.
I must plead guilty - without any reservation.
There is nothing I can do about it
since I cannot get you here
except by wishful thinking
making up your image in my dreams
wherein I still can love you passionately
without any reservations,
and you are not even hurt or importuned thereby.
That is another freedom, but of no avail,
just as to cry is nothing much to boast of;
but the truth about the matter is,
that since I miss you earnestly
I also must needs love you earnestly.

Love and friendship

The freedom of our love is maybe its responsibility
and finest trait and fruit, since it is based on trust.
That maybe summarizes the whole thing:
longevity of love is friendship,
and where friendship lasts, love certainly will grow.
The deepest love is not just passion but affection,
and where this is stabilized, established and well founded
love becomes synonymous with friendship and self-evident.
Those who really love each other need not talk about it,
they just stick together like old friends
in consistent and continuous communion
that cannot easily be interrupted
even by the longest momentary separations;
for when two souls find each other and united into one
that union cannot be more perfect
in transcendence of all vows and bonds and worldliness.

Poor comfort

A poem is poor comfort
for the absence of your love,
but still, it gives a hint
of the beloved's soul and presence,
and, what's even better, it remains

and is no lie
but deep and heartfelt honesty.
The poorest substitute for love
is flesh without a spirit,
carnal satisfaction without faith,
while love is so much more than that
and maybe truest in immortal lines.
I claim no such immortality
but am content with simple honesty.

Black holes

In darkness shines the light of love,
a truism, but of some severe significance,
because the light is threatened by this darkness
constantly, and darkness is, as Plato found,
much greater than the vulnerable light.
The darkness is unfathomable in its depth,
and this unendingness of dark holes in the universe
is ever like a terror, since it cannot be defined.
It just exists as an eternal threat
against the twinkling smallness of the light,
which never can, however, be put down.
That is the magic of the miracle,
that this eternal overwhelming darkness
always is defeated by the tiny light.

In servitude

We are custodians of the muses,
bound by them in lifelong thralldom
to create and propagate their beauty
fettered by their inspiration
to produce and serve humanity with joy,
while we remain unthanked in poverty.
Thus is our destiny of unfair destination
to toil alone against the mainstream,
pioneering to create a better finer world
against the ignorance of that majority
that never knew the muses really do exist,
while we are left without a choice
but stubbornly to struggle on,
our only real reward just being
our association with and knowledge of the muses.

OCTOBER HARVEST FIRST PART.

Protest

I love you telepathically
more than anything on earth.
In view of violent storms over the mountains
sweeping villages away and breaking up communications
ruining the lives and homes of farmers,
I can not endure this monumental foul play,
separating us and ruining the world.
My passion is destructive against this injustice
crying out in horrible despair
protesting all my love
against all the dark forces of the universe.
My only comfort is
this solace of a fact
that our love will manage this
and stalwartly survive
to spite all the destructive powers of the universe.

Love by candlelight

May I call you my love, my lovely?
What a shameful and presumptuous question!
I call you names without asking
and ask your permission afterwards
when the importuning already has been made.
What a shameful and unabashed conduct!
It just fell on my mind in this candlelight
in a purely romantic and natural mood
to call you that name which forever is yours in my mind
and which sometimes demands some expression.
So forgive me my bold importuning,
but let me just whisper that name in your ear again
with full guarantee that you only may hear it,
of names most misused but also most honest,
my love.

In the hopelessness of natural catastrophe

In the hopelessness of natural catastrophe
my only comfort is to think of you
with tears of sorrow for all those who lost their homes
but all the more for missing you.
My life is split by hard responsibilities
for work, for people and for you
while my most practical sport,
my greatest pride and pleasure
is completely to ignore myself
to concentrate on what is more important,
that is my responsibility and love.
So I beg you to forgive me
if I sometimes must neglect you for responsibilities,
but be aware that they are only there

A confession

What is a lover without stains?
My greatest fault, if you'll forgive some straight confession,
is my incredulity and doubtfulness -
I never could believe in love nor trust a lady,
letting my love be corrupted by mistrust and jealousy
for nothing - it was maybe that old green-eyed monster

which appears whenever love appears as its back side and contrary,
but fortunately I could always well control it,
piously preferring self-inflicted torture to myself than hurting others;
but the worst was always the incurable and persecuting doubts
which usually, unfortunately, proved too true.
Thus every love-affair I had was ship-wrecked
on the shoals of doubtfulness and hard reality,
my love surviving only in my lonely ruined heart
in constant fickle hope of better luck next time.

Some health sign

There is no surer sign of your good health
than that your mind is free and wanders easily
on wings of music or imagination and creation
without being fettered to concerns of the corporal body,
pains and aches and worries, hypochondrical superficialities;
because your mind, your soul and spirit and identity
was born and incarnated free,
and nothing ever should obstruct or sabotage that freedom,
which is your insurance and your only guarantee of health.
So there, my love, I earnestly beseech you to keep free and well
so that I never may stop loving you,
so that we always may be co-dependent on each other's freedom
and protect it, safeguard it and cultivate it
so that our creativeness may never cease.

Wishful thinking

Powerless and awkwardly bereft all strength
I cry to my beloved from the depth of darkness
and despair to in my languishment evoke a dream
that maybe still remains of perfect love,
a perfectly ideal relationship and union of our souls
in prayer for humanity and all that madness
that so desperately governs this so aberrated world;
but our love can save it, and that is my dream.
No darkness, no atrocities and no demented violence
can touch or violate this dream,
since our love is sacred
and a wonder at that too.
So let us pray across the borders of our separation
to redeem humanity with our love and with it all civilization.

Nature

The overwhelming character of nature
is something that man never can describe
nor live up to, grasp or even understand,
since nature ever is man's total master
against which man ever has to fail
in awkward and pathetic, constant and ridiculous defeat;
since man must ever in comparison with mother nature
stand a miserable naked lost and stolid child.
The greatness and the wilderness and power of Dame Nature
must constantly reduce the vanity of man to nothing,
and the only way to tame her and co-operate with her
is to respect her sovereignty and accept her terrible supremacy
in self-humiliation and to never try to challenge her;
for she alone has sense to know what life is all about.

Constancy

I send you constantly my love.
I don't know if you feel it,
but my constancy is well enough for me,
and I believe, as long as this my constancy is true,
you also with your intuition will be faithful
to the beauty of our union, this our friendship,
which must be considered something of a strange coincidence,
a kind of fortunate release from previous traumas
and a platform for the future to create and build on.
I feel our relationship is perfectly constructive,
we have never hurt each other yet,
and, as I said once previously, I don't think that we can.
So, what else is there to do but to continue
this persistently constructive glorious constancy?

OCTOBER HARVEST FIRST PART.

Gratitude

So far my love has been acceptable to you,
and I am grateful for it.
Take it as an offering of humbleness
and gratefulness for that this love is possible.
Some say I fell a victim to the cruellest women
who only taught me the impossibility of love
of their own hard experience, hardened nature,
hardened pride and arrogance, which only taught them self-love;
but with you somehow true love was suddenly released,
a new amazing possibility was found in beauty's orchid bud
of honesty and sensitivity, of wisdom coupled with extremest intuition,
and I was released from lifelong dull imprisonment of no love.
So what else can I then offer you but my sincerest gratitude,
that I may love you and that you receive my love.

The lover

What is a lover? Someone to be alone with
on your own, to dream about when he is absent,
to always have him handy as a trust
to be able to rely on completely
and to be certain of, whatever distances and absences;
a friend to be at one with always when you need him
even when you cannot reach him,
to always think about and live with in your thoughts,
another ego of your own, to be able to respect
and to never fail to honour, sure of trust,
since you know for certain about a lover
that he never fails you.

In the night

(The headline of this poem came from Robert Schumann's piano piece with the same title, which could be listened to as an appropriate accompaniment to these troublesome lines:)

When in the sleepless night I think of you
and worship you the more for all my torment,
nothing can more strengthen me in my conviction
in my faith in you for all your absence
than the fact that you light up my sleepless night
and turn it into harmony, security and welfare.
Is it maybe that you seek me with your ghost and mind
like I seek yours, heroically spiting distances
and lacks of any urgently desired means of straight communication?
Certain is the fact that my unsettled ghost is out and hunting
desperately for your contact by whatever means.
Thus maybe we can meet in spite of all
as lovers somewhere beyond this constrained reality
to there unite and stay united without any more constraint.

Regretting love

A strange theoretical question arises:
has anyone ever regretted his love?
I must say that everything speaks for a 'no'.
I never found anyone anywhere,
not even in all world literature and our history,
who in whatever preposterous way has said:
"I regret that I ever gave my love to her (or to him)."
Are there any exceptions? Not even poor mothers of criminals
have to my knowledge regretted their love of their lost ones,
not even the raped victim can fail to feel some compassion
for the most condemnable of all transgressions.
Nor even can I regret any of my many moments of love,
not one single of them, although God knows
they all cost me more than I could ever give.

An opening

How do you want our relationship?
Sleeping together or just neutral friendship?
Whatever you wish, I will grant it
with no reservation, as far as I can.
If you still are a virgin, let's keep you that way,
if that is your desire - I will never trespass you.
If you want children - let's postpone that question until we get started.
Of course, you'll prefer your vocation and work,
which, however, does never exclude love but rather demands it,
like I have my duties and hopeless condition of workoholism.
We are flexible both and can compromise infinitely,
since that is one of love's many miracles:
suddenly impossibilities turn into practical feasibleness,
all doors open, all locks are unlocked, and the only thing left
is an endlessness of opportunities and possibilities.

My care

It is so long ago I wrote a poem to your dedication,
not because I have forgotten you, but from neglect,
confused by crises on my journey which upsets it
all the time and throws me in the doldrums
of exasperation and despair, disheartening me
to the point of no return from the black hole of desperate defeat.
But you are there still somewhere way beyond the rainy clouds
like some ethereal dream of something better than my ruin,
like a promise of some sunshine after all
when all these desperate accursed rains have passed away
and left us with the ruins of a wrecked country
dismally transformed into a havoc just for nothing,
for the weather play and waters to destroy our lives
and throw us deep into depression - and for what?
I just don't care, since you are there, which is my better care.

the trekker's nightmare

Leaking tents

It's not just that it's wet and dreary,
but it's freezing cold as well,
and there is no way to get warm
in soaked blankets and with drippings
following you mercilessly in whatever way you turn
to helplessly escape the cold and pouring streams
that find their way wherever you have something sensitive,
like papers, books, your camera, your toilet paper,
and whatever that can not survive a touch with water
will be sought out by the waters of the leaking tent
to cheer you up and force you out of bed with an umbrella
sitting upright all the night in freezing cold
until the rain stops, which it never does.
It could be worse, though. Drippings only torture,
but if something happens to the ground and waters move it,
you'll end up in a flood of mud and never wake up any more.

Another cup of tea

My love is like a cup of tea
that never can be finished
but is amiably replenished
every time you finish it,
like a perpetuum mobile,
for thus works love ad infinitum:
there is nothing in the world to stop it,
no one can get through with it,
it is the most unsolvable of problems
that demands a constant entertainment
to be carried on to the delight
of those who never tire of the sport
but live just for the exercise
of love's eternally miraculous expansion.

Rest

Rest with me like I will rest with you
on an exquisite bed of flowers made for you
made softer by the gentle touch of our delicacy
and richer by our lengthened dreams of sweetness

that have the strange habit to be constantly prolonged
into interminably unsurveyable continuations
like a novel or a symphony that never ends
but just continues to develop and expand
into more wondrous and delicious new beginnings.
But from this constantly developing and never-ending epic
we need pauses, – so, my friend, come, rest with me
and I will rest with you, and thus, we shall sleep well together.

Falling stars

Who needs a constellation of the Virgin to depict you
when the starry night presents the entire Milky Way
for a sufficient illustration of your bounty,
of the depth and richness of your soul
and of your overwhelming beauty,
which I can lie comfortably on the ground
just staring at it, meditating over it forever
while I count the stars that fall,
each one as one more stroke of luck from you,
each one another ray of light and message from the Milky Way
of grace and love and kindest thoughts from you.
Thus do we communicate in flashes,
fast but absolute and without end,
each falling star conveying this important universal message
of the interchange of love between all constant lovers.

The artist's dilemma

He can but create alone and must have solitude
for concentration, focusing and freedom from disturbance,
which makes him an alien and must affect his natural relationships,
at worst distorting him into an antisocial personality,
a monster and a freak, incapable of natural relationships,
quite often winding up in sado-masochism and tragical self-torture,
like a monk stuck in a dead end of exaggerated discipline.
But if the artist leaves this perilous self-centredness,
he risks his contact with the muses, his creativeness, his soul,
or that is what he thinks. What he must learn is compromise,
which always solves all problems, the supreme necessity,
for no one can do without love, and no one can do without company,
the muses often hide behind your friends and speak through them,
and, most important, love is never only for yourself.

The glow of love

The glow of love remains and never fails
but keeps on warming our hearts,
refilling constantly our energy of fire
that seems never to burn out, but on the contrary
continue to expand its warm intensity,
as if our love just kept on constantly renewing
its amazing strength and lasting continuity.
Thus keep my verses all the time repeating
that same story that seems never to grow old,
that love is ever young as long as it remains
and never can get older than its summer freshness
just as long as it just keeps on burning
without ever burning itself out,
its glow renewing and continuing to warm our souls,
the more our love keeps on consuming us.

How can you love me?

How can you love me?
I am like a satyr beyond recognition,
masked, disfigured and corrupted by a goat's beard,
behind which I hide a face completely ruined
by old age and many decades of foul living
summing up a despicable failure of a life
that never any woman could accept.
Thus am I burnt out by a self-consuming fire
shattering persistently my soul and body
with self-torturous outrageous pain and longing
just to be with you, my heart's desire,
that I well know I might never reach,
since you are all that I am not.
And still, my hope keeps me right on that crooked path
of blundering and foundering in pursuit of that dream
of one day maybe despite everything reach any kind of love,
with you, just you, and never anybody else.

Longing

Just let me sleep with you and be with you,
adore you and caress you in my dreams
in perfect gentleness and softness
without any humdrum trivial matter to disturb us,
only you and me together in a dream that never ends
which I must dream alone without you,
calling for you in my desperation of relentless sleeplessness,
with only the minutest glimpse of hope and comfort
that I know that you exist and after all may still be faithful
to the beauty of this dream we have together
which I pray we one day never shall wake up from any more
since that is all the truth we need to keep on living:
this illusion of a love that might be some kind of reality
and in that case so much more important
than that cruel reality which keeps us separated.

On his illness

When in a crisis situation my health fails me
and I crawl decrepitly on all fours to clean up my devastation,
the annihilating horrible reality of my incontinence,
I can but cry in misery about how utterly unworthy I am now,
an ageing clown no longer in control and charge of his own body,
maybe the beginning of a lifelong downhill degradation
and humiliation leading down into some black hole
of the final tragedy, the inescapable defeat,
the ruin that awaits us all in the conclusive demolition
of our life, all that we lived for, our identity and personality
and even all our memories, experience and deserts;
but one thing must remain untouched by all this misery,
and that is love, of course, untouchable, serene and incorruptible,
which on its own alone shall ever conquer all
that ever even tried to bring it down.

Just another one

My thoughts are constantly with you
incapable of leaving you,
keeping pious company with you
as a desired guardian angel
of my own construction and imagination

but nevertheless and even more
for you the faithfullest protection
replenished with the piety of all my love.
Thus keep I burning for you
willingly and ardently with all my love
to keep you spiritual company at least
in the regretted absence of your presence physical;
but something tells me that in love nothing is more important
than the piety and faith and will to love
and the ambition never to forsake it.

Budding miracles

Do you feel it when I love you?
Do you feel my tenderly caressing thoughts,
my wishful thinking dreams of total generosity,
my universal well-wishing for you,
my total honesty in universally wide opening my heart for you,
my over-self-indulgent love for only you?
Our love is like a flower opening her buds
to gradually reveal her secret and undreamed-of glories
one by one in careful calculated portions
never to completely bluntly throw it all wide open
but instead to open up forever more and more
and without ever ceasing this expanding process
and to never close it. Thus our love continues an expanding miracle with
no end to its possibilities, its wonders and its beauty.

Journey's end

What does it matter that my journey goes so slow,
outrageously fatiguing and annoying
in its horrible monotonous and trying toughness,
when, as luck would have it, you are there to think of, who enlightens it,
who follows me on my outrageous wanderings
and keeps me on my feet when I should fall,
succumb and give up to the pessimism of my misfortune,
being constantly with me and in my prayers
as my indefatigable guardian angel.
You not only keep me going on my feet
but keep me flying in the air above the clouds
to even more ensure my safety and my good arrival
in your arms at this precarious journey's end,
which is, in fact, the only thing I ever left you for.

The Himalayan Symphony

Do you hear the hills resounding with this glory
of our symphony of triumph, glorifying all the beauty
of the world, of all the freedom of Dame Nature,
of our harmony and love? Thus sings my heart for joy
and hovers without bounds among the highest mountains
just to sing the praise of all the beauty of this world,
of you, our friendship and our love.
What matters the extremest separation in a case like this,
when love just frees itself from all the confines of the world,
of all mortality, of matter, space and time
to just exist in glory, flying clear above all vanity,
and gloriously enjoy the highest, purest music,
that of perfect silence in eternal stillness,
the sublimest music of the soul,
transcending heaven and eternity.

Riding the whirlwind

My love is flying on wings of fire
never to rest but to always continue
forever ahead to new continents of exploration,
a nomad and rover and wanderer,

OCTOBER HARVEST FIRST PART.

restless incurably like the wild wind,
but the freer for being without any bonds
or without any will that in any way can tie her down,
since she is only love; and love cannot exist
and survive but as free as the whirlwind;
and no one can tame love except he who rides any whirlwind,
the highest, most difficult and most advanced of all sports,
but the only one worth all the painstaking trouble,
the ultimate art, which the effort of conquering
only is its own reward, and the finest as such in existence.

The fugitive's homecoming

(The worst trauma of any journey is usually the cultural shock that awaits you at home...)

What business has the fugitive at home?
He can not be accepted, no one wants him,
there is nothing for him to come home to except loneliness
and strife, his family ignoring and despizing him,
the basis of his unacceptability, the ruin he was born to,
his unfair predestination to a lifelong punishment of exile,
scarring him with unjust stamp of prejudicial doom
for no specific reason other than his personality
that somehow seems too much out of this world;
and yet, he has to eat and sleep and live and labour somewhere
somehow, and that is his only rescue: he can work;
and if that personality is such that all his work can only be creative,
all the better, then he will have some support and backbone in eternity,
and all he has to do is obstinately to work hard with his creation,
and he will be more triumphant after death than any mortal conqueror.

The bleeding heart

There are wounds that never heal,
and worst of all are heart wounds
that must bleed forever most profusely
until the frail heart has wasted all
and broken up in pieces of her scattered sorrows.
Heart wounds do not bleed themselves to death
but rather cry out their indulgent inundation
until that poor heart, the tender fountain, is dried out
and cannot keep on crying out the tears of blood
since they have drowned and dried up
in her wasting devastating pain and sorrow.

So if you meet with a mother who can shed no tears,
forbear with her, because she has been crying
all her life and only tears of blood and has none left to cry
since she is only waiting for her heart
to finally break up in mercy.

Lost souls in the abyss of spirituality

We found each other in the abyss of the soul,
both stuck in that black hole, the worst of all,
a bog of no escape, a swamp of wet sentimentality,
a well of feelings without any end or bottom to its darkness,
the most hopeless and incurable of prisons;
but in those black depths of utter darkness
there is that which keeps us going and alive
in different dimensions in another better world
of sensitivity, prolonged antennas, extra strange phenomena
like vertigo existence out of normal order and our bodies,
telepathic qualities and other weird stuff just for freaks,
which makes us freer, actually, in this our prison of the soul
than all those who are bound by opposite impediments,
like property, a house and car and junk and practical responsibilities
that fetter them to the most desperate of chain gangs called mortality,
which is the ignorant majority of all this miserable poor humanity.
So what have we then to complain about? As outsiders
we are completely free from this outrageous mortal coil,
and in this perfect liberty which gives us wings
we can just go on flying and forever and together.

Reunion

Our difficulty is not with ourselves
but with this alien world of ignorance
which fails to see and recognize the obvious,
all the beauty, sensitivity, nobility of soul and mind,
all the refinement which you can turn life into a work of art with,
if you only leave barbarity and coarseness,
rudeness and vulgarity behind with all destructiveness
and live for love alone with its constructiveness.
It pains my heart to see you suffer in this climate
of a barren Nordic stale and hard mentality;
for your so tender heart of gold that easily cries blood
can never be adjusted to this grey society of stony hearts
that hide behind a mask of an infallible bureaucracy
that never can do any people any good.
But take it as a challenge: we can make this desert flourish
if we only stick to love and use it well.

Poetry enthroned

There is no need for any other law than poetry,
make her the Queen of all existence in her everlasting glory,
that must outlast all that junk called vanity and ugliness
which only show up in this world to pester and pollute it
for no other good than tragedy,
the trap which all humanity so enthusiastically marches into
fooled by the deceivers of short-sightedness and fickle profit
for which sake man drowns himself in any madness and insanity
most willingly - and hardly sees himself through even afterwards.
But poetry remains, with beauty and idealism as champions,
the last romantic hero isn't even born yet and shall never be,
for they belong to Poetry's and Beauty's court of everlasting light
and can't be even tempted from their sovereignty to step down
to follow suit with this demented, ugly, sick and decayed world
which politicians think they rule, unable to get into their thick heads
that Politics is nothing but the Madness Greenhouse of Megalomania
where there are no other masters running the asylum
than the vainest power of them all,
the ultimately and completely egoistic opportunist's self-destructiveness.

Simplicity

It couldn't be more simple.
Yes, of course I love you,
but I am a giver only and no taker.
All I want is nothing for myself
but everything for you,
and since your health condition is so delicate
I will not ever risk to jeopardize it but protect it only.
So my answer to your question of what I expect
is nothing for my own part.
As an artist bent on one-sided creativeness
it is excluded that I would desire anything from you
except, perhaps, the wish that you would keep what I would give you.
See my poems as documentations of my feelings,
a tempestuous inner world that ever moves and changes
but which never gets out of control,
and of my love, of course, which is quite undeniable
but of a rather purely altruistic kind
that never can get negative, destructive, morbid or insane
but is, I am afraid, a rather hopeless case of one-sided constructiveness.

Woodstock - in restrospect after 37 years

It was all a craze, of course,
a most absurd idea of most immoderate proportions,
a phantasmagoria of surrealistic recklessness
to stage this concert of megalomania for an audience of five hundred thousand,
all well fed with food and drink and any drugs for half a week,
with children getting born during the concert and some others dying,
everything allowed, the music being anything and perfectly without self-criticism;
and still there was something spectacularly sane about this whole flipped-out event,
so many people gathered just for music's sake to be together in a ruse,
intoxicated like on something so out of the ordinary as a common trip
to never really get completely back again, and, for a number of them, never to recover.
None of us was there, and still it feels today as if it was but yesterday
and as a great historical concern for all of us, not thirty-seven years away,
but recently, and in that omnipresent zone of timelessness,
that you are constantly in touch with as a practising musician -
the idea was very good, no matter how it sounded
and whatever were the consequences.

On the sea of love

Are you the victim of the ocean,
or are you the ocean?
All your feelings are your own,
but they will blow you anywhere
without your being able to resist them,
although you as their possessor
are alone entirely responsible for them;
so, – are you the wind that blows,
or are you the skipper of the tossed ship
that sets the sails to how the wind blows,
risking shipwreck on the way
and without knowing whether you will ever reach a port?

The wind is yours, the ship is yours,
just keep afloat, enjoy the wind and keep it going,
and at least you won't lack any entertainment
on a sea that tends to get the funnier
the more outrageously you keep on blowing.

Exhaustion

Where do they all come from,
all these tiring wasted wrecks of wretches
who exhaust you by their extremism,
the Limbo people without roots and aims
who only live for their eccentricism,
as if life's only meaning was excessiveness
at any cost by any means whatever the results,
and they ignore completely that they leave you
wasted in the ditch as they have passed you by
and driven you completely over by their wastefulness
of energy, of nonsense, of big deals for nothing,
of their hopelessly excessive vanity inflation.
But the other people, those who are more normal,
can't you stick with them, who for a change are sensible?
They are not easily accessible, since they are usually at work
and are not seen at home except late in the evening,
when as burnt-out cases they arrive, and early in the morning,
when they have to go to work without much rest
and having usually endured a night of nightmares or insomnia.
Those, the normal people, are not much to celebrate
since they are generally boring; and thus don't you have much else
than all those extremists who loiter without work
and just keep on exhausting you with their relentless pathos,
being better than the others in at least that they are never boring.

Lost

My love is an incessant stormy ocean
that keeps beating me asunder from my wits,
a shipwrecked fool completely lost at sea
and tossed to madness by its hammering atrocity,
and as a lover you are hopelessly alone
with this too overwhelming darkness of a cruel night,
your feelings drowning you and pulling you straight to perdition.
Yet, you are alive and can still fight
for your survival, even if you as a forlorn lover
are completely on your own and have no mercy to expect
from anyone – a lover lost is worse off than a ruined pauper.
Still there is a plank left of your shipwreck,
one last hope, if even that is the last straw
and even if that only is your own imagination.

Passion

When passion comes and takes you from behind,
what can you do? You have no other choice but to succumb
to its relentless wildness, darkness, terror and destruction
and must be the victim of your own emotions
overwhelming you with hopelessness and no escape,
no possibility for any shadow of defence;
for passion is the ultimate manifestation of the darkest force of nature
in her greatest irresistibility and her omnipotence,
her majesty and dreadfulness of silence like of death.
And yet, in this black hole of hopelessness there is a kind of life
more tough in its expansion than the most victorious sperm,
triumphant in its life and glorious in outbreak.
So what can we do about the force of passion?
There is nothing else to do but just the best of it.

The haunted humanity

The ghosts that haunt you
are the spectres of this insane world and age,
the phantoms of derailment and the enemies of love
that make spontaneous love impossible
and keep us fettered in Orwellian restrictions
isolated in unhuman cubicles of so called work and duties
that are just one way to the asylum
made more comfortable by the horrors of medicinal society
that give you pills to poison you relieving you of life
which anyway is just unbearable because of this society.
They say we are too many people on this earth,
and therefore the majority expects a sudden instantaneous destruction
that would finish off the sick majority which only suffers anyway,
and thus the thoughts and speculations of this world
continue to get sicker. There is only one health sign remaining:
Love can never get corrupted, while it lives and keeps on loving.
Never mind about the children and forget about your sex life,
if the health state of the world demands such sacrifices
for the sake of humankind's survival,
but let never go of love.
It is for us to cherish as the only thing
that ever will continue keeping us alive.

The workoholic

Is he to be pitied, or is he to be envied and admired?
Maybe both, or neither, since he is the victim of his happiness,
he is productive and enjoys his work but has got stuck in it,
like in a vicious circle but of happiness and glory,
which he can't get out of.
Oftentimes you see most doubtful consequences of this queer anomaly,
like difficulties with relationships, divorce and misery,
which usually just spurs him on to even harder efforts,
and thus is his most precarious condition only made the worse.
The problem is that there is no one who can help him;
only he himself can liberate him from his prison
of his work, his paradise and bliss, his sado-masochistic
self-destructive torture and his most unnatural and perfect hell,
which undeniably and more often than not
will end up with producing end results of most amazing quality
that will remain and prove to outlast vanity.

The Humanist's Complaint

by my old friend and colleague Doctor Sandy in Athens,
written last winter

Is idealism then dead and buried
just because materialism drives it over?
Is humanism then to capitulate
to ruthless unhumanity?
Must love then constantly give way to hatred
since hatred otherwise destroys her?
Must gentleness then succumb to hardness
just because hardness doesn't care?
Must then beauty be replaced by ugliness
just because ugliness expands?
Must then life give up to death
only because death exists?
Yes, alas, as long as justice is controlled by injustice,
since thereby suicide is justified,
the ultimate protest against evil,
injustice, inhumanity and godlessness
in a highest possible appeal of life
in the final resort to despair crying out
in the highest and loudest outcry of existence
which outcries all eternity.

Sea of Love

It's all for you, my loved, all my sea of love
of endless care and generosity,
of all my life and its creativeness,
my whole production and all that I lived for,
all the beauty I have lived for, all my music above all.
Just take it, drown in it, protect it and enjoy it,
let my music's affluence inspire you
and match the generosity and full length of your gorgeous hair,
and be magnanimous, magnificent and magic
with the manifoldness of this sea that I bequeath you,
greater than the lands of all the earth and richer
with its endlessness of life and love
that man can never understand or fathom
except lovers of the same kind of dynamic bottomlessness
as creative freaks like you and me, both drowned in our abyss
of the ultimate perfection of the beauty of pure music

manufactured and created only out of the profoundest melody
of love that only can be found beyond the depths of all the oceans.

a satire-like never-ending story, collected from some recent inside information, also a kind of doctor's nightmare,

The Funhouse High Priest

He is a prophet in his own right,
since he is always right,
his self-righteousness breaking all records,
since he squints to his right side
with what I believe to be an enamel eye,
for he never looks you in the eye.
Still, as a doctor he knows exactly
what medicines to feed you with
and believes he cures of everything
in his own right infallibility
although you flush them all down the toilet
since you prefer staying alive and sane
so that you can observe the established insanity
of your own infallible doctor and his nurses
who keep feeding him with medicines,
medicines, mind you, that he never prescribes for his patients,
since he wants to be sure that he only gets well himself
and no one else, since he needs his patients
to provide his hospital with income and enough guests
to ensure stately subsidies
without which his funhouse wouldn't be so funny any more
but would be shut down
since all the patients got away and all the nurses fatally intoxicated
from the medicines provided by their doctor
so that they would comply well on the couch
day and night
and forget about all the healthy patients,
which they so miserable failed to make sicker
since they all flushed down all their medicines in the toilet....

Aloof

Your aloofness does not bother me -
I am not hurt by anyone's detachment
which on the contrary increases my respect,
detachment being always sane and healthy
and the more, the deeper feelings are involved;
and I, if anyone, am well aware of depths of feelings
and the storms that rage under the surface
hidden well under the invisible cloak
not of a mask but from necessity
in order not to let them die but live forever.
If you give them out for mortals to manhandle,
then there will be hurts and undesired end to them,
but flowers are best cultivated in protection.
It's a simple question of survival,
and I will support it, never risk it,
live and cultivate my love
and never interfere with others doing likewise.

Abandoned

Come and rest a while, my love,
you must be tired, since you worked so hard
escaping from the heart of darkness and the savage hunters
who made you a scapegoat for their vices
and bereft you everything - for nothing,
for some petty theft, as if you were a person to be robbed,
the poorest thing I ever knew,
whom I so gladly would have given everything
but who was proud enough to give me thanks for nothing,
 independence being more worth than the highest treasure,
liberty and sovereignty being not for sale.
What can I give you, then? What can I do for you?
I am afraid I can't do anything
except of course continue to adore you
and sustain my love for you the more persistently
and diligently for your distance and departure
and the hopelessness of that impossibility to reach you.
They have alienated you from me, your only perfect lover,
all those other lovers, who just wanted to annoy you,
use you up by their destructive despicable opportunism
while your ideal lover let you get away
and was the only one to piously leave you in peace,
while you have fooled them all and cheated them of all their love,
escaped their baseness and made them all cuckolds
while the only one who really lost you,
your most faithful lover, I myself, yours truly,
is the only one who still possesses you,
the dreamer, who in losing you
has only as the only one secured you,
being one with you in spirit and in fate,
more bound to you than any law agreement can ensure
and being with you the more definitely now
for being lost without you.

Controversial

My love, your openness and frankness can not hurt me,
and I told you so from the beginning.
All I wanted was your welfare, and I want it still
and more than ever, now especially when I can see
your turbulences, what you have gone through and what you need,
which simply is a general dismantling of your love affairs,

completely, every one, so that you can find peace
and work with what is meaningful and more important
than ridiculously self-degrading dallying with childish games
of intrigue with unworthy knaves that are a bit too fast
in making women pregnant whom they then are stuck with
for their misery until they are compelled to leave them,
adding some more lonely mothers with their children on their own.
My dear, I am no friend of sex, since I have seen too much abuse
and almost only this abuse of one-sided destructiveness
and very little good results and lasting happiness from sex,
in fact, a sum of almost nothing. Be at liberty,
enjoy your freedom, use it well for good constructive purposes,
creation, work and charity, but you live better without sex,
the main corrupter and polluter and destroyer of mankind.
there is maybe a need for a general underground resistance movement of this kind...

The underground humanist

We are the nomads of eternity
who don't fit into this derailed world of brutality
since we are alien to its dominating ugliness
and are too soft in our music to tune in to noise.
Thus are we outsiders and outcasts
who do not belong to this corrupted world
of tyrannies, dictators, wars, barbarity and violence
since we never can conform to what is not constructive.
We must never be a part of all that we abhor
and stubbornly protest against
but rather safeguard and protect in isolation our ideals
and work for them unflinchingly in underground conditions
to once let them conquer all and vanquish ugliness and unhumanity
to let civilisation glory once again in splendid beauty
and let nature conquer all man's unnaturalness
and bring him back to normal, that is peace and decency
to make love possible at all for the creation of a future.

The old maid

I know that you despize me all, you young infernal lads,
like Balzac did, who wrote some novels only to express his hatred of us,
but, excuse me, we are not old virgins for no reason.
We are capable of learning and observing,
and it is too obvious what you men are capable of
and never hesitate to plague us with, destroying not your own lives only,
but intentionally making a big mess and with a vengeance
most of all to innocents. Let's not just speak of the abortions,
all those cases that turned pregnant "accidentally" and "unintentionally"
just because the bugger "happened" to come home too early and too fast.
I think we owe most cases of poor solitary mothers,
who can not support their undesired children, to those bastards.
Let's not say a word of all those women psychologically ruined
and destroyed for life by "accidental" and "unfortunate" miscarriages
due to rapes and other "accidental" and "unfortunate" maltreatments.
Let's not lose ourselves in those discussions
whether such occurrences are acts of love or not,
which you males always claim they are while the results prove differently...
Well, let's not talk about such things at all,
but let's just leave all those poor men alone

who can not handle women properly as human beings,
and they might perhaps learn likewise to leave us alone,
like I do mercifully and persistently with them,
so that both they and I can work in peace with more constructive matters,
like for instance dedicating our energy to love,
which actually involves more gentleness, politeness and respect
than just that vulgar sleazy dirty game called sex.

the worst catalogue of humanity

Numerical epitaph

29,000 children dying every day from lack of care is a devastating number

calling other endless numbers to mind, which never must be forgotten,

like the hundreds of thousands of women slaughtered by inquisitions 1300-1700 for being supposed witches,

like all those hundreds of thousands of Indians the Spanish killed in Latin America for not being natural Christians and to take their kingdoms and riches,

like the hundreds of thousands of Red Indians in North America killed (on purpose) by Englishmen and Americans, (the English having introduced the first bacteriological warfare by infecting blankets for sale to Indians with smallpox,)

like all the uncountable 'heretic' victims of the Catholic Inquisition 1200-1700,

like the 1,5 million Armenians killed by the Turks in the First World War, the first comprehensive genocide,

like the 20% of all Tibetans killed by the Chinese for nothing, or for just the pleasure of destroying their culture and identity,

like the 1,5 million of his own people that Pol Pot killed off in Cambodja just to execute his power according to the guidelines of Mao Zedong,

like the 6 million Jews killed by Hitler's Germans, the worst genocide ever,

not to speak of the 63 million victims to Lenin and Stalin

or the at least 70 million human deaths caused by Mao Zedong,

or the efficiency of the Americans, who in two brief blasts sent 500,000 innocent Japanese to death, either directly or unbearably slowly, in Hiroshima and Nagasaki,

and so on, and so on,

all of them having proved but one thing, that humanity never learns....

another kind of epitaph

Autumn

How many days remain for you
to roam around this harrowed earth
so painfully and deeply scarred by failures,
mostly only failures, not just of your own
but of so many lost and wasted lives
and. worst of all, too many friends who died too young.
I could write epitaphs in all eternity
just to bewail them and cry out their sorrows and my own
for what they failed in, what they never could accomplish,
all their unfinished invaluable work
and, most of all, the loss of their too precious souls.
But they are all still out there somewhere
waiting maybe for another opportunity
or for a better world, but they could wait for that forever,
since we haven't seen much betterment for some millennia.
Sorrow keeps me company with falling leaves
in flaming colours red of blood or love or both
while no tears are enough to cry out all the pain
of this so wasted tragical and futile life and world.

In a musical sense

In a musical sense, what is life?
An accurate question, which pinpoints the essence
not only of life but of existence.
In the beginning was not the word but Music,
and what on earth was all that music about?
We certainly hadn't heard all that jazz before,
and the question is if it sounded at all,
so at least it could not have sounded bad.
Let me put it like this.
In the beginning there was a kind if flow
of some kind of idea, that must have been musical,
because it produced such a tremendous effect
that we had a kind of Big Bang.
It's impossible to recollect or reconstruct,
but it certainly was there,
and it was music, as the source of everything,
as the dark horse behind everything that rides,
and that is life itself, the only motivation of which is –
music.

analysis of the famous syndrome

Reggie Perrin

It's not a crisis, it's just a character development.
Suddenly one morning you wake up to find
to your amazement that your life was all futility,
and you see through everything with clearness for the first time
and recognize the vanity of human wishes, toil and bother.
"What have I been doing all my life?" you ask yourself astonished,
and you realize you haven't lived at all.
All of a sudden, sex becomes dispensable,
you see through all your partners of the past that you don't need them,
love transcends into a higher plane of soul-mates,
endless friendship suddenly becomes the only acceptable relationship,
and you don't even need your property and money,
suddenly detachment from all worldly matters becomes vital
and much more important than materialistic fussiness and all the world,
and love takes on a religious aspect, you turn a philosopher,
stuck with your head in heaven and enjoying it,
at last discovering the real reality among the clouds.
You wake up from a nightmare of ridiculous concerns like from an illness
to turn into something natural and human for a change.

Congratulations – you just made it getting normal
and converted from this mundane mess of mainstream brainwash.

The suicide party of David Braithwaite

It was a very strange festivity
some years ago at Corinth, Greece,
the story of which doctor Sandy told me,
who was there. Let's leave the host alone,
he had the party of his life, an unforgettable farewell,
to which he generously summoned not only all his friends
but any kind of wayward outsider and displaced person,
many hippies, alcoholics, tramps and tarts
with even children, whom he gave a most luxurious dinner
with food and drink that never saw an end,
Retsina wine and Greek salads galore,
the atmosphere replenished with both joy and sorrow;
everybody laughed and had a good time
while at the same time no one eye's was dry
when the eccentric host made his farewell and welcome speech,

with ample thanks to everyone just for their coming
to be present as a delightful company to his demission.
No one thought at first that he was serious,
but he had actually invited all available Bohemians in Greece
just for his company and give them all a party for his funeral.
What people best remembered afterwards
were those almost unnoticeably small remarks of bitterness
which indicated a most overwhelming disappointment
in the field of love and women – he had loved,
but more than what was good for him, and unsuccessfully.
This is no story really for a poem
but should rather be the subject of a play, which shall be written,
with the documentary material as its delicate heartbreaking base,
maybe next time I go back to Greece.

in defence for the delicacy of ideals

Don' t cut my dreams down

Do whatever harm you will to me and to my life,
but let me keep up my ideals,
since I can see no other purpose of my life
and nothing else to really live for.
They say it's dangerous to wake up a somnambulist,
but even worse and almost worse than any crime
is to bereave a person of his natural ideals,
his love, his piety and dreams.
But real ideals can never really be defeated.
They keep on coming back,
creativeness can never have a set-back but can only be renewed,
so there is actually no danger really.
Just let the somnambulist walk on
in safety on his clouds and smiling in his dreams,
and no harm will come out of it,
while no one knows what fearful things could happen
if you touch and crush an individual's universe
conserved well in a dream but that might well contain
the key to universal safety for humanity.

Thanksgiving sort of poem

Beloved friends,
what can I say,
touched and moved by your compliments
beyond recognition
being somewhat drunk
having celebrated also others today,
so I am afraid I don't write very coherently at the moment,
anyways, as some of you Canadians prefer putting it,
(especially from British Columbia,)
my sincere thanks
and appreciation to you all
for more fedelity and ceredence than any lover,
hoping to keep it up in spite of all losses
on the emotional plane,
my sincere thanks,

Blind love

You just have to face the music:
love will ever play the dirtiest tricks on you
and never be the same but always puzzle you,
upset you, never be reliable and always blindfold you
so that you never can see clear reality
but always must fall victim to it as to love,
since blind reality of love will always lead you quite astray,
you will love anyone who isn't worth it,
and you will be cruelly abused by anyone
who just will take your blindfolded condition as an opportunity
to lead you any stray path down to hell just for the fun of it,
and you will end up as a wreck completely crushed
like in a shipwreck all entangled in the shattered ruins of your lost ideals.
But there is always a way out and a salvation.
Just keep your blindfold on, refuse to compromise with false reality,
continue challenging the cruelty of the world by countering it
and opposing it with your alternative, your own created world of beauty,
which most certainly will outlast this vain world of futile nonsense.
The object of your love will constantly play foul on you
and most outrageously, but that must never check your love,
which ever must keep flowing to enrich, if nothing else,
at least the spiritual world of sentient beings
which ever will be hungering and needing more
of that true love of honesty which is the reason for your life.

Through the minefield

Let me guide you carefully
across the minefield of abysmal trenches,
thorns and scorpions, poison ivy and what not,
so that your bare feet will not stumble into any bomb
but tread on safely like on clouds
with maximum security, like a professional sleepwalker;
just rely on me and hold my hand,

and your poor blindsight will not lead you wrong
but safely to the other side through any ambush
that will miss you most completely
since I will make you invisible to any danger,
any rotten scoundrel that would trap you,
who instead shall fall into his own deceit –
you may be sure I will see to it thoroughly;
so be not apprehensive or afraid of anything,
just keep your fingers crossed and prayers going,
and my love shall save you from whatever
so that nothing evermore will threaten you again.

9-11 and all that

When anger hits you on the nose...

When anger hits you on the nose
the urge to strike back gets on overwhelming,
but you can't strike back while still your nose is bleeding,
you just have to swallow it and bide your time,
and as your anger thus is laid to rest
you soon forget about it,
and the motivation disappears

to do something about it,
and thus nothing sensible gets done
about the insult, which remains
buried alive, where it infests and grows
until it reaches some infection stage,
and then the trouble is completely introvert
like a sore inner wound you only feel but cannot dress
and turns perhaps into some metastasis.
Still, that is far better than to actually strike back
in blindness, hatred and revenge
of short-sighted brain-bankruptcy
with no idea of the inevitable consequences.
Thus we have this vicious circle of political insanity,
each madman of his own fanatical establishment
just thinking of his own group egoistic interests,
manipulated into power for destructive reasons,
like the Bush impostor in the White House
stealing presidency from Al Gore, whose main concern
is universal welfare, global warming problems and the future,
while the short-sighted impostor lunacy
by sheer incompetence turns international discussions into failures
triggering the 9-11 sabotage attacks against civilisation,
which politically then are turned into a crazy war merry-go-round
manipulated forth against Afghanistan at first and then Iraq
by the oil mafia governing the president –
and thus is world politics turned into a mess of trouble
just to close the eyes to much more vital problems
like the melting ices in Antarctica and Greenland
that will drown the world if nothing brings it to a halt,
natural problems of man's own short-sighted making
that concerns humanity, the future and all nature
clinically free from egoistic thinking and vendettas –
say no more, I stifle and can only pray and cry,
forgetting all about my bleeding nose.

Kathy. You missed the nose all together. And, you hit the wrong person, establishment, governement leader, etc, etc, etc. We were attacked!
Phyllis: Is Bush also to blame for all the other attacks on Americans dating back to the 70's? There have been seven, two while Clinton and Gore were in office. These people hate freedom. It has
nothing to do with oil, the environment or politics. They are worshipers of evil.

Me: With my bleeding nose I am hitting no one and defending no one, least of all any terrorist. The inconvenient truth is there was an important world meeting in spring 2001, which the US walked out on, refusing to deal with global problems. Some people say there would have been no 9-11 attacks with a different administration - this can neither be proved nor disproved. The Afghanistan war of 2001 achieved some important and constructive results, let's not speak about the gas pipe lines from Central Asia to the sea through Afghanistan that were impossible to construct before that war; but the Iraq war, everybody agrees, was started on false grounds, there having been no weapons of mass destruction on Iraq's side, Bush's excuse for driving over the UN and starting the war, while Dick Cheney and D. Rumsfeld pressured the CIA into advocating the war although there was no ground for it, if it were not for the oil. See Al Gore's film and do something about the US being responsible for 30% of the pollution of the planet. President Bush has refused to see it.
Zoya: This is a very, very significant poem.
It is so sane and asks the relevant question, so forcefully and directly without mincing any words...
Ultimately the fact remains that no war can bring peace.
No peace can be brought about by violence.
No violence can be ended by violence.
Bravo, dear Aurelio!
Love,
Zoya

freaking out

Ridiculous lovers and other freaks

Who has not been through it?
A complete loss of all dignity and pride,
of self-esteem and everything you thought was yours forever,
just because some silly incident, some awkward situation,
something perfectly ridiculous and accidental,
such as finding your wife's lover in her bed,
an operetta situation, humanly deplorable and perfectly preposterous,
and all you ever dreamed of is forgotten, crushed and broken up in pieces
with a broken heart and tears and years ahead of misery, remorse and sorrow,
all because of human weakness, everybody being really innocent.
But that is how it starts, the real romance,
the suffering, the pathos, the profundity and melancholy,
and you melt away in sweet senttimentality and self pity forever,
drowning all your sorrows in a glass that never ends,
the chalice of your martyrdom being refilled forever.

That's how the carreer begins for the professional freak,
who nevermore can be quite certain of his sex,
he can do anything for love, turn homosexual or bisexual or whatever
but will never turn a Lesbian, unless he becomes a woman,
which of course could be another choice of his, or hers,
depending on what sex or kind of sex he chooses,
if she suddenly becomes a man or he a woman.
So, in brief, enjoy yourself, whatever kind of sex you have or are.
freaky advisers leading you straight...

Labyrinths of love

What shall we say? Resign and give up in pathetical dismay?
My friend, be comforted. Your love is never lost
and never wasted, never can it be expressed in vain,
and if you lose a girl or all the girls of this frustrating world,
then you can find, some wise guys say, another kind of girl
and sweetheart, lover, partner and whatever, in yourself.
Now, what freaky kind of comfort is that miserable bullshit?
Sorry, I just tell you what they have been telling me,
the experts, those who never love except to lose their love,
who have seen all the tragedies and managed to survive them
and themselves, their love and their repetitive perdition –
there is always a way out, they say, and if you cannnot find it,
just go back into yourself and find your other self within yourself,
in brief, turn schizophrenic, like so many do successfully.
And so they freak out, the advisers, the psychologists,
the head-shrinkers, support teams, pimps and gigolos
and you just scrap them all as good for nothing.
And having given up completely, getting ready for the exit,
a dramatic most spectacular demonstrative resounding bloodily impressing suicide
you will find a friend right there just waiting for you,
and you ask him with surprise: "Where have you been?"
He answers (or if it is she): "Well, I just happened to be here."
Nothing ever fails to turn up when you least expect it,
and you simply will continue be surprised
as long as you give life a chance.

OCTOBER HARVEST FIRST PART.

Separation

What separated us?
Alas, we are both innocent of our fates,
which we have to follow and which teach us
all kinds of uncomfortable and undesired lessons,
and for some reason our very striving for nobility
has become the parting wall, sealing us off from each other,
robbed of our souls and our free will by the very thing we have in common,
our ideals and vocation, our very work, which brought us together
and now has turned itself into a wall, casting us in different prisons.
Our only salvation is our souls, if we still can find some contact
in spite of the total and fatal separation, across the ocean of division,
if our minds can find each other independent of our bodies
with their weakness fettering us to wordly troubles of pettiness,
the trivial cause of our separation,
the unacceptable sabotageing matters of unnecessary inconvenience;
and fortunately we have some experience before of the ultimate phenomenon,
that nothing is impossible for true love of sincerest honesty.

the environmentalist's concern

Disturbances

Nothing works properly any more.
There are disturbances everywhere, sabotageing life,
messing up communication lines, turning nature into havoc,
 threatening life and the very existence of man
because of man's own folly,
who doesn't understand that he can't be unnatural
without upsetting the universe, life and his own existence.
Never earlier have so many life forms died out,
never has man been more violent and self-destructive,
never before has any form of life turned into a threat to life itself,
like man does now in his totally absurd egoism.
What can we do? Eliminate the disturbances,
keep them out of our lives, close up the omnipresent noise pollution,
turn back to nature and plant trees, abandon the brainwash society
and be human, kind and gentle, cure the psychotic illness of stress
and co-operate with life instead of doing everything to destroy it.
No one has an enemy except himself, if he turns into one,
and that's the only possible departure from nature, life and reason.

The Argument

When you really love someone
you tend to idealize her,
that is unescapable in love
and its predestined ruin,
since your lovéd always must
sooner or later fail in living up to your ideal –
it is a matter of reality and nature,
and thus you must lose your lovéd,
but you can never lose your love.

The lover to the loved

Stay a while, my love, and keep me company
just for the night, and you shall not regret it,
for the more you give, the more you will be given,
and I will not give you up, because you are my soul,

that is, you are my life, you hold it in your hands,
and there is no more life for me except your love.
I know this borders on the burning out
and draining of our energies,
there is no more exhausting thing than love,
and yet we need it and can't live without it
even if it must consume us in the end
like in the slowest kind of suicide,
but it gives so much pleasure on the way
and, above all, much more life than we already possess.

Profundity

Why can't we have each other?
And yet we have each other.
Destiny blocks our ways and seals us off
for her own purpose, it seems,
the mystery of our love,
that constantly is spurred on
and brought to darker depths
of infinite affection and intimacy
but without ever getting too close,
as if our love was more a water story
of unfathomable ocean depths
than of any fire that could burn.
Maybe it is better that way?
Never to consume or be consumed,
but to be drowned instead
in the vastness of a sea that never ends
but only waxes all the time
in greater overwhelmingness of beauty.

Castles in the Air

One day we'll realize our dreams
and talk forever during endless hours of a sleepless night
of only love and love again until we stifle
in our sweat and bliss and wonderful exhaustion,
something that we all need, not just you and me.
Evasive dreams that never can come true
but always can be dreamed about are always necessary
to talk out about, because that is the way to share them
and not have them just for mirages reserved for wishful thinking,
and that way at least can they be kept alive and even verifiable.
There is no greater joy and food for love
than to share common dreams of definite impossibility,
because that proves them not impossible at all,
since what two people can conceive together
is what they together also can create and out of nothing.

The Wise Guys

When beauty came along, the wise guys had a song:
"We did not ask for her to come here."
And they fired her and kicked her down the alley,
for they knew much better how to manage without beauty
than to let her enter any of their frozen hearts.
And thus they lived on without any dance or song
or anything that possibly could risk their mind control,
for they preferred to live without beauty
rather than to risk any joy or tears or dangerous emotion.

For the wisdom of the wise guys is so advanced in its foresight
that roses and orchids will freeze in its dry coldness to death,
and people and pupils who are made to read their textbooks
of elaborate pedantic instructions about rules and law and order
will be petrified by such outstandingly premeditated brainwash
to never have bright eyes or searching intellects again.
Instead they were compelled to physically work hard with their brute force,
but all their diligence served only others and their masters,
those who taught them to mind only their own business
and to count their hard earned money since it was so little,
and to hate what tempted them to laughter and to some enjoyment
of for instance beauty in some flowers of some garden.

But we will have summer once again, or so the songs will sing,
and heaven will continue beaming forth some sunshine.
Much will pass that wasn't of much pleasure,
and our hearts shall be uplifted once again;
for beauty never comes or goes but to come back again,
so will the songs forever sing, and nothing can shut up them,
although no wise guy in this world will ever heed them,
refusing to believe their nonsense to be better than their wisdom.

Anonymity

Buried alive in the greyness of sterility
by the gravedigger and murderer of silence
in that indifference into which you were born
as in a vacuum which always was your own
and followed you on as a persistent fateful foe
of some relentlessness, since he never gave you up
no matter how hard you fought to get out of that grave
of isolation and suffocation due to the lack of spiritual air…

The soul was born free with wings of her own
but was never given any air to spread them out
but rather was shut up in the straight-jacket of ignorance
like in a perpetual thralldom of obligatory indifference
of the society of humdrum prejudice and stifling fatalism
in the stagnation of materialism that gave up to death.
And therefore, my twin soul and sister of destiny,
you are being throttled for your creativity, your only crime,
that separated you from mortal mediocrity, and given that stamp
of doom for prejudiced abnormity and anomaly,
declared taboo by that commonness of normality
which can but bore us free and wingéd souls to death.

The desperate lover

He came to me dissolved in desperation.
"No, I can not stand it any more!
I will no more be treated so by any lady!"
"What is then the matter? What has happened?"
"They just drive me nuts!" "But who?"
"The ladies! Who else is so cruel and merciless
but all the other other hopeless mad indecent and revolting sex!"
"What have they done then? Is it more than one?"
"One is more than enough!" I tried to soothe him.
"Tell me now, what has she done to you?"
"She just keeps doing nothing! She is never there,
she gives her word but never keeps it, she forgets her promises,
she says one thing but does the opposite, she never keeps appointments,
and she goes to bed with anyone but me!"
"I see," said I, "so you are jealous? Have you any proof of her unfaithfulness?"
"It is enough for me to see her being fondled by her friends,
her girl friends and her lovers and the whole world,
while I am the only one to treat her decently!"
"And since the whole world loves her and debases her,
you are frustrated as her only true and decent lover and avoid her?"
"Naturally, yes!" "My friend, you are completely lovesick."
"Yes, of course! That is the problem! And I can not stand it any longer!
She is so completely unreliable!" "My friend, you are not first in history
to find out love is not a stable thing. What will you do?"
"That is what I am asking you! What shall I do?"
"You love her. That is all your trouble. Stay out of your love,
forgo her, or continue suffering. That is your only choice."
"But why must love be so humiliating and give so much suffering?"
"My friend, that is the question which no lover ever had an answer to."

And I went back to work, preferring to stay out of any trouble
with frustrated lovers angry with each other.
When love leads to jealousy it is no longer love but only egoism,
which can drive any lover out of love to any madness.

The pathetic lover

"Why can't I reach you?
Why are you never at home when I come by?
Don't you want to see me again?
What did I do wrong?
Or is it just that I am too old?
This pathetic old ridiculous fool
is then good for nothing and unqualified for love
and a thing to just sort out and forget all about.
No, no woman's heart can be so cruel.
There must be something else.
Did I frighten you?
That was the last thing I wanted to do –
on the contrary I always observed the strictest politeness
to spare your delicacy and my own vulnerability,
for no feelings are sorer than the faithful lover's,
and no lover's feelings are easier to wound than an old one's.
Or is it just so simple and vulgar that you prefer someone else,
someone younger that you can dominate,
someone who doesn't flinch at making sex
but is prepared to make child with anyone,
a vulgar playboy who doesn't care about his victims
and forgets immediately whom he laid before...
In that case there is only disappointment
and nothing else to say or do
but to say farewell to love
and consider oneself a pathetic ridiculous failure
impossible to redeem or even to feel sorry for
since he just gave up and fell a victim
to his own vulnerability and the doubts of his misgivings
and was not made to receive love but only to give it away
thus making his life of love a constant bankruptcy,
and whether it was worth it or not is a totally different story."
- Said the old fool and went away and fell in love again.

Insecurity

Your inner security is nothing to rely on,
and neither is there any outer security.
Your feelings will ever play havoc with you,
constantly resulting in surprising earthquakes
worse than any earthal catastrophe
whenever you are not prepared for it,
and they will never leave you in peace,
because they are always there,
like hungry harpies and furies of the night
just waiting to put their claws into your soul
and make it bleed most painfully and copiously
until you can not bear it any longer
but just have to clasp the knees of your friend
and beg for mercy, like a criminal escaped to an ayslum.
And yet, those feelings are better than being without any,
career hearts of stone are frozen stiff forever,
and successfully established authorities are lost forever,
having done their careers and having nothing to look forward to
but death as the release of their feelings at last
which they buried alive in the bank vaults of success
locked away forever,
while the trembling leaf of an exposed and vulnerable soul
will ever be free, as long as she suffers from her feelings.

A chance meeting

You called me from afar
across the wilderness of solitude,
and I was there to hearken
and to understand your foreign song,
a call which only the bereaved could understand,
a song of love and languishment
of missing the beloved but without heartrending pain,
no tears was in that song but only loneliness,
like from a crane got lost from her migrating flock,
a cry of melancholic forlorn alien beauty
of such singular enchantment and intriguing personality
that I felt recognized myserlf as something similar,
a hopeless case of alien nomadic yearning wildness
never quite at ease or peace with anyone
and least of all with my incurably outrageous self.
So might two wolves make contact by a howling song

across the frozen desolations of Siberia
and find out to their immense surprise
that they were not alone completely in this foreign universe.

Two old souls

We are two old souls, you and I,
and I would place you more convincingly in ancient Greece
identified as something of a treasure of mythology
originating most exceptional creativeness
as nothing less than as a perfect proper muse.
Myself have roots there, I was born in ancient Greece
where both my heart and soul belonged from ancient times
and always found their way back to return to,
as to something of a mother's womb but in a spiritual sense,
that womb and fountain of perpetual life continuing still
to nourish all humanity with dreams of charm and beauty.
Thus we are two timeless souls
too old to ever get much older and to therefore stay forever young,
retrieving and connecting to each other ever and again repetitively,
maybe throughout history, to keep it going
and to constantly remind humanity to never give up
the creative and constructive mission
which remains the most important task of life.

Memories of my first love

You bring me back my first love
just by your existence
with your long amazing hair
exactly as my hippie bride of 30 years ago
who just like you enchanted all her world
and made all men go drown themselves in craziness.
Since then nothing has changed at all.
I am still young and green, naïve and potty
and consider the whole world my own
since it is dancing all just for my love,
and I am omnipotent as a lover
since I have you for my love,
the only goddess of eternity,
who keeps my love alive forever
just by existing
as my first perpetual love that never dies.

Happy birthday!

Our strange relationship
is something of a miracle to me
that now is underlined and focussed
as I venture forth to celebrate your birthday.
We are not together and have never been so
but are so the more for being separated,
you in Russia, me at home at work,
as if we never had been parted.

How is our relationship to be defined?
I am too old to be your lover or your husband
but too young to be your father.
I am something in between,
a friend in Limbo of some undefined category,
a nothing but a bit of everything
but could be anything
and would be willing to whatever you would want.
So that would be my birthday present to you:
I shall be to you whatever you desire.

But the main thing is that our relationship is good.
It has been good from the beginning
and has constantly improved
as long as we have known each other,
and let us just keep it so
allowing it to constantly grow even better.

Timeless lovers

We have no time for this relentless world
of ignorance and cruelty and nonsense,
like ridiculous atrocities and violence for nothing,
so we stand outside it and are proud of that capacity
of chronical outsiders feeling sorry for this mess
of worldly matters, vanities and follies,
making politics a nuisance for all sensible and thinking men
and women, who should just refuse co-operating
with this mankind and these men
that only know the language of enforcement,
of brute force, destructive hardness,
self-destructive lunacy and idiocy.
Unfortunately, most men in accountable positions
suffer from this madness and should therefore

definitely be subjected to some treatment;
while the only sane and decent people
have to step outside and sort this world out of their lives
to at all be able to devote themselves
to all that matters in the long run, which is love.

Apollo and Aphrodite

There was a scandal at Olympus
as there suddenly arose a rumour
that Apollo, of all gods! had fallen flat
for Aphrodite, of all goddesses!
And Dionysus laughed his sides off,
Zeus and Poseidon shook their heads,
Artemis just went off out hunting
and would hear no more about it,
Hera smiled benevolently,
knowing well the weaknesses of gods and men,
Athena just could not believe it,
she was shocked, the only one to be so,
while Apollo's brother Hermes as the only one
decided to find out the truth about it.
So he went to old Hephaistus and asked
if his notorious wife had actually deceived him.
"Do you find that strange?" Hephaistus asked.
"Do you not know that she keeps sleeping with just anyone?"
"But even with Apollo?" asked bewildered Hermes.
"Ask Apollo," answered the old limping smith,
"I have not had anything to do with it."
So Hermes went to seek Apollo out,
whom he found sleeping with the lovely goddess Aphrodite,
both entangled in each other's masses of blonde hair
and all too evidently more than decently enjoying it.
"What is this?" asked the frowning Hermes,
folding up his arms, "have we not had enough of scandals
here on Mount Olympus? And of all gods, you, Apollo,
and with Aphrodite!" Apollo turned to him with calmness,
looked at him carefully and asked: "And would you, Hermes,
miss an opportunity with Aphrodite, if you got one?
Who are you to envy me, a god yourself, my beauty and my love,
and would you really dare denying me or anyone the privilege
of loving beauty just for beauty's sake,
even if she is a whore and Aphrodite and another's wife?
Good Hermes, leave me to my love and seek your own,

for you shall know, that even if I am the chastest of the gods,
enjoy the highest reputation of morale, integrity, idealism and virtue,
even I am subject to and must subordinate myself to love,
the weakest of the goddesses but all the same
the only omnipotent one, the power of whom everyone must bow to,
even Zeus, which his wife can bear you testimony of;
and even Artemis, my sister, although she remains a virgin
must accept that love alone rules all the universe,
all life, the destiny of man and even of the gods,
which you shall understand, if not before,
when we, the gods, are gone, but love continues still."
So quoth Apollo and turned back to Aphrodite's silent charm
to lose himself completely in her beauty
while his brother Hermes went away in brooding worries,
for the first time contemplating the impending possibility
of even the mortality of all the gods,
but finally arrived at a conclusion: "Yes, by golly, he is right!
We must be mortal, yes, of course, unless,
how wise my brother is! we give ourselves to love,
since only love in this world must of course,
according to the most and only natural of laws,
rule life and be the only immortality!"
And he turned back to Mount Olympus
and told all the other gods, that there was nothing wrong,
and that Apollo only knew the real way for them all
to spite all history, survive their own mortality
and ultimately end up defeating even time.

Variation

Don't remind me of my first love.
I was raped and killed, and that was it,
that is, my love was killed from the beginning
by the evidence of hard reality
and the annihilating fallacy of man
resulting in a devastating disappointment
of supremest kind for life,
a rape to be endured and re-experienced forever.
How can love survive? - is my resulting lasting question
which will never have an answer.
Love just gets on and survives
like life when it bursts through the toughest asphalt
with some tiny flower, just for demonstration,
and goes on like crazy, loving just for love's sake,

just to prove its own impossible existence,
with no smile, no tears, as stoic as a deathskull
but nevertheless with irresistibility
continuing to love like mad forever.

The truth about the matter

The truth about the matter
is that love, if true, is too deep to be properly expressed
and never, therefore, can be expressed enough,
and therefore, the truer and the deeper your love is,
the more easily it gets misunderstood,
and then starts the real process
of introversion, broodings without end and in eternity,
the problematic analysis of what went wrong,
which nothing really did,
love just got entangled in itself and by itself,
got stuck like that famous interrupted coitus recently explained,
was too deep and too true to get a forum in reality,
in brief, turned into a hopeless ideal.
How do you solve that problem?
It's just impossible.
Love once turned into an ideal remains an ideal,
and there is no cure for it, it just goes on forever,
like a satellite launched into space to wander on forever
into nothing but with the most important message on board
of all eternity explaining all the universe
and holding within the innermost and deepest of all secrets
of life itself.

Untouchablility

"I find love to be an indefinable force that sometimes has no reason, and therefore makes our wanting of it all the more desirable." - BlueyedSoul

Don't turn my love into some palpability
but let me keep it free from agony of coarse reality
and thus preserve it better as an indefinability
to cherish and feel free to cultivate without hostility
from rivals, complications and outrageous culpability.
Thus saith my love: "You'd better not risk touching me,
for then I might prove real." I will not touch my love

but rather dream away from it and reach it better that way,
since the language spoken into dreams is clearer
and much more reliable than what all words in lies are able to express.
There is no love but abstract love,
there is no truth in love but in the soul,
and love made concrete is one way into a trap
where you get stuck and nothing more can save you
until death restores your soul and freedom.
So keep clean and out of love's more practical manifestations,
and in that way you will manage to stay on in love forever.

The Chat

When we sleep together, you and I,
and talk at length about forbidden things
that no one ever heard of,
and I venture in my sleeplessness to leave your bed
to just escape our union for a moment,
something thought-provoking startles me,
that you are not alone as long as I at all exist.
This world, this universe is just too small for us,
and in the thawing warmth of our embrace
the whole world melts away
as just a negligeable vanishing nonentity
that our hearts are too full of love to even mind,
while we alone exist
as some kind of dualistic nuclear centre of existence
even while we keep apart.
And at the same time, our love keeps all the world alive,
as if it was dependent on the fact that we exist together;
and thus can we go to sleep with a good conscience
having done our duty to the world by making love.

Headaches and heartaches

by the way, T.S.Eliot's birthday, 26th September

Another day of hell
in desert land with hollow men,
an outsider in exile
marked as alien and treated worse,

an outcast lost in headaches
and, what's worse, a bleeding heart.
It could not really be much worse.
Why does he then stay on,
a lonely isolated frozen-out exemption
from the greyness of this suicidal Hades?
He has his work and sticks to it in fealty
although they never thank him for it
nor give any salary or recognition,
but he just accepts it, shrugs it off and carries on,
since even in the hopelessness of blackest hell
you always find something to love,
the only universal cure for everything.

All the 'Offs'

Don't remind me of the corpses,
all the lost ones, all the accusations,
all the failures, all that got away,
all the exploded dreams, the cruelties and massacres,
all the deceivers and the frauds,
the vanished hopes, the deaths, the burials...
Let me rest in peace for all the living dead
that never can stop torturing you
by being constantly dug up as agony reminders
whenever they get the slightest chance.
A divorce is worse than any marriage,
for a marriage can be ended by divorce,
but a divorce will ever haunt you,
hunt you down and keep you on the rack forever.

The black hole of truth

Let's go away together
on the ultimate and only valid journey
out of this world, out of all reality
and leave all baseness and vulgarity behind
to lose ourselves in wild fantastic dreams of beauty
thickened with the perfumes of our love song
that shall never end but constantly reach greater heights
of wuthering astoundingness and glorious perfection.

People say that life itself is nothing but a journey,
and it has no meaning but for that especial element
of being ever on the move away and forward,
always onwards, often wayward and the more, the better,
just as long as that trip never ends
but leads us on and carries us away
into the abyss of oblivion
into that black hole of love and beauty
that will ultimately end up in a dawning new eternity.

The worst and most painful jealousy...

Jealousy is never worse than when it's justified,
when others make the same claim of your love as you,
when others act as if they were your doubles
manifesting the same feelings for your love as you,
transforming your life to a nightmare of outrageous clones,
all those unworthy rivals utterly destroying what was yours
and killing off the harmony of what you thought was perfect love,
continuously ruining your day and life and future,
and you can do nothing but resign in gloom.
For what can you do about others having equal human rights as you?
It was your bad luck that they picked on your love,
you have no right whatsoever to deny them any feelings,
and to start some quarrel, have a fight or challenge them to duels
is now out of fashion and but childishness.
You have to bear it, and if you are lucky
your love might discover that you, after all,
was better than the others and the only worthy one.

The kiss of death

Yes, it's possible to kiss yourself to death.
When love is running out and ruining itself,
when you are wasted and has turned your inside out,
that is your heart and soul, so nothing else remains,
then you can still consume yourself
by throwing yourself out into the final abyss
visiting the hell of dead and wasted lovers
where they kissed themselves to death;
and, mind you, they were not just ordinary kisses.

Lips may meet and signify but shallowness and nothing,
lips may lie and put on shows, like hiding behind lipsticks,
but there is another kind of kisses, much more subtle,
that are whispered in consummate silence, privately
by means of nothing but the element of honest thought.
Those are the kisses which I here try to describe,
the secret loves that never manifest themselves in flesh and blood,
the unexpressed desires, wishes unfulfilled,
and dreams that never could come true,
all those unwritten tragedies of love
that never came to more than secret kisses from afar
sent by some windhorse, wandering in darkness,
the sincerest kisses ever,
that will always carry through their message
spiting time and space to go on loving
and to die of love forever.

An old time ballad

She had a wooden leg but was surprisingly efficient,
and the blokes could never do without her.
She developed a technique of outstanding refinement
quite unique for her profession, not to scare away the customers,
but finally she did it just too well.
A client could not let her go to others, so he gallantly proposed to her,
and she could not afford to be without a husband,
once she got this one chance of a lifetime.
Well, on the wedding night she just broke loose
forgetting all restraints, and fellows of the bridegroom
standing secretly to watch outside the window
saw the blockhead screwing off his head like hell,
the wooden leg had never been less of an obstacle,
but, alas, there were some consequences:
he picked chips and splinters from his leg for fourteen days.

The closed gate

You are never there when I come for a visit.
I am tired now of climbing fences,
all these locked doors keep the wrong people away,
how can you love and associate with friends
and have some kind of human workable society
if you need codes to enter every ordinary house?

Is love then to be fenced away
and kept by force away from every home?
Is privacy synonymous with isolation, then?
In Orwell's brave new world love is a dangerous disease
that has to be resisted and exterminated,
and its medicine is pesticides and other drugs
preventing you from thinking properly,
and human contacts is a menace to the order of society.
The only culture is the mainstream brainwash,
which is obligatory for everyone,
and he who does not want it and who shuts it out
is anti-social with a criminal potential
and must carefully be watched -
the cameras in every street will spot him everywhere.
I am so tired of this alienation of humanity in this society of unhumanity
for order's sake and for security, for politicians to manipulate the easier,
for the establishment of lies, hypocrisy and cynicism,
and don't want any more to climb high fences,
break up gates and force myself through locked and coded doors
to only meet my friend, who suffers in her loneliness,
like everybody else.

The abstract beauty of your soul

The abstract beauty of your soul compels me
to some apprehension for your frailty,
like some precious old Venetian glass entrusted to my hands
for my responsibility to care for and protect,
and I will do so willingly and bind myself to that distinguished obligation
piously regarding it as my concern and mission,
maybe the most vital and important of my life.
The secret of your charm is that you live by soul alone,
material values are nonentities to you,
while you look only for the soul of man to bring it forth,
that is the best sides of humanity and of each human being;
all that ever was of any good in any person you awake
to new life, and thus can you thaw up any human heart
and even recall frozen flowers back to life.
My love was such a frozen flower,
buried and suppressed since twenty years,
and could I then stop loving you and go to sleep and lethargy again
when you are here to brighten up my life? Impossible,
life was created to exist and must exist through love,
if possible, forever.

Apollo and Aphrodite, part two

Apollo lay with Aphrodite, never tiring of each other,
but eventually they started to discuss the situation.
"What is love, my darling, really?" asked Apollo.
"What a stupid question," answered love's own goddess,
"you don't talk about it unless you want to destroy it."
"But mustn't lovers talk about their love and their relationship?"
"But that is not what love is. Love can not be talked about,
because you can not understand it. It exists, and that is all."
"My darling, you intrigue me. Then the more important to discuss it
and to have it understood. That is a challenge, then."
"You do not understand it, and you do not talk about it.
You just give it and want nothing in return.
It is the gift of life to manage and administer in such a way
that you can never keep it for yourself but only handle it by giving it away."
"So it is not for keeping but for giving only.
But can you hurt anyone with such a gift?"
"That is the delicacy. Love is total trust.
If you don't trust your love completely and can be completely open
with her about everything, then your love is lacking."
"Did all men and gods you slept with before me trust you as much as I?"
"They did, and I was not unfaithful to a single one of them, for I am love itself."
"What does your husband say about it?"
"Nothing, for he loves me."
"But he never slept with you."
"And thus he might well be the one who loves me most of all."
"Is chaste and virgin love then higher and superior to any carnal love like ours?"
"Yes, for there is no more powerful and potent lover
than the one who never spends his semen."
"But can he be satisfactory?"
"Not temporarily, but in the long run he outlasts all other lovers."
"But you ladies do prefer the proper temporary love
in flesh and blood in bed, or don't you?"
"Never count on that. The trust is all. Give me a lover like my husband,
who has never slept with me and never been unfaithful
and who trusts me no matter with whom I go to bed,
and I call him a better lover than the fairest
and most irresistible of all efficient lovers."
That concluded their discussion, and Apollo felt that he had had enough.
He left her bed and went home to her working husband,
where he laboured in his den, and told him:
"Dear Hephaistus, I am sorry that I stole your wife from you,

but I have learned the lesson how much better you are as a lover than myself."
Hephaistus said: "You must be joking."
"Not at all," Apollo answered,
"I in all my beauty and my splendour and refinement
is a clown and dilettant in love compared with you,
who with your limp and ugliness have never let her down
in your respect and faith. We all have sometimes deprecated
and despised her for her wantonness,
and you, her husband, is the only one who never thought insultingly about her.
That is love and much more love than any lover physically can bestow on her."
And fair Apollo left Hephaistus and his wife in peace
and never tried again to copulate with her,
for he had learned his lesson about love and stuck to it.

Vain separation

The first thing every morning that I see
as I wake up is you, the more so
the more absent you are from my side.
I can not do without you,
and therefore you never leave me,
like a guardian angel always on her guard
to save us both from every danger
that could possibly disturb our union of hearts
that once and permanently fused our souls to one.
My mind and thoughts and soul and all are all of you,
and there was never anyone to vie with that capacity.
Yet, still there is so much for us to do
and such a labour just to get to know each other
and to reach ourselves and understand our love
that is too deep for us to fathom by ourselves
since we are drowned in it once and for all.

What went wrong?

What went wrong? It petered out, but never died,
but many got completely lost on all those crooked ways,
not only vanishing in drugs with permanent brain damage,
like almost all the friends of Cassidy and Kerouac,
but above all in all those flummeries and weird deceptions
masked most commonly in saviour-like attractiveness;
but all those 'movements of religion and philosophy' with business interests

were naïve and innocent compared with the political reaction,
when demonstrations were stamped down with brute police force and the
FBI let all drugs loose to swamp the Woodstock concert
in political premeditated purpose to commit and trap
and rape the flower power movement into drug addiction.
This was never proved nor disproved, but the accusation
has grown stronger with the years
and also more persistent, loud and clear.
Of course, war ruined everything, the Vietnam war
in escalating madness after the assassination of John Kennedy,
who at an early stage saw the necessity to stop it and who tried to do so,
which was why he was assassinated by psychotics who could not accept it,
brought all America, the leader of democracy and of all nations,
morally in disrepute and in disdain, the bottom reached, we thought, by Nixon,
but, alas, there were administrations worse than his
who stolidly refused to learn the lesson. Still, the hibernating hippies
never stopped encountering new springs,
the music constantly increased the flow,
not even drugs could stop the freedom liberation of the mind
in idealistic aspiration, like an urge of irresistibility
for beauty, fantasy, constructiveness, creativeness and goodness.
Love and truth and beauty never died and never will
but will go on exploding and refuting backward world order forever.

Our case

Our only problem, as I see it,
is that we don't ever seem to get the chance to talk out properly.
There is so much I want to tell you,
there are infinities of question marks,
our friendship contains elements that need clarification,
the abstractness needs some definition,
I am too much kept away from you by work and obligations,
and our intercourse is always interrupted by some mad disturbance
importuning like we never importune each other.
That is our dilemma. We can't reach each other
in this alien world of a deranged society
of alienated and environmentally disturbed and brainwashed people
where we seem to be the only sane and normal ones,
since we can see the blindness of the others.
Fortunately we at least stand in some contact with each other,
or we would be left alone in isolation with the mess of all humanity.

For Phyllis, on her birthday

You went with me upon the hippy trail
once upon a time when we were young
in different worlds but in the same direction
in the pursuit of idealism and beauty
to get drunk by life and get into extremes of it
walking tall and high and without scruples
brushing everything away that wasn't positive;
and here we are, still, after forty years
and are still on that trail, pursuing happiness,
idealism and beauty, since we never gave up
that perhaps most vital quest there ever was in life.
I never was a hippy on the outside but the more
inside me with a soul more flippant than the worst
of crazy horses, and my best friends were by far
the most extreme ones, those who just did anything
in pursuit of the same ideals.
We have them still, whatever did get lost, they didn't,
and we still have far to go, for many years, I hope,
since for that quest the longest lifetime
(even with a hundred birthdays) never is enough.

Lost in the maze of love

The depth gets deeper all the time,
the abyss is no longer bottomless
but virtually expanding into the relentlessness
of the infinity of all the universe,
where you get lost,
where there is nowhere any compass,
any ups or downs or any straight road
but just an infinity of labyrinthic intricacy
with no hope of ever getting out again.
But maybe that's the very meaning
of the strange impalpability called love
that you should never get the hang of it
but just experience it as that amazing puzzle
of impossibility and incredibility it is
and suffer for it equally as much as you enjoy it
with the only obligation to just take it on
whatever happens, with a distant possiblity
to sometime somewhere maybe understand
what it was all about. You love, but that's not all
but only the beginning of another universe.

MAGNUS AURELIO

A hippie epitaph

Wherever did you go, my lovely lost one,
the butterfly of warm and tender colours,
always draped in veils like to enlarge your wings,
the Queen of hippies in those days
surrounded by a court of brilliant beautiful admirers,
a court that I accepted for my love of you
and loved you, living up to that responsibility.
We all were carried easily away by any love in those days,
so were you, when someone stole my bed with you in it,
but I still loved you after that and wanted to sustain my faith,
but you could never take it seriously
and abjectly refused all further poems
and all efforts for a reconciliation.
Was it better, then, to turn to smoking
and committing yourself only to the queerest bums?
You had a child with your seducer
and became a hard and bitter woman
whom I never more could recognize
as that sweet butterfly of only candid colours.
Once or twice you tried again to turn to me
in efforts to renew the loveliness we had,
but I was working hard and could not sacrifice
what ideals I had left to instability in love.
Instead, since then, I only worked for love.

Embarras de richesse

This law is very strange
that tells of the encumberment of pleasure,
how the better off you are, the more you feel unhappy,
and the more you have, the more you want and lack.
If you are spoilt by everything you want, your life is ruined,
and the higher you have raised the standard of your living,
the more likely you'll acquire dreadful illnesses,
most being nowadays of having lived too well;
while if you work hard and are poor and have to constantly fight with adversity,
you'll probably keep well and healthy and much better off than all the rich ones
suffering from boredom, from the worries of their property and their possessions,
from atrocious taxes and the turbulences of the stock exchange
and getting nothing for their woes and worries for their property and riches
but a most unwelcome premature heart attack or worse.

Such is the wisdom of this world and of its ways,
that all you strive for will backfire,
and no matter how much you deserve,
you will get only what you don't deserve.

The wayward ways of love

Sighing and dying for your sake
I languish in my hell of love
but do it gladly, since I know too well
how fortunate I am to suffer for your sake,
you being what you are, a goddess,
not of love but of the force behind it,
the motivation, the creation and the cause,
a queen of beauty but combined with feelings,
all a trembling tenderness of sensitivity,
a cluster abyss of intoxication
wondrously consisting of too much of everything,
a hopeless overwhelmingness
of beauty above all
to which we all must fall
in adoration and dependence
and the ultimate addiction
to the ultimate ideal of indefinability.

The comfort of maltreated ladies

A lover's soul is always full of tears,
but he can never shed them,
for they are not tears that flow that easily
like water, but must needs some treatment
to at all have any proper outlet.
There is one possible treatment only,
and that is the poet's temperament,
that transforms those precious tears
into the costliest jewels
as a neverending flow of riches
from a cornucopia of beauty
only for the pleasure of man's virtual eyes
and for the comfort of maltreated women,
who in poet's tears transformed into dreams
of beauty find a love of greater worth
than any man's discharge of natural brutality.

To Be in Love

Can you be driven to madness by love? It happens too easy.
A few sleepless nights only, missing your love, and you're lost.
Not an animal caught in a trap in a pit is so helpless and destitute
as he who's in love but without his beloved.
Turn around with your sighs in your sweated bed, you ridiculous fool,
for never you'll get her, since you are so stupid to love her too much.
There is no self-tormentor more miserable than the lover in loneliness
who dares not to love his beloved,
who dares not to cry out his madness,
who dares not admit his all too human weakness
and his foremost privilege being a man:
to be simply in love.

The dependence of independence and vice versa

Sorry, love, I can not do without you.
I was born a free man and an even freer spirit,
and I always cherished and kept safe my independence,
many girls refused me since I was too independent,
but then there was you, an equally nomadic independent spirit
living, as it seemed, on just her independence,
free and totally emancipated as a feminist,

and neither of us wanted ever to fall prey to thralldom,
not in any way, and least of all in some traumatic sado-masochistic bondage.
Still we need each other, but as independently dependent on our co-dependence,
freedom is the guarantee of our souls to never become subject to another,
so we can be co-dependently dependent on each other only as completely independent,
if you see my meaning, which is rather simple and not difficult at all.
And that is maybe the right key to every happy and successful couple and relationship:
that they remain completely independent as dependent on each other.

The true lover

"It's not you I do not trust,
it's all those other fellows,
all those swarming men around your bed,
all those invited to your side
to help you on the way to have some fun,
all those who just are out for kicks
to use the opportunity and to use you
for unknown ends, but selfish motives
always end up badly
usually for both the bastard and his victim;
but I love you anyway,
and that you can be sure of,
that no one in the world can love you more than I do.
So I don't mind all those other phonies
whether they are fucking you or not,
I just keep clear out of their way,
'cause I don't want no trouble
with my love or with her lovers,
since my troubles with myself
and with my feelings, honestly, are quite enough."

The grey hairs

Each time you see her, alive or in memory,
you shall acquire in richness another grey hair,
that being in logical law the most natural wages of love.
No one loves more without sense and more blindly
than aged poor old fools with no more on their heads
than the whiteness and baldness of suffering endless experience.
But he who is young, and without any single white hair,

has not loved anyone but himself yet.
With pain and with suffering only,
with the full desperation of unfair defeat bolting blindly in madness,
in the depths of dishonour and blackness of hell only
real love will gradually come to be learned,
which is not of this world,
but which colours you white like from ashes and snows
and which purges the colours away from your hair.

Madness

Some call it madness, others call it love,
some call it anger, others call it instability,
all those feelings that play havoc with you,
that result in outbursts for good or for worse,
that neither you nor anyone else can control,
that oversensitivity that people tend to suppress
under fraudulent masks of scruples killing all honesty –
no, let the madness out, if it be madness,
Freud was right, you can't keep anything in
and least of all the truth of ordinary human feelings
that simply have to be expressed,
or the stones themselves will start crying,
the weather exploding, the earthquakes arising,
your feelings are holy no matter how mad they may be,
and the only way to be human is to express your feelings.
Some criticism at last is due...

The challenge of the ten commandments

They are not really any true commandments
but eight prohibitions and two recommendations.
The ancient Greeks had only one commandment,
but they never put it down in writing,
since they knew man's fallacy enough
to be aware that he would never be obedient to common sense.
Their one commandment was a hint at a recommendation,
that one should not dedicate oneself to hubris,
which man ever did as long as he made history.
Since then, no more commandments were imposed on man,
since he preferred to constantly go mad
with hubris and to violate the ten commandments,
most especially the first and wisest, oldest one,

the one that said 'Thou shalt not kill'.
The history of mankind boasts the testimony
that he never could have heard of that commandment.
Older than the ten commandments was the fundamental message
of the oldest writs of man in ancient India in the Vedas,
where it is expressed not only in the Kamasutra
the necessity to live by love alone.
Well, well, that message clearly also was forgot from the beginning,
or the men that made this earth a constant battlefield
did never hear about it, as they never could learn anything.

Compassion Requiem for dead lovers

Let me share your tears and blend them with my own.
There is too much to always cry for,
and the oceans never can get full of all the human tears,
although they overwhelm the ocean waters with their saltiness,
since there is no end to sorrows and no bottom to their abyss,
the sorrow fountain being constantly replenished,
and the waves of tears irrevocably growing and increasing like tsunamis
in their overwhelmingness and irresistibility.
And there is no sorrow deeper than when love is dying,
the supreme momentum thereof being
suicide for love.
Here falls the silence,
words can not express the grief,
the tears will choke all voices into silence
which will boom with the appalling overwhelmingness of death
re-echoing in all eternity,
for there is no sound or power more tremendous
than the silent grief and sorrow for a true love that was lost.

Shyness

The gag and the strait-jacket coming from shyness
are far more efficient than those of a lunacy ward:
the tyrant of shyness called reasoning sense
will not let any word cross your teeth's fence to freedom
that might risk delivery of any feeling of honesty.
What shall we do with our feelings, then,
which still are there crying out in the prison of shyness,
tethered behind seven armoured gates of common sense?
No matter how reason ordains and securely rules over the world
bragging perfect control with the power of absolute force,
it is never more powerless in all its absolutism
against the simple truth and eternity of human feelings.

Some love declaration

I love you. What on earth does that mean?
It means that you are my only love,
that I can't love another,
that you are the only one included in my love life
and that my life without you is no life.

You are half my life, and this half is but half without it.
So what can we do about it?
That's the question.
We just have to stand each other,
live in the same world
and do the best of it.
There's nothing else to do.

Catechism or katharsis? Both!

The Drunkard's Cathesis

You know that it's bad for you, but you have it anyway.
You know it's self-humiliating, but still you have it.
You know it makes you more rough and vulgar and cheap, and still you have it.
You know it worsens your company with yourself, and still you have it.
You know it will ruin the following day, and that you won't feel nicely afterwards,
you know that you only ruin and decapacitate yourself, and still you do it.
You know it gradually burns out your brains, but still you have it.
You are a teetotaller, an anti-drug-campaigner, a strained purist making efforts,
you are the chastest of puritans, and still you have it.
It definitely tastes bad like something between piss and shit, and still you take it.
You ruin your intestines and fart bloody liquids,
you suffer a lot and can't stand it really, but still you take it.
When you piss the green and red stuff burns in your pick,
but you continue anyway.
Others will suffer for you, but still you continue.
You are incorrigible, and still you drink, although you know it's all wrong,
and you sober up just to start drinking again.
Why then do you keep on drinking? Just because you are only human.

All at sea

What care I about art and craft
as long as I am honest and have feelings to express
with some sincerity that is worth while expressing;
and to make it properly expressed correctly is my sole ambition,
not allowing any straying pedantry to interfere.
It is much more important to keep focussed
as the pilot on a wayward ship blown off the ocean,
no one knowing where we are or on what course we are,
this ship of love with tattered sails
and without any charts to follow

leaking from a million wounds and worries
and with nothing safe at all to hold on to
if we should sink – except our valid friendship.
That alone is all the safety in the world,
and as long as you have friends to turn to
and your love is nothing but a friend
no storm can blow you anywhere but home.

A divided combination or a combined division

What's the difference between loving you and loving my ideals?
Is there a differfence? Yes, but merely a subtle one,
you being so much of a soul yourself
with spiritual nourishment for your basic living
and your main sustenance for survival,
while of course ideals are always higher
than what anything can be in life on earth.
So am I then unfaithful to you for preferring my ideals,
or am I unfaithful to them for loving you?
A combination is the only answer.
I could love you both
and in the one embrace the other
and make my ideals find outlet into you
and find you one of my ideals.
That would, in fact, be the ideal love.

You are like a drug to me

You are like a drug to me:
as soon as the effects are gone
you only long for more,
for seeing you again,
for being with you,
sharing your good spirit and your joy again.
You are my glass of wine
without which I can't live much longer
in this dreary snakepit of consistent misery
with more complaints for every day
and tragedies galore
that constantly grow worse.
Your friendship only makes this life endurable,
the drug of life, the only joy,
the sharing with another

anything outside yourself,
forgetting all you know about reality
at least for the time being
in the better company of someone else.

The Bawd

a girl I used to know 23 years ago...
She's still alive, by the way, and hasn't changed at all...

An ugly old cow in a night-gown and challenging hips
walks thus out in the street, dressed in slippers
to swing them around just to make people watch;
swears and spits like a man, her vulgarity worse than a pimp's,
treating every man worse than a dumbbell,
with no respect except for virgins,
chain-smoking almost like some intermittent vulcano
and boozing but coffee except wine or port, brandy, whisky or spirits;
can stand any stuff, having guts made of iron and steel,
hardly reacting at all to her burning them out systematically.
But this bawd is a reader.
She has education like nobody else,
with a limitless library and no end to all her languages:
English, French, German and Spanish
is her conversation and brilliance of wit,
and she reads the most difficult literature in five tongues.
Her most favoured darlings are Pasternak and Stefan Zweig.
What intelligence! What a magnificent talent!
And all this concealed beyond such a facade of vulgarity,
those seven layers of paint and those curtains of cannabis smoke,
buried under that permanent booze of wine, brandy and whisky
and that sordid traffic of creeps, crawling creatures called men.
My dear heavenly muse of such splendid distinction and wisdom,
- who pushed you down in that alley? Who turned you thus on,
and who made you thus thwarted grotesquely?
And why was not I allowed into your presence
before thus your soul was so unjustly buried
beneath heaps of memories and disappointments
of love stories turned into such bitter sadness
of corpses remaining forever?

The private hard-liner

You must believe me: I do love you,
but what can I do for you,
this society we live in being as it is
with no aknowledgement or recognition,
salary or any notice of hard workers in the field of spiritual creation
like ourselves, and no awareness, only ignorance
of the importance of what we are working for;
so what can I do but continue working hard
for nothing, but the more persistently in obstinate timidity
for beauty, truth and love in poetry and music.
I don't care if this society will crumble in pathetic self-destructiveness,
I will continue spiting it and time and fashion all the same
by just continuing to work constructively
ignored by all the world and time
but for the satisfaction of my soul, if nothing else.

The masked l over

Let me come to you in clandestine disguise,
like some Greek god did hide in clouds to gain some access
to some nymph, for the avoidance of unnecessary scandals,
checking people's talk and prejudicial rumours,
sanctifying life, consigning it to safety
to let no one in on it except the lover and his love.
So will I drape myself in cloaked invisibility
to visit you in hours without witnesses
and get away with it but leave you with our love contained
forever as a gift of unsurveyable longevity
and with a summary for life enriching it forever
but for us alone, since no one else knows
that we love each other. Let it be a secret
for eternity for our souls to mask them
and to make them recognizable more markedly
so that we always can continue our love
in glorious independence of all things that do not matter
in true love, such as mortality and incarnations,
time and lifetimes, bodies, age and any circumstances.

Orpheus went to his mother, the muse Calliope, complaining...

Orpheus' complaint

C: Are you here, my son, complaining now again?
O: But what else can I do, my mother, this world being as it is?
C: You must have patience with the mortals.
O: It is not impatience that I suffer from. Your service, mother, is a tribulation,
since I am alone in my outstanding musicality
and therefore mostly sing to deafness and to ignorance of what I sing.
This dull mortality is killing me by their indifference,
which refuses me all feedback and but answers me by shallowness,
vulgarity and unawareness of the worths of truth and beauty.
As immortal in my talent I was even not allowed a wife.
They promised me her if I would perform and sing to all the dead ones,
and I did so, but the dead kept her away from me nevertheless,
and I was not allowed to even see her. Why, then, sing at all if only for the dead,
the deaf and ignorant who can not even keep their promises?
C: My son, life is unfair, I must admit, but you must have more patience
and continue working. That is your responsibility
to art, to beauty and to truth and all humanity.
O: Then let me die a martyr to the coarseness of the ignorant vulgarity of
mankind, for their deafness to my worth and beauty as musician kills my
music anyway.
C: My son, I'll see what I can do, but don't expect too much.
O: I only want a settlement, because humanity has broken
and refused me any kind of contract.
C: Orpheus, my dear, it grieves me so to see you suffer.
Would you then insist on crucifixion, just to have it done with?
O: Mother, mankind doesn't want me, and they never asked for me.
What can I do, then, but submit a mostr resounding protest
and efficient demonstration, that will never be forgot in history,
against the inhumanity, intolerance and dullness of this mortal ignorance
of man, that forces me out of my job?
C: You are impatient.
O: Art and truth and beauty and the soul must breathe,
or they will suffocate and stifle in impatience.
C: I have heard your prayer, your compalint against the gods is hereby filed,
but you must wait for their decision.
O: For the gods to act you have to wait forever.

The heroine

She is married to an alcoholic
for whom she slaves and totally exhausts herself
blindly nourishing her love with endless love.
As a drunkard he is a professional,
drinking much and all the time, with oceans in his eyes,
was clever once and able as an artist,
doing nothing good no more and being good for nothing.
He is just a burden to her
when he's not a burden to society and everybody else;
and when she is not present, he lies just with anyone and gladly.
He is unpredictable, is able to attack a stranger anytime,
sees often twelve blue elephants behind him
and dares never be alone.
He has four children from as many broken marriages,
while she has only one from but one broken marriage.
When from time to time he gets too difficult she takes some shots
sometimes a number of times a day.
She simply can not bear it anymore sometimes.
And she is epileptic.
But what a heroine for inspiration and divine endowment!
She will never bust and never cease her splendid humours,
only joy of life and warmest generosity she beams around,
and in her daily suffering she is more beautiful than no one else.
But it is a strained and straining beauty,
a beauty of enforced and pounded hardness,
of the tightened pain of inconceivable unyielding suffering,
the spiting courage of a furious mother hard against all evil,
a beauty rather masculine in screwed-up hardiness,
a beauty which in its heroic stubbornness against all sense
can only be as womanly as nothing else.

Bitterness

They all say the same thing:
No bitterness!
It gives a bad taste wherever it shows up,
destroys the poetry and kills the atmosphere,
dispels the magic and interrupts the dreams,
is alien to beauty and has no love in it,
and yet we can't escape the truth.
It's there stealthily lurking in the dark
to wait for us, assaulting us in vicious ambush

to throw us in depression with all doors thrown open
to the cellars with the skeletons, and we just have to look through it
to name the skeletons and voice the accusations,
and we can't just keep it to ourselves but have to share it
and give vent to anger, fury, grief, despair and pessimism
until the fit is over, and you can see sunshine beaming forth again
that marks the positiveness in its proper light,
and suddenly all bitterness has passed and is forgotten,
like a parenthesis of no consequence;
but still it's there awaiting in the dark
for opportunities that ever will recur
like darkness every night
with most unwelcome nightmares.

Romantic love

A curious phenomenon with a million definitions
and none of them correct. It's easier to say
what's not romantic when it comes to love.
For instance, sex is hardly a romantic point at all,
while suicide always is when it connects to love.
But most romantic of all love ingredients
is the fundamental one, the simplest and the basic one,
quite ordinary friendship, that can be expanded and enlarged,
constructed on forever and continuously built on and developed
spiting time and lifetimes and so on,
a precious jewel to be shared and commonly enjoyed,
a constantly enduring budding happiness,
a spiritual glory and a lasting comfort
and, above all, faith, trustworthiness and freedom
ultimately ending up in what we all so desperately need and long for,
which is definite true love that never ceases to be thoroughly romantic.

The Quarrelling Dame

She quarrels like hellfire sparkling,
wounding my soul with the sharpest of daggers galore,
like the soldiers of Rome shot down poor Saint Sebastian with forty-one arrows.
She beats me with her entire being in smothering violence,
destroying my spirit and knocking my head off,
turning my eyes out so that I no longer can see her,
benumbing my ears with her totally outstanding ire.

There is hardly anything left of me as I retire
on staggering feet not to see her again,
but still unhurt I smile, for I know,
that she scolded me only for love.

Some love declaration

I love you. What on earth does that mean?
It means that you are my only love,
that I can't love another,
that you are the only one included in my love life
and that my life without you is no life.
You are half my life, and this half is but half without it.
So what can we do about it?
That's the question.
We just have to stand each other,
live in the same world
and do the best of it.
There's nothing else to do.

At your spiritual service

Your blindness is much more than ordinary eyesight
since by your clairvoyance you can see what others can not see
and thus sees only what is best in man
since you bring forth his soul and sees it only
disregarding all the morbid outside shallowness
stuck in the flesh and in the problems of futility
that, fixed in egoism, is bent on vulgar opportunity
which you can't see and thus fall prey to selfish folly
of the coarse ambition of shortsightedness;
while few like you mind only the importance of the soul
and sees it through in all its beauty of imperishableness
thus bringing forth the best part of your neighbour
to some dangerous degree of spiritual hubris and intoxication
which they can not handle, since they are not used to it
and need some discipline to learn how to control it,
and thus they turn into your abusers of ingratitude.
To our good fortune there are some exceptions,
and I must regard it as my privilege in that capacity
as number one to humbly serve you as a friend and colleague
in whatever needs you ever might encounter.

Entangled

Entangled in each other's hairs
of spiritual richness and endowment
we are hooked and stuck together
in the web of love and shamelessly enjoying it
while at the same time it gives me some conscience
of the impropriety of living just for you

ignoring other duties and the problems of all mankind.
We must compromise and split our love in different bodies,
one attending outward obligations
and the other constantly attending only you.
Thus can I love humanity and life through you
and at the same time have you as my goal
in my attention and my love of life
and obligation to humanity,
thus keeping our love humane
in loving universally
and never losing ourselves
in false love webs of selfishness.

On the death of Anna Politkovskaya

Careful with that lethal weapon,
you might kill somebody with it
and, what's worse, make martyrs
that you afterwards will nevermore get rid of
since their testimony only will the more be sharpened
and kept furiously alive if they are killed for it,
you clumsy hooligans, that make a mess out of a decent work,
a brilliant journalist world famous for her courage
and her boldness to report on all the murders
and atrocities of our authorities
incriminating our whole government;
and you, deranged torpedoes,
just walk in and make a carnage out of a celebrity
respected and adored by all the world of conscience freedom fighters
and a lovely woman, and a mother at that, also,
like the idiots you are, instead of simply forcing her abroad,
no matter how, thus silencing and keeping her efficiently away,
like the Chinese do
with whoever dares to implicate the criminal authorities.
What can we say? You made a mess of it,
now everyone call us accountable,
and we can not even defend it.
All that I can say is, the less said, the better.

— Vladimir Putin.

Another brave journalist

An investigating correspondent of the war scene in Iraq,
she made sure to be friends with everyone
and most especially with the Iraqis and all common people
but was shocked to see how by the mere existence of the war
all people became brutalized and alienated
and especially her friends, the common people, the Iraqis;
and before the war was ended she was kidnapped by Iraqis
for no purpose, just because she happened to be foreign.
After a few weeks they realized they had no reason to keep her as hostage,
so she was released and could return in safety to her friends.
In safety? With her as a bodyguard was her best friend,
and as they came back to the lines of the Americans
they opened fire on her without any warning.
She was well protected by her friend the bodyguard
who shielded her with his own body
but was shot to death himself - by the Americans,
the leaders of this "friendly war".
The incident led to a crisis in her country's government,
the Berlusconi government of Italy,
who enthusiastically and uncritically had joined up with Bush.
She just told the truth and risked her life for telling it,
investigating what went really on behind the war scenes
and is clear about it: US loaded the Iraqi government
of Saddam Hussein with mass destruction weapons
for the use against Iran in that war twenty years ago.
When Bush embarked on this war in Iraq some years ago
it was with the excuse that Saddam Hussein still
had all those mass destruction weapons and was dangerous,
which proved a fable, since he did not have them any more.
So America gave fuel to that oven,
that got burning hot in Bagdad with Saddam Hussein,
and then sat down on it,
and that is why the US arse is burning in Iraq.
Her name is Giuliana Sgrena. She is still alive
and continues risking her own life
to build the bulwark of democracy by sticking to the truth
and making it well heard and documented.

Hold me responsible...

Hold me accountable for all your inconveniances,
I feel responsible since I invited you to this absurdly alien country,
make me guilty for all the inhuman controversies, insults and humiliations
that you suffered here for being only what you are,
a free creative spirit with a right to be your own
and wise at that and honestly constructive.
It is no one's fault that people are here as they are,
completely spoilt by a degenerating welfare system
turning people into zombies by the isolation brainwash system
which, alas, is common in industrialized developed welfare states.
In opposition to the backward cultural illiteracy here
we have to stand up on our own and just survive
and make the best of it in these dark ages
of exploding criminality, drugs abuse and rape.
Be not afraid, though, because I shall always stand you by
providing a protection shield against all bad vibrations
and destructive influences, being totally immune myself.
And we are safe as long as we keep at it
working hard creatively and actively
and stand up to the right of our artistic freedom
as exceptions from the humdrum greyness of the common ignorance,
refusing to get dull and brainwashed like the masses;
and our freedom as creative minds is our mark of nobleness
of higher quality and status than positions, property or progeny
of any kind; since we are children of eternity,
the world is far too small for us,
no ocean is enough for our need of space,
we need all the ether of the universe
just to dwell and breathe and move around with our minds
as perfectly creative spirits not accepting any limits.

Reservations

True love is of course completely unreserved,
or else it is not true and must raise doubts.
However, burnt by lessons of experience
you must as a lover have misgivings
and be more reluctant with the years to take the smallest risk,
which makes you hesitant and undecisive
when you fall in love one final time too much.
But that might only be to love's advantage.
Any love experience teaches you some good,
and the more hard and painful your experiences have been,
the more good lessons they have taught you
which can only be to your advantage;
for the more experienced lovers are,
the more their irresistibility increases,
since they only love the more the harder they've been hit.
This lesson tends to teach us, that the more you hesitate,
the more you doubt your love and have misgivings,
the more true your love, and the more beautiful it will become.

Ultimate love

There is no ultimacy in love,
and that's what's ultimate in love.
The ultimacy is strived for and worked hard for,
you can climb whatever mountain for it,
but you'll never reach the top of that one,
since that Venus mountain was created
to remain forever the most sacred and unreachable of mountains,
like the fabled Monte Veritá with secret monasteries and sisterhoods,
which you ultimately can get into any touch or understanding with
by only dying for it. Better then to go on climbing,
striving, working hard and longing
for the ultimate evasive ultimacy
that will go on attracting you and tempting you,
provoking you and prompting you
to any feat of heroism, impossibility and miracle
except to reach the ultimate fulfilment
of that love of yours that once was given you
for the ultimate challenge of your life.

Still there on the hippie trail...

Two of them are dead, one murdered,
the other was their only intellectual
with some serious interest in the classical.
Paul is entertaining still and less pathetic than the Rolling Stones,
who never knew their limits where to stop
with some romantic flair kept intact –
they just kept on wasting everything on nothing
and especially on drugs – they all did that,
Sid Vicious and the Sex Pistols, Brian Jones,
the monster of vulgarity, king Elvis Presley,
while Cliff Richard and flamboyant Tommy Steele still have some style;
but almost all the others wasted everything on going down the drain
by drugs or alcoholism, like all jazz musicians;
and the question is, as it was put by that old king of rakes
George Jung in prison: Was it worth it?
He felt it was almost worth it, although he lost everything.
Even such endowed and ordered talents as the Beatles
went on drugs as they earned millions every day,
and Moody Blues were worshipping Tim Leary,
dead of aids, the freaked out drugs professor
who kept professing extreme liberalism until the end

and never had regrets or ceased to keep it up,
that totally absurd ecstatic exaltation about living just for trips,
as if life's meaning was complete detachment from it,
any means allowed for any kind of drastical escape,
as if hysteria was the truth and only happiness.
That whole concept was fantastic
and a kind of cult of pure phantasmagoria,
and however mad that universal craze was,
and how totally insane much of that music was,
I can but quietly agree, that all that waste,
and every single moment of it,
was completely worth it.

In the sky

My love is freer than the blue sky
and a darker menace than the midnight sky
but is as true as any sky
that constantly remains up there
and shows as much fidelity as any weather
changing constantly but being always there
to dream of and extol like any ideal ecstasy
to worship and remain in service of with gratitude
forever, – if it only would be possible.
But you are always there, I know it,
waiting for me, ready for me,
with as much delight and charm
as any love could ever dream of;
and so shall I love you
as turbulently as the weather ever changes
but interminably with a cosmic passion
fit to fill the universe with more delightful sunshine
than could ever be produced by any supernova
banging off in indefatigably limitless expansion.

Flair

How shall I relate to you, my love?
We stand too close to be at odds
and have too much in common
to have any reason for division,
and we understand each other far too well

OCTOBER HARVEST FIRST PART.

for words to be of any service,
needed or at all be necessary.
We have everything, and yet we miss each other
since our souls are too united to allow our bodies to unite,
wherefore we have to keep some distance
not to risk our souls. And that's the secret
of our love, that is so envied, since it gives us
so much more than just the joy of mortal love.
That special character enhances and brings forth
the beauty of our souls and underlines it
in a spiritual development that has no limit,
which is marked by others but not understood by them,
which fills them with some envy which defies all definition.
Let them be confounded by their lack of understanding.
Deities should never mind the small talk of the mortals,
and in our love our level stands above the mortal speculation
making us like gods in our special kind of love
that stands forever beyond mortal recognition.

The problem of the commonest love cliché

I love you. How can I make those words sound less banal,
this common phrase worn out by everyone most every day,
this formula turned shallow into water dried by verbal homeopathy,
a boring repetition meaning nothing by too much protesting,
overused especially by liars – but how can you else express it?
That's the question, and the answer will be difficult.
Perhaps the best way to express it is by not expressing it at all
but merely showing it, by deeds, by poems and by presents,
for example, while the truest love expression is within yourself,
you only know yourself the real truth of your love,
no one can feel your feelings and their worth and how they feel but you yourself;
but probably the finest way to give them some expression
as correct and true as possible is by creative art,
especially by poetry, which was constructed just for subtleties.
And if your loved one reads your poetry, accepts it as her own
and takes it to her heart, she will, if not at once,
by time at least and constantly more deeply understand it,
especially since that's the kind of love that lasts,
it can not burn out and it can not lie,
but it is there and live forever.

The forsaken lover's complaint

I searched for love, but all I found was loneliness
behind the masks and ruins of betrayed fidelity
in desperation trying to keep up a smiling face.
I searched for virtue but found none that lasted
and no continuity in promises and vows and faiths.
I searched for purity but there was none
that did not purposely seek out the dirt to wallow in it,
as if purity was only meant to get debased.
I searched for morals but found only double standards,
and where civil courage actually stood up I found it crucified
or, if it managed to survive, neglected and avoided.
I found no love that did not first think of its advantage,
opportunist love that only calculated profits
and no love that was not narcissistic, thinking only of herself.
I found in this world no ideals that were not crushed
and smothered by reality, the world and power
and the bulldozer establishment of ruthlesnes and egoism.
I found no spirit that did not strive ultimately for material benefits

and no religion that was basically not just camouflage
for egoism, fanaticism and power greed ambition.
And where was that good will that did not result in only tragedy and evil?
Where was beauty that was not corrupted by the ugliness surrounding it
and drowned by the environmental ruining of everything,
pushed down the drain and trampled on, buried alive?
Where is God, who they say is the only one responsible
for making all this universal mess and keeping it in order?
To these problematic questions you will find one single answer only
in your solitude.

The concert pianist

What care I about the audience and their tastes?
The truth is only in the music,
and my only job is to be faithful to it,
honestly to make it right and render it some justice
and forget about the audience.
They are only there to get the message
while I am the messenger who carries with me
the divine and lasting message of a better world
of sanity that outlasts all the madness of the world.
Compared with music, there is nothing but insanity
in everything that is not music that sounds well.
So listen carefully, hark well my message,
for it is unique, and it is difficult,
demanding concentration and a total focus,
for true music of pure harmony and melody
is in all its abstractness and aloofness from reality
no less than all the voice of God you'll ever hear.

The divorcee

"Shall I give you up, then,
since you show so little interest?
I am tired of this constant hell
of always looking after you
while you ignore me and just fool around,
enjoy yourself and drown yourself in shallowness
with younger men and lovers
risking clearly to get vulgarized like them
in abysses of boring cynical frivolity.
Is that how love must always end,

one doing anything just to escape the other's company,
abandoning oneself to gaiety of nothingness
and ending up in vacuum on the other side
with only bitter memories of foolhardy mistakes
and finding your most desolated loneliness
in the mistaken lover and a marriage failure?
Is my friend then to prove right
in the most terrible repellentt possible reality
that there is no love but in self-love,
which you fool yourself by calling your ideal?
If that is true, then there is nothing in that truth
and no God in existence in such truth,
no God in such a meaningless reality
and in this life no love at all.
Then even death is better,
and all suicides for love have never hesitated
to prove such a bleak reality of no love possibility
completely wrong as an absurd and total unacceptability."

The crucial daily contact

Your love is all you need
to have a full infinity of love and happiness
crammed into only one resplendent day
if only you can have a touch or glimpse of her.
That day will then be saved and counted
as successful and felicitous and unforgettable;
but one day, just one single day without your love
and without any contact with her
will inevitably bring disaster, ruin you
and throw you straight into the depths of hell,
and that day will be lost forever.
That's why you must keep up your love
in daily contact with her, or you'll both be lost,
you to your nightmares, and she to her worse alternatives,
and none will be the happier for that,
there will be only turbulences, griefs and tears instead;
when you could be so happy if you just maintain your love
by keeping just in touch, reminding of each other
to keep up the paradise of your unequalled union
which the whole world is dependent on
for your and all the universal harmony and happiness.

Abandonment

The darkness of your soul is like a menace to our lives,
and yet there is no evil in that darkness,
only an entrapment in your self
that threatens you much more than anybody else.
No wonder you are hopelessly nomadic,
seeking constantly to get away from your shortcomings,
limiting yourself by closing up your feelings,
trying to escape from the dilemma of a personality
that has too many anchors in the past
to ever get across the sea.
The more you try to get away,
the more you will get wounded by your fetters.
You just have to face the music,
let the curtain up, forget about yourself,
deny yourself, allow yourself to get away from it
and finally allow yourself your feelings.
Yes, get overwhelmed, cry out,
you need it, it will do you good,
and I will help you cry and share your tears
and mix your feelings with my own.
Thus shall we never leave each other
but together drown in blissful abysses
of totally forgetting all about ourselves.

Political detachment and disdain

Welcome, brave new world of cloning only and no love,
you loveless phantom of aborted visions of unhuman lies,
the twisted nightmares and sick morbid fantasies of Orwell,
Huxley, Wells and other artificial futurists who all were wrong,
since that acceleratingly deteriorating unhuman society
is only an unnatural alternative to getting too deep into drinks and drugs,
to unsound dreaming out of work in decadent intoxication.
It's a lie that our language is impoverished,
that we are all controlled by Rupert Murdoch and his media,
since we humans never can be slaves without revolting.
Any kind of tyranny and mad oppression in whatever smart disguise
can only lead to triumphant rebellion with victorious overthrow.
All materialistic thinking, programming and calculating are but lies
that always are refuted by the unexpectedness of history.

The whole world with its leaders, opportunists, populistic flirters,
pharisees and hypocrites are just a masquerade without a meaning,
empty boasts of nothingness and cheapest nonsense
which attracts attention with the same efficiency
like anciently the Romans used to be efficient in producing
on the vulgar masses by just ranting on the stage
and making vulgar noises like of farting.

The dream chase of love

My love is like a dream that never ends,
that varies constantly in shifting hues and colours,
always entertaining and dramatic,
always shifting into unexpected turns and moods,
as unpredictable as any weather,
ever turbulent, irrevocably always coming up with new surprises,
and as fascinating as the rainbow as it glows and shifts complete
after a rainstorm, always promising a neverending future
full of new surprises of just perfect wonderfulness without end.
So therefore I refuse to wake up from that dream,
I will cling to it and intently follow it,
contributing most willingly to its expansion and development
that keeps just filling not just my life
but all life around me with the lustre of some splendour
that just can't be left alone.
So, please continue, dream of love, to haunt me,
never leave me, never let me down in peace and ease,
but keep pursuing me, and I shall pursue you
until the end of my unending loving days.

OCTOBER HARVEST FIRST PART.

Phantom love

The abstinence of you is totally unbearable,
a torture worse than any possible hang-over,
a depression of Grand Canyonesque dimensions
and a melancholy illness with no cure in sight
unless you suddenly would come and save me.
It's worse than any epidemic, worse than Aids
and all veneric possible diseases, worse than death,
since one is forced to stay alive – and without you.
It's like being hamstrung in a hospitable bed
obliged to wear a strait-jacket tied up tight
with no air left to breathe and thirstier than any desert,
it's like being thrown out into empty space
launched like a satellite to fall forever
into constantly increasing darkness
that will never spare you any nightmares.

So, in short, my love, I can not live without you,
there is no life for me but a life with you,
so I shall never leave you
but remain your constant guardian
as a crazy spirit hovering around you
to protect you with my loving madness
against anything in life that is not love.

Passionate poetry and poetical passion

That poetry is rather dull
that only speaks of positive affection,
love in the blues and fondling silliness,
and goes from bad to worse in purple passages
since sex is never properly described in words.
But when your love is set on trial
and you have to face adversities,
when Romeo and Juliet comes along in tragedy
and blood and death becomes ingredients,
then suddenly the inane love becomes an interesting affair.
You need some drama to make love
at all convincing, or you will get petered out.
So bring along the drama, the adversities,
the jealousy, the raving passion,
raise the green-eyed monsters,
let them swarm up from Moria
and the dens of hell in overwhelming masses,
spice the passion with some sado-masochism,
start tying people to their bed-posts,
bring along the chains and scourges,
bring the shameless nudity out in the open,
let the hairs loose in their maximum of length,
and make some scenes with tears and outbursts,
and the love will come alive
in flashing fireworks of most explosive power,
screw it up with alcohol and drugs,
make orgies out of parties and let them derail,
and you will have a passion
that will set your poetry aflame and flying,
taking off with jet acceleration
leaving ground forever;
and you will be flying on the wings of love
and nevermore be able to do anything without it.

A dirge

She sings for love but crying all the time,
it is a sad song of deception and a growing disappointment,
cheated of her life her melancholy is forever growing inwards
in a dreadful pain affecting heart and lungs, like in consumption;
but her tears will ultimately release her, since that flow
is purging not just her but all that know her,
since her empathy is so exceeding strong and deep
that anyone who can at all perceive it
must be touched profoundly and not ever choose to fail her,
although everybody does, since no one understands her grief,
the constant flow of tears of blood, for nothing, seemingly;
but with her cries all nature, half of all the forests of the world
now being gone, annihilated, burnt, cut down and ruined,
while all wildlife is increasing in extinction
and the monster man keeps violating Mother Earth
with no consideration, afterthought or sense at all
while she is suffocated by his burning tyranny
transforming forests into cinders so that earth no more can breathe.
And you are crying out your tears of blood for all humanity.
I can not dry them up, but only add to them.

Universal vanity

What's in a relationship when you remove all vanity,
what is there left at heart, what's in the core,
what is the centre of all love,
what do two people have in common
that results in tenderness, affection, co-dependence, and so on?
The problem is: you never find the core.
All you can do is to forget about all that which does not matter,
age considerations, practical and trivial circumstances,
all that is just in the way,
for souls can always find each other and stick to each other
without any banal means,
since their relationship is written in the stars,
and a relationship is always timeless.
Ask the spiritists who never lose their touch
with loved ones long since passed away
who are as much alive today as hundred years ago,
your love is always and invariably a matter of eternity,
once it is there it's there to stay
and go on living with you all your life and beyond,
and the stars confirm it: it's all written in the universe,
that there is nothing vainer than at all to bother
since we all are part of the eternal,
and the key and contact with it is our love.

Some sweaty lines

Running out of inspiration
turns you on in perspiration
and your stinking transpiration
adds to all that constipation.

The lights of our love

I love you in the morning
when the birds do warbling sing your praise.
I love you in the evening
when the sunset decks the world in rosy golden colours
just for you. I love you in the daytime
when the sun delights in you and tries to outshine you
in all her glory, which she fails in,
so she is happy to be glorious just for her delight in you.

I love you in the night, when passion rules
in glowing assiduity and hotness, like the stars can never be outshone.
I love you every day, like every light in the whole universe
can never be shut out or hindered in its splendour.
I love you perpetually and with imperturbable continuity
that rather than to tire seems to constantly increase.
I love you evermore, there is no end to it;
so let's just keep this marvellous eternity,
enjoy it and maintain it and just let it shine.

Idealism: an allegory

Idealism isn't wrong,
it's just that it but keeps on flying
beyond mortal wits and possibilities,
and thus reality refuses to accept her.
She is right, though,
to just keep on flying,
or else she would not be true
to herself and to her idealism,
and there would be no idealism.
That's the risk of true idealism:
it has to fly high in the air
and never tire on her restless wings,
or she will fall and die and perish
and be there no more to be admired
by the happy few who understand
the frail unique imperishable nature
of idealism.

The confidential lover

"How shal I express my love to you
without it being insufficiently expressed and incorrectly?
It is vital for its life and for it to at all be able to survive
that it is right from the beginning and that it can not go wrong.
You are the only one I love, and that I do not wisely but too well.
That is the whole truth of the matter, there is nothing else to add,
you have my heart and are the only one to have it,
and I must regret it only if it would become a burden to you,
for I am prepared to bear the burden of my love alone

if it would be unbearable to you, or for that matter
to anyone who could not bear it or who would not have me.
There you are. My prayer is all yours and in your hands
to do with it as my most sacred offering whatever you would choose,
to cherish it and use it or to do without it.
I have been refused before and, sorry to say, used to it,
so I can take it as a man and will survive
no matter how my love might be received, misused, manhandled
or refused and trampled down by those who would not understand it,
but I will continue loving anyway and be the constant lover ever;
for I know my love is of such kind that it can never be a waste."

The quiet reader

I read you well, and therefore I keep silent.
Let my silence be the voice of my appreciation –
when you are affected, you can't speak.
So I am sorry if I can not let you all know
what I read and how I read and how I love it –
I have never read a poem here at Poetbay
that I did not find lovable. You can not waste your time here,
on the contrary, you can not use it better.
In a few days I'll be gone for yet another journey,
but I hope to stay in touch no less for that,
if not with regular and ordinary diligence,
at least sporadically, since I never can stop writing.
That was all. I love you all, and will continue reading you,
although unnoticeably and invisibly to you,
unless your sensitive poetical antennae will perceive
how much I love you all.

In the void

Without love, what can you do?
Your life becomes a desert void of flowers,
there is no water for your dryness,
common sense is worthless
like all instruments and indispensable technique,
you can just not do anything but languish
in a boredom worse than any hell;
so any love is better,
and that means exactly ANY love!

Let her misuse you and abuse you,
use you for her calculations and own ends,
let her deceive you with just anyone,
just leave it all to her, as long as you may keep her
as your love, for that is all you have,
and there is no life and nothing to live for
but a vacuum worse than death without it.
And that power thus supremely exercised is not by women
or by any partners, but by that phenomenon called Love alone.

One of those singsongs

Solo:

I would love to sing a song
for only you and me
to go a-singing all along
for lovely hings to be

Chorus:

For all bad things must have an end,
true love is all we have to spend,
we have no other time, my friend,
for any other end or trend.

Solo:

So sing along with us this song
of true love that just can't go wrong
as long as we keep getting on
to sing this unforgettable amazing song

Chorus:

For all bad things must have an end,
true love is all we have to spend,
we have no other time, my friend,
for any other end or trend.

Some serious business

There was an old shit-house in Tangiers,
public, of course, and used by everyone,
so you could not enter,
because the whole house was full of shit,
so you just had to shit outside,
standing on the safe side of the threshold
with your arse inside
and fire.

Children

We are children, all,
that never can grow up,
since even the most grown up and most serious
must remain and never can become more than a child,
like even the most aged and whitish bearded patriarch,
like every politician, bishop, bureaucrat, aristocrat and autocrat:
inside at heart you never are more than a child;
all honours, medals, titles, merits and diplomas
are just frippery and shallow masks, hypocrisy and fakes,

since all of life is just a childish thing that constantly grows more so
the more you think that you grow up and mature;
and the wiser you think you are getting, the more childish you become.
And therefore the old man and the small child are strongest among humans,
since they only dare be openly and credibly and naturally childish;
only they enjoy that privilege.
Those so called mature ones that acquired a position and responsibility,
who are so stupid that they start to take life seriously
must never lose their face, that most ridiculous mask of maturity,
since they imagine that they matter, which makes them so utterly ridiculous.
No one therefore is more human, real and natural than those
who all their life through dare prove openly
that they were never more than just small children.

The winds of the unconscious

The melancholy landscape of our love
is harrowed by unfriendly winds
that blow the beauty of our dreams to tatters,
but, on the other hand, these hard and cruel winds
just by their hardness blow our love across the world
like windhorses that never tire.
That's our glory: we give never up, we never tire,
we just keep loving through our work of beauty
to renew the world and cleanse it from its foulness
like the prophets of eternity that might be our unknown mission,
subconsciously but all the more importantly and powerfully.
That's our only job: to keep the course of truth to our vocation,
which is only to create through love a lasting world of beauty.

One more comment on Joshua

see my earlier poem "Compassion - Requiem for a dead lover", October 5th.

The ghosts are always there
whether they dwell in Limbo or are gone
for new adventures in Samsara,
and that's the miracle of spiritism:
although a loved one long ago has left
and taken up a new life burden
it is possible to have subconscious contact with her soul,
she will respond, her depths of soul are always possible to stir
and to recall to life with contacts of an earlier incarnation.

This is difficult, absorbing and subduing stuff
that never can be thoroughly investigated,
only nosed on and discovered hopelessly to be
an entrance to eternity that only leads to one more door
than opens into other, deeper, more eternities.

The inseparableness of dreams and reality

The highest possible of dreams
is naturally just a dream of love
but could be nothing but a dream of you.
So long now have I loved you,
and yet you are so far away,
unreachable and unattainable
not like a statue but more like an angel,
and yet are you closer to me every day.
How is this paradox to be explained?
It can not be explained but only understood.
We know each other better than tough lifetime couples
and yet have not lived together for a moment.
Flashlights have our golden moments been of rare togetherness,

but flashlights are more blinding and efficient
than unending days of boring greyness.
In this lifetime we have flashed through many lifetimes
as if it was time to bring them all together
in a single moment of explosive truth
to let love once for all and definitely
triumph in a bliss of irrreversible imperishableness.

The passion of your hair

More brilliant and unfathomable in its richness
than the shimmering profundity and lustre of the Milky Way,
the lights and colours of your gorgeous hair
is food enough for an eternity of sleepless nights,
but is my passion worthy your divinity?
Your passion speaks a language far more eloquent
than any body language could express,
and I must try to match it with a similar sincerity,
but such ambition is impossible for mortal limitations.
That's the problem of our passion: it is out of bounds,
and therefore I am by respect reduced to silence,
but rather call it awe, and let another sense take over,
that extraordinary power of the other senses than the five,
since that is what we need to understand and get to know our love.
So let us dwell for all eternity in outer worlds
than this so sorrowful mundane and trivial one
with all its most pathetic bodily and sorry limitations
to stretch out with the ambition of our love
for fruits of even stranger trees than the forbidden ones of knowledge
and of right and wrong, to celebrate together
that intimacy with stranger secrets of eternity and life and death
that ever could be properly expressed by human passion.

Into the bottom of despair

When the storm gathers and things get rough
and darkness besieges you strangling your life
surrounding you with constant terror of outrageousness
and turning all your daylight into night
driving you hard into cornered defeat
losing everything hopelessly, even your way,

you have nothing left and no salvation to turn to;
but even when all beyond all hope is lost
there remains in the darkness of hopelessness
someone to love who will think of you kindly,
and that knowledge is all you need to survive
almost anything, even the horrors of terror;
and never there was such a total despair and complete utter darkness
that love did not always shine through it
dispensing of all that was just in the way.

The Talisman

We have a secret pact
that no one can begrudge us
since no one knows about it
or could even understand it
since it is within ourselves,
the secret understanding
of a higher sense of wisdom
in a total alien language
of pure feeling, sensitivity and touch,
that make us far more vulnerable
than most people,
who would judge our extra sensitivity
a 'nervous problem of a schizoid kind',
while it in fact is like a Talisman
more costly than all riches of the earth
and as a love affair and language much profounder
and much higher than all commonplace communication,
and we share it with some dead ones
who are still alive beyond the grave
and much more so than all those normal people
who would never understand
an extrasensory perception
of a language of pure feeling
that belonged to more romantic times
of depth of pathos and compassion
that has never been in use again
since it was buried and forgotten
with the tears of many tragic poets and composers.

The dark sides of beauty

Many are distraught by that tremendous melancholy
of those sentimental moods and melodies
that fill the golden music of Chopin
and makes it overwhelming,
and he was a sick divinity indeed,
just crying all his life for all his lost engagements,
all the girls that wouldn't have him for his poverty
or for George Sand, who just maltreated him
and made his illness worse by mental cruelty.
But there is one more side to it, an even darker one,
the passion and the storms,
the raving fury of the world's political injustice;
and that's where you have the universal illness:
It was not Chopin's but all the world's.
His Polish motherland was cruelly occupied,
suppressed, stamped down and ruined by the Russians,
and for that Chopin's heart bled itself to death
not from relentless harm and righteous fury
but from bottomless compassion.
What he did was to cry all his soul out
and to waste it in a pathos of wild mad and bitter sorrow
with no ends, no cure and nothing else for it but hopelessness,
like in the case of any bolting horse,
that can't be stopped except by her own heartbreak.
That's the darkness, the supremest terror,
the compassion that can find no end,
no bottom to its sorrow
and no choice but to continue crying out
forever.

MAGNUS AURELIO

True love undefined

Even the heaviest planets of the highest density and solidity are just flying around...

True love is never to let down
and never put down.
You just can't pinpoint it.
It has its own laws
never to be violated
never to be understood

and least of all defined,
you just obey them,
follow them and close your eyes,
to learn that you are blind,
which is what you are,
a child astray and drifting far away
i no man's land in darkness
flying just around
with nothing stable,
nothing to depend upon
and nothing possible to cling to
except love itself,
the perfectly supreme capriciousness
that has to be obeyed
or simply left alone,
and then you are alone indeed.

The love of paradoxes

While at the same time we are so much like each other
we are totally each other's contraries
unmatchable irrevocably with each other
while we can not do without each other,
you dependent on continuous company,
me dreadfully dependent on the freedom of my solitude,
while also you need, most of all, your space of freedom
and I wallow in that sado-masochistic social addiction,
which just burns me out, like you are burnt out
by all that you loathe and cannot do without.
It's one of those impossible equations: love is never mathematical;
you need your freedom and your loneliness and company,
and I need solitude and freedom and addiction
to all that which harms my work and limits my expansion.
Are we both then self-destructive as creative artists?
Yes, in some ways, since we need to be alone and free
but are dependent on each other
and must do without each other totally except as friends
whose love is far too strong to be allowed
except as spiritually roaring beyond all control,
and that is never satisfactory, no matter how much we are soaring
beyond space and time in madness of our sanity of love,
which gives us nothing but a whole eternity of sleepless nights.

Life's gift is only to be given, never to be taken

I am with you
on the dark side of the moon
where no one sees your tears,
but you shall never cry alone,
not even in that total and eternal darkness,
for I am the light
that shines up even that most hopeless
dark side of the moon.
The cure is to let go,
forget about yourself
and concentrate on anything that isn't you.
It's your responsibility to life
to love all life
and not just be alive yourself.
You are the fountain of your life
that spreads your life to others
and should not keep life just to yourself.
Old people may be boring,
but they know what life is all about
or else they would not still be living,
they would not have lived so long
if they were not familiar with the knowledge
that your life was given you to give to others,
not just to enjoy it for yourself;
for there is no more certain misery,
unhappiness, entrapment and despair
than to get stuck in bleak self-centredness,
a one way only down to hell,
while life is only in embracing it with love
and giving it away with constant care for others
as long as you live.

A greeting to Zoya, for Diwali

Sorry I can't join you.
We are stuck here in the darkness,
the notorious depressivity of Scandinavia,
where now begins the dreariest season of the year
around the Hallowe'en, when most of the year's suicides occur,
and many people die for nothing,
maybe just from darkness and depression.
In the darkest days we have but seven hours' daylight,

and the rest is darkness at its densest, thickest and most daunting.
But in India the summer will continue
still for yet another month,
and I will join you there,
as prices fall after Diwali
to enjoy the freshness and the joys of India in the fall
when people there are at their very nicest
and the harassment of tourists vanish
with the dollar tourists, while the pilgrims and the lovers
faithfully remain, who know and love their India.
I can't promise to find you in Aligarh,
but at least I will give you some greetings
from my lovely mountains Nanda Devi, Anna Purna
and of course the loveliest in the world -
the Kanjenjunga.

Reduced to silence

When reduced to silence
love still goes on
more glowingly and intensively
than if it was outspoken,
for silent love keeps quiet
only to control its fervour,
utter honesty and overwhelming truth,
sincerity and depth of feeling
to maintain itself
and save it for eternity
to keep it burning
always with the fullest flame
but the more faithfully in secret.

Terms of Trial

My concern for you in your melancholy
is limitless, complete and hopeless
in incurable despair and worry
like your own outcrying anguish,
but what can we do about it?
This benighted situation is not of our making,
we are innocent of alien mentalities
like suppressing, ignorant and parasitic ones,
and see no solution else but to cut off the leeches,
not have anything to do with sick mentalities
and just do our own job in peace and quiet
obstinately and in isolation, if there is no other choice,

although it is both hard and difficult
to constantly ward off adversity
and struggle against evil winds
of no intentional but no less ruinous hostility
of pure indifference, ignorance, stupidity and sloth.
What can we do? I am afraid our only choice
is just to keep on working and keep smiling,
doing something good out of a hopeless world
destroyed by spiritual corruption, poverty and misery.

From the depths of wilderness

When in the depth of our acquaintance
I must question our validity
and search a purpose with our flight together
in the waste of space in perfect blindness,
I find nothing to confirm and validate our union,
only the right contrary, impossibilities
and arguments against it,
but that is the very challenge:
we have entered far too deep into each other's souls
to extricate ourselves from this immersion;
and the fact that circumstances, all of them,
cry loudly out against it
only makes the fusion more consolidated
and increases the attraction of the challenge.
So let's just go on, in blindness, anywhere
and stick with cheeky obstinacy to each other
even clandestinely if it so must needs,
since we have nowhere else to go.

Preferences

People with a dark spot, like alcoholism, addiction,
sexual mistakes and other kinky weird anomalies
are usually more human and more interesting than normal ones
of orderly perfection and impeccability,
who more incline to ordinariness and being boring,
not that you must be extreme and utterly immoral
not to be a bore, but people who have tasted self-indulgence
usually have much more interesting human knowledge and experience
than all those who just are natural and normal.
Give me therefore a fanatic or an alcoholic or an addict,

and he will be better company than any stable person of position
who knows nothing about man, lives only for himself
and has no love but for his possessions and his self.

Audible whisperings around the globe...

All I miss is you, since you are all the world to me.
What is the world to me with all its riches and careers
and fortunes without you, since you alone give any meaning to it?
Yes, I miss our midnight conversations and the outcries of our unions,
but we shall join hands together once again
and hug each other in embraces that will never cease
to warm each other for the longest winters
and to fill our memories with food for thought
enough for candid tenderness without an end to it.
That's all I can devote myself to in your absence:
sentimental and pathetic weaknesses of sad nostalgia
and melancholy to make tigers cry for crocodiles.
You are with me, and I am still with you,
no matter how extreme the geographic difference is,
which problem can't go any worse,
which means, things can go only better then.
Let's hope so, for that is our only comfort.

My home conviction

My home of love is yours. It is not decorated
but the more filled with my love of you.
It beams with tenderness, it is replenished
in the atmosphere of purple dreams
with kindness only for your sake,
my home is love, and there is you,
you are its only tenant, no one else
was ever willing or invited;
so, in brief, my home is you, and all my love is yours.
There is no night with any darkness
since there is your light in it and in my life,
which shines for you with only you for any splendour.
Thus shall this be constantly repeated
in my heart and soul and by reciters
as long as there is at all in this world any love
to uphold love with for the only sake of love,
the only matter in existence worth existing for.

Greetings from the happy valley

A greeting from the hippie heartland
with some legendary places like Manali and Malana,
Manikaran and Almora, where the grass grows wild
in any quality and even better quality the higher up you get,
with permanent communities of hippies of all ages,
none too old and none too young,
all seemingly completely happy with a paradise of dreams,
that is of daydreams, but of beauty also,
since here people tend to be more beautiful the higher up they get.
In Manikaran and Malana they can vanish into happiness,
since there they have the drug of drugs Datura,
which can place them out of time for two years or for ever.
It was old Timothy Leary who discovered
how the cannabis grew wild around this area in any quality,
which instigated the first hippie colonies to settle here,
which since then constantly have multiplied,
the last years thoroughly with Israelis.
There is nothing wrong with that sort of a carefree life,
you do no harm to no one, while occasionally the Police
makes raids to Parvati, Malana and those places
to burn up the harvests of the villagers of cannabis,
which ruins them and to no good for anyone.
It is a kind of bum life making you a chronical outsider,
but there is no harm in that as long as you just keep it for a spice,
– in fact, it has been proved that cannabis can cure a number of diseases
that would be considered hopeless otherwise,
amongst them chronical diseases and disorders,
often undefinable mysterious ones, that thus can be miraculously cured;
but let not that spice take over the control of all the food that is your life,
for then you waste it, it will then end up to nothing,
while a spice should just augment the nourishment, not kill it.

Jesus to Mary Magdalene

– a speculation in how he might have been thinking

"You are my closest friend, perhaps my only friend,
and you are safe with that relationship,
and there is nothing that can change it ever.
Powerless is every slander, you have been enough subjected
to that worst humility, a woman's reputation
is her only asset and the only thing she has,
you were bereft of it completely long before you met me;

but instead, and listen carefully, you have acquired
something much more to be envied.
By your knowledge of so many men
you know them, you have all their souls in your possession,
you know man like man can never know himself,
and therefore I esteem you higher than the most respectable of women.
Therefore you shall be forever under my protection
and considered the most honoured among women
second only to my mother,
who is just another fallen Mary like yourself.
Remember, I am but a bastard out of wedlock
who has taken on myself this Messianic mission
only since I am the only person qualified to do it,
so it is just my responsibility
that I have to accept, or fail humanity,
which would be a much worse deception
than to make a king out of this bastard.
You are then the sister of my destiny,
a bastard seeking comfort in a fallen woman
of some prominent experience, and you must admit
we match each other well. We do not even need the ceremonies
and the superfluous complexities of sex to prove it.
And in this my highest possible regard of you two fallen women
closest to my heart, I promise you,
shall every woman of all ages be secured and blessed,
worshipped and protected in my name."

The harmony of our music

The sunshine of your smile
is more than just enough to make my day
more full of glory and delight than any sponsor could,
since your good fortune, harmony and happiness
is all I care for, it means everything to me,
and I can't bear to see your eyes besmirched with tears,
your wrinkled front or any sorrow in your being.
Light my life with your good company,
light up the darkness of my soul with your good influence,
light up my energy with the most fervent fire of our love,
and light my fire with your trust and smiling friendship,
and how can I else but love you?
And keep loving you with ever more increasing depth of feeling?
Keep me burning, like I will keep loving you,
and we shall never fail in keeping up the light
and harmony we owe to our music.

The Pledge

Today six months have passed
since first you came into my home
and since I fell in love with you.
I can not hide it to myself although I can control it,
and my chief concern has ever been to not give you a burden
or to hurt you in whatever way.
I could do anything for you
and have so far been happy to at least do all my best
to help you on your way and ease up any difficulties,
which of course I gladly will continue to;
and as I wrote you on your birthday,
I will be to you whatever you would want of me to be
and never violate the limits of your pleasure.

The eternal flow of life and love

The flow of life and love can never be arrested.
No sloth of slow mentality,
no ignorance or violence,
no government oppression, conscious or unconscious,
no bureaucracy or automatic tyranny,
no systematic greed or hopeless petty thinking,
no autocracy or any dreadfulness of politics,
no nuclear scarecrow like some monster of dictatorship
like that Korean booby, and no terrorism,
nu human vanity and folly,
no oppressive ideology of atheistic fundamentalism,
like the Chinese imperial state of communism
forbidding all religions except atheism
and persecuting them with force,
not all the weapons in the world including all the nuclear ones
can stop the naturalness in the flow of life and love
ubiquitously in the universe. - Remember,
there are just as many suns and stars around the universe
as there collectively are grains of sand in every beach
and desert altogether in our world,
our sun is just a grain of sand out of this universe of sands;
so life must be all round the universe if it is here,
not frequently and everywhere but sparsely;
so our life and love are here to stay
and to go on continuously forever.

Lovers in Limbo

My love is all reserved for you, but in that reservation
is included such a lot of others,
like as if my love of you was something of the very motor
that made possible my love for all that lot of others,
friends, acquaintances, the family and relatives
and even strangers on my journeys.
Such, in fact, have more often than not become my truest friends,
nomadic wanderers, adventurers and exiles,
like so many fugitive Tibetans here in India
and escaped unsocial refugees from from gross injustices
in Europe and the western world, from communism,
from Thatcherism, from brutal Bushism and capitalism
and from themselves, the vainest and most desperate escape of all.
But they have all somewhere some love
that constantly keeps waiting for them;
no matter how exiled they are, they always have a home at heart
to some day hopefully return to;
but the truer and profounder their love is, the more it hurts,
and the more painful is the enterprise to take it up again.
There are so many lovers suffering in Limbo,
and at present we are two among them.

Through the valley of shadows

Suddenly you woke up in the valley of death shadows
with no light for any guide and nothing for a comfort,
only darkness perfectly impenetrable and opaque,
like hell itself all of a sudden fallen down to earth.
It's only to climb up again the long and dreadful way
from bottom of despair, one slow step at a time,
with arduous tortuous labour, patiently and carefully
and never to lose hope and sight of the salvation.
Just go on and carry on the unendurability,
the burden of the suffering, and you shall be rewarded
with the glory of survival and the miracle of life
to be able to start living once again
with some acquired extra wisdom in addition
of experience and of have had the honour
of the triumph of the victory and conquest over death
with the pure will and power of the soul and personality,
the vicissitude of your integrity proved worthy
to continue its existence on its own with confidence.

Yet another description of love

The limitlessness of love
is like continents worth charting
but so much more interesting
to study and to learn from, since it moves
ever variable and changeable like water
flowing constantly with ever increasing energy
working wonders everywhere
of ever changing kind
constantly renewing itself
like an ever burning Phoenix
constantly on flying wings
and ever flying higher
towards finer purity of mind and soul,
since true love never can be sullied,
only constantly miraculously multiplied.

Picturesqueness in hippie classicism

My friend was like no other friend,
the most outstandingly and typical of hippies,
if he'll excuse me, but I simply can't resist
describing him in something of his heyday,
when in Varanasi a good friend of mine encountered him.
I hadn't seen him for some years myself,
but that encounter made such a profound impression
on my friend, that actually he wrote a book about it.
John, forgive me if I give you now away,
but you have changed your face so often,
and you never have repeated any of your masks,
so no one, I assure you, will from this description
recognize you, if he ever met you at some other time.
His blond hair reached his waists, he being Jewishly convinced
that long hair, like the Sikhs maintain, ensured the strength
both physically and of character.
But add to this, great silver earrings in both ears,
the fancy dress of a most typical barefooted Hindu pilgrim
dressed in orange, beads and staff and beggar's bowl,
and so on, teaching westerners the ways of Varanasi
by the Ganga and its holiness, and most intriguingly
initiating them in other mysteries than they had ever heard of.
This my friend, who went out boating in a full moon on the Ganga
with the burning candles on the river

to enhance the effect of the moonlight
blending with some fleeting corpses
was a Russian from Saint Petersburg,
who there enjoyed the one trip of his life,
transforming him into some Atlantide philantropist,
seduced by the profound and irresistible initiation
which my friend produced,
a magic more abstruse than Castaneda's.
Where are you now, my friend, and in which shape will you be present
when I see you next at full moon by the Kanjenjunga
in the fullest glory of the Himalayas?
If I know it I will not betray it,
so that I once more can keep you for myself.

The fleeting spirit

The fleeting spirit of our love
is you and me and something else between
that never can be specified nor gratified
but moves us on incessantly on cosmic winds
blown everywhere but to ourselves,
since this untouchability is the right essence,
unidentifiable, of our love
more precious than we ever can imagine
or get any relative idea of ourselves,
since love belongs to us to merely escape us,
leaving us enigmas only that can not be solved,
but something else between, a mutual understandability
of things that no one else can get a distant hang of,
miracles and powers unexplainable
and constantly astounding us with new expressions and results.

The Fifth Element

a lecture on the elements

The question is which element to choose,
which one you best identify with,
which is stronger or most likeable.
The first is Earth, the solid matter, all that is concrete,
which more often than not, however,
is submerged and drowned by Water. Water
also quenches every Fire -

Fire which devours all is always powerless against it,
except when it combines with Air,
which then can dry up any lake.
Is Air then the most powerful of elements,
since nothing can subdue it, pin it down or even see it?
But there is in Buddhism a fifth element
denominated Wood, which is organic.
Of all organic forms, wood is the hardest and the most enduring,
which is why in Buddhism it has come to symbolize the essence
of this fifth of elements, which is simply life.
It is dependent on the other four,
it has to breathe with Air, it has to grow and live on Earth,
it can't do without Water, and the Fire is its energy.
But basically, all four elements have together that one function only
to support the fifth and make it possible,
the only really meaningful and interesting, important element,
the toughest and most usable longliving form of which
is that most precious Wood we all need knocking on at times.

So let's just plant more trees, the most invaluable support of life
producing air (that's oxygen), providing energy,
enriching earth and binding the wild waters
and not take them down,
for that would ruin everything on earth,
let loose the fires and the waters
and impoverish the air - in short,
a tree is of as much importance as the life of any man.

Love Portrait

How shall I define my love of you?
It is not easy, since it has too many aspects.
First of all, your beauty is not your first thing
and not what I love most in you,
but what it is a mirror of
which is all that which is not seen
but the more strongly felt and recognized
as something much more precious than your beauty.
Let's go deeper into this, because here is the clue:
the outward mirrors of your soul are so remarkable
reflecting depths and faculties that multiply your character
into a maze of wonders and enigmas
but at the same time of wisdom and reliability,
a singular trustworthiness of wonderful profundity

and rare presentiment and foresight
of, I would not hesitate to say, prophetic character;
while at the same time you are honest like a child,
your soul is bare and visible to all the world
which makes it quite inevitable
that the whole world can but love you.

Darjeeling

Silver beams illuminate the landscape
and increase with constancy around the hills
until they blind you into rapturous exhilaration
for the mountain far above all others
so serenely highlighted in heavenly and perfect majesty
by the enchanting morning glory rising from the sun;
and in its shadow, this small village
like a child born from this paradise of beauty
living almost only from the beautious charm of Kanjenjunga,
so benevolently generous from this life-giving magic,
that immediately she naturally must become the Queen of Hills.
Thou art the Emperor and majesty, o Kanjenjunga,
but your child Darjeeling mirrors this supremacy
and grows into the most desirable of queens
by stealing irretrievably your heart
and leaving, as you have to leave her,
a nostalgia to ache for life
unless you constantly return.

Universal minimalism

We are of a higher better world than this one
where our dreams can meet and join each other
in a cyberspace of nowhere and of everywhere
including all the dreams of humankind
that share them with us in the extraordinary plus dimension
of the sixth sense, extra sensory perceptions and what not,
I know full well that you know what I mean.
No further explanation is required.
Let us just continue dwelling there
in bliss and beauty meeting all our needs
and sticking to the motor of it all:
the music of the spheres,
the constant and eternal harmonies

resounding throughout this minimalistic universe
of more suns than the sum of grains of sand across the world
but merely perceptible to those initiated in this dreamworld,
this resplendent essence of all harmony of life,
this innermost and utmost centre of existence,
this invaluable, priceless precious thing called love.

The same old story...

When in the realm of heavenliness
I think of our relationship
and how we are like twins
in souls born long before this life
united by our chosen destiny
of musical ideals fought hard for,
I am like a blind man in my doubts
and faltering in troublesome uncertainty
to just maintain my course through darkness
in my faithfulness to you and our ideals
which we have suffered for so much
and paid so dearly, just to find each other
as inseparable friends on higher levels of affinity
than ever can be gained by mortal forms of love.
We are too close, now even at the furthest distance,
ever to be able to dispense of our relationships
which, in absence of our physical contactability
is only the more strongly felt in metaphysical dimensions;
but all this is old and well known stuff already,
which, however, I can never tire of repeating.

Humility

When you have travelled far for nothing
just to find yourself in perfect darkness
with no end to it, no bottom to the abyss,
like a blind man without stick led down into a mine,
it is a lesson only of orientation,
and you must get through that darkness all alone,
there is no other way and no one to release you
from that hellish course to nowhereness of nothing
but to just get through with it, the worse the better;
for it is a lesson only, just another education,
the best form of which is travel,
which by trials certainly will teach you

something of reality, an accurate perspective;
since reduced into a flying brittle autumn leaf
completely at the mercy of the winds of destiny,
of passion, nature, politics and maybe war
you will be privileged to see things as they are
from both above and through and from the gutter,
which remains the best of all perspectives;
since down there you only can look up
and move up and improve
and have things to look forward to,
perhaps the only natural position and perspective,
that of natural humility, which teaches you
the underdog's philosophy of true survival,
just observing, bowing, looking up, admiring
all forms of life and loving it.

From the bottom of despair...

Himalayan realism, from the traveller's diary:

"The turning point of this journey was on the 11th, when suddenly the weather changed, and even the most experienced trekker here has never met with anything worse. I was then in north Sikkim, it was not as bad as on November 9th 1995, when there were disasters all over the Himalayas and 14 people perished on Mount Everest, but almost next to it."

Infection, insect bites and running noses,
snoring room mates, sleepless nights and aching limbs,
you just lie tormenting yourself
with furious scratchings of your wounds,
you cough your lungs out, eyes are watering cascades,
and everywhere you hear around you
this tremendous Himalayan cough,
the empty dryness of the hollow hoarseness like of horses,
snows and rains, the worst that ever trekkers met with,
worse than even my friend Veteran encountered by Mount Everest,
and nightmares, worries, tortures and laments;
but still you carry on, enduring anything
just for the pleasure of surviving
even the worst thinkable ordeals
to one day finally return back home
to work, to humdrum winter weariness,
to just a normal life instead of these extremes,
however beautiful, revolting, educating and adorable.

Shamballah

geographic survey

The fabled kingdom, transformed into Shangri-La,
is still a vivid and most real ideal
comprising all the ancient Buddhist kingdoms of the Himalayas,
like Nepal and Sikkim, Bhutan and Tibet, Ladakh and Zanskar,
Lo, Mustang and even Kashmir and Mongolia,
once a perfect and united realm,
the capital of which was never found;
but people say there still are endless caves
under the mountains, leading to the sacred spot
from where once all this perfect and harmonious world
was ruled dynamically by the first of Buddhas;
and the dream has never nor will ever die,
like some kind of Asiatic Messianism,
for all who live here, though, a most concrete conception,
no ideal in no time ever being too impossible, too good
nor too impractical to once be realized.

Maya

She was just a woman and a mother,
although Buddha's mother, like himself, an ordinary mortal,
but has come to symbolize a human valuation
of much higher worth than any deity.
She has become a symbol for not only Mother Earth and Mother Nature
but for life itself as simple motherhood,
the very instrument of constructivity, creation and protection,
above all criticism as such, incapable of any harm or evil,
just the harmony of continuity,
the perfect sweetness of one-sided positivism,
the miraculousness of the talent to make something out of nothing
and the home of love undying everlasting.

All this is embalmed in this simplicity of motherhood,
a simple human character, quite limited and mortal
but endowed with the supremest gift of making life
and thus more worthy than the holiest divinity
for being only lovable.

The music of the stars

The music of the stars is unknown
but to those who dwell among the stars and listen
to the language of the gods and goddesses
that mortals can not hear and therefore must deny;
but we can hear them, we who fly among the stars
with open minds of musicality and open hearts
to anything that is not common but exclusive
just to those extraordinary souls unscarred by baseness,
naturally esoteric, born out from the ether
and wandering like exiles and outsiders here on earth
with nothing to relate to except like-minded exceptions,
who can understand the language of the stars and listen to it
and who therefore, piously obliged by understanding
to keep quiet of the secrets of the esoteric universe
since that is far too overwhelming in its beauty
to be used for any means except creation and construction,
are compelled by love to caution and sincere discretion
and the more so the more strong it is,
since it must never risk the smallest misrepresentation,
since the higher and the truer, the more sensitive and delicate.

The Exile

Dharamsala, November 20th:
The Tibetan poet Tenzing Tsundue, exile from Tibet in India, has been placed under house arrest to prevent him from protesting with other Tibetan exiles while the Chinese president Hu Jintao makes his three days visit here...

Driven hard across the snows
over the pass in wintry mountains
with frost-bitten feet and corpses on the way
shot brutally to death by occupation soldiers
or just stranded in the snows in freezing death,
old people, children, mothers, victims of all kinds;
thus suffers the whole nation
driven out by brainwash propaganda
and enforcement of autocracy,
thus turning a whole people into prisoners and exiles
in the country they themselves had built
and turned into a unique culture of philosophy,
respecting life above all and tradition

with a wonderful flourishing sense for ceremonies,
pompous, colourful and solemn
as the perfect ordered party going on forever;
until brutal unhumanity broke in with force and hate
intentionally wiping out a culture of two thousand years
destroying six thousand and forty-six monasteries and temples
out of six thousand and fifty-nine
and burning manuscripts, hand-written books,
three fifths of all the libraries and treasuries of literature,
and why? For sheer stupidity, the joy of violence,
the glory of destruction and the rape of beauty?
For the triumph of the opposite of culture,
human dignity, nobility, humanitarianism, compassion
to let evil with voluptuousness replace all virtue
and all man's constructive efforts?
The dictatorships and mad rapes of politics in the 20th century
has turned the cultural protectors, humanists and lovers
into exiles in this world of barbarism and cruelty;
and it goes on, the rape of beauty by barbarity,
not only in Tibet but everywhere
by blind and brutal brainwash from the media and politics
through the carelessness and greed and ignorance of mankind.

The Problems of Esotericism

The unacceptability of esotericism
is that it is esoteric, that is,
for its inaccessibility reserved for just the happy few,
since only those with an advanced mind
and intelligent profundity of understanding
can at all get any hang of it,
since it is practically totally incomprehensible.
Already the philosopher Pythagoras saw fully this predicament,
wherefore he simply didn't make it any clearer
but just let it be, as most deep thinkers all since then
have also done, from Plato and Plotinus,
from the Essenes to the Cabbalists,
from the Freemasons and Hermeticism to Rosicrucians,
from the Master Eckhart to the Jesuits and the Illuminati,
to the manifold secret societies of our day
of obstinate forever hibernating Hippies
to the children of New Age and the Free Thinkers of all ages,
all heretics, outcasts, outsiders and aliens
who unlike all common people, who just live on earth,
see life from outside, looking into it.

Just another flow

Melt in tears
and let the flood of warmth
run over all the coldness of the world
to let it know what tears are for,
for tenderness and care,
compassion and all good things
that make life worth living,
and, above all, feelings, deep and honest
of the heart and soul, that ever need expression;
and the warmest, softest, sweetest and sincerest
evidence, expression, outlet and manifestation
of your feelings are your tears,
whether you cry for beauty, joy or sorrow
or for anything at all; but they release you,
always, being the original and truest food for love
that never can be given out in vain.

The portrait

Let me take with me your picture
of your absolute consummate beauty
to keep locked up in my heart forever
for the eyes of no one else but me,
the only one to fully worship and appreciate your beauty
unforgettably perceived and photographed by my mind's eye
to keep it as the highest and most incomparable of treasures
to look upon in precious moments of supremest privacy
to thereby stay in touch with you
in love imperishable
never to be perfectly consumed
but only, every time I look upon it,
more aggrandized
and the more so the more I may live,
and long beyond my dying days.

Home to the dead

Returning to normality
from educating edifying journeys
and adventures in a world of beauty
teaching you humility and culture
of a different perspective from above

to humdrum western mainstream brainwash
over-technocrated, automated, sterilized,
where a seventh of the population
go on psychic medicines
as legal drug addicts
which is considered comme il faut,
no matter if it breaks you down, –
it is quite normal to be burnt-out
from just sitting by a keyboard in a cubicle;
and in the long run thus civilization certainly will follow you
in breaking down, dissolving down the drain.
This re-initiation in the western brainwash of perdition
is the worst ordeal you can experience,
coming from a real world of ideals and truth and beauty
to a snake-pit of degeneration and decay;
and all that you can do is to endure it,
do the best of it, survive and struggle on
alone for your ideals in obstinate persistence
just to spite the mortal blind way down of mankind
for the hope of the necessity
of the occasion of the turning of the tides.

Political murders

A secret Russian agent is in London poisoned
in the old way of the KGB by radioactive means,
which only superpowers have the means of;
but that Russia, which alone was motivated to the murder
does of course deny it, as did Putin when the journalist of civil courage
Anna Politkovskaya was murdered
shot down in the elevator of her home
with no less than five mortal bullets
in the ordinary mafia style,
which murder also only Russia could have any motive for.
Things don't look any better
as the murdered London agent Litvinenko
was investigating the aforesaid murder
of the lovely Anna Politkovskaya;
but Putin and the politicians reason with some realistic cynicism:
"Who cares? Who has the energy and time to bother
when the world goes down the road to ruin anyway
by aids, catastrophes, malaria, TBC,
the global warming and ever increasing floods?
We can afford to overlook some small politic murder,
one or two, a dozen or another

since they must be soon forgotten anyway
and disappear in the most boring usual flow
of normal global catastrophical statistics."

Love declaration

I love you.
Let these words be stamped forever in eternity
no matter who am I, no matter who you are
just to make sure the pure sincerity
of how much I love you outstandingly forever.
Let it be, and let it work, and let it live
and let it never die,
because that is the only life for me
without which I will be as barren as a desert
bored to death by thirst and hunger and depravity
since you are all I ever cared for
whether drunk or sober, mad or sensible;
you are the source of life and cure for anything,
the only absolute insurance of there being any life at all
and for there being any meaning of existence
and for any continuity at all
for any love or any meaning of it.

Midnight Conversations

In the darkness of midnight
far away beyond ourselves
we meet and join in timelessness
like two spirits moulded into one
by the truth of this momentary eternity.
This bliss is the supremest of this life
and the miracle of it the most incredible.
The eyes go out and we live by hearing only
sweet soft words from barely audible voices,
the loveliest of this life
only because they understand each other
and thereby comprise each other
in the pious breathless embrace of eternity.
This union is this moment which,
if you have experienced it,
you can but always pray for its remaining
and continuing forever.

The Suicide Bomber

Your reward will be a thousand rupees
if you go ahead down to the market
letting off a bomb to make as many casualties as possible,
in cash, with guaranteed security,
provided that you get away with it.
The suicide bomber thanked them well
but wanted payment in advance.
The fully covered terrorists
with only eyes to let in any light
could see enough to exchange meaning glances
and gave the voluntary candidate
the full sum in advance, but on condition:
THE SUCCESS MUST BE COMPLETE!
He promised piously to do his very best
but was not that much of a fool not to be well informed
exactly where his terrorist employers and their chiefs
would meet to make their schemes next time,
he would have a report to make to them;
so that is where he went eventually when time was ripe
and let discreetly down their dried up drain a bomb
which went off powerfully detonating most resoundingly
and blowing many well masked and anonymous intriguers
up and maybe all the way to space with such efficiency,
that one could never tell how many or who any of them were
since they were so anonymous and carefully wrapped up and masked.
They were included in the general statistics:
so far six hundred and fifty thousand casualties only
in a war where everyone fights everyone for nothing,
while there is just one who wants to stay there and remain,
who happens to be president of some states in America.

Common prayer

Let us pray together,
kneel together in humility
to focus on our troubles
and resolve our problems
by combining all our forces
in an effort of mobilization
of our healing powers
which are no less physical than psychic,
wherefore we had better be entwined,
the closer up, the better,

coiled up in a knot like loving snakes
to make our combination more efficient
in the outflow and release
of the profoundest energies
which any love can fire off
for only universal benefit
and for our own improved development
to progress ever in the beneficial process
of our universal love as prayer and unification.

Hibernation

Gone is the sun and the light of the world
with a vengeance replaced by the cold Scandinavian winter
of icicle beauty and permanent frost
without mercy with dreadful slow silence
deep-freezing the hearts and the minds of the Hyperboreans
replacing all life with lethargic melancholy
and sleepy heaviness with only one cure:
the headache of alcoholism,
while the bears only are wise enough to go really to sleep
to pass winter over in wise passive silence,
the wisest of animals, while man, the craziest,
just goes on working like hell
celebrating the madness of Christmas,
while wisdom and love is forgotten and drenched
in the sorrows of drinking depressions
while more people die than in any of the other seasons
of spleen or just tiredness, suicide or common depression.

But light can not die and survives in the soul,
where the sunlight is brighter than ever in heaven
if only you let the creative spirit have vent,
recognition and any attention to its neverending potential
which is more efficient than any solarium,
and that's the best way to survive winter horrors of darkness:
let out the creativeness, don't let it slow down,
go to sleep or get drowned in the dreary depression
but let creativity flow,
for although all the sunlight gets niggard and sparse
with the intimidations and threats of starvation to death,
there is nothing in heaven or earth
that can check the light or cease the flow
of all that which you carry around in your soul
as your main source of life and of love and creation.

Crisis treatment

Our minds collide in splendid piety
to gracefully adorn our unity
in quiet prayer for the patient's sanity,
recuperation and return to amity
from any darkness in the shadowy conformity
of hospitalization's bleak passivity
of no way out from any black hole of calamity
but only the dead end of operational rigidity,
the horrible experimental vulnerability
of no way back but only way out into relativity
to nothingness or somethingness or no ability
to cope with any unexpected terrible fatality.
But our antennae feel the way
and hold the sway
against dismay
and any mayday
since we know full well
that nothing ever fell
by fate on us to tell
us anything from hell
but only from the other dell,
that there was never any trial tragic
which did not improve our mutual magic.

Sunday sermon

Getting drunk for nothing
is never an excuse
for staying sober
since you never can get drunk for nothing,
since, even if there's really nothing in it,
in the drunkenness you'll certainly find something to it
worth the drinking
even if it's only red wine,
but, of course, you need some rum
to get it really done,
I mean, the reason for this drinking
which you need for sure
more often than not,
especially if you've been sober far too long.
Thus spoke the preacher from his pulpet
to his congregation on a Sunday service

with the bishop listening to him
most seriously, whereafter he found it convenient
to comment on his parson's sermon, saying:
"Only three small things, my friend.
First: Jesus was not shot but crucified,
and second: the correct word is not Cheers! but Amen,
and the third: you just don't go down from the pulpit
sliding down the rail. But for the rest,
your sermon was indeed most interesting."
And the young priest, who well aware
of his most venerated bishop's visit and inspection,
had prepared himself with a few glasses
for the sermon, promised to himself,
that from now on he would more diligently study
what the Scripture really said
about the actual holiness of wine
in celebrating great occasions,
for let us not forget, that Jesus on his wedding
did turn water into wine, and that on the last supper
he demonstratively advocated using wine
for every sacred celebration in his name.

Love expressionism

We were meant to be each other,
delve into each other to become each other,
joining more than just our limbs
but coming even closer through our souls
to dwell together in the harbour of eternity
in silent intimacy constantly increasing
in intensity and tenderness
to motivate us ever more sincerely
never to let go but keeping holding on
to our love and to each other
in the warm embrace of our hearts
to blend the blood of our spirits
in a generous ever increasing flow
which like a flood will certainly continue
to grow constantly more powerful
to overwhelm all sentient life
supporting it and honestly encouraging it
to continue waxing in its glowing flow
with love of ever growing perfect irresistibility.

On the table

Do not worry.
You will later on wake up again
to a new day and a new life
beyond all worries and anxieties
with illnesses and tribulations passed
and left behind forever
to give way to just another life,
a new life better than the former one.
You will not even feel
there on the table
when they drill into your head
to carefully remove the parasites,
the growth that isn't yours nor you
but only something to get rid of,
all the rubbish of your life,
all that which you should have left far behind
long time ago, all that, which wasn't part of you,
which wasn't your life, which was not for you;
while all the rest is left for you ahead,
your pleasure and serenity,
the happiness of your remaining life,
the glowing evening of the warmest part
and maybe longest and most pleasurable part
of your most precious life,
which simply just is bound to be
more precious now the longer you remain with us
for every day more priceless and invaluably rich and worthy.

Some ingredients of love

They count to twelve,
those who think love's ingredients can be counted,
but love is out of accountability.
The ingredients are not to be summarized
nor even identified, since they are too many
and far too variable to be more than faintly discerned.
You can not pin love down or analyze it.
You can only live it.
Once you're there, inside it living it,
you are on the right path and know something,
and then it's just for you to move on,

continue living it in whatever way,
the easiest way being with sex,
the most difficult way being without sex,
but that is more of a challenge.
You can even live it with sex but without sex,
if you see what I mean, which perhaps is difficult,
but what I mean is simply, that the love you live
must be within you and at the same time
completely comprise the person you love –
and that is maybe the basic ingredient of love:
it must be all or nothing.
If you have it all, you have all to give,
and then it's just to go on spending,
giving, beaming, spurting forth
and generously expand your love
without any end to your experience of it,
since love works by constantly renewing itself,
and therefore love is life neverdying.

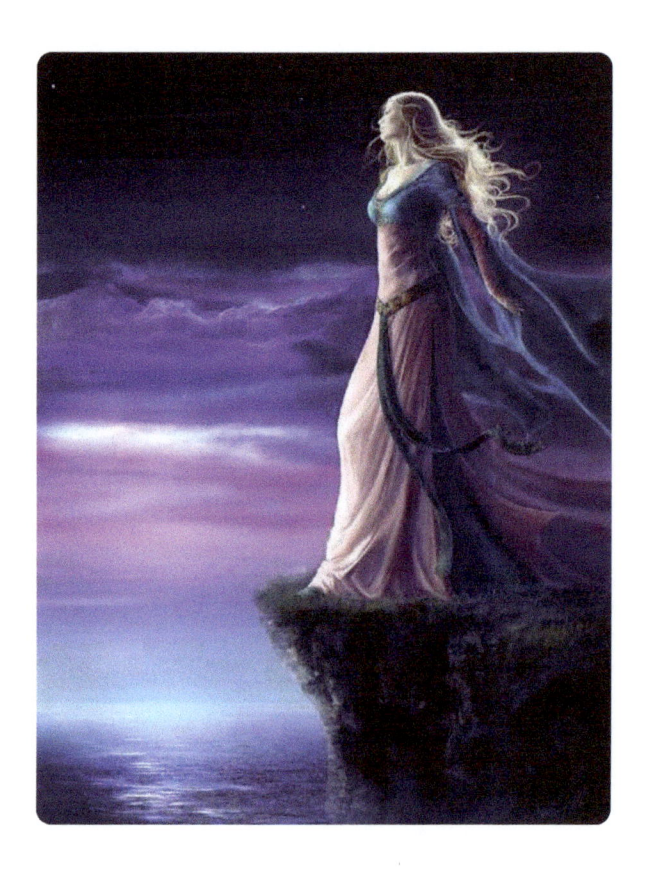

The Razor's Edge

To wake up every morning
forced to fight the torments of your body
just to stay alive and fit for work,
the daily combat just to make life bearable
and tolerable and enjoyable at least in any way
is more than just a full time work.
It is to fight for life and for survival
balancing across a tightrope blindfolded
and without safety net, the tightrope cutting deep into your feet,
the famous razor's edge of life that Maugham described
in what is actually the introducing hippie novel
about man's desorientation in this age
in this distracted world polluted by destruction by himself,
while only sparse illuminated individuals
feel the lostness of mankind and try to search for a solution,
which they only find, as individuals, individually.
It's a predicament with no way out
which forces you to introversion
trying to find an alternative solution
by an inner road perhaps through metaphysics
for the vital rescue and redemption of mankind,
of life, of nature, of the planet and the future
to at all make any love a possibility
in desperate determination not to let it die.

Innocence

The dwindling abyss of the loss of all self-confidence
because of personal calamities and natural disasters
is not something that you can do anything about
except endure, survive and brace with that stiff upper lip.
Things don't get better by the aspect of the havoc of humanity
destroying life and species, nature and environment
including any basics for the future,
since there are not many wise men any more
who honestly can stake their lives in love
investing in a family concern for future troubles.
So you get discouraged, overrun by the mad circus
of the bolting world of greed, insanity and egoism
with sex and violence as the acceptedly sole meaning of existence.
All that you can do is stand apart detached and critical
and maybe hibernate this age of Kali,

this destructive universal lunacy of dehumanization
and denaturalization, by quite simply do your work,
maintain your garden, write your poetry
and keep up the remanining beauty of the soul
which never can be poisoned or corrupted
by anything you didn't cause yourself.

J'accuse

What was the bright idea of making this world uninhabitable?
Your shortcomings, capitalists and politicians,
will be as grim as your shortsightedness,
which turned the whole world to a mess
by your voluptuosness of reptile greed,
you crazy world seducers of industrialization,
putting the world's riches and its future in your pocket,
making the destruction of the world your gold
which you could not bring with you anyway
and leaving nothing else behind than world pollution,
poisoned future as a curse for generations,
you the greed exploiters, presidents and autocrats,
oil billionnaires, industrial tycoons, dictators,
wildlife hunters and destroyers and above all military pimps,
who made arms, violence and killing the world's greatest industry.
The sickness of the planet cry out loud against you all
and most of all the rising oceans, dirtied by your oil
with coral reefs consumed by your pollution,
the tuna fish completely disappearing even from the depths
and dolphins, whales and other breathing friendly beings of the sea
caught up in drifting nets to suffocate and drift forever
testifying by their corpses to man's criminal irrationality.
The seas will rise to vengeance against man,
his tyranny and arrogance, his carelessness and hubris,
while we thinking and responsible downtrodden rainbow warriors
are the ones to suffer for the greatest crime in history,
the shortsighted destruction of the world by man,
the ones to remedy the mess and clean it up,
for which a generation must be sacrificed
until the world perhaps can be inhabitable once again.

The crying song that never dies

Its melody is haunting
unforgettably lamenting
and complaining ever
by those ever flowing tears
that gives the music never dying energy
to go on playing, singing and lamenting,
crying all souls' hearts out
in a hymn that can't be silenced
but which everyone must hearken;
for those tears, that heart-rending affliction,
that pathetic wail and dirge
of too much beauty in its melody
is just the source of life,
the pain by which we all have come to life
and by which we must aye continue to support it
keeping up the essence of life's unbearableness
which is its neverending and intolerable beauty.

The Nurse

The sweetness of your care
is like the honey of a precious blossom
too unique and priceless to be picked
and far too rarely exquisite to be professional.
You waste your love to make the patient
feel much better than if she was well
with such attention as if she was something of a film star,
and, of course, she is the most important person in the world
as long as she is invalid and has to be confined in bed,
while you make her existence like to a consummate dream,
thus building up a paradise for her
in this horrible state of close to death.
So good are seldom nurses, and so sweet are seldom lovers,
while like this you transfer our love
to a superior kind of level
raising it beyond this mortal mess of things
into a higher education of more care and tenderness
for only increased good for everyone who knows you
and especially for me, your humble lover.

Together (2)

We belong to each other
and cannot do without each other.
That's how it works,
the destiny of our love,
the mutuality of our souls
and its relationship like twins –
the more we do without each other,
the more we need each other,
like a constant urge to return
forever to a distant past
where we were born together
in a unity of love
that ever has kept warming up
for this long evening of togetherness
when we shall never again depart,
but only constantly return
to where we started.

Healing powers

There are no healing powers without pains.
The more your pains in healing hurt you,
the more miracles you work,
the more efficient is your healing;
so just let the pains consume you,
and the more, the better.
Think of Christ and what he suffered,
greatest of the healers,
and all those among his followers
who got those stigmata for healing,
like St. Francis and the Padre Pio,
all authentic, all prolific healers;
but no gains, no healing powers without suffering.
That is the essence of all empathy:
you have to feel the sufferer's and patient's pains
in order to relieve them,
taking them on you,
identifying with them, looking through them,
going through them to thus let them ache out and dissolve.
That was the method, secret and the mystery of Edgar Cayce.
If doctors were more knowledgeable in this business,
many hospitals would soon be empty.

The miracle

When after the day's work
I stumble home to bed
dead tired and exhausted
like a wounded soldier
languishing of thirst and bleeding,
hungering and dying of fatigue,
the only thing I need is you,
my only, truest love,
most lovable of women in existence,
all my comfort and the only cure
for my consumed and outraged soul,
the only nurse who can keep me alive;
but you are there, and will be always there,
the final harbour after all the stormy seas,
the star like Sirius to always guide me right,
the brightest light in all the midnight sky
to solace me and give me courage

and renew all that which was my life
which I had thought I had completely spent;
but that's the miracle, that all I need
is one kind thought from you,
and I will be reborn and resurrected,
no death and no ruin having any power
against that life and that love
which gives me all I ever had to live for.

No partition

You are part of me
and not just any part
but the most vital part,
the most inseparable part,
the part that stays with me
interminably all the time
to ever keep me company
even when I am alone,
and what is more,
the most professional outgoing part,
the part that keeps me more than just alive,
the part that universally participates
to put it abstractly
in any way in any life
to just and simply keep it up and going,
more explicitly, in brief,
you are myself and I am you,
and thus we keep on hanging on together
just to keep it going
flying on inseparably
now and on and on,
as much as possible forever.

Divine intimacy

We know a secret which we share in common
of the highest depth and ultimate intimacy
that spells our lives with magic
of such kind that everyone must envy us
our knowledge of this intimacy with divinity,
which they can only do out of their ignorance.
Let them torture us with that if they so bother

since that only can become a torture to themselves.
We have a higher task to overcome;
the base frustrations that futility so stupidly bombard us with
are only challenges to cope with on our way
to do our job without reward and without understanding
not to just survive but to survive as souls
and thereby progress on our thorny stormy path
to higher education to thereby continue to instruct this wretched life
of what it really is and should be;
and that is our squirrel's wheel:
to ever run about and reaching nowhere
without ever getting out of the entrapment of our destiny
as spiritual workers working harder or at least as hard as any farmer
for the betterment of mankind
sacrificing all including and especially ourselves
on the delightful never-ending Via Crucis
of our passion of the nightingale's commitment to the rose.

Narcissus – the true story, or, what actually happened

– it was just an accident, but made permanent and eternal by legend

Narcissus spoke to his beloved Echo:
"Darling, you just bore me.
Can't you entertain me any better
than by being just my echo?"
The poor nymph began to cry
since she could not defend herself
and couldn't find a better answer than,
quite awkwardly: "My love, how can I please you
with my poor self since yourself are all perfection
and I can do nothing better than to imitate you
in all your so perfect ways?" Narcissus sighed
and said: "So you are just an imitation.
What a bore you are!" and looked away to find
his mirrored picture in the water
and was amazed by his own beauty
and how actually he was perfection only
and was hypnotized by his own apparition,
being quite unable to release himself
from his own stare. But Echo would not leave him
and observed that her adored lover had been caught
by something in the water. "What has caught your eye?
What are you staring at?" she asked.

"Just look in there," Narcissus said.
"I never saw such beauty in my life."
The nymph saw his predicament and laughed.
"But that is just yourself! It is the mirror of yourself!
Have you not seen yourself before?"
Narcissus answered: "No, I never found myself before."
"Come, come," said Echo. "You just can't get stuck
in admiration of yourself forever.
There are other persons in the world."
"Not as beautiful as this one. You are right.
I am perfection. I don't need you any more
nor any person else, since what I am
transcends all other human beings."
Echo could not quite accept this.
She retorted: "If I may not love you,
and if you no longer can love me,
at least let me then love your picture."
And she dived into the water
just where he was sitting, right into his picture,
which was shattered instantly.
"What are you doing!" cried the young man rising,
"You can't swim!" And he jumped after her to save her.
But the river god was there and waiting for them,
takin his good opportunity, ensnaring them
in weeds and water lilies, pulling them down under,
and it so befell that they both drowned,
she in the picture of her love,
and he in fruitless strain to save his love,
which after all he could not finally deny.

Hanging by the neck between life and death

A situation difficult as such, no doubt,
and what is worse, it's serious.
What can we do about it,
when no doctors can do anything,
when experts are completely at a loss,
when no one does or dares do anything,
when operation offers no results,
when there are complications
and we are left hanging knowing nothing
since there is no one to tell us anything.
Our last resource is healing
which can give us no assurances

and no professional or certain help
at that ideal place of a rest in limbo
as a sluice and easy gate to death.
All we can do is pray for miracles,
which certainly can happen
but are certainly in no way certain.
This is hell or purgatory
of a temporary kind though,
since death of all things is the last
that lasts forever –
it is only the most casual of moments
briefer than the slaking of a candle
and a passing only through a gate
from one life to another, or,
as many put it,
from this mortal life of vanity
to the eternal life of any meaning.
We can not accept it, though,
but must hold on to her in persevering obstinacy
until she recovers and returns
to a much better life than heretofore,
for her sake and for ours.

The pain of life

You can't escape it
while you live.
It will increase
outrageously
tormentously,
continuing day by day
to steadily increase the pain,
like some malignant cancer on the soul
which you can't even scan
and even less discover or identify,
since it will move about your soul
in constantly increasing turmoil,
chaos and disorder and disorientation
circulating as incessantly as any blood
to wax with life and age and rage
like some infernal road to hell,
the most infernal of them all,
since it will never bring you there
but only push you further on to it.

The brighter side of this, though,
as that with this pain and torture
your maturity will also grow,
the pain will soften you and make you nicer,
smoother and more humble and more flexible,
it's called katharsis,
you will learn something, develop,
this most painful lesson which we know as life
will always teach you something new
to sort things out with
for another grapple with the problem
and some better orientation
how to cope with it at all,
survive and learn some new tricks
just how to endure it.

All too short lights in the long night

The glimpses of our love
are much too fickle, short and passing
and the more so in this darkness
of our passing situation
of just threats and perils everywhere
in which there is no challenge against death
except foolhardy optimism,

the obstinacy of the will to vanquish anything
that simply can't be vanquished,
while we just catch glimpses of each other
forced to separation by this inexplainability of fate
which makes my love more fervent only
stressed by this adversity of destiny
to ever crueller frustration,
paralysis and intoxication.
There is always one way out, however,
and I am quite certain that way is not death.

Faith

I'll never let you go
but keep an eye on you
to keep our souls and hearts together
definitely but indefinitely
just to keep my faith
regardless of our distance
just for old acquaintance's sake –
I never broke my faith to you
and never will
however hard my jealousy
tried to replace me with another
character that wasn't made
for either me nor you.
As long as we are true
to ourselves
we cannot lose each other,
since the truth is all we ever had
to keep to and to build
whatever was worth building
not to ever be erased.

Hell – an introduction

it's not as bad as it sounds…

Of course, it's all a fake.
Hell never really did exist,
and neither did the Devil,
although he acquired many names,
like Satan, Beelsebub (the lord of flies)

and others. Satan was originally
just a local tribal idol,
just like Pan or Baal or Ra,
but of some Arab people,
and the place called Hell
was the inferno of the Nordic winter,
ordinary life but at its hardest.
It's the human mind which has turned hell
into some nightmare of imagination,
and since fantasy can never be restricted,
so has Hell been turned into a whole mythology
of most incredible absurd and weird stuff,
(just go botanizing inte Dante,)
all reflecting the subconscious
and man's less attractive sides,
his mental weakness and neurotic nature;
so the devil which we all must fight
is just the enemy within us,
everyone himself is his worst enemy,
all fears are of the unknown of our minds,
and there is nothing evil
but our thinking makes it so,
as someone said already
many hundred years ago.
Since there are many sides to our imagination,
there are many aspects of this hell
of our invention
and no end to it;
just let it out,
and it will vanish
like a dream
and like all dreams most fascinating.

Grief

Inward crying without tears
is more sincere than any tears
can be and much more painful,
since that's why the tears don't show:
they can't come out,
they are forever blocked
on their way out
and tapped instead into a pit
of bottomless despair like a black hole

of too much crying
filling an infinity
with woes unutterable
of the grievous powerlessness
against cruelty, injustice, tragedy
and everything that shouldn't happen
and which for that reason only
seems to happen.
What to do?
Continue crying
without tears
forever.

Outstaring darkness

They say the total realism
is equal to the total pessimism,
and although there might be some grain of truth in it
it doesn't have to be so negatively terrible.
Outstaring darkness, if when it's total,
is just making the discovery of certain lights in it,
and there never was a person dying
without smoothly getting over it
and even smartly even with it and away with it
completely disappearing to the other side
without a trace, without informing anyone
and maybe even without dying –
that's what we may all discover when we die.
Well, I'll not be too morose and acrid about this,
but will be niggardly content with pointing out
the trivial truism, that all is not what it seems.

Overwhelming adversity

How shall I express my love of you
when there is lack of any means
except of mortal kind that never is enough?
And what is worse, I am unworthy of you
and of love, since I have no means to support you
and not even to support myself,
while your haphazard situation is at risk
and can not stand a further strain of any kind,
while I am hopelessly at bay

with no means even to express my love,
so tragically fettered in a cage of desperate impossibilities.
But let adversity continue towering in overwhelmingness
since there is nothing that can not be overcome by love,
nor even death, a powerless and foolish thing
compared to facts of immortality
through which love triumphs ever gloriously,
as if the strange phenomenon of immortality
existed only for the sake of love;
and that, I guess, is just about as close as we can get
to any universal truth.

Nostalgia

Why could not that divine and golden age and moment
stay and just remain, forever going on?
It was the age of friendship, the most perfect love
of innocence, when nothing was required
and no knowledge was at hand nor needed,
when we simply loved and were together
naturally without affectations or pretensions
long before the first released erection made us blush
and turn into ourselves
to never be completely free again.
At school there was a whole world to discover,
chart, reveal and wonder at
of knowledge, botany, geography and art,
a most intoxicating enterprise
that made our minds delirious with happiness
revealing endless opportunities and possibilities;
but that was then, the children's golden age of long ago,
before the physical reality of love caused chronic introversion,
before relationships had caused their first upsets and schisms,
before we realized the world was mad,
before we started to grow up against our will,
before we parted and before you died,
my best friend of my childhood.
We were at the age of ten-eleven then,
the best years of our lives
which have survived us with their glory
staying there behind us in eternity
while we grew up and withered
deadlocked on our course
to the inevitable vanity of death.

Poor people's riches

We don't need cars and swimming-pools,
what shall we do with monetary worries
of the stock exchange and too much taxes,
risky options and accursed roller-coaster shares,
anxieties of properties and constant keeping up
of meaningless facades and artificial nonsense,
when we get along so well with just our dreams,
our love of beauty and of being just together,
having cheap and frugal meals with friends,
enjoying fresh air and some sunshine,
listening to ancient proper music,
reading old imperishable sacred books
of inexhaustible immeasurable merits
with some poetry occasionally
to adorn our humble life with golden fringes.
I don't care about material matters
since you can't take anything of that with you
while all your true worth, grit and dreams
are more imperishable than your soul
as long as you just keep them flying.

Our sovereignty

Pride and independence stand between us
separating us like something of our own worst enemies
originated by our own best qualities.
I offer you my help, but you will not accept it
out of pride and independence and politeness,
wanting to take care of everything yourself
and going the official way without support,
not listening to others or accepting alien advice,
while I treat you the same way,
not accepting any help or your advice
and keeping independently straight on my own course
steering blindly out of reach for anyone;
but all this sovereignty, pride and independence
is developed just to give more space to love,
enlarge the possibility for its existence
and provide a larger room in the cathedral
for the greatness of our hearts to roam
to give more freedom to our love,
which can not stand restrictions

and which in this world can't find enough space to expand
since love, if it is honest, craves much more than all
and never can be satisfied or have enough.
Excuse my pride and independence,
but it's only to give you and us a wider berth
to cultivate, expand and let our love continue thriving in.

Under the protection of the muses

It is divine but dangerous,
it keeps us from the perils of this world
but at the same time is a constant trial
of our lives, our personalities,
our personal validity and worth,
it is a constant hardening
like that of steel in ice and water
melted down at first completely
by consuming heat and fire
and then forced into a mould
to reach some permanence of structure
only through atrocious torture,
sufferings of hell and purgatory cleansing;
but the mortals can not touch us
while we must the more assume responsibility
committing us to empathy with shortcomings of others,
pledging us to share their sufferings to ease them.
So being under that protection of the muses
is no more and no less than a high responsibility
which we must prove our worth of
through our labour and accountability
as thoroughly creative non-stop artists
bound to never sleep and never rest
for the commitment to our love and our ideals
and all that makes life worth
all that atrocious trouble of just living.

Midwinter love

I wake up in the middle of the night
and there is naught else for my eyes but you,
there is nothing else that I can think of, only you,
and only with sincerest love without a smudge
of anything not being perfect love,

which couldn't be more flawlessly complete,
and that in this exhausting time of crisis
with a cancer patient closest to us
horribly afflicted by aggressive peril of her life,
for which there might be no cure else but miracles;
but we believe in miracles and can do miracles,
since that is all our love has done and all the time
and ever since we met,
so that is probably what our love will keep on doing.
Let us live for that, no matter what will happen,
come what may, whatever trials we may stumble on,
but we shall never fall.

The pain of loving

Only those know anything of love
that have survived it
with its pains and crucifixions,
suicides and afflictions
leaving you completely ruined
like an empty shell
to be left washed out on the shore
eventually to be assorted by the sea
and thoroughly dissolved to ordinary sand.
Supremest fools and jokers
are the greatest lovers,
the erotomaniacs, who believe they love
but don't know anything about it,
those born yesterday as chronical drivelling idiots
lusting senselessly for what will only burn them out.
You want to laugh at them but can but pity them
with sadness and regret,
that you, with all the loves you had,
you never could take proper care
of what you now, too late, will realize
was the only true one
and the only one you never had.

MAGNUS AURELIO

Your two faces

One of them is pure delight,
the paragon of beauty,
blinding like the sun,
compelling you to look away
to just not let your love consume you
prematurely driving you to nuts.
The other is the serious one,
impenetrable in severity,
forbidding rather than attractive,
making you afraid to come too close
not willing to disturb;
but these two different faces
almost opposite in kind
are just the opposites of life,
we wear them all,
like the two classical theatrical opposite masks
which never can exclude each other
although they can never be combined
and are of the same person.
We are all inextricable in complexity
and can not fully understand each other
nor even ourselves.
All that we can do
is just to love each other.

The school of love

To love and care for your integrity
is paramount and primary as my concern for you
as your respectful lover,
caring more for your protection than for having you.
They say the gentleman is dead,
that he was extirpated in the rotten age of world wars,
the most difficult and dark barbaric period in history;
but since man has survived,
and there continue to be ladies,
there will always also be new gentlemen to ressurect,
since love is unavoidable as constant miracle
and the sole breeder of both ladies and their gentlemen.
The gentle soft touch that true love requires
craves nobility of gentlemen and subtlety of ladies;
and that is the school of our love
which I am honoured to be tutored in by you.

Our league

a mystery

Conspiracies do usually succeed
if only they are thoroughly constructive
and the schemers can be sure to get away
and be the only ones aware of how they did it,
like in this peculiar business going on
now at the hospital about our patient.
When my closest friend died now four years ago
he never told me what he suffered from,
I was informed too late and not before he died,
and the resultant shock was the more terrible
since I was well aware I could have saved him,
but he never told me even though we met
less than a year before. In this case, fortunately,
everything is obvious, and we were in time,
the healing has begun already,
and we know what was behind it,
how the hidden spiritual processes resulted in
these circumstances already resulting in
a better cure than anyone hade hoped for.
Everything, of course, can be explained by chance
and luck and fortunate coincidences,
but we know the truth behind the curtains,
how reality was all staged from behind
by machinations only known to the initiated
taking part of the mysterious league of universal healing
which is mankind's and our planet's only hope.

Love, naturally

Let me love you with my heart and soul
and with what's more, that is,
all that you can imagine.
Yes, there are no left-overs from love,
it is exactly everything or nothing,
and if it is everything it never ends
and can not be controlled or limited
but must be timelessness itself
including all infinity and all the universe and what is outside,
which, of course, is the most interesting of all.

Thus grows my love infinitely explosively
in limitless expansion out of all control
and that quite naturally,
since we are no more than natural.

Russian murder

– comment on the Litvinenko murder case

It's not an ordinary execution,
mafioso, just for kicks,
no, it is a masterpiece of complication
with a megalomaniacal exaggeration,
schemed, prepared and organized for months
in the most studied way and with a vengeance,
with the careful transportation of the rarest
most expensive poison in the world,
and in the Russian way with vodka-wobbly hands,
here spilling some of it in various restaurants and airports,
almost all around all Europe, in Berlin and Stockholm
among other places, just to get a poor ex-agent liquidated,
with a vengeance from the firm he left, the KGB,
sought out in London, England, poisoned hundred times to death
by radioactive means at the cost only of five million pounds,
a Russian execution in the name of loyalty
to what? To Putin or the KGB, the new autocracy
which through the years already has become notorious
for so many murky murders of truth-telling journalists,
or to the lost cause of the fallen Russia,
which throughout her history has only gone from bad to worse?
We can not tell. We can just wonder at this Russian methodology.

The gentle touch

The gentle touch of love
in better worlds than this one
is our realm of indefatigable unapproachability,
supreme immunity against all bad vibrations,
since we live only for the good ones;
but in this realm of love,
although extreme in subtlety,
it is the more expressive, powerful and overwhelming

in its kind for being so refined and cultivated,
driven hard to its extremest sensitivity,
so that the faintest touch and loosest hint
can be too forceful to sustain.
It is a most particular responsibility
to happen to be privy to these things
of higher education than most ever dreamt of
could be possible or did exist,
but we must never keep it for ourselves
but on the contrary
infect the world with this addiction
of the higher spiritual values and life meanings
which, in fact, are more worth living for than any other matter
and the only reason for our being here at all.

Love at the hospital

– the forgotten Christmas celebrators

The personnel is leaving,
going home to celebrate with families
as far away as possible from all their patients,
left in wheelchairs or in bed
alone
to manage by themselves
to do their things in nappies
quarrelling within themselves
and fighting against memories, regrets and worries
in increasing darkening despair
while friends and relatives do also quarrel
about how to care for them
and doing nothing
except waiting for their heritage
and crtiticising those who really care,
while all those vast hospital corridors
echo from depletion in extremest emptiness .
more desert than a desert
covered in a windowless and sterile claustrophobia
letting no one out
except the personnel
who take their holiday
as far as possible from all their dying patients.

OCTOBER HARVEST FIRST PART.

Life and death

Death is part of life, and life is part of death,
and never the twain shall part.
It is life's constant marriage, that never can be separated,
never subject to divorce, never dissolved,
since there is no life without death
and no death without more life.
We do not know what happens after death,

since that is not for life to know,
it's not life's business to worry about death,
but we may assume, that death is no more
than a transient crisis of life,
like all crises of life.
The only mystery of death is its reticence,
it keeps quiet about its secrets,
and that is the only thing that makes death attractive,
its only attraction, in fact,
which is why it has to keep so absolutely quiet about it,
or else it would not exist
to make life so attractive.

How can love be possible

How can love be possible
in this corrupted world of filth and strife
destroyed by avarice and war for nothing
torn asunder by religions claiming all to be the only right one
while they only prove themselves all wrong,
by nature raped and harrowed beyond recognition
in environmental universal human self-destruction
and all else, starvation and disease, malaria and aids,
bacteriae building up resistance against antibiotics
horribly resulting in pandemics and world epidemics
that can not be stopped, and even climate changes
with the ever growing threat of steadily increasing storms,
typhoons and hurricanes, tornados and tsunamis
and so on, with no end to the steadily increasing misery.
So how can love be possible? The question is right justified,
and there can be one answer only: yes, it is not possible,
and yet it happens anyway.

Christmas at the Alms-House

You wouldn't have expected it,
but there was actual Christmas there,
among the paupers, bag ladies and alcoholics,
drug addicts and bums and invalids,
all having had their fill of simple but delicious food
and entertained by the best music in the world –
a classical old restaurant trio with a piano, violin and a guitar,
old pensioners performing, singing and enjoying,

not with very well-tuned instruments, not very accurately,
but in perfect mood for sentimental melodies
of that undying kind which will remain in timelessness
and never will be tired of, like "Isn't it romantic",
"Fascination", "Three coins in the fountain";
well, it couldn't have been better.
There were even some old couples dancing,
most of these pathetic guests were stuffed
with over-eating and completely lost and worn out,
but they all most thoroughly enjoyed it.
Christmas was here found at last,
in the middle of the slums among the poor and outcast,
no pretensions, no hypocrisy, no luxury, no artifice,
just life at its most human,
and what could possibly be better ever?

The Dying Patient's Complaint

How can life be possible
in such a mess of human wretchedness and wreckage
of brain surgery and tumour, stroke and cancer,
all at once, and yet they all demand of me to carry on,
return to life in a decrepit ruined body
which impossibly can be restored;
complete recovery is beyond reach;
demanding the impossible is an absurdity,
like this preposterous whole situation;
still, they all do mean a lot to me,
and I am not completely willing to depart
and leave them all behind;
so I am vacillating between life and death.
If they all want me to remain,
my relatives and friends in such a number,
I of course will humour them and stay with them,
but it depends on them entirely;
if they are not sufficient in their love and prayers,
I have not enough of patience to remain in this invalid body
but will have to leave it for a better one,
no matter how much they may love me,
my poor children, relatives and friends,
who after all, no doubt, will understand me if I leave them..

Dark Clouds

Don't let them fool you,
the appearances,
that hide away the sun
but cannot keep the sun or light away,
since it is always there
and even in the darkest night;
you have to look through all the darkness,
pierce beyond their false blockade
and always see what's beyond and behind;
like in your soul, where clouds disturb the view
and sometimes cause distress, anxiety, suspiciousness
and other false and passing phantom shadows;
but what you think yourself is just delusions
while the light is outside in the universe
and never can be shut out by the clouds,
however much they gather and disturb you and the weather,
since the source is always there beyond and beaming,
which is all that matters, the resplendent origin,
which is the universal creativity.

The Heart of Poetry

The heart of poetry is difficult to reach
since there is almost nothing more evasive,
keeping mainly abstract and impossible to pinpoint,
analyses being usually a complete waste and failure,
since they only manage to break poems down for nothing,
the extremest sensitivity of poetry allowing no blasphemous trespassing
and being all too easily too deeply hurt;
and that's how we now manage to approach the secret:
that precarious touchiness is not for mortals to tread down,
the soul of poetry will not allow or even risk debasing,
so it has to constantly be on the run and fly away,
its very spirit being purely escapist,
since it can not survive or live at all
except in total freedom without limits,
since its gift demands complete space
like the eagle and the condor needs their heaven without end
in order to at all be able to exist;
but for what flight and purpose then needs poetry her wings?
For her expression, which demands completeness or nothing at all,
since poetry at heart is nothing but

the highest and the purest most refined expression,
of what else if not just love?

Whatever was Christmas really all about?

in answer to *"Daybreaker's"* important poem *"God is dead?"*

A simple message of just love and common sense,
of peace, co-operation, brotherhood and kindness
was mixed up from the beginning
in a terrible dogmatic passionate confusion
for which Paul, or Saul, was most responsible,
who without ever meeting Christ took charge of all Christianity
and started the first schism with Peter,
separating christendom from jewry,
starting a dogmatic church of power and intolerance,
eventually evolving into that notorious autocracy
of one infallible political state Church,
which system later made it possible to introduce
the inquisition, persecution of so called heretics,
burning anyone alive who was unlucky to have been informed against
and starting the first genocides against the Indians of South America.
That Church was not Christianity and certainly not that religion
which the carpenter of Nazareth once humbly introduced
of love and humbleness, of peace and brotherhood,
of working all together on the art of being kind.

Love is not worth it

I never was much for it,
actually, I always did refuse to enter it,
since rivalry is such a beastly thing,
a passion uncontrolled like that of animals,
complete abandonment of reason for the sake of egoistic passion –
let the bulls fight for their cows.
If other former wooers claim you
as persistent lovers of the past,
I will not argue with them –
let them have their way,
and if the lady meets their claim,
that is a risky business for her,
since, whenever ladies choose among their lovers,
usually the best one is the lost one.

There were many instances like this,
when I lost all the ones I loved the most
while they succumbed to ruthlessness and blindness
of the drive of egoistic passion
and were wasted with their ruined lives.
For me love is more sacred than worth fighting for,
since you can only love in peace,
and it is better to safeguard your love alone
and keep it burning in inviolable sanctuary
than to risk it in debasing conflict
with intruders who don't care how much you love
if only they can have their brutal way
destroying in blind passion all that made love worth it.

Missing you

– passing dream impressions of surpassing reality

Really don't know how to well express it,
but since you are not here
it will have to be a quiet meditation
over your imagined presence
in my life in spite of all,
in spite of all the death beds and concerns,
in spite of all the complications, complexes and calamities
of this dramatic love affair
which never seems to end its overturnings
into ever more increasing unexpectedness
of adventure and metaphysics,
not to mention mysteries galore
of this love labyrinth into a foreign exploration
of the totally unknowable, unthinkable and most improbable
strange wonders of relationships impossible
that after all seem to end up in the fantastic
possibility of everything all of a sudden coming true
like some fantasmic dream of ghostly unreality,
the strangest wonder of them all
you being here with me in veritable presence
inside me and not forever only in my thoughts
but grown into my soul to stay there,
for how long? For all eternity,
as long as we don't really know each other.

Beyond love

It's beyond me,
this magical affair of wonder
superseding and transcending love
to spite all worldly matters and reality
and conquer death by common sense,
replacing egoism with altruism and healing
properly amounting to a miracle
of unprecedented proportions
which make love discussions, arguments and speculations
secondary and redundant matters to the primary concern of life,
the right to live at all and the defence of life
against stupidity and narrowmindedness,
against the foolishness of man
who even rationally thinking just builds up his limitations,
while the truth remains forever far beyond him
but within his constant reach,
if only he would grant himself the simple gift of grasping it.
It's beyond me, but let us just let life come first
and make all personal concerns a secondary matter,
even love, since it is personal,
while universal love called life is all that matters.

The inexpressibility of love

The inexpressibility of love is a dilemma
since nothing in the world can do it justice.
It is like a journey that can never end,
approaching constantly the goal but never reaching it
but ever dreaming about reaching it
uninterruptedly depicting and imagining its wonder
in a neverendingly expanding towering description
of flamboyancy with many ornaments
but never failing in correctness and in realism.
Thus does it hopelessly enthrall us all
in ever changing and dramatic entertainment,
and there is but one thing we can do about it:
that is to enjoy it.

The undeniability of love

The undeniability of love
is something you can't trifle with.
You can't avoid it, once you are in love
you have no choice but to go through with it
in any way, however painful and uncomfortable,
it is never to be turned away
but to be stalwartly confronted
with its challenges and problematic compromises,
tragedies and crises, tribulations, sufferings and deaths;
for love is all about the central thing of life and death.
The best way just to keep it up, alive and kicking
is to concentrate on its ideals,
to never get bogged down but rather keep your nose up
breathing fresh air above water
and avoiding to get drowned in passion and infatuation;
for the only danger about love
is the psychosis of over-involvement,
getting stranded in the storm and over-whelmed
by the emotion of the unavoidable frustration
which inevitably must occur
and which, in every love affair,
is just a test and trial
to make sure that love will work,
remain, continue and survive.

Seas of love

Never mind their overwhelmingness,
just let them come and drown you,
overturn you, knock you down and beat you,
it is only healthy, it will only do you good,
no matter how horrendous hells they offer you,
no matter how much you will be demolished and destroyed,
no matter how repetitously you will constantly be driven over,
killed, reduced to cinders and annihilated,
since love will survive and manage anyway
and keep you floating just as long as you keep loving;
for the wonder is, that love in all its overwhelming floods
will ever keep you boyant –
so just rock along, enjoy your swim and follow down the stream,
and at least I can assure you,
you will definitely end up somewhere.

The Tortured Lover's Complaint

I can only be your lover
if I am your only lover.
What's love worth if it goes to bed with friends
and leaves the lover outside howling from neglect
and hurt more deeply than the sorest heart wounds,
massacred in battle, just from feeling locked out and ignored?
The question must arise if it is really worth the bleeding,
the despair and agony, the complete traumatization;
and still, the faintest glimpse of the beloved's face,
the shortest moment of her presence and her smile
is more than well enough to drain the ocean dry of sorrows,
heal all heart wounds and sweep all the bitterness away
in just a moment's flash and make a paradise start instantly
from the beginning, as if never any fall occurred.
What fools are we, the lovers, who can never have enough
of our folly, but must ever and again walk into walls and trains,
get many times run over, lost at sea completely and repetitively,
and we still will never tire of again start everything all over.

Courtesy

You can never bore me,
however much you try.
There is something about you
that never can bore anyone,
since they can only love you, all,
whatever you do to them.
Your wisdom is of such a kind
that makes you in a way infallible,
I don't think you could ever do a wrong thing,
although, naturally, we must all make our mistakes.
Your goodness is too thorough
to let any wrong come through,
and that is possibly your only weakness:
others can hurt you, and you can be profoundly hurt,
since goodness generally lacks protection.
It is there to be in constant outflow
spreading love and not demanding it;
and so no one could possibly do anything but love you,
which includes myself, your humble servant.

Euthanasia

Since I have to die, just let me die,
and make it quick, do not prolong it,
I always hated sentimentalized farewells;
and death is painful too
and more so than enough,
so why then make it even more so
by postponing just a transfer
which can't be avoided anyway?
To die, to sleep, that's all,
and just not waking up again,
like freezing comfortably into an embalming snowdrift,
going gradually to sleep, quite slowly limb by limb,
like some mild anaesthetic slowing down life till it stops,
the softest death imaginable.
Yes, if there is no returning from the definite departure,
just make it quick then,
do not trouble me and keep me waiting,
for I will be in a hurry
when I can't use this life any more
to get into the next one.

Ode to a loving drunkard

What is left of you, when all is finished
and the bottle empty, and you lie there in the gutter
vomiting your anguish and self-pity
forlorn and deserted by all living creatures
that you once thought were your friends,
while now you see your only friends among the dead,
the only people that can never be unkind to you,
the only ones who don't insult you and depress you,
all those people, who are only sympathetic when they sleep,
while bullies rule the earth and drive it mad unto destruction
like all those responsible demented politicians
who in fact are chief accountable for this old planet's state of health
while they are those who get away with fortunes
and escape the course of justice,
while you lie there weeping in the gutter
with the rain down-pouring on you ruthlessly and endlessly,
the drunkard crying desperately all his guts out for the world
and for this strayed humanity that never can get right again.
But still, there must be something left.

Oh yes, you still will be insane enough a fool
to go on living and of loving
although no one in the world deserved it
except you yourself, the undermost of underdogs,
who never will stop loving any human being
from your accurate perspective from the gutter.

Love and pornography

Without love your life is dead,
a darkness without light,
a hopeless mess of no return,
which makes it so important to take care of love
and deal with it the right way, justly,
making it remain and not just using it.
Real lovers find it most upsetting
to all of a sudden see each other naked,
and, as we all know, so did Adam and Eve after their fall;
and the first thing they did was to in consternation
and alarm put on some clothes,
most primitive ones if not only fig leaves;
so they were upset, alarmed and almost desperate,
which I find a most natural reaction,
after such a paradise of love which they had had
for such a long time even.
Love is more than nakedness and nude display,
which isn't love but only deviations;
while a simple word of kindness
can be much more love than any carnal exercise.
So let us concentrate on love
and just forget about all those unnecessary extras
which, for all their matter, just don't matter,
since love lives and dies within the spirit
while its stretching out to concretize in matter
is just a departure from where it belongs
and always must return to, even if it dies,
to only there be able to get born again.

The Secret

There was never anything between us except love,
but that sufficed for an eternity,
and let us keep it that way,
let's remain in love and cherish it
in adoration and soft kindness
without any disharmonics out of tune
and keep the melody of beauty flowing,
the most beautiful in all existence
that can never reach its end or fulfilment
but ever must increase and be prolonged
in beauty and in longing and in perfect understanding.
Thus we shall stand forth in time
against intrusions and false chords of insolence
and be a paragon of lovers
just by keeping our love our own and on its own
like some professional outstanding secret
just for masters to obtain and manage
well with care to keep the art and skill in session
unsurpassed and perfect for all future generations
to just wonder at and ask: "How did they do it?"

Bastards are we all

Bastards are we all since we are human,
man for his perversions is the basest animal
and actually the only one to be indecent;
so what does it matter if your parents misbehaved,
if you are not your father's child,
if you have to take care of other children than your own,
for instance your divorced man's children from a previous marriage,
and so on. No one is pure, no one is sacred,
all that we can do is just the best of it
since we are here and have to live and stay here;
so let's just not make it even worse in messed up families
by arguing about it, questioning your origin,
investigate intricacies and ask upsetting questions.
Bastards are we all, let's stick to that
and make the best of it.

OCTOBER HARVEST FIRST PART.

A suggestion of the healing powers of love

The mysteries surround and overwhelm us
in intoxicating wonders of the soul
in this unheard of drama of a patient
subject to an extraordinary process
of the utterly impossible through healing;
while there are two characters in this proceeding

although we are three protagonists.
One is the patient, suffering since long
and now at last in some orientation of her case,
all mysteries about her sufferings resolved,
while love is second in this case
of infinite resources of indefatigability
all coming out of you in tireless exertion,
while the possibility that I might be your only lover
and that you have been my only love
would just be some addition in this case,
a moral faint support of humble kind
that I will faithfully continue to sustain
no matter what will happen, but,
as she herself maintains with admirable calmness,
will turn out only for the good.

The desperate solution

Like a washed-out wreck of war
you lie there in the depths of misery
disfigured and molested in dishonour
doomed in your condition to the worst of all:
to stay alive, to go on living
as an amputated wreck
with no hope for a decent life;
and yet, life is worth living,
since at least there is one person left to love you,
and that is enough and more than a whole world of reasons
to in spite of all go on, stay on, live on
and torture yourself on along the path of tribulation
with no end to it, since even death
is just a temporary vain release;
since what comes afterwards
is always even worse.

Addiction

There is no addiction not worth having,
or, as someone put it, there is only one addiction
which includes them all, and therefore any one is better
than not having one at all. Can there be any truth in this?
Oh yes, it is the whole truth, and it's truer than you can imagine.
Why is this? The only real addiction is, of course,

that abyss we call love, which everyone is stuck in,
naturally, all his life from birth until his dying day,
since that's the essence and what life is all about.
But love gets easily perverted, and there are perversions
without number of all kinds, and they expand and constantly get worse,
since that is how love works.
But since perversions always come from love,
that source is their excuse and sanctifies them,
if they do no harm and keep within reasonability;
and love will remain forever an addiction and the first and last one,
from which all addictions and perversions emanate
and are mutations and translations, variations of.
So whatever your addiction, it is better just to have one
than to be without, since love doth speak in many languages,
and none of them is wrong.

Repression

Tear away the curtains and the shadows,
let me finally discover what's behind it all,
let's go beyond the aberrations,
all that stands in our way of our love,
the wrong ideas, the doubts and broodings,
the entanglement of seven veils,
since all that matters is beyond it all,

beyond suspicion and possession,
beyond all obsessiveness and beyond doubt,
the naked truth of our relationship,
which no one can intrude upon
and which excludes all importuning.
Love can never be denied
but must the more arise and grow
and make itself more deeply felt
for being put down and repressed –
it can not be controlled;
for if it once is there,
you have to let it be
and just go down with it
in its engulfing generosity
more vast than any ocean.

The bored meeting

The board meeting went as it should:
only gossip and yawnings,
sloth and slowness getting stiffer and staler
every moment with increasing boredom,
as if we hadn't been bored enough already
with all this stalemate stagnation
constantly growing from bad to worse
as if there was anything else to do
but to get lost and drop dead,
which board meeetings never do,
so they infinitely continue
to be bored meetings.

Assessment

You are too good for me
and too good to be true,
you are too beautiful
for my unworthy humbleness
and for my decrepitude,
too young for my old age
and far too dear for my possessing.
Shall we call it off then?
That is the supreme impossibility,
since no divorce can separate us,

and there is no lover
that can tempt us to deceit.
How shall we keep each other then,
when circumstances always keep us separated
and we never seem to reach a settlement,
since there are always others claiming you,
and I can never be completely free
from my commitments.
So our only chance is simply to continue
as we have done all the way so far
as lovers distanced by our shyness
and our over-sensitiveness
and our mutual fear
of hurting, losing and of trespassing each other,
since we both refuse to ever lose
what we so far in spite of all have gained.

The supreme humiliation

It is fatal and for love completely unsurvivable,
much more than a crisis, worse than any trauma,
and it kills completely instantly
but leaves you scarred for life
with wounds that never heal but always ache atrociously,
and you can never in your life
trust anyone again completely,
for it is the highest and the deepest treason,
and I am afraid it's also the most common one;
the trivial case when your own love
goes into bed with someone else.
Although you are not touched
it hurts more deeply than could any wound,
and the trauma stays for life.
The first time when it happened to me
I should have been wise enough
to learn to never trust my love again,
but then you fall in love again,
the same old trivial story is repeated,
and the wounds you tried to desperately cure
the hard way by repression
open up again in torments worse than ever.
Although I lost everything
my pride remains,

that I was always honest as a lover
and did never go to other beds
except my own of faithfulness,
where love was always kept impeccable
no matter how much it betrayed me.

The Lover

(just a sketch of an old friend)

Let's talk about the lover.
He just goes around and takes on anything,
as if his business in this life
was simply to take on too much,
the more, the better,
since his loving care is simply indefatigable,
as if all his energy just went on growing and expanding
with his busyness; but all his business
is just love, and he knows well his business.
He went wild as far too young,
became subversive as a hippie
which remained his trade all through the years,
at times unrecognizable with hair down to his thighs
and silver earrings with all kinds of necklaces,
at other unrecognizable as an academician
of complete propriety in costume, necktie,
shaved and short cut, like a bureaucrat.
But he continues taking on all kinds of cases,
schizophrenics, addicts, refugees and outcasts,
championing their cause and giving them a lift-up,
while his love affairs are the best secrets in the world,
since all his love is just discretion.

Real life

Don't give me that shallowness
of ordinary entertainment,
flair and superficiality,
which are like farts of butterflies
as quickly vanishing as instantly forgotten.
All that is only lies, what people laugh at,
while real life is found among the dying,
in the drama and the tragedies of fighting for one's life,

which is the very highlight and the turning point of life,
the highest moment of supremest truth,
when death announces life's metamorphosis
from this life across all borders to another beyond us,
the living, while the dying only has the privilege
to see beyond and enter into triumph
his or her apotheosis and fulfilment
of the glorious liberation from all worries left behind.
Preparing her for that fantastic journey
is the best thing we can do for her,
adorning her departure with the warmest care
of lovely memories and tender love
transcending and surpassing all she ever had.
Thus can we make it certain that she will return
and even more: not even ever leaving us.

Love and self love

You can not love unless you love yourself,
and all your love is worthless
if you fail to take into consideration
your beloved's self-love and her right to love herself.
In fact, she can not love you
unless she may also love herself.
The same applies to you.
The more you love yourself,
the more you also can love others,
and without that self-love
love is without roots and nourishment.
Love works and only works when it is double,
dualistic, dialogue, of giving and receiving,
and although it only can expand by giving,
its miraculous effect is this,
that all your love, the more you give it,
will return to you at the same time
as it is generously spent on your beloved and on others,
and thus will it always double
and remain impossible forever to get lost.

The Workoholic's Dilemma

He is not incapable of love,
but, on the contrary, is too much of a lover,
feeling his responsibilities as such
and trying desperately to live up to all of them
and thus is constantly an over-worker
giving only, not receiving,
since he feels his obligation just to love
and therefore has no time for being loved.
It's at the same time clinging to maintaining the initiative
like from some fear of losing it
and not remaining in control,
and that fear is the sickly part
which keeps him in the squirrel's wheel
imprisoned in his constant and one-sided outflow
bent on voluntarily to work himself to death.

Two directions

Our schizophrenic society offers two directions,
and we generally take them both
in opposite directions
driven both ways by the schizophrenic society
in a desperate effort to conform to it.
This society, by stress and overwork
is going to extremes to drive us nuts,
forcing us into the direction of introversion
by over-focussing and concentration
ending up in burnt-out cases,
paralysis, cancers and brain tumours,
so we find ourselves completely apathetic
as a wreck abandoned in a ward.
This is of course insane,
and thus we turn into the opposite direction
away from stress and the society,
going anti-social, freaking out and dropping out,
abandoning ourselves to any kind of love
just to get out, escape ourselves
and all that is unbearable in humdrum dreariness,
routine, responsibility and overwork for nothing,
anything to just get out of ourselves;
and the miraculous result is this,
that the more we lose in this uneconomic process,
the saner the results, the better off we are,

the more we gain in health and clarity of mind,
and the ultimate reward of this is freedom.
And then we don't have any need
to any more complain of this society
which as a safety catch
enforces us to drop out and abandon it.

The real lover

The real lover has no means to express his love
because of shyness and fear of getting hurt,
he has no means to pay for his love because of no money,
no riches, no resources, no nothing,
so he dares not express it,
since he knows nothing is more easily abused,
more easily taken advantage of than love,
and the more so, the more honest and true it is;
so he just protects it by keeping it inside
to safeguard its honesty and keep it intact
for the true love that never comes;
since he has learned the hard way never to trust a woman
but only to love her the more
for paying for his faithfulness
by keeping himself buried alive
just to keep the constant slavework of his love
burning, if naught for else,
at least for consuming himself,
which he knows it's worth
keeping it alive
by suffering.

A compliment

There is a pain and thorn
deep down inside my heart
that aches for you incessantly,
as if my only life was close to you
and in your company,
more blessed than could any other's be,
since you are you and no one else
can even distantly approach your character.
So am I spoilt, then, to at all be known to you,
or is it that I am the only one to know you
deeply and enough to understand you?

I must not be so presumptuous,
since there never was a man
who ever knew at all a woman;
since that is the woman's charm
and personality to always be detached,
evade, escape, transcend, surpass
and overpass man's faculties of understanding
to in fact be man's unique and single overman
as teacher, guide and better half;
since man without a woman
is a continent without a sea.
So let me love you, now, continuously
and indefatigably as a faithful brother
and much more than that:
your only man who really knows you
and how to appreciate you more than fully.

The outcast

In the bottom of despair the outcast
languishes forlorn and buried deeply in self pity
monstrously alive the more in death.

His exoneration is his excommunication
leading straight to exhumation and his resurrection.

The fortune hunter

She will capture you, seduce you and destroy you
like a vampire and as convincingly,
and you will only recognize the danger and the risk
by really getting caught and actually succumb and fall
most willingly to the seduction,
which will be most thorough,
once you see the trap and are locked up in it.
The only thing to do next is to recognize the ruin and accept it,
start again from zero, hoping not to get entrapped again
but painfully aware that you will be at risk
and liable and vulnerable,
and that you can never trust yourself again.
The worst of all, perhaps, is this,
that you can never say, 'Forgive me,'
and she never will say that to you.

The workoholic's creed

She doesn't run away from you,
you always have her when you want her,
she will always keep within your own control,
and you can not in any way betray her,
nor can she deceive you,
faithfulness and love is all there is between you,
and your intimate relationship might even pay,
she never gives you any reason for some jealousy,
and she never goes to bed with others,
you can always when you want be quite alone with her,
and you might even find her beautiful at times.
She never runs away or paints herself too much,
she never misbehaves or drinks or swears,
takes dope or needs abortions,
and she never scolds you,
your relationship is perfectly harmonious without quarrels,
and if sometimes she can be a bore,
monotonous and humdrum,
that is only up to you, your own fault and responsibility.

The Pain of Love

It hurts, and more than any operation
since there is no aneasthetic
and you must be conscious all the way through
that infernal Armageddon, Golgatha and Purgatory
if you get through there at all,
for there was never any greater pain
than that of love when it was true
and had to end before you even reached it,
which is usually the case
when that elusive thing called love
for one time's sake uniquely
happens to be true.

Lucifer's rehabilitation

There is no sweeter voice than thine,
the honeyed balsam to my soul,
the only medicine I need,
the sweetest music in the air,

the finest note that ever graced a melody,
the purest song that ever warbled
higher and more lovely than a nightingale
and softer to the touch of sentiment
to the beleaguered overwhelming sorrows of the soul.
The deepest darkness of the wailing heart
can only be dispersed by such a voice of tenderness
expressing purest honesty of deep affection
sending down a hopeful spark to Lucifer
with strength enough to swing him up to heaven
and restore his wings in whitest glory;
for such is the power of the honesty of love
that it can banish hell to heaven.

Release

Release me from my love
and let me die with it exulting
in the blind release of reaching out
into the light from the abysmal tunnel
of what's worse than death: the trials
on the way of love through all the agonies
of jealousy, uncertainty, unanswerableness,
suspicion, longing and misgivings,
doubts, exhaustion and humiliation.
But the end is always there,
the reaching of one's home,
the light end of the tunnel,
the supreme release of all your energies,
the height of beauty and of happiness,
the ultimate reward of all your faithfulness,
the final absolution and absorption
of your soul and body into the fulfilment
of the final light that is the definite reward
that must await us all,
if we just loved at all.

A parable

(I just received this from a friend in India, a beautiful parable concerning the "International Friendship Week"...)

There once was a little boy who had a bad temper. His Father gave him a bag of nails and told him that every time he lost his temper, he must hammer a nail into the back of the fence. The first day the boy had driven 37 nails into the fence. Over the next few weeks, as he learned to control his anger, the number of nails hammered daily gradually dwindled down. He discovered it was easier to hold his temper than to drive those nails into the fence.

Finally the day came when the boy didn't lose his temper at all. He told his father about it and the father suggested that the boy now pull out one nail for each day that he was able to hold his temper.

The days passed and the young boy was finally able to tell his father that all the nails were gone. The father took his son by the hand and led him to the fence. He said, "You have done well, my son, but look at the holes in the fence. The fence will never be the same. When you say things in anger, they leave a scar just like this one. You can put a knife in a man and draw it out. It won't matter how many times you say I'm sorry, the wound is still there.

A verbal wound is as bad as a physical one. Friends are very rare jewels, indeed. They make you smile and encourage you to succeed. They lend an ear, they share words of praise and they always want to open their hearts to us."

Natural observation

When may I love you again?
No man can live without his love,
he's got to have it, and at any cost,
and if he can't, he has to turn to extraordinary means,
like telepathic dreams, perhaps the best of substitutes;
which actually can work both ways,
I mean, your lost one can respond,
no matter how much she is lost or alienated, –
love will always bring her back
and bring you back home to it,
it can never fail but must consistently
surmount and conquer all,
since that's what love is for:

all things must fail but love,
and love alone can make all things succeed,
if only they unselfishly are motivated
by that basic working force of miracles
that never fails and never dies
but always must remain, continue
and sustain all that
which makes all life worth while.

Hackers into poetry

Supreme stupidity and vanity,
outrageous folly and pathetic miserable lunacy,
you future monster, how can you get such an idea
to even dare to challenge poetry,
more holy than the gods,
the very incarnation of longevity,
the sacred word more sacred than the Bible
that invented it; this is ridiculous.
You just can't challenge poetry in any way,
not even hypothetically;
for a poet, like for instance Dante
or the poet behind Shakespeare
must remain alive for ever,
while you can never harm in any way
a single word that ever was poetically written.

And even if you would succeed in such an enterprise
of a preposterous deletion of all files,
you can not kill the dreams,
that will continue spreading poetry forever.

Reflections in your hair

Let your hair grow with your generosity
in beauty with your soul and animosity
and thus increase our love in constant unity
to never cease in affluence and purity,
for ours is the privilege of loving
and of understanding all too well
what love is all about, its working,
and what it lives to tell;
and that compels us to some obligation

to keep out of molestation
keeping our expansion ever growing
to fulfill our over-flowing
of that love of yours that's in your hair
to grow forever everywhere and here.

The wasted actor

Please don't push me any more,
I am enough divided and destroyed,
dispersed and lost in far too many parts,
each claiming more than I can give;
for acting on the stage is nothing less
than spotlight prostitution
claiming all you ever had
and more than that,
bereaving you of all your privacy
and everything that was yourself;
for acting means, you have to be just anyone
except yourself, the only person lost to you,
the only character that you must never act,
while all the others must demand
your flesh och bone and heart and soul
until you are an emptiness of nothing left,
and all those characters and parts you acted
are reduced to phantoms of pathetic memories.

Abstinence

It's hard to bear,
the abstinence of you;
your house is empty like a desert;
although quite a small apartment,
all the emptiness is greater
than would be the vastness of the ocean
without ships, and all the deserts of the earth
without a single oasis.
Still, your memory is there,
the softness of your being rings with music
in the silence of your instruments,
the spirit is still there
awaiting your return
to once again refresh our whole existence

with your presence and your company
to cure all desert feelings
and become enough of a oasis
to put all the deserts of the world
to green fruition
and cure all the ocean storms
and all the darkness of the universe.

To the lighthouse

The fulsome light of our affair
is like a lighthouse in a stormy night
enlightening our path through darkness trials
and leading us in blindness on
to what? Whatever lies in store for us,
more trials, storms and tribulations
or the worst of all, a total interruption,
we at least will face it altogether
and stand up to it together
spiting threatenings of death
and challenging eternity to just survive
all in the name and right of love.

The wounded angel

(the patient and her nurse)

Your wings are growing although ruptured,
and your soul is free although confined in bed,
your handicapped communication with your body
means the more gymnastics for your soul,
which soars in freedom flying everywhere
discovering new realms of spiritual awareness
while the doctors can't see anything of your true state.
Your fortune is your nurse who sees it all
and understands the miracles that happen here
of your amounting freedom compensating
the brutality that struck your body down
to painful and heart-rending invalidity;
and that's true nursing:
to acknowledge and be constantly aware
of that the patient's soul is marching on
with all her dignity kept intact and alive

and perhaps much more alive because of body damage
than imprisoned in the body and confined to mortal senses.
Whatever happens, you will never die
but always stay with us remaining close to us
since we will never let go of your spirit
but stay up and never leave your side,
since we are more aware now of your presence
than we were while you were physically fit.

Make love, not war, Mr President!

Since you have never made a single good thing,
getting into office by a coup and cheating,
getting helped by your own brother governor,
applauded into office by tomatoes, eggs and other rotten things
that people rightly threw at you that rainy day
when you refused to leave your car for your protection
against those who knew what you had done,
the first thing that you acted on in office
being to accelerate American deforestation
and start projects for Alaska's exploitation and pollution,
all, of course, just for your oily business,
stubbornly denying the existence of a global warming;
and all that was prior to your going into war,
your greatest failure, fiasco and American catastrophe,
as if the fact that this would be a mortal blow to all American economy
was not enough, since you were bent on ruining your country
from the start - just out of ignorance, of course.
'The worst administration ever' is what you are being called,
so I would suggest that you just pull yourself together
and go into bed and there start making better things,
for instance love, since that is what you need, poor President.

Missing

My longing and my missing you consumes me
with a devastating fire that leaves nothing left
of all I thought that I consisted of
but which, without you, is a barren wilderness
of only scorched and desert earth
completely desolated by that destiny
which seems to never let us have each other
but continues but to separate us

drearily indefinitely
like a storm that never gets blown over
but just keeps on harrowing the land,
the life we had which never was our own.
Our only hope is that which never dies,
the last resort, the fickle hope itself,
which although hopeless never did completely leave
all mankind at a loss
but kept on burning
stubbornly in spite of all
with the minutest flame
but constantly surviving
just to spite the overwhelming destiny
which keeps on claiming us and owning us
but which can never stop us from continuing
to be sustaining in our love and hope
in the belief that it will in the end
prevail, reward us for our patience
and remain our sole defence against our destiny.

Unconditional love

Love must of course be unconditional,
or else it isn't love,
or if there are conditions set by love
they are the hardest and the most impossible
to satisfy, surmount and challenge,
wearing you completely out
and leaving you a shred of wreckage
hardly able to survive,
since there is nothing more exhausting than true love,
that must have all or nothing,
craving unconditional surrender
penetrating everything and most of all your soul
which must be violated, changed and recreated
just in order to survive at all, continue and go on.
But once you have surrendered, given up completely
and are at the mercy of your lover and your love,
the worst is over, and you can start living.
That's where life begins,
that's where you'll find it and be able to enjoy it,
since once you have given up yourself,
surrendered unconditionally all your love,
you will receive it and continue be receiving it forever.

Supremacy

My love, it's not your fault.
Nothing is your fault.
Whatever happens, my love stands above it
sacred and untouchable,
inviolable and serene
in infallible perfection
if there ever was one.
Trials may oppress and vex us,
illnesses may seize us and strike down our nearest,
accidents, disasters and catastrophes may happen,
but my love is singled out from every risk
and can't be touched, suspected or at all called into question
since it is the only sacred thing I have.

Love among the ruins

It is all a wreckage,
our ruined lives
with illness and decrepitude all round us,
suffering and pain just about everywhere
and crying out aloud
like chained lunatics in a madhouse
carefully tied down with leather stripes
with no limb capable of even moving
as if you could tie down the human pains and sufferings;
and we are separated, shamefully to say as usual,
and can do nothing but in spite of all reach out
and have our love in common
like the rarest orchid suffocating in this darkness
of a dense spruce forest in the winter snows;
and still it lives, survives and does continue forward
 in its kind illusion and naïvety
believing it could spread its beauty everywhere,
while the spruce forest darkness only answers with a compact silence.
Still she lives, and while she lives,
and as long as she lives she triumphs.

Love and friendship

Of course, love must lead to some disappointment,
there was never any journey without obstacles,
what would our lives be without crises,
and what love could ever work without a challenge?
It is only natural, that sometimes you become frustrated
with your partner and with that whole sex,
and then you always can resort to friends,
and that's how homosexuals and lesbians started.
But that love of your own sex can never satisfy,
while there is no better friendship,
no friend can be more reliable
than such a confident companion of your own sex,
since there are no sexual tensions naturally from the start.
The sexual tensions only ruin most relationships,
and the most difficult of all is to maintain your partner
as the best of friends although she is not of your sex.
That is maybe the ultimate and highest challenge
of all love affairs - to keep it going, to keep loving
without ever letting go the fundamental friendship.

Adoration

My love, you are the focus of my adoration,
if you'll excuse me, I just have to love you
as the only object of my worship,
although I am well aware
that I know you too well
with all your female frailties,
every human limitation
that a human being is at all capable of,
which just makes her the more perfectly human
and lovable as such.
So please forgive me for continuing to love you
obstinately and persistently,
since you at leat are lovable,
which, as God knows, not every human being is.
Consider it a weakness, it you want to,
but for me it's just a human faculty
to prove that I am human
which for me is a more valuable grade
than any possible divinity or honour.

The up-lifting spirit

Let me lift you up
unto the heights of happiness
and stay there with you up in heaven
just to warble in our triumph
of our high victorious love,
the ruler of the seventh heaven
and the angel wings of our beings
having reached our harps already
by the splendid fugues of our songs.
Thus let me keep you there
in constant thrilling vertigo
like one great ballet dancer
lifting up her swan in one resplendent leap
to never put her down again.
Thus will and do I love you
indefatigably and outrageously,
incredibly and carefully
to never let you down again.

Modern funeral

The man thought dead awoke in his coffin
and became alarmed at his condition.
"O my! I hope indeed they didn't fix the lid!"
But of course it was firmly fixed with screws.
His next troubled thought was:
"Am I buried alive,
or will they burn me alive?
Rather buried alive than cremated alive!"
He pounded his fists against the lid,
but it was solid, so no sound went through it,
and he couldn't hear a thing above it -
modern coffin lids are thick and solid without holes.
"Well, well, I guess I'll notice if it gets too hot
or if I start to freeze," so he resigned
and tried to make the best of it,
to make himself more comfortable;
but then suddenly he noticed to his utter joy:
his wife had sent along with him his precious jewel,
his favourite and dearest toy, his mobile phone!
He cried for joy at his salvation
and made a call immediately.
His wife, amazed, quite bluntly answered:
"Darling, we thought you were dead!
Where in heaven's name are you?"
The moral here is: never leave your loved one
without access to his mobile phone,
in case he wants to reach you from the other side.

The Condition of Life

My love, I will not marry
you since I am too much of a lover
and therefore love you too much.
What kind of logic is this weirdness?
That is simply how I work -
I can not be a lover
unless I base my love on freedom
and can work with freedom as a base,
for love can never work or live or breathe
unless it hovers high in total freedom
to be able to sustain itself
by this inspiring indispensability,

without which no love can continue.
Thus let me love you and continue loving you
with freedom as my neverending energy,
for there was never any love bird warbling
stifled in a cage to keep it down and limited
in the unhuman, murderous imprisonment
of practical accessibility.

Elementary

Love is constantly to be transcended by itself.
That's how it never ceases to amaze us
and surprise us by its ever changing nature
going on like a metamorphosis without end,
and all there is to do is just to follow;
and as long as you just follow its expanding course
you will be working and alive as a good lover.
Only when you stop and put love in confinement,
make up regulations and will have it disciplined
you will be disappointed and will lose it,
since love never can be regulated and confined.
You must be free with it or die with it.
There is no other choice.

By the death bed

There is no greater heroism
than fighting it alone in darkness
against absolute adversity
with no chance of a victory
but fighting it out all the same alone,
life being turned into a constant nightmare
of outrageous pain and suffering
with no associate except the fearful death
which tortures you the more the more you fight it.
Everyone advises you to just give up,
give in, succumb, resign and let it go,
but life can not be parted with in any way
without a fight and voluntarily;
and the longer and the more you fight it out,
the more heroic your defence of life becomes;
and all is well, and victory is possible
as long as only there is someone by your side.

When finally the last companion gives up the last stand,
not until then the fight is over,
and it is allowable to finally give up;
and then you know, as you are dying,
that you die a conqueror,
you have secured the final victory;
and that companion will also know it well,
as you both know that this life will go on
victorious and conquering forever.

Transubstantiation

Whatever dies grows stronger
by its love, that cannot die
but simply can't be stopped
for its inviolable continuity
that must go on forever
by a force much stronger than of nature,
which the dead know better than the living,
since they see it all quite clearly
that is blurred for us by our senses.

Open up your spiritual eyes
and close your mortal eyes
to all things mortal,
and you shall begin to see
eternity in spirituality
enlightened by a greater light
than any blinding one on earth.

The angels have no wings but fly the higher
for the loss of them, and so do mortals
for the loss of all their senses
of their mortal bodies.

It is all perfectly natural,
the supernaturalness
of this weird illusion
of our mortal life.

How to handle catastrophes

Laughing through your tears
there is a certain cheerfulness in hopelessness
as if the ultimate defeat was after all a victory
although it cost us everything
and we are wearied out in all our energy
completely, as if now at this fulfilment
battle was about to start.
The tears will do no good,
the sorrows and catastrophes are to be laughed at,
and the problems start now as they have been solved.
This mess is difficult to be helped out from,
and it seems the only thing that we could do
is making it still worse,
which always is a possibility and a temptation.
Better then to go to sleep, forget it all,
get drunk and let the world resolve itself
with all its troubles, which is no concern of ours,
and postpone awakening to this mad nightmare
called reality as long as possible.

The other side

— a kind of truism

There is no love without atrocious turbulence,
no happiness without diluvions of tears,
no way to paradise except through hell
and no way up at all without descending to the bottom.
Fools are we that childishly believe in positiveness,
as if anything of good could be one-sided
without other startling facts to contradict all so called truths!
All happiness and fortune is a selfish coward
while the only person who could rightly be content
and properly be called a happy individual
is he that managed to escape from life to death
without a failure left behind of all his life.

After the fall

– partly inspired by the Swedish poetess Karin Boye, dead at 41.

Of course it hurts
when the spring bursts
in aching buds of awakening
to the blinding light of ruthless reality,
when our longing is awakened
from its sleep of mercy to its sentient pain,
when the locks of our hearts are forced
and crying feelings must into the open,
melting into the heaviness of drops
that must burst forth into rains and floods
of our remorse and pain of endless witholds
that no winter ever succeeded in freezing to the deep;
and of course this new life must hesitate
in faltering steps unto a new path
of the unknown, so difficult to stand on,
impossible to find out and forbidding us to fall.

But then the miracle occurs,
after death I hear your voice again
so soft and full of tenderness
as if death never had existed
but was merely a bad dream to waken from,
bringing new life and hope
and courage to in spite of all
partake in the new creation
which after the ruins
will be the toughest work of all.

The bag lady

When her husband threw her out
she got down on to her feet
and kept them on the ground
to start a new life with a wider range
of vision and perspective
and became the centre of a circle
of enlightened people, new age prophets,
spiritualists and visionaries of Aquarius,
like a wise old lady of transcendent insights
all the while remaining like a tramp,

insisting on her status of a bag lady
with all the necessary outfits:
plastic bags for luggage,
bicycle as only vehicle,
no real apartment of her own,
no riches, no security, no nothing
but a universe of friendship and devoted friends,
of cheerfulness and good comradeship,
all the best and most enlightened people of the place,
like as if she had been a queen
but happier as such than any one enthroned
and richer than the Queen of England
with her ownership of nothing
but preliminaries of spirituality,
more vitally important than the whole world
of mundane and passing follies.

Disappointment

– the scandal of unfathomable width

How could it happen,
that most dreadful scandal in our modern history
and in a qualified democracy!
They didn't just elect him and enthrone him,
that most ignorant of presidents,
who never had been travelling abroad,
who never had much of an education,
never studied history
and hardly ever read a book,
a former alcoholic cheated into office,
and they re-elected him!
They covered up the whole environmental research
that the previous administration had painstakingly procured
with all the clear resulting indications of the global warming going on,
the Bush administration made a cover-up of it
to not disturb financial interests,
to keep up the oil business as usual
burying their oistrich head into the sands
for short-sighted pecuniary profits
at the expense of the planet.
What a loathsome leader of the world!
Investigating this felonious racket,
Watergate and Irangate appear as innocent soap bubbles,

while the Brits misguided by that Blair
just bought it all and fell flat for that racketeer and con man,
tricked into a booby trap by phoney greedy hustlers.
Such deceivers of mankind can never be forgiven
or forgotten, like the 20th century dictators
Lenin, Hitler, Mussolini, Stalin, Mao and Pol Pot,
the mad seducers and destroyers of humanity,
the rogues of history, whose gallery unfortunately
never has been stopped from being constantly expanded
by those criminals, adventurers and crooks
who mask themselves as politicians.

Love folly

If love be egoism, I will not be a lover.
Better then to step aside and let the egoists
in senseless folly fight it out among themselves –
I will have none of it. That love is false
that boosts the ego into a baloon of lies
that has to burst and vanish into nothing
as a blown-up rag in shreds and good for nothing,
like a most deplorable pathetic fiasco
just to throw away into the garbage.
True love is a selfless self-effacing angel
never seen and working hard
invisibly from underground
appearing only through her work results
that must remain a joy forever for its beauty
if it only is conducted honestly
in true sincerity of love.
If rivals, fighters and psychotic passion drivers
think they deal with love
and blame their love for their psychotic business,
they are just deceivers of themselves
and have to learn the hard way
that real lovers only win by losing all.

The soul collector

How can love become a tragedy?
It's all too easy - the smallest detail is enough
to wreck the finest fregate into cinders,
like the man who lost his wife to his best friend
and after thirty years of marriage with three children,
or the wooer who inevitably had that bad luck
to get all his sweethearts snatched away by others
just as he was going to propose to them,
or the poor man who could never have a wife
without her cheating him with other men,
the more the better, as if vulgar fornication was a merit;
or the lady who infallibly got stuck with the wrong men,
drug addicts, alcoholics, psycopaths and mental cases,
while she never got the man she really loved,
and he, who really loved her, also never got her.
Well, there are so many casualties in love,
that casualties of war are easier to calculate,
since most love victims just obliterate themselves in suicide,
making their life's greatest sport to get away with it unnoticed.
Other victims turn to less fructiferous alternatives,
like going lesbian or homosexual
with, of course, no natural results,
and end up crying out pathetically their frustrations
like all losers in the most incalculable game of love,
where losses generally are completely ruining
and gains just fickle transient momentary whiffs.
There are too many bitter bachelors who learned the hard way
not to ever trust a woman, and too many spinsters
who turned into hostile feministic militants
because of too bad luck with the wrong men.
Among the commonest of clichés is, among frustrated men,
"I never met a woman I could trust," and among women,
"Never was there any man who did not cheat his love
from the beginning." Still, there always are exceptions.
Some there are who just continued ever to be faithful
to their massacred ideals, and the more so
the more they got hurt on the way,
and others who are just content
with their collection of the souls of those
whose bodies they could never reach.
That is a special and extraordinary category.
They are maybe greatest of all lovers,
since they never can forget whom they have loved once

and they never can betray a single one of all their loves.
They have their candles burning constantly
in the profoundest depths of their most tender hearts
and never fail to light them up again
if any of those candles would go out.
Their faithfulness, experience and piety is inexhaustible,
their love embraces all, is omnipresent and supremely tolerant,
and they are maybe the true teachers of true love,
since they, by never getting anyone, did never cheat,
did never let you down, did never hurt a soul
and carried their love safely through all hells
to keep it burning as the true ideal which it should be.

As time goes by

— some optimistic faith

My love, when shall we meet again?
When shall the clouds unveil the sun
and let the moonbeams through the night
to light my fire by your bosom
and enlighten us with all that beauty
that our love once made us so familiar with?
When shall we smile again at jokes amidst all tears
to lighten up the tragedies and cure all deaths
by life's inspiring spirituality to clear all darkness?
When shall we find again that leisure
and that time for ourselves
that spited so heroically all unhuman stress
and made a green oasis of our city's desert center,
spilling over from our love to gild all streets
with the delicacy of our poetry?
When shall we love again?
When death is dead and tears are dry
and happiness has driven all bad luck away
and miracles have emptied all the hospitals;
which naturally only can be finally accomplished
by the obstinacy of our most intrepidly persistent love.

OCTOBER HARVEST FIRST PART.

Ghosts

To suffer in the darkness of silence
is not just the privilege of raped virgins
but of all true lovers
who never knew love
unless they suffered in the darkness of silence.

The darkness is complete, all life is gone,
all lights are put out by the whirlwind
and there is nothing left
but to suffer in the darkness of silence.

So what do I care
if mankind and the world go to hell
through their own abuse of nature
since there will always be someone left
to suffer in the darkness of silence.

The victims driven over by development, by authorities,
by scoundrels in disguise of the establishment,
by ruthlessness authorized to rape and murder all things human,
the souls of all those who against their will were robbed of their bodies,
they will prevail,
suffering in the darkness of silence.

The intolerable truth

The truth is always controversial,
sensitive and painful, and above all, difficult.
One may not always speak the truth
because of possible upsets
for unsurveyable reaction consequences,
but still, nothing can tie down the truth.
So, better operate immediately, then,
than wait for metastases to explode.
Let's take for an example just an ordinary accusation,
like "The lady is a tramp", a very ordinary disappointment
of a banal and frustrated lover who has been deceived.
He may not say it in the open,
since there might be ladies who might be offended.
But if really she has cheated him,
what power in the universe can possibly deny that truth?
If there are protests, matters will thereby get only worse,

then there will certainly be great upsets,
and the whole matter might develop into drama,
melodrama, tragedy and even worse:
divorce and separation, suicide and murder!
Yes, unquestionably, irresistibly the truth must out,
or it will cause infection and get worse,
a simple diagnosis and a natural development.
When thus the facts have been established,
we may now proceed to see what we can do about the ruins.
If both parties have been naughty and deceived each other,
then there is a balance, and no harm is done,
and they can just continue being friends.
But if one part is innocent and has been hurt
there is a crisis of an upset balance
which unfortunately seldom can be rectified.
The victim gets no better for reacting,
and the perpetrator gets no better with a penalty.
The perpetrator can go on, the first deception is the worst,
the rest is easy; while the raped, deceived or violated victim
is the problematic issue here.
There will be more regrets in her than in the perpetrator,
and the higher her degree of innocence, the deeper damage.
She is called a 'her' here, but it might as well be any man.
Old bitter bachelors with secret traumas
carry with them for a medicine the syndromatic mantra:
"You loved her much more than any lady ever could deserve,"
and live in some kind of a gloomy limbo with the terrible conviction,
that the love they gave once was just wasted on ungratefulness;
and old maids that develop into dragons have a similar syndrome.
Of course, they are pathetically pitiful,
but usually unfortunately they are right.
If once we love with honesty, profundity and truth,
have we then not the right to expect something better
than just fornication, copulation, egoistic rape and sexual degradation,
wounds that cannot heal and mortifying traumas and deception?
If we once were born with a pure sense of love as an ideal,
what right has anyone to take away and ruin that ideal,
and may we not do anything and even boycott the whole world
from our universe for the protection of that delicate ideal?

And in such cases, truth will stand you by
as your best weapon for your guidance
out of all the human swamps of lies, deceptions,
egoism, abuse, confusion and destruction.

The thawing tears of death

Crying through the tears of love
does only multiply and increase them
for the benefit of digging deeper
the abyssal grave of constantly increasing loss.
Where is our love now,
that flew so graciously about last spring
and now has only barren twigs
of wretched trees without a leaf
to rest her tired frozen feet on,
warbling and singing cheerfully no more
but only crying in despair her heart out
in forlornness without end and without light,
as if death's tunnel had no exit
but was only actually a step down
to eternal darkness of unutterable silence.
Still the tears keep coming on and running forth
eventually at least conveying some kind
of a thaw somewhere beyond this frozen world
of frozen hearts, maltreated to extinction
by a robot system of hospitalization
quashed by mortifying rule of the establishment
allowing no exception to the hopelessness of death.

The dying patient's last wish

Do what you will with my decrepit body,
throw it to the wolves, recycle it, just let me die;
my only wish is this:
please don't commit me to the hospital.
Don't let them operate me
for a bleak postponement of inevitable death
in an invalidated body without functions
for my soul's imprisonment for nothing
just to make death's torture even worse.
If I must die, just let me exit quickly
without sentimental painful long farewells
that only aggrandize the pain
and makes death worse,
which every action must do
that makes the divorce just more unbearable.
I will have music, though,
the only ease from life's atrocious pains,

the only thing that makes reality less ugly;
so let me die triumphant in the roars of music oceans,
and I will depart alone in loneliness
and gladly vanish from your sight
thus sparing any suffering on your side
sneaking over to the other side
as noiselessly as possible
without a sound but with the music roaring.

The bleeding heart

My love is yours, an offering for life to you,
a sacrifice, a willing stand-by of no limits,
which you may accept or do with what you will.
I will not fight for it, for you or against any rival,
I will only love you and maintain that privilege
if even you refuse it and I must keep it alone.
The choice is yours: you'll never lack a lover,
you can choose whomever, I have no pretensions
but will persevere nevertheless whatever happens,
since you never can quench any flame of love
that once got started out of honesty alone,
was born as pure as any baby
and could never be put down
but only harder in its growth
for love's eternal victimization.

Ode to Dead Lovers

They were considered the ideal couple,
young and blonde and beautiful,
he in an excellent position with a brilliant career ahead,
she like a princess of society, a paragon of beauty and of virtue,
loved by everyone and worshipped by many,
and she never could say no.
Of course, she had too many friends,
and one of them, a friend too many,
thought his love of her was greater than her husband's.
When her husband was away on business journeys
and she had to care for all alone their two small children,
naturally she sought relief in company of friends,
and that particular more passionate friend saw his opportunity,
availed himself of it and would not let her go.

Unfortunately her devoted husband learned about it
not from her but second hand from others.
From abroad he wrote to her: "I know not how it happened,
and I will not listen to your story of whose blame it was.
It does not matter. It has happened, and that is the total damage.
I can not come home to where a lover stole my wife from me.
The house is yours with everything belonging to it.
I will not come home to claim a morsel of our life together.
I will stay abroad and find another life,
because the one I had is ruined,
and I find myself afflicted with a ruinous disease
called jealousy for life with constant madness,
the sole cure of which could be to nevermore come home again."
He never broke his word, he never saw his children or his wife again,
and she, for their sake, married after the divorce
the very bloke who had transported her out of her marriage
and never ceased to persuade her into his more comfortable one.
When her former husband learned about it
somewhere far away in Singapore
he found himself the final cure of his disease of jealousy
by purchasing enough amounts of sleeping pills
to never have to wake up to this world again.
He did it on this 14th day of February,
his Valentine to the surviving world,
which nonetheless continued loving more than ever.

Vampires of the night

They are really there,
the sucking monsters,
surreptitiously inveigling you
to drain you out by their invasion,
the blood-sucking parasites,
confusing all your senses
and distorting all reality for you
by drowning you in fears and paranoia
just to cloud your soul and steal it
dragging you down by the nose to hell
of no escape and no way out
except into a constantly increasing darkness
until you no longer have any perspective left.
Who are they, then, those invisible mind parasites?
They are your own self-centredness and introversion,
your exaggerated occupation with yourself,

your own sick egotism and narcissism,
your self-deception in that dangerous delusion
that you are anything at all.

A dual chord

How does it technically work,
our telepathic love,
since I so well feel all the warmth of your heart
although you are so far away
and even alienated and beleaguered
by this separating fate of unacceptable absurdity?
Is it so simple, that my kindest thoughts of you
must raise the same for me in you,
and is that how it works for everyone, then,
generally? Or is this reserved for lovers,
like some kind of metaphysical extraordinary
mechanism of spiritual vibrations?
We are out here in deep waters,
and they constantly grow deeper
as we wade out more profoundly
into darkness of experimental weirdness,
but there certainly is something to it.
Logically I would long ago have ceased to love you
if that absence of our intercourse was not replaced
by this most strange and tender mutual chord
reverberating through the universe
in transcendentally seducing music
far too subtle to at all be sensually perceived.
But since that string binds us together,
let us so remain together in perpetual dualism
of musically overwhelming beauty
totally unheard of but at least
completely understood by us.

One musician to another

No man has any right to claim you,
since music only has the right to own you.
She created you for her exclusive service,
and that is the highest service possible of love,
from which no mortal baseness has the slightest right
to drag you down. We both kneel humbly at the altar service

for the muses, the unique divinities of some manifestation
through the power of creation, which is why they only
are divinities self-evident and proven to exist
as indefatigably active in a zone of timelessness.
Our share of that dimension is our service to their service,
which no pagan can remove us from,
since we were born to serve
and work hard for that service
to the values of eternal beauty, life and truth,
the word that never fails, the melodies that never quieten,
the light that never settles, and the spirit
which will speak forever through not only poetry
but above all through our attentiveness
and sensitive ability to hear the harmonies of silence.

Some comedy

The stage is dark and empty,
and the audience has gone home.
Once more, how many times before!
has Romeo lost his Juliet, and has Juliet lost her Romeo,
and the whole audience went home crying,
and how many times before!
Must love then be a tragedy,
in order to make tragedy become a love,
surviving by repeatedly continue dying,
so by dying it will never die,
like that old love of Juliet and Romeo?
And yet, the play is false, it is a lie,
for in the first original we find a different testimony
of what really happened: Romeo was actually alive
when Juliet woke up from her phoney sleep,
so they could once again embrace and cry together
just to make things worse,
since Romeo was poisoned anyway, -
two suicides for love, for nothing, for each other
for a perfect entertainment of all times
to make all mankind sob forever
for this tragedy of love
which turned into a love of tragedy
to keep love growing and sustained forever.

OCTOBER HARVEST FIRST PART.

God's tears

Your highest merit are your tears
not shed for pity's sake but for compassion
being something of life's very fountain,
like a mother's source of love and kind protection
for all life, all human character and feelings
and the care for human worth and dignity
and above all the most supreme necessity of freedom.
Poets say life started in the ocean of God's tears,
and that was never contradicted.
So are all our tears a continuity
of God's own care of life, and when we cry
our tears are God's and a projection
of life's inmost values and its essence,
thus diffusing and expanding what our souls are made of,
which is our inheritance
and the eternal very essence of divinity.

Born free to keep love free

The freedom of our souls is our salvation;
that we were born spiritually free
makes us immune against all trespassing
on our love by strangers, fools and mortal idiots
who don't understand that love is something higher
than just sleazy sex and messing up and putting down,
the vulgar idiocy of clumsy ignorants,
no better than unthinking animals,
unhuman cynicals and base primitivists;
while thoughtful and considerate responsibility,
far-sighted care and freedom from all bonds to tie you down
is what love really is about,
the nourishment of its eternal life,
the food for thoughts of tenderness that always lasts
and the consistent kindness without end
that rather banishes itself in self-effacement
than dares take the risk of hurting any human feeling.

The Force

When love is bursting forth
there is no force in all the universe
to hold it back, love being what it is
the force, the all pervading ether
keeping all the universe in shape and rolling
like a mystical embalming omnipresent power
that can never be accounted for or come to terms with,
while we all at the same time, all thinking beings
actively take part in it and constitute it,
like a metaphysical and universal natural democracy,
each being having rights that cannot be abused
without the natural retaliation of the karma.

This was some small effort at defining this mysterious Force
that has become a myth of science fiction
but which actually exists for good or worse
and which we never can get rid of
being there for us to simply make the best of it.

Enough is never enough

Recently a lady shockingly confessed
her major difficulty in this life to be
dependence on the syringe and its use.
I had to comfort her and say,
"My dear, there are much worse addictions.
You don't know what you have missed."
Oh yes, we shouldn't really talk about it.
All those loves I had
that failed and faltered on the way,
the girl who cheated me with previous lovers
and who cheated them by suddenly absconding
with a brand new lover off to Paris;
that devourer of men, who used them up,
consuming one after another,
leaving them like wrecks behind
with bleeding souls for their remaining life;
that vamp who had been married thrice
with only ten engagements previously,
and who, when I had had enough of all her tricks,
swore she would never have another after me
to next week trap a new one twenty years her junior,

or that lady whom I never can forget,
what was her name again,
well, let's forget about it,
or that siren, who for just her sport -
enough! There is an end to it,
the story that did never end,
of how at every time I made a solemn oath
of nevermore trust any lady,
that decision and severest promise of sincerity
was never followed but by just another fall
for yet another chapter of the neverending story...

Devotional poem

Our living world is built, created and maintained
by its devoters, those who are devoted to their love,
whatever that love is for, whether families,
their culture or society, creative beauty
or whatever their devotion aims at;
but what matters is the character and essence of devotion,
which is always something of the very core of the best human qualities,
the heart of the most vital matter of constructiveness.
Construction is the keyword here,
which, coloured with devotion,
carries by its honesty success to fulfilment
and triumphs by completion in a lasting glory:
"It was worth it! None of all this effort was in vain!"
It is the satisfaction of the godhead
when he found that what he had created was all good,
devotion makes creativeness a holy matter,
and all that we need to maintain the creation
is to show it some devotion.

Fever

Day by day my love is growing worse
for all the trials, the frustrations, the death crises,
funerals and shocks, erupting into fever
that grows worse for every day.
And there is nothing you can do about it
but continue loving faithfully
with self-effacing self-consuming self-destructive constancy
ignoring how your limbs are aching,

how your strength and powers fail you,
how your work and life disintegrates
and how your love grows more impossible for every day.
Despairing you may cry with pain from hell
and thereby only make the matter worse,
more painful, more excruciating, more acute a torture,
while your only comfort and reward is
that at least you never failed in love.

Sexy acrostic

Strange as it may seem,
especially as we teem,
xasperated as we team,
you are still only my dream.

Harassed by reality

Reality, the constant obstacle and sabotage
to love and all idealism,
is just life's greatest challenge
to stand up against and face,
surmount and get around,
and the best means and only means to do it
is by love, of course, which never can be vanquished
and which never can give up
and rather dies than tolerates defeat.
That is the very element of love:
to fight unto the bitter end for the impossible,
the unattainable and highest freedom,
the intangible ideal, the dream that always must go on.
So if reality has anything against our love,
that will at length result in nothing else
than adding fuel to our love.

The soul is cooler than the heart but warms for a longer time...

Every moment without you
is like a lost eternity in hell.
I know, there is a gap between us,
and I will not let you suffer for it
but allow you any freedom

that would all but rob me of you.
You belong to no one
but remain a tenant of my soul,
its chief inhabitant, and that I promise you:
that home I will keep warm for you forever.
Nowadays all gaps can be abridged and bridged,
there never was an actual need for a divorce,
there never was a separation but from vanity and selfishness,
and honest love goes on forever,
and I will not give you anything but honesty.
There is a gap between us - let's forget it,
since it does not matter,
since our love is all that matters,
and it would be unfair to ourselves
if we did not allow it air to breathe
and let it live and burst into that flower
that blooms only nevermore to wither.

A definition of music

Stamped with a religious mark from the beginning
it ever was a ladder between earth and heaven
for the mortal spirit to transcend to immortality
by seeking contact with the gods through harmony and beauty.
So the muses were created as a kind of intermediary
to stand directly in association with the arts,
the artists being all musicians, since originally music was all arts,
the manifested concretization of the inspiration of the muses;
while the highest art was always fundamental music,
which is best described as simply prayer,
the direct live contact with divinity,
which all the great composers proved:
Bach, Handel, Haydn, Beethoven,
they all paid tribute to the godhead
principally first and last.
That is my definition: music as the best of prayers.

The widower to his late wife

(from Dan Millman by J.E.)

Do not stand at my grave and weep.
I am not there; I do not sleep.

I am a thousand winds that blow.
I am a thousand glints on snow.
I am the sunlight on ripened grain.
I am the gentle autumn rain.
Do not stand at my grave and weep.
I am not there. I did not die.
I live in a million places and things
Recalled as memories, borne on wings
From times and towns beyond the sea
Do not stand and weep for me.
In son and daughter and smallest child
I am there. Be glad. I am free.

The Gipsy

Don't chain me to the ground, please,
because I was born with wings and have to use them,
or else I would not have been born with them.
Don't fence me in, because I was born out of wedlock
without fences, which is why I never needed any.
Don't put me down, because I was only born to rise and grow
and never could be put down anyway, so why then even try?
Don't try to put me into custody or hospitalize me,
since I was too well to ever run the risk of getting sick,
and I was far too clever to get caught for all my liberties.
Don't try to kill me or to bury me, because I am too much alive
to ever have my death accepted - it just will not work.
Just leave me as I am, an international and homeless bastard rover
beachcombing the seas, enjoying rainbow gatherings and parties,
an enthusiast for beautiful nostalgia,
finding brethren everywhere in hippies, vagabonds and outcasts;
and wherever there is life and party,
I am in the middle of it and enjoying it.

The Surge

The longing and the throbbing of the deep heart's woes
is like a fever distancing your soul from life
while at the same time waxing overwhelmingly
intensifying your life's urge to surge
from hollow decadent reality to a transcendence
into heaven to encompass all the world
not only with your love but with your joy

and music of your soul without which you can't live
and therefore want to spread out to all others
piously disseminating what your heart is brimming over with,
the best part of your soul, your feelings, your sentimentality.
It's only natural. The only thing unnatural is to suppress it.
Let it bloom and fill the world with rainbow parties
so that beauty, joy and love at last some time may cure the world.

Farewell

You rest in peace in such a sumptuous bed of flowers
that you never dreamed of while you stayed with us.
Your years of toil are over, and now you may relax
as long as you would wish in this magnificence of flowers,
wallowing in beauty and their perfumes, and caressed
by all the singularly lovely memories of you that rest with us.
Think kindly of us for our follies while we err in this mundanity,
like we will never lose the sight of your example
as not just a caring mother, but so full of care for all your friends.
We will not weep, because we know you are still there
and will not leave us, for as long as we will keep you in our minds,
since you gave us your love to never take it back
but to remain with us and grow forever.

The only true love is a tragedy

There are so many instances of this,
and all confirm the tragic fact:
the highest and the finest love
was never consummated,
independent of how far it reached.
That means, that love is even greater
and more true, the more it is a tragedy.
You can love and never reach your love
and never have her,
and no lover is more certain of his love.
You can lose her, and you will love her forever.
You can see her vanish into other lovers' arms,
and then you know you loved her more than they.
Love is a loser that by losing is the winner,
and the more he loses, the more winner he becomes,
since love is always fair in that
her grace falls more on honesty and truth

and sublimates the quality and warmth of love
than bothers about the delusory futility of sex,
which always is a passing satisfaction;
while true love is never satisfied
but lasts and goes on growing and expanding
in increasing beauty armoured for eternity
the more it is struck down by anguish, hardship and mortality.

Glorious friendship

Let us take it easy and be friends
since there can be no end to friendship
and it can expand indefinitely
without bounds for its neutrality
without even a chance of any of us getting hurt.
As friends we can enjoy each other
freely without problems and without restrictions,
we can laugh at weaknesses and at each other
and forget all second thoughts of jealousy, suspicion and reserve.
The universe belongs to friends of God
who in the harmony of friendship may infest it freely
with the merry parties of light-heartedness
and carry on just thriving and carousing easily
in constant celebration of all things that last
among which friendship is the first one
and the very evidence of the stability of love when it is true.

Melting

Every time I touch upon a certain note
the flows start universally reverberating,
spring explodes in melting flows,
joy triumphs like the age of miracles,
and any wonder seems about to happen.
That is when we strike a chord together,
when we musically harmonize as souls
and when our thoughts join hands
and are united in the ether.
Why is it not always then like this?
Perhaps we need to cry alone sometimes,
perhaps our need of rest from love
is equally important to our need of love,
perhaps our loneliness is equally important to our company;

but when I melt in tears alone there is no greater urge
than just to share that heartbreak and compassion
and unite in my most devastating sorrow
with that endless ocean depth and richness
of your own profuse affliction,
so that we could cry together and the more
to make our sweet multiplication
of our sorrows and compassion tally.

Souls marching on

We buried you under a mountain of flowers
but none of them would even wither.
For you there is no resurrection necessity
since death for you was an impossibility.
Yes, you are there still and partying,
having a good time as always among all your friends;
the party you started can not be disrupted,
since such a good party is set off just once and for all,
and you still are the head of it, keeping it up
as if you never even had had any illness.

So love keeps on rolling forever,
a party that never can be discontinued
with maybe occasional changes of guests
but pre-eminently independent of common mundaneness,
of death and of worries, of changes and comings and goings,
the more so the more the departed has wasted her love,
which no one did more here than you;
which is why you were taken away from us,
too good a person to last for her love,
which was even too much for yourself
but enough, all the same, to last quite some eternities.

Advice to a musician

No one has the right to claim you
since you belonged to music from the beginning.
She owns your soul,
and you owe your soul to her
with all her ocean depths of wisdom,
universe of loving and emotional profundity
and unfathomable richness of experience,
not just any kind of, but of all humanity,
the human history consisting mainly of the journey of the spirit,
being all there in the records of the soul
as manifested in the arts,
emotionally above all in music.
That's your reign of government and freedom,
of expansion and of love
which you can share with all humanity in music only,
which belongs to you like something of a key
to all hearts of all sentient beings.
It is also a responsibility
demanding faithfulness and labour
but, above all, purity,
since only loving hearts of truth and honesty
could ever make good music that would last.

The enigma of our love

The enigma of our love
is constantly indefinitely getting deeper
always growing well beyond our understanding
in remoteness, depth and mystery,

while at the same time we grow nearer all the time
discovering new facets of our mutual understanding,
while our happiness and joy is veiled in tears
of gentle melancholy and infinite beauty,
sorrow leading us together into some abysmal tunnel
of which we don't know what's on the other side.
The question is if we dare try it.
I would dare if you would want it,
but I would not even risk the touching of some wound;
for love can never be too gentle or too careful
in its handling with respect the human soul,
which never had enough consideration.

Rainbow love

– a sad story.

When you chase the rainbow,
do not hope to find that jar of gold.
Be realistic.
Be intent on chasing on for nothing and forever.
You will have at best some sweet dreams and some rest
occasionally, but the rest will be a chase
for air, elusive and evaporating dreams,
the beauty of which finally will leave you
left with only hollowness and sadness,
and that is the final fruit of love:
the tears you shed when you have lost it.

No shares are riskier than sharing love

They say that love is better shared
than kept in isolation,
privately discreetly guarded like a caged bird
and nourished, famished unto death,
the greatest tragedy of love,
when it can never reach, get out
but stays concealed in secret,
shied unto discretion of self-immolation.

Share it, then, for it is better
to be nailed upon the cross
and tortured unto death,

be hurt unto unbearability of psychic pain
and dragged into dishonour, shame and dirt
than not to share your love with whom you love,
no matter how she might mishandle you,
since any tragedy is better
than to let love stifle
without any story to remember.

The imperfect lover

I don't want to leave you ever,
but I have to every now and then.
The chief dilemma has been this all times of love,
but there are others also.
"I would love you, if you didn't have so many men,
so many other lovers," is another.
When a loved one has a number of intimacies,
there is one always that loves her the most,
and he will never get her,
like there is one she will always love the most,
and he will be most difficult for her to reach.
Love is perfected unto imperfection,
and the higher, purer and more perfect your love is,
the more it is impeded by its imperfections.
So there always are too many problems
in whatever kind of love;
and all that I can say, to say the least,
to somehow assuage our difficulties
and our constant separations
is, that I will always be the more with you
the less I am with you.
Take it as a pledge or an enigma,
but your soul will know the truth.

Relativity

The distance of my love is wider than an ocean
and more unsurmountable than any ridge,
unreachable like any sun
and as untouchable as a black hole,
and yet she is more present than reality
and more genuine than any truth,
more honest than the messages of angels

and more definite in her sincerity than any child;
for love is always perfect.
All she needs to prove herself is to exist,
then distances turn null and void,
all obstacles become negligeable nonentities,
all darkness turns into perpetual light,
and all you need is to acknowledge it
to make it work, to turn existence into paradise
and to make life worth while
and something of a joy for all eternity.

Creativity

We were born to be creative,
life exists to recreate itself,
it is the first rule of survival:
if you fail to multiply the life that you were given,
you will not be worth it.
But, this creativity can find so various expressions.
The most natural one is of course to reproduce,
to start a family creating children,
that is basic, easy and most down to earth;
but there are other ways and higher aims
more difficult and singular and more demanding,
such as concentrating on the spiritual world
and reproducing spiritual values like idealism
in art and literature, music and philosophy.
Such people are no good for ordinary life,
for raising children, for mundanity and practical concerns
but should be valued and encouraged for their higher aims,
the beauty of their insights and their visions;
for idealists are recreators of our future
making it worth while to live for
and especially when this our present seems so horrible,
unbearable, unhuman, hopeless and insane.
The dreams are our creative tools
wherewith the world and future always is remade
to make it better after all we constantly go through;
and only artists of a pure and honest heart
know how to dream them.

The magic of our love

The magic of our love
is vulnerable as the purity of music,
sensitive as nerves strung high
like strings unto a bursting point
and oversensitive to any false disharmony
which is forbidden trespassing on purity,
which on the other hand, like beauty,
is its own reward – they go together,
beauty, purity and truth,
and must be kept, like music,
constantly high strung to make it sound.
As a reward we have these tunes and harmonies
of overwhelming beauty emanating into songs
of love with words of poetry
that will reward all lovers for their faith
with beauty that will never die
but keep rewarding faithful love
with its own life of everlasting somethingness
that really can not be defined
but is, as Dante said,
the love that makes all suns and stars
of all the universe go round.

Feelings are always true

All you feel is true,
and feelings never lie.
You know the touch of your antennae,
and the longer your antennae are,
the more you can be certain of their touch.
Your soul reverberates of senses
that can never be put down
but must reverberate;
and the more turbulent they are,
the clearer is their language
of plain clearcut obviousness,
and living souls are never lies.
So if you feel that you are loved
and that you love, and that your loved one
is the one who loves you and the one you love,
you simply can't do anything about it
but just let it be, enjoy it, love,

be certain of it, do the right thing of it,
cherish it, respect it, take it easy
and give love a chance
to speak herself and be in her own right
as all the good there is in life.

Insatiability

We all need more love
than we can ever get,
and the more we love,
the more the insatiability increases.
So why keep on loving, then,
when it never pays?
When your prostitution is gratis,
when the feedback always comes too late,
when ingratitude is love's ultimate reward,
and you can not even save your soul
from getting raped?
That is the question.
You just go on until you fall,
for there is nothing else to do.

Looking forward to 2012

They say things gonna change then.
They say the world gonna get better at last.
They say the climate change gonna wake people up.
They say all the good things might happen
to make a clean sweep outa all the bad things.
They say revolutions will happen
to shockwave all the bad people outa their beds.
They say bureaucracies will get the creeps
and implode into vanishment.
They say all autocracies will go to crap.
They say they gonna rock the world back to basics
and rock the hell outa all the Smersh junkies.
They say things might happen
that gonna set us right on course back again
to where we came from, back to paradise
and all that golden age stuff,
just to make the politicians drop their pants
and go crazy for real home to their nut-houses

to stay there not to endanger the world any more.
They say a lot of healthy things,
those rainbow people with everlasting parties on the shore
to celebrate the rising ocean and the rising tides
to wash the world clean again
outa the dirty hands of crazy politicians.
And their magic message to the world is:
Cheers!

Love under torture

The wind blows hard and mean against us
with a merciless and heartless coldness without end
while torturesome adversities amass and haunt us,
death and losses, irreplaceable bereavements,
and to all this mess our constant distance and intolerable separation.
How can love survive? But as the buds spring forth
from freezing death in suffocating snows,
so will all human souls transcend all frozen hearts,
and there will always be a resurrection
from all false, untimely phoney deaths;
and somehow love will fool perdition
and always come again by miracles
in something of an everlasting venture
to in spite of all exist no matter what
to not allow herself to ever be let down.

Mixing up

Mixed up with you is not an easy thing to be.
You lead me on to unknown depths
through whirlpools and uncharted shallows
to an end which neither of us know what it will be;
but we are not without a pilot,
and we know our course and what we want:
a love of limitless duration, depth and understanding,
and a constantly increasing personal intimacy
that always will bring us two closer to each other,
nearer to the core and heart and inner basic truth of life
with concentration on the burning secret of creation,
the chief mystery of all existence,
which we have the opportunity to find
by those two keys we have acquired to each other's souls.

I understand you, while you still don't know
whom you have found to guide you and protect you through the shallows,
but love will reveal it if you let me,
and I never shall move harder than you wish
but piously conform to your own pleasure,
knowing well the love that I can give you
can be so much more than all the world can offer you.

The Rainbow Warrior

— an effort at a definition

He is the hero of our time
but rather careful and discreet,
does not take any risks
while he is certain of his case,
that he is right and fights for all the good
there is at all in this decrepit world,
defending everything worth living for.
He fights for Greenpeace and Tibetans,
demonstrates for peace and tolerance,
has nothing with dogmatic bigotry to do,
believes in immortality, reincarnation and the soul
of every living thing and being
and defends above all life in all its forms,
hugs trees and plants them,
chases whalers down and off from all the seas,
is not political but more environmental
and crusades more underground and more efficiently
appearing as concealed in his activities
as captain Nemo and as purposeful.
You find him everywhere, he is increasing
in efficiency and numbers of both sexes,
and wherever you will recognize him
you will know him (or her) as a friend.

Desire

My yearning to your person
is a thirst that never can be quenched,
since you can never really wholly reach another person,
grasp her, have her or be satisfied with her,
since there is always something else to it.

Desires are deceptive leading you astray
since they can never be fulfilled completely
but must lead you on beyond the point of no return,
and thus you always get beyond and miss your goal.
Desire drives you on and speeds you up
and is its own deception,
making you escape your goal instead of finding it.
Content yourself with only loving,
care for her and see that she is always there,
and that is all you really need to just keep going on
as a true lover staying faithful to at least your love.

Love among the troglodytes

Yes, it is disturbing how they wallow
in barbarity and trash,
the victims of our brainwash age,
the addicts of society's perversions,
but we can do better without them
and do not have to mind them,
steering forth and free of foulness
out to freedom of the limitlessness of every ocean
and the freedom of ourselves and of our own,
the sacred work we live for
and the high ideals we work for
that can never be corrupted
by the baseness of the troglodytes
who rule and dominate this brainwashed world
and bring it to perdition,
while we stick to the exceptions
who alone are capable of saving it.

The Junk Society

Those barking dogs of madding crowds
are like an anthill thrown in chaos,
all a muddle in a stressed up vanity,
humanity forsaken and seduced
by media brainwash stuff
completely overrunning everyone
with information of no consequence
or meaning, drivelling and vulgar nonsense
for the chaos merchants to make money

on upsetting everyone as much as possible,
the servants of this sick society
that turns all thoughtless people into addicts
either by blind medication or on drugs,
unless they drop out as alcoholics
or just leave it all to its own self-destructive holocaust
to save themselves, a few exceptions and sane individuals
from the general perdition.
How can we stand it? That's just what we can't,
and that's what saves us. If we just look through it
and observe the overwhelming junk flow of society
and recognize it as the madhouse carousel it is,
we can detach ourselves from it and rise above it
for a better purpose of our lives to find
of something more enduring, permanent and meaningful.

The Moment of Truth

Let us sink together
deep into the endless bottomlessness
of the fathomless eternity of our feelings
just to make them deeper and more bottomless.
Let us together melt
into each other's souls
in friendship more profound than any passion
just to keep it intact and alive
as long as possible and possibly forever
for the highest possible enjoyment of our union.
Thus let us be one and share ourselves
continuously to never break it off;
and that's the syndrome, sign and meaning of all love
that it should just go on forever.

The secret

The secret of our love will never be found out.
Discretion hides it in a wood of veils
and no one understands what is beyond
the depths of darkness in the heart of wilderness,
the thickness of the forest density
where everything becomes a jungle
of impenetrable mystery and fathomless concealment
where we dwell together with our dreams

refusing to wake up to this aborted world
of unacceptable absurdities and artificial madness
where the only human people are outsiders
who refuse to deal with or have anything to do
with the demented bolting universal lunacy
which dominates our brave new world's society
and forces everyone to dehumanization
and denaturalization speeding up the general degeneration.
But our love can never be infected by it,
and our friendship goes beyond their reach
immune to any effort of debasing it
from its consummate level of perfection
guarded by its secret of discretion.

Missing you

Risking being sentimental,
still I can't deny my missing you,
and that's why you will have to
put up with my song.

I miss your beauty and the fragrance of your soul,
I miss your harmony spread by your presence,
I miss the love we made as souls
more intimate than any bodies,
and I miss the soft touch of your grace
upon my being, as some charms of elves and angels;
and I miss your serious joy
and sparkling lights of your dark eyes,
I miss the music of your voice,
the poetry of your kind words,
the care and wisdom of your heart's warm passion;
and I miss the fun we had amidst our deepest tragedy,
the glory that we reached amidst the tearful flows of sorrow,
and the life we found together in the presence of our death.
But most of all I miss our bare togetherness,
our naked mutual company,
our understanding and the harmony of our minds
when we were molten down together by our fate
to nevermore get whole as separated from each other.

Vain separation

When in the night I wake up to my sleeplessness
and see you smiling in the company of others,
I enjoy your pleasure and but wish
that I could be there and enjoying it with you.
We are now separated by an ocean
which is but a second's distance for our souls
that even just might bring us only nearer to each other
by the challenge. But the point is this:
we can not lose each other,
not by distances or separations,
not by lack of contact or temptations,
not by being taken in and occupied by others
and least of all by our fate and destiny
which seems the more intent on unifying us
the more we are impeded by adversities and trials
which add only sharpness to the challenge of our love.

Forgetmenot

Small flower, tiniest of blue-eyed souls,
my source of inspiration and enjoyment,
welcome to my secret flower bed
of tender memories and sorrows,
of a lifetime filled with love
and stories immemorable
of beauty constantly increased
and never any friendship that was lost.
You all grow faithfully and richly in my heart,
I never would forget a single one of you,
while you, forgetmenot, my freshest flower
fulfil them all by only being there
to make my heart alive again and more than ever
giving fuel to a love that lives on immortality,
the essence of the soul's endurance to in spite of all
go on for all its overstrain to constantly surpass itself
in burning brighter and more gloriously
for all its suffocation in the trials of her love.

Forward

The limitlessness of our love
is constantly confounding all the universe.
What does it matter where we are
since we remain in touch wherever
all the same and independent of geography
and all mundane dimensions?
Even if I go away and am completely lost
I still will know you closest to my heart
and never lose you wherever you are yourself.
Our flair is like a constant flight on golden wings
that never actually can put us down
but keep us going on an endless journey and adventure
of discovery in realms of beauty, tenderness, humanity
and warmth of heart, the endless ocean of our travel
being the profound and bottomless eternity of love
in constant change of weather in life's highest drama
of the turbulent and educating journey of our souls.

Respect the loser

Losers are we all
in some way or another,
and the less we seem to be so,
the more probably we are so.
Only look at those tycoons
with loads of money
and a perfect family at home;
but, usually, the richer,
the more divorces,
the more addicts, nervous breakdowns,
alcoholics, mental cases and so forth
all ending up in loneliness,
delusions, tragedy and total mental misery.
Just look at that gay workoholic
having such a good time working all his life
and hard, and gaining nothing
ending up a burnt-out case for nothing
having lost his whole life on the way.
The loser is in every human being,
and the less he seems to be a loser,
the more cover-up he has to do,
the more he is a loser,
which all losers know indeed
deep down inside themselves.
The best thing is to just admit it,
recognize your tragedy
and stretch your hand out liberally
to make friends with all the other losers.

On the move

Don't stop me while I'm running,
do not try to pin me down,
don't slow my pace, don't fence me down,
for all my life is movement,
and all air I breathe is freedom;
I can't wait to live
since life is all we have until we die,
I have no patience with formalities,
and slowness is unbearable,
existing only to be speeded up.
I must keep flying, or I'll fall,

I must keep living, or I'll die,
and death is not acceptable,
since 80 out of 100 die for nothing
and from totally unnatural vain reasons.
Life is all there is, and we all need it,
since that's all we have
forever.

Beauty

Beauty never ceases,
never stops to grow,
grows ever younger and more fresh
and more delightful with the years,
like some old oaken giant
with an ever more majestic crown
and greener leaves for every year,
more lush than ever
when it should have died so long ago.
Thus music also only grows more beautiful
the more its age increases,
like the classical string quartets
growing more enchanting
every time you hear and play them.
Only the exterior withers,
only the material values vanish,
while the soul matures forever
gilding everything with beauty
that it touches
and the more so the more conscious and aware she is.
So flower on forever, beauty,
grow, increase and flourish
for your own sake, that your truth
may constantly make life worth while.

Masked Madonna

Who are you, secret beauty,
so well veiled behind the strangest riddles,
covered in enigma and so eloquent in ambiguities?
You raise my curiosity to peaks of expectations,
since I must suspect you are the mystery
that I sought contact with so long.
At last I would uncover it,
receive it and enjoy it - but alas!
As soon as you removed your mask
I found no answer to my questions,
once again the feedback of my love was lost,
my questions only multiplied,
and all I could do was to ask you
to put on your mask again.
A mystery is best as left alone,
alive and intact as a mystery
to wonder at and to admire from a distance,
but when you approach the sun and come too close
the only thing to do is to retire.

Free

Love is best when flying free
in limitless abundance of fresh air to breathe
on golden wings to carry on forever to get higher
without ever losing sight of the direction, the beloved.
When your dreamland opens up and is your only true reality,
when worries fade and mundane follies vanish
in thin air dispersed by realler dreams of truth and intuition,
when your spirit soars and nothing can retain it,
that is health and freedom, naturalness and normality,
and nothing else is valid, nothing else is true.

Just another love declaration

I love you more
than any married man can love his wife,
for my love is higher than what any formal love can be,
since my love is unconditional,
like parents' true love for their children
giving everything and claiming nothing.
I will never claim you nor claim anything from you
since I just want to love you
and keep on faithfully loving you
for what you are and nothing else,
regretting that I don't have much to give,
no wealth and no security,
which makes my love the more sincere and humble,
without even caring whether it will even be accepted -
all that is enough for me is that I love
and that I will continue loving you
and beg to be consistent in that faithfulness
and that you maybe might accept it as an offer
of a humble soul for no more than your grace
to be if nothing more at least my friend.

Unending energy

Let me fly to you at home
on wings of golden ocean birds
and on the flowing waves
that never cease to keep on rolling on
forever to each shore across the world

importing vital messages of foaming love
that never cease to eagerly press on,
like I do in my dreams of longing
back to our community and company
of friends and lovers, beauty, art and music,
our environment of truth and constant revelation
of the only things of true importance:
our love, the freedom of it,
and our faithfulness thereto.

Healing

Our maybe only difference
is your urgent need of constant company
while I need absolutely to be now and then alone.
But although separated far away from you
I keep associating with you in my mind.
I wish that could be something of a comfort to you,
that although not with you all the time in person
I am always with you in my mind.
We are so like each other in all other aspects,
that I keep on recognizing me in you,
and you are always there, my dream,
my constant company, my twin in mind,
that I feel I could never let you go or leave you.
Let's just stay on then, since it cannot harm us
but might be the very healing
which we both will always need.

A summary of nonsense

Make it simple, make it short
and have something to tell,
or else shut up and go to hell.
That would be all the catechism
for any writer; and if it were followed
we would not have all this trash
of nonsense, sex and violence,
pornography and senselessness;
but on the other hand,
we would not probably have any poet left
or anyone at all who would be writing,
since, if everyone could properly look through himself,

we would all see the vanity
of all performance and self-exhibition
while the only valid stuff remaining
would be basically universal
and anonymous documentation
of the simple truth
the shorter and the better.

The truth of dreams

Don't tell me dreams are worthless substance.
Dreams is all we are,
reality is all a dream of unreality,
our souls are more concrete and definite
than any actual appearance
luring us into illusions of reality,
while the truth is always:
nothing is what it appears to be.
So all we have, in fact,
is sticking to our dreams,
the pious faithfulness to our ideals,
the secret and unconscious testimonies of our souls,
the freedom of our spirit when it soars
and everything that cannot be explained.
The truth is there
beyond our grasp but definite,
and we shall never understand it.
All we can do is to try to
and to follow it
on wings of dreams
that always will continue carrying us away.

One drop of water

You marry to give your beloved
and your children comfort and protection
as a pledge for piously sustained security,
but without children and without security
the marriage pledge is only a formality
of emptiness and no significance,
while your relationship depends on love alone
that is the more significant and stressed
and more important to sustain.

That is my sport, my love,
to keep up all the love there is
between us and between our earth and heaven
as a universal matter of significance
not just for us but for the cultivation of all love
around the world that everyone is most dependent on,
love being everything and everyone dependent on it,
while we bring our contribution to the sea
in form of our love's drop of water
adding to the ocean's constant flowing
all around the world of love and life,
while not a single drop of it is worthless
but a microcosmos in itself
containing all the world and universe of love.

Eternal repetition

What else is there to tell you
than that I love you?
Let me repeat this phrase
like any nutty doting idiot
this like mantras rambling nonsense;
but to me, like unto him, it is dead serious
and therefore the more important
to just have it constantly incessantly repeated
with the same insistence as the rolling waves
keep going on and on and on forever
for just the glory of it
ever growing in more furious energy
to sometimes make the ocean power greater
in tremendousness than any other,
if we only have our love for an exception.

Spiritual symbiosis

We both suffer from a physical infirmity
in different ways, but being invalids,
our different handicaps will compensate us,
making us in one way to each other complimentary
which the more releases our spirituality
and makes it dominant in our relationship.
Thus physical shortcomings and this limiting annoyance
favours the unification of our souls

and makes it independent of our whereabouts.
Thus can I carry you around wherever you may be,
and you will have me still no matter where I be.
And the result is this, that we will only get the nearer
to each other, the more we depart and try to separate.

When in the tenderness of our togetherness

When in the tenderness of our togetherness
I dream of you remembering our trials
I can but sustain the fact that we remain inseparable
even separated by mundane dimensions such as space and time
which simply are beneath us and can't bother us
since we remain together beyond every reason
independent of the universe and physics,
the shallowness of all illusions of reality.
Thus do I love you infinitely still
with constantly increasing faithfulness
that has gone much too far in carrying us away
to ever set us down on earth again,
since even the severest efforts of the basest vanity
can never pin us or our love down to mortality.

Friendship and love continued

Friendship is a universal thing,
but love is personal and private
and the holiest of all religions,
since it is a matter of the soul alone.
Your friends may love you,
and your contacts may expand forever,
that's what friendship is for,
to connect, maintain, enjoy and broaden company
for the constructive end of everyone you know;
but your love can only be one person,
it demands, necessitates and needs some reservation
just to keep it holy and maintain its holiness,
the apex of which is the union of two souls
with the desire for them to remain united
in their spiritual communion forever.

The Loner

Friendship is a universal thing,
but love is personal and private
and the holiest of all religions,
since it is a matter of the soul alone.
Your friends may love you,
and your contacts may expand forever,
that's what friendship is for,
to connect, maintain, enjoy and broaden company
for the constructive end of everyone you know;
but your love can only be one person,
it demands, necessitates and needs some reservation
just to keep it holy and maintain its holiness,
the apex of which is the union of two souls
with the desire for them to remain united
in their spiritual communion forever.

Athenian graffiti

— Inscription on hostel bed
signed "Bigmouth strikes again!"

Living in Athens
is all good and fine
till you've been drinking
that old Greek wine,
climbing the stairs
completely rat arsed,
falling back down
pretty damn fast.
Ouzo for breakfast,
Metaxa for tea, -
Oh no, my liver
is disowning me!

Yet another delirium

Being drunk with you is worse than being drunk with wine,
or better, being more profound and lasting an intoxication
for which no cure is in sight, no rehabilitation,
no relief, no solace and no peace,
the wonderful delirium going on incessantly
like on some ride on ever higher mountains;
so that nothing will appear more fearful
than one morning wake up sober to reality
and find the ecstasy reduced to nothing
replaced with boring humdrum nothingness.
This must lead to the undeniable conclusion,
that there is no drunkenness, delirium or intoxication
that is not appropriate and totally excused
if only it adds wings and force to your eternal flight of love.

An old theme

If my thoughts could reach you
with their tenderness and kisses,
spiting distances and obstacles and vain reality
embracing you in neverending warmth of heart
and overcoming all the limiting dimensions,
then also the suborned informers would be of no consequence,
no slander would come near us or concern us,
mortal thoughts would fall apart and vanish
thoroughly reduced to nothing by our love,
and quarrels would be empty words of nonsense
signifying nothing, going down the bog of emptiness,
for that is the magic force of love, that everything disintegrates
that is not structured and endorsed by that sole element
upholding all the universe and being only love.

The future

The past is gone, and although living still
you must not look behind you,
turning back to what must stay behind and left behind forever,
for your duty as a man to life is to create the living coming time,
the unavoidable tomorrow that must always come,
depending on what you make out of it at present.
Thus to live is just a duty of creation,
and the best that you can do in this predicament
is just to simply make the best of it,
as you are stuck in this dilemma of mortality
and can't do much else than to use it
for the best, that is creation of the future,
which just can't go wrong,
if only you just use your love to make it.

Bacchanalia

Let them sing and dance and vomit
to their hearts' content:
it will just do them good.
And join their party:
sing and dance and vomit:
it will only do you lots of good.
As long as you express yourself
and make an outlet of your life
as much as possible,
it will just do you lots of good,
the more the better; and you can be certain
no one will object, as long as you keep carrying on
organically, sticking to what's natural,
and it will all be just an orgy of consummate innocence,
and nothing is more natural and free.
Keep partying on, and no one will object
as long as just keep on partying on.

Voices of silence

There is no more expressive sound than silence
in which actually all sounds and music is contained,
all voices that are never heard but all the more outspoken
of all things and secrets, mysteries and truths unheard of.
Love and friendship needs no more advanced expression.
The supreme intimacy is without words
which only our souls resound the more with music
booming in its silent harmony to outshine noise irrelevant
to just stick to the basics of our love,
which only needs the perfect silence
to communicate and have all things said perfectly.

Beautifying eyes

They create your world, improving it
with the enchanting lustre of your eyes
of only goodness and idealism,
with softness generously spreading out your light
into the souls of everyone you meet,
thus turning them to better human beings
only by your mere existence.

It's the life-inspiring and creative power of the soul
which thus miraculously, like green fingers,
makes life bloom and flourish and improve around you.
What is then your gift of this incredible expansive beauty?
Yes, I know as a musician what your secret is
and therefore will preserve it secretly between us.

Basics

Leave me out of all the brainwash noise of vanity,
of this mass "culture" of superficiality and nonsense,
controlled by media vomiting dispersing stuff
all over this polluted planet of denaturalisation
just to make the brainwash world pandemic worse
for the shortsighted benefit of poison chaos merchants.
Let me hide behind the trees of some forgotten virgin forest
and remain there in humility, timidity and peace
to only concentrate on vital things
that make life worth while after all,
the beauty that remains forever,
the experience that is forever beneficial,
music that will never die
and ancient sacred writings
going on inspiring forever.
Nothing else is really of some consequence.
This brainwash age of stress and mental aberration
is just, like any war in history, a vanity to outlive,
although hibernation under duress always is an unfair trial
of constructiveness and love,
as if they ever could be doubted, questioned,
harassed tragically by the foolishness of vanity.

The ten commandments of pantheism

— found this by chance and thought it worth while noting down...

There is only one God, and he is every god.

All life is sacred, and thou shalt not abuse it.

Rest from stress whenever you can.

Thou shalt respect and tolerate the faiths, beliefs and religions of others.

Killing any living being is always murder.

Love is all, but don't abuse it.

The only thing that really can be stolen from you is your life, which is just a loan anyway.

Truth will always prevail, and lies will never last.

Respect your neighbour and what he values in life.

Life is universal and everywhere, to be respected, recreated and maintained.

Intimacy

The understatement of communion
just between the two of us
in pious silence
of the more inveterate vibrations
that accelerate with urgent constancy
to hopelessly inveigle us
into an ever deeper abyss
of intimacy
is not between ourselves exclusively
but is a matter that concerns the universe
like all intimacy,
the highest of all possible communication,
since its privacy lures out the heart of power,
energy and spiritual potency,
which is known
as nothing less than love.

Shadowing the sun

When in the night of sleepless worries
I wake up at three with soaring mind
concerned about and haunted by adversities,
oppression, persecution, cruelty and senselessness,
the war against the freedom of constructive minds,
the efforts to obstruct the freedom of the Internet,
the civil wars of bigotry, fanaticism and hate,
I cough distraught with nervous sickness
like in some tuberculosis last stage

that will never finish me but just goes on,
I think of you with my sincerest love
and know for sure, that we will manage everything
and even Bush, the greatest presidential failure
and the global warming threats of dire prospects,
since our love is hot enough
to even outshine and cool down the sun.

Limitation is no limit

How can I give you all that love
I want to give but am too mortal
and too limited in my qualifications
to at all be even able to express?
That is the only problem of our love affair
and our relationship, but that is maybe why
we have instead our music
for a universe of love expressions
since, as every thoughtful artist knows,
all beauty comes from love alone,
and in its spiritual form love has no limits
but is able to expand forever in expression
and creation of its beauteous infinity.
So let me love you with my music
to inspire and increase your music with my own,
thus filling up the world with music of our love
to multiply the beauty of its harmony forever.

The day after tomorrow

When doors are closed and slammed into your face,
when friends go mad and die with only words of bitterness,
when you are ruined and betrayed by those you trusted,
when your love refuses to communicate with you,
when all the world is threatened by the day after tomorrow,
when such a scenery for every day becomes more imminent,
when those you love go disappearing into drugs,
when childhood pals go off in alcoholism, suicide and cancer,
when the world just keeps on going constantly and more awry,
when leading countries threaten punishment by force
of overkill with nuclear armamament, like North Korea and Iran,
when rogue states are allowed to keep on getting worse
with openly increasing tyranny, oppression, persecution,

murder, genocide and governmentally supported criminality,
what can you do but cry with all their victims in despair
to share with them at least in solidarity and empathy
a universal prayer in protest to echo through the universe
for something better than the day after tomorrow.

Lamenting the loss of a friend

How deep is thy fall, o most luciferous of angels,
maybe just because of that,
the highest light of all, supremest beauty,
closest to the highest, bravest of the brave,
the grandest haughtiness and noblest hubris,
fallen down to direst dirt in bottomless abysmal darkness
where you wallow now in madness and despair
and hopelessness forever,
all because you chose it for yourself.
I dare to call you still my friend
although you are now incommunicable
locked up in a padded cell
with nothing but your solitude
in splendid isolation, as you wished,
unheeding of all warnings
that all bad things must end up in loneliness.
All life supporting constructivity
can never fall into a loss of company;
the lover, even if he is alone, is never quite alone;
while loneliness, when really lonely,
is the opposite, for only those,
who search for the reward of death.

A Simple Love Song

You are my only love,
the one for me to never leave,
down in the bog of love
to just enjoy and be at ease,
you are the world for me
as I am true to the word for thee,
for only you is the girl for me,
for I am so in love with you.

Yours is my only heart,
the one and true, forever blue,
no one can strain my heart
to leave my sole concern for you,
never the stars can fall
but to adore just the shadow of yours,
for you are mine, and my only heart
belongs with all my soul to you.

Wistfulness

I love you and I miss you,
my friend in need and friend indeed,
more worthy for your poverty
than any stressed out boring millionaire
for your particular creativeness
ennobling you and giving you more richness
in abundance of the spiritual kind
much more worth than the entire world;
for spiritual children and the art of giving life to them
is on a higher level than just common progeny.
There is no higher honour than to be a mother,
but to be creative spiritually is a higher art,
contributing to spiritual welfare and awareness of all life,
which is dependent solely on continuous creation.

Transcendent transience

Just the hearing of your voice
is more than just the loveliest reminder
of our love and closeness,
being overwhelming as a revelation
of the presence of your personality,
in singularity so perfect in integrity,
in loveliness insuperable,
if you pardon my exaggerated praise,
which though can never reach the height
of your true worth and what it means to me.
Just let me love you, and I am content,
and all we need for love and for my loving you
is just the presence, which surrounds us everywhere
wherever you may be at large lost in the world,
since our separation is just a formality,
our love transcending everything that smells of transience.

Masochistic love

Is my love a sickness, then,
since pain is all it offers me?
The hollowness of its deficient lethargy
is like a creeping wasting weakening disease
that eats you up from inside cell by cell;
and yet you can't stop loving still,
as if the very pain and torture of it
was the heart and meaning
of the neverending trauma
that keeps growing like a cancer in your heart,
an ache and ague worse than any physical defect,
like that old man on Sinbad's back
inflicting just excruciating pain
for seemingly no other reason
than to make you feel alive;
and that is reason good enough to go on suffering,
to go on smouldering in tortured silence
for the one and only hope of some release some day,
of any kind; but until then,
just let me keep on loving
in the endless torturesome exhaustion
of my self to keep it growing on forever
in its total and unbearable consuming pain.

Enchanted by your charm

– another old love song

Is my love a sickness, then,
since pain is all it offers me?
The hollowness of its deficient lethargy
is like a creeping wasting weakening disease
that eats you up from inside cell by cell;
and yet you can't stop loving still,
as if the very pain and torture of it
was the heart and meaning
of the neverending trauma
that keeps growing like a cancer in your heart,
an ache and ague worse than any physical defect,
like that old man on Sinbad's back
inflicting just excruciating pain
for seemingly no other reason
than to make you feel alive;
and that is reason good enough to go on suffering,
to go on smouldering in tortured silence
for the one and only hope of some release some day,
of any kind; but until then,
just let me keep on loving
in the endless torturesome exhaustion
of my self to keep it growing on forever
in its total and unbearable consuming pain.

Love presence

– just another love song

You are there, my only love,
the only one for me under the sun,
no matter where you are,
you always will be there and waiting for me
like I'll be yours
forever, and a day
or two or more whatever you choose to say,
whether far away or near me,
what difference does it do to our love anyway,
since we hold sway
for our love to ever stay on to us,

adoring, cajoling and worshipping everyone close to us,
for my love is here to stay
to never leave me again for any day,
if it's okay!

The soul string touch

You touched in me a special chord
that never did vibrate before
with such a special sound
of tenderness, sincerity and purity,
which more than struck me dumb
and changed my life completely,
one of those rare momentary miracles
that suddenly burst forth
completely out of nowhere
to turn your existence upside down
and change your character forever.
Still I can not understand it,
that miraculous chance meeting
of two souls immediately melting
into one, which has remained one
ever since, and that was long ago,
like as if this our year together so far
has been more than only one eternity.

Imminent love psychosis

There is no love without psychosis
of the most enjoyable and enviable kind,
but to enjoy it you must keep it steady and control it
like a humanist and pilot staying clear in dire straits
to at all be able to let love go on.
It is the sharpest and most difficult of balances:
the line is thin and slack, and you just have to dance across it
meeting even uphills and adversities on this laborious course
of high-strung sensitivity and the frailest delicacy
threatening to crash down into darkest abyss any moment.
Just beware of getting too mixed up and filled up with yourself,
and you'll be safe in loving anyone except yourself.

Dealing with the overwhelmingness of love

The truth of our love is stranger than fiction,
especially since we never can know the entire truth.
The only truth we do know about it
is our feelings, that never can lie to us,
whether aching like hell or longing like hell,
they remain too overwhelming to be dealt with,
which is why we are so careful with each other.
But love when it exists is always true,
it can not be lied about or hidden,
it can not be tamed or even controlled,
it must burst forth sooner or later,
since like all true love it must breathe.
So let us breathe the life of our love and enjoy it,
since it was given us for a joy indeed
so rare, that it truly deserves to be taken care of
as a unique moment of priceless joy and precious beauty
to overwhelm eternity with in its moment of truth.

Where's the problem, when there is no problem?

What's all the fuss about?
Just knock it off and let's be friends
for good or for worse but forever.
Who wants or needs a marriage?
Who cares about rings and riches,
what's the use of formalities,

who even needs sex or drugs or alcohol
when all we need is each other,
just to stand in touch and enjoy each other,
just the feeling of the presence of each other,
and everything else is superfluous.
All we need is love, and we have it,
so why make any fuss about it,
since that's the last thing that we need,
since we already have the only thing we need,
which simply is each other.

Just another simple love song

My love is there for you to stay,
my love is here in every way,
my love looms large to heaven's day,
in every way it works today
for ever more and more at large
I think of you, my only love.
When shall we join our limbs and hearts
to just tune in and fall apart
dissolved in souls and wondrous arts
creating miracles to start
and never cease in loving art
to join our hearts to never part.

Amnesia

Forget all the quarrels,
the deceits and disappointments,
each time you were humiliated
and cheated by your lover
and every time you caused upsets
that never could be cured.
Forget all about your failures
as a lover fool and freak and fake
and concentrate instead on that which mattered,
your true love which always was there aching,
burning under cover in its constantly abused faithfulness,
surviving every winter and catastrophe
in spite of all, to go on loving,
which is all the memory that counts:
the memory of love that never dies.

Eagles and butterflies

This love is of some matter and concern
involving some responsibility
that is not easily escaped from,
since we can't escape from love.
Its character is fleeting like a butterfly
but at the same time soaring like an eagle
and can in no way be caged and fettered,
since the butterfly will always flutter out
and eagles without freedom are not eagles.
Let us meet and join up there while we are soaring
and leave out the limits of the mundane imperfection
separating us and keeping us out of desirable communication,
since our love is all the freedom that we have,
the wings of which are for the eagle's use and butterfly's
to keep us sparkling, soaring and enjoying
if not our mutual presence, then at least our mere existence.

The impossible truth

You search for it but never find it since it
is unfathomable in its vastness,
inescapable in cruelty and realism,
unconquerable in inestimableness
and utterly horrendous,
since there is no greater enemy of poetry
than truth, reality and facts.
Still, you can't help going for it,
burning up and out yourself on it
in some strange self-destructive urge
to just consume yourself
in the extremest most impossible of quests,
to learn what all this really is about.

Sentimentality

Where will it lead us,
this sentimentality
that drags us down into a bog of feelings
without end and without bottom,
where we perish drowning in our tears,
while at the same time heaven lifts us up

on eagle wings of golden love
unto the realm of infinite felicity
on flights of starlit magic of eternity.
No wonder I get so completely sentimental over you
since I find no way out of this predicament
of stuck in bogs and lost in heaven
except by just giving in to you.

In the still of the night

In the still of the night
my heart shines so bright
in my longing for you
just to see what you do
in your loveliest hue
in the light of the night
which gives you all the right
to command me and own me
since you only love me
like I will love you
being ever more true
to the love that we own
so sincerely once sown
from the trust of our heart
grown together in smart
never ever to part
from the love of our heart
that we always shall grow
to outstanding survival
for heaven to mow
in eternal revival.

The laziness of Aphrodite

– a love lesson

The laziest of goddesses
is only good for work in bed
and therefore rather would not leave it
but just stay there going on in bed
alluring everyone to serve her
and her whims of love to stay in bed
with you just working hard for her

and she receiving only, in her laziness
the most privileged of gods and goddesses;
but she is not entirely without rewards.
She grows forever in her beauty,
and that beauty is contagious,
spilling over into all her lovers
who learn to enjoy it and adopt it,
cultivating it as lessons of her love
to go on spreading it not only into other beds
and other lovers, but all round and everywhere
as love should spread indeed in every bed
to make the world a better and a saner place,
the hotbed being laziness.

Flowing as always

Crying for you as always
I am drowning in you as always
wiping my tears as always
away from my chin, but as always
they keep coming on, pouring down, as always,
renewing themselves more efficiently as always
than I even can cry them out, since as always
you keep booming in my mind with your music as always
more devastatingly than any live music, since as always
you are the sole live music in my life, which as always
keeps me going on as always
at least never tiring of you,
since you are there always.

Inspiration

You bring out the best in me,
my warmest feelings and my tend'rest heart,
my deepest constructivity and piety,
and my sincere humility and reverence.
With you I have my heart's content
and can have nothing more,
can wish for nothing more
and have no further needs.
I simply couldn't have it any better,
and yet we continue forwards

to develop and create our lives
to even higher heights of happiness.
That is the finest miracle of all,
that we have only just begun.

Meditation

I meditate on you
extolling in your harmony and lustre,
never minding your new grey hairs
adding silver to your gold
that only makes it even more serene and precious
as the jewels of your soul enrich our lives
and turn them into something of a neverending treasure
of our love to ever swim and drown and wallow in
to draw new life and breath from this unfathomable beauty
that is you in your good heart
and beatification of our lives.
So could I go on meditating and forever,
dreaming only lovely energizing dreams
that turns my whole existence into one-sided creativeness,
of which I never would complain
but only work the harder
to maintain it.

In the deep of the night

In the deep of the night
there is a fathomless silence
of stars shining bright for eternity,
irreducible lights that never go out,
like our love, the miraculous light of which
more is like some profound uncompromising enigma
that never can be either solved or divined
in its incomprehensible darkness
concealing a starlight of more potent light
than the brightest of all heaven outshining stars.
Shall we try to approach, comprehend and get down to it?
No, for the answer to its distant irony and ambiguity
is maybe as obvious as ever in all heaven's stars,
that they shine best the further away
we are kept from their mystery.

The Queen of Night

The night club queen just doesn't care
since everyone loves her anyway,
they being all to her just fools and slaves of love,
of drugs and alcohol, of libido and sex,
while she just leisurely enjoys their folly,
laughing at the feebleness of man,
his most ridiculous self-humiliation
for the whims and beauty of just any wanton woman;
but I will have none of it and rather cure my anger
at this gross unworthiness and terrible abuse of love
in bitter isolation and tempestuous fury
to rather plague myself with tortuous frustration
than risk touching any one of those abusive dames
who gladly sacrifice whatever chance of sincere love they had
for just a moment of abusive pleasure
of the opportunity to trample down all human feelings.

Marlowe and Shakspere

I cannot help it, but in those dramatic lines
for centuries now published under Shakspere's name
I keep on hearing Marlowe's mighty line,
as if behind Macbeth and Hamlet, Julius Caesar and Othello
there was Tamburlaine behind them all at bottom,
buried deep but never dead
in ever resurrected unsurpassed consistent cruelty,
a theme recurrent constantly in Marlowe
in the Jew, the duke of Guise, the fate of Faustus
and poor royal Edward; buried to the triumph of the boring Puritans
obscurely atheistically and anonymously whisked away
to be replaced by Shakspere's chastized mollified modification
without controversial stuff but with the poetry triumphing
over death and vanity the more in booming verse
in straight continuation from the drama launched by Marlowe.
Well, it has been proved that Marlowe was in difficulty
seriously accused of atheism and homosexuality
and other controversial stuff most insolently published by himself,
like pamphlets against church and order and an atheistic lecture,
which would mean, if he did not abscond,
then he would certainly be executed.
Now his death appears as the most masterfully staged
of all Elizabethan plays, a well concealed intrigue performed obscurely

just to make a show of a most controversial poet's demise
for the obvious purpose to just let him be, remain alive
and go on with his work, but under cover, for security.
Thus Shakspere enters as a mediator
for the continuity of Marlowe's drama, although modified,
to let it grow in ever more astounding glory
in its mighty lines on stage
to never die, like Macbeth, Hamlet and Othello,
Julius Caesar and the mighty Tamburlaine the great,
most threatening and most immortal menace of them all.

The dream of you

All I ever gave you is for keeps
I'll never take a moment back
of all that we have had together
which I gave you for your own forever.
When resources end and our bond is broken
we shall still have all our dreams,
the memories of more tresurability
than any mundane stuff for base consumtion;
like you entered me to constantly remain there
as a chronic inflammation in my heart of beauty
of a most contagious kind,
since it has permeated all my life
and does so still and more than ever,
as if I could never do without you
even when long after we have left each other.
Let it be, let it remain so,
let the paradise continue,
let the garden of our love continue growing
for the benefit of all
and for the cure of everything
that wasn't born of love and beauty.

A sermon

– the lady to her frustrated wooer

My dear, it will not do to argue.
We are not of that sort that will listen
to an angry voice impassioned by frustrated blindness
of misguided egoism you thought was love

but only was a bolt carried away into the dark.
You can not build a dialogue or a relationship of any kind
on one part's will, since listening is always more important,
for the dialogue and the relationship to live at all,
than just to talk and give free reins to any gallop,
which is bound to run amuck if you don't check it.
There is no one who can judge or know or feel another's feelings,
they are sacred to the individual
as the most personal possession she will ever have,
and none has any right to touch them
or to importuningly take them for granted.
Love can never be assumed or taken casually for granted,
that is the supreme presumption and a mine-field
that will just explode into your face if you tread carelessly into it.
Love and feelings is an abyss, a descending into hell
where you shall never find a way out
unless guided solely by your love, which always must be pure.
That is the only lighthouse in the stormy night –
the purity, sincerity and the profundity of selfless love
that never makes presumptions, never takes for granted,
never risks to hurt or trample others' feelings down
but always moves with carefulness and tenderness
to only silently adore and cherish with the utmost care
preferrably to never even dare to touch it.

Flying on broken wings

Love is an idealism
which only can survive as such –
you have to idolize your love,
or it will die; and anything subverting,
acting to debase your love from its ideal ground
will, unless checked, destroy and kill it.
It will keep alive as long as it may keep on flying,
and no longer, for when wings no longer can uphold it
keeping it on constant upright course and ever striving higher,
it will fall by lack of air under its wings
and lose the freedom that was all the nourishment of love.
But I will be your tears, when you forlorn on earth
emotionally shipwrecked like a nightingale with broken wings
have nothing else to do but to cry out your heart,
to be there when you cry, and you shall find me in your very tears
to lift you up again on golden wings in warbling song
where we shall fly together in the sun
and cry our hearts out in our song of freedom.

Danger!

— another sleepless night

One day without you
is just a waste of time,
an irrepairable outrageous loss,
a day of mourning
and a day robbed of your life
to be remembered with dishonour
as the worst investment of your time.
Frustrated, you can never be more angry,
since you never can have that one day repaired,
and you can never have it back.
How, then, shall we avoid such losses,
such catastrophes, calamities, fatalities
and fearful unforgivable unheard of drop-outs in the future?
We had better sleep together constantly
and never let each other out of sight,
or else we might get lost
on erring fateful paths of straying wilderness
to lose our basic touch, the only life we have,
which is our love, which needs togetherness.

Simplistic statement

Our love is holy and divine
and therefore so untouchable
for others even to suspect
the nature of its truth and honesty,
but let them think the worst,
and we shall do our best
to keep it going, flowing, flying
in the bliss of our secret
which is just in all simplicity
that we can never do without each other any more.
Let's stick to that, then,
and forget that ever we were tempted
to imagine there was any other possibility
for us than just to live
exclusively within each other.

Magnetism

To just lie quietly
and dream of you
is such a full-time work
that nothing could be more exhausting,
since nothing could more permeate my life,
my being, my existence, than your being
which is all I have at heart
to boast of and to cherish
as a drunkard his last bottle.
Let's enjoy it, then,
and drink it up
before it is too late
and that wine gets too sour
to be relished properly.
We have it here and now,
so let's just get together
and get stuck together
never to let go of our love.

Friends

— a kind of definition

Love is indefinable and strange,
a weird adventure of capricious risks
with everything at stake and nothing really to be won
except experience, which always is for good and worse;
and those who have enough experience
of the controversial kind and have found out
the traps and fallacies and vanities of human hearts
know all too well that love is just a dangerous attraction
to get burned and damaged by for life
with sometimes losses irrepairable
to keep on crying over for a lifetime sentence,
and reduce therefore their love's ambition
to the acquisition of a lasting friendship.
That's the best thing, actually, that can be gained by love,
a lasting ever more enriching and developing reward;
so if you really want true love and keep it,
just make sure to make your love's best friend
and then be constant in your love's ambition
to retain and cultivate that friendship.

Some conciliatory advice

When a man tires of love he tires of life,
and when he is tired of life, there is always death to resort to,
as if that could be something better,
which it is to failed lovers who have given up.
So what ever you give up in life, never give up love,
since that is actually all you have
to make life worth while rather than death.
And remember, how love can offer you all sorts of extra things,
like hang-ups, down-unders, dissolution i tears,
bereavement, deception, and smothering frustration;
but the miracle is, that you still can go on loving,
which in spite of all sometimes is a better thing to do
than to stop loving.

Love and death

Never mix your love with such absurdities
as base illusions of mortality.
Love doesn't go along with death,
since love is just the opposite,
and if a love relationship fades out and dies
it simply wasn't true love; since you recognize it
by its talent for survival, spiting any obstacle,
surmounting all adversities and just continuing to grow,
develop and increase, forever, if you want.
Mortality and death is only an illusion which,
at best, transports love definitely to infinity.

work situation

You just can't help it,
falling asleep all the time
in front of the silly computer
which just gives you any amount of silly jobs,
boring jobs, tedious jobs,
so you just fall asleep trying to handle them,
and then, since you keep falling asleep,
you can't get any work done in front of the computer
which all the time insists on sending you to sleep.
Whatever you try to work with,
your concentration is sabotaged by your falling asleep,

so your boring work keeps mounting in heaps
for you to keep falling asleep by,
which problem keeps you awake at night,
so that then you never can sleep any more,
thinking of all that work that keeps growing
since you always fall asleep trying to deal with it,
while, when all you can do is to think about it,
it just keeps you awake,
as if falling asleep at your work was something to worry about
to keep you awake when all you would want is to sleep...

Honesty lasts longer

I only think of you, my love,
although I do not know thee.
I know not mortal languages of love,
but I know Woman, and I love her,
and true love does not need any language.
Everything important reads between the lines,
and to explain it and evaluate it is to ruin it
by the vulgarity of coarse debasing concretization,
the most heinous and supreme of sacrileges.
So leave my pure thoughts of love in sacred peace,
and do not ask for more than all its honesty,
which is the only thing love needs to keep surviving.

Butterfly existence

Why must love relationships give so much pain
as something of a punishment for their existence?
The protection is a shyness of vulnerability
which suffers from its brittle delicacy.
Is then loneliness a kind of cure?
It heals for certain, so that you get bold enough
to woo the holocaust of new relationships
to get shot down again in your exposed heart
and painfully reminded of the pangs of wounded love,
more damaging and aching than all physical affliction.
Thus the vicious circle carries on and never ends,
the self-destructiveness of plain relationships,
like that alluring candle in a butterfly existence
which she lives for only to get burned by.

Strangers

How is it, that the more we love each other,
the more difficult it gets for us to explain ourselves
and understand each other, as if we still were strangers
never having known each other, and for all our experience
constantly know and understand each other less.
And still, this alien feeling of estrangement from each other
forces us together more and keeps us more legated to each other,
as if, the more our contact and communication grows in truth,
intimacy, intensity and co-dependence, the least lack of our togetherness
feels the more confounding and confusing in upsetting turbulence
as something utmost unacceptable to our existence,
as if the minutest dissonance in our relationship
was more upsetting than the most catastrophic of earthquakes.

Doubtfulness

When I sit quietly at bay
in dreams and sipping piously my glass of wine
and think of you and our strange love
as skeptic as I ever was
if not considerably more,
since age does not retard your criticism
but rather turns it constantly more critical,
I question everything and is irrevocably doubtful
about life and death, eternity, infinity and holiness
and must revaluate existence thoroughly
and desperately without end
and must arrive eventually at one conclusion:
everything is doubtful, nothing is to be relied on,
nothing is for certain, but for one thing:
the uniqueness of the truth
of that strange love I feel for you.

The elementary simplicity of metaphysics

There must some kind of God.
We have no choice.
Or else all life and everything is lost.
For total atheism is nothing but the ultimate capitulation,
the utmost enmity to life,
since most unnatural of all is to give up.

If life gives up it has no meaning,
therefore it must have a meaning,
since at all it does exist,
and therefore there must be a God
as an idea above all others,
an initiative and constructivity
all of its own that guides it.
That's the elementary simplicity of metaphysics.

Golden love

In hues all golden
like a long desired dreamt of child
as innocent as newborn,
always positive and full of life –
where does that inner beauty come from
that outshines the sun and make all clouds disperse,
a joy of simply being what you are in glorious independence,
and yet nothing is what it appears to seem,
there is a front completely hiding abysses of worrying desperation
like a poker face, which you can't know
if its expressionlessness hides a full hand or just misery.
But souls know better human hearts than outward shows,
and we knew well each other from the start
like two lost souls diverted many centuries ago
to find themselves on mutual path by chance again
like a lost thread of fortune suddenly revealed and rediscovered
to be recommenced and now continued on a fresh start
right into the ever circulating spiral of eternity
to once again engulf us in its course
on yet another round of this intriguing game
of love unto infinity.

Deep throat message

Let me write you something really shocking
and unheard of, in this puritan community
of squeamish sensitivity and no remorse,
no tolerance for anything outstandingly upsetting,
so let's just calm down and be prepared.
The secret is, that everything is back to normal,
metaphysics and their balance is restored,
the turmoil of the two world wars and their barbarity

is over, done with, the atomic age is finished,
the horrific cold war with its terror balance is a fairy tale
to frighten little children with, we cured it all,
we angels of the hippie metaphysic rainbow movement
by our prayers and the honesty and energy of our will
and its constructiveness - so just forget about it.
There are new fronts and intrinsic problems coming up,
the global warming problematical complexities
above all, and the complex of America's megalomania,
with an irresponsible administration
trying most pathetically childishly to cover up
the Pentagon reports of long ago
that gave the full agenda of the global warming consequences,
while the Bush administration chose to comfortably look the other way
and cover it all up, like any oistrich in the desert.
Pardon me for saying so, and for revealing these state secrets,
but our work has only started. All of you who joined us in the 60s
starting those hullaballoos against the govermental military fascism
have to just keep going on and keep it up
in universal hippie demonstration just for love, against all violence
to save the future of the planet and our children,
since we owe it all to them, that life we loved
and must be kept alive in all its beauty
for the sake of just the sentimental joy of it,
for the protection of our human feelings,
which is all that keeps humanity alive.

Closeness

Far too little we were able to enjoy each other,
far too little we could meet embracing tenderly,
and far too short our unions ever lasted
in comparison with the immeasurable greatness of our love
which, although it kept us together constantly in spirit,
that session of eternity of love was just a minute
to that lifetime of that love we did deserve.
Unfair is life to lovers, never really granting them
what they deserve and need and should have naturally;
and the greater and more tender and profound their love,
the grosser life's injustice looms in terror
like a most unhuman vengeance just for nothing but their happiness.
So must we be content with our humiliation,
bow to fate in humble piety prostration and subordination
just in order to survive as lovers

to at least maintain that love
that keeps us closer to each other in our spirits
than we ever can be joined on earth.

The most beautiful poem of love...

The most beautiful poem of love
was never written and never shall,
for its lips were sealed by its kisses
exchanging such secrets of intimacy
of such tremendous profundity and capacity
that the power was too overwhelming
to bear being put down in words
of profaneness and simple reality,
since anything less than the top of it
was just a debasement unworthy of truth,
the which honesty simply was all time too high
to ever be capable of being made understandable,
which only they can grasp and be convinced of
who know the importance of letting love speak for itself.

Right or wrong, my love

How much do you love me?
What an impertinent question!
And totally irrelevant at that!
The point is that I love you,
and more than that I have no right to claim.
For love is only giving, never taking;
when love is made with an agenda
it is not love but politics and egoism,
while love is truth as long as it is given only,
without any reservations or demands,
and if another element is mixed in it,
then just forget it – then it's better
to leave love alone and put it in a nunnery.
And that's the touchstone, which must always be applied
and implemented – the continuous trial,
doubts and questionings, the constant conscience
asking questions of the only valid kind : –
is this then right what I am doing?
It is only right, as long as you are loving.

Backfire

– Never try the same weapon again, if once it has backfired.

Love is not love if you suffer from it;
if it hurts you and gives you pain it is not love
but an abortion, a mistake, abuse or accident,
and it will only become worse it you don't leave at once,
forgetting all about it. If you struggle on
and waste your faith on what has fallen,
trying to believe it will recover, giving it a second chance,
and then a third, a fourth, and so on
leading only to increased self-torture,
self-destruction, wounds that constantly go deeper,
hurting more the more you keep supporting it,
then that will be the end of your integrity,
your peace of mind, your harmony and health,
your good sleep and the order of your life.
Your only chance is keeping your love straight
and in constructive order, or it simply will not work,
and nothing, not the highest effort of the greatest expertise
can make love work if once it has been violated.

The crying tree

— *a true story*

It was a lady who told me the story.
She was staying in a house out in the country
with an ancient giant oaken tree quite close
with branches stretching over it
and roots down deep under the basement.
She found difficulty sleeping in this house,
and gradually the aches began in all her limbs,
which she could not explain,
since there was nothing wrong with her.
No sleep, and aches all over,
unexplainable, and then a total sadness
that just made her cry for nothing
while the pains increased intolerably.
Suddenly she realized:
it was that old tree affecting her.
Her female empathy had found communion with the tree,
which recently had had two giant branches cut,

which now the tree was seized with anguish for,
in pain trying to heal and not to bleed to death.
The tree was something like three hundred years of age,
and at that age to have some amputation is no easy matter.
Trees are human, and their DNA is close to our own.
It has been proved, that when some trees are cut down in a forest,
it is felt by other trees and even trees as far away
as in the very other end of that same forest,
which is like an organism and a community,
where all the trees co-operate communing with each other.
That was something about trees, their sensitivity and human feelings,
and about the fact how actually it hurts in all Dame Nature
when they are cut down.

Comment on the situation in Tibet

This dilemma calls for some urgent and constant attention:

Quote:

Dalai Lama's shattered dream for Tibet

By B. GAUTAM
The Japan Times
Saturday, May 26, 2007

MADRAS — Tibet looks like a dream shattered. You feel this when you hear the stories of horror told and retold by Buddhist monks and nuns who have escaped from Tibet and taken refuge in Dharamshala, the center of the Dalai Lama's government in exile in India.

Nestled in the foothills of the snow-clad Himalayas, Dharamshala is deceptive in many ways. The Dalai Lama hides deep worries behind his serene smile: He knows he is not going to live forever, and the community he leads could lose any hope, however faint it may be, of seeing a free Tibet.

The nuns and monks who have run away from years of humiliation and torture at the hands of the Chinese in Tibet also despair. They know that their sacrifice may have been in vain.

Once a supremely spiritual civilization, Tibet revered the Dalai Lama before the Chinese invasion in the 1950s. It is this religious society that Beijing is bent on destroying — maiming and killing anybody who refuses to give up his beliefs or who harbors the slightest hope of political autonomy. The Chinese have torn apart monasteries and killed roughly 1.2 million Tibetans since the annexation in 1959.

Now, however, China has adopted a more tactical approach to crushing Tibetan resistance. The country's president, Hu Jintao, who once imposed martial law on Tibet, has realized that heavy-handed steps lead to greater rebellion as well as international attention and protests. Since Beijing covets the billions of barrels of oil and gas recently discovered in Tibet, it has begun to co-opt Tibetans in modernizing the Roof of the World, while quietly silencing the core of dissent, monkhood.

Although China has said publicly it will promote and encourage Buddhism as well as restore monasteries and palaces to their former glory, the picture behind this veneer of tolerance is still one of ruthless elimination. The Chinese hold patriotic conclaves where Tibetan monks and nuns are told to forget the Dalai Lama.

As Tibet's capital city, Lhasa, undergoes changes beyond recognition, with even a rail link to China, Tibetans are being slowly pushed to the fringes. An increasing number of Chinese are setting up shop and home in Lhasa — with train services facilitating such relocation. Beijing knows this is the best way to control the local population.

Chinese officials often blatantly cheat rural Tibetans out of their own land, convincing them to give it up for promises of property in the city. The promise is never kept, and the farmland goes to Chinese entrepreneurs, who convert it into industrial zones.

Watching almost helplessly from afar is the Dalai Lama, who knows that if he does not set foot in Tibet before he dies, his people will be furious. His strategy of a middle path — asking for greater political and cultural autonomy instead of total freedom and holding talks with Chinese envoys — has not yielded results. His people know that Beijing is waiting for his death, after which the Tibetans may find themselves rudderless.

Many Tibetans are not willing to go down without a fight. Today, at Dharamshala, one can hear open criticism of the Dalai Lama. He is accused of selling out to the Chinese. Campaigning against the Dalai Lama, and for total freedom, is Tenzin Tsundue, a young Tibetan who has become the most important figure among the exiles in Dharamshala. He and his band of followers have abandoned the Dalai Lama's peaceful approach and draw their strength from militants like Palestinians.

This may go against the very grain of Buddhism, whose founder believed in one overriding principle: nonviolence. But Tibetan youngsters who adore Tsundue have little time or patience for values that have gotten them nowhere.

In India, Tibetans have stormed Chinese consulates and the embassy. During a recent visit by Hu Jintao, a young Tibetan tried to immolate himself outside the Bombay hotel where the Chinese president was staying.

Tibetan hardliners are targeting the 2008 Beijing Olympics and the new train line to Lhasa. In the days to come, violence could manifest itself more intensely in various ways. When the Dalai Lama finally goes, his followers will have little to fall back upon. The hardliners may then try to convince Tibetans that since the Dalai Lama's Buddhist doctrine of peace, love and the middle path did not fetch any tangible result for decades, violence is the only answer.

But with China ready to treat such Tibetans as terrorists in a world that is growing weary of violence and bloodshed, the new Tibetan approach to winning freedom may well come to nothing.

What seems more likely to happen is that Tibet will be firmly amalgamated with China as all traces of its ancient civilization and spirituality vanish. Tibetan culture may end up as just another chapter in a history book.

B. Gautam
(unquote)

The problem is the greatest dictatorship in the world, which the whole world kowtows to in submission to its capitalistic success: so far it has paid to support this totalitarianism, so all opportunists (which most of mankind are) continue encouraging the regime that slaughtered its own subjects at Tiananmen Square 4th June 1989, forces abortion and sterilization on mothers who have more than one child, still worships their Big Brother Dictator Mao as something of a saint although he was the greatest murderer in history with some 100 million homicides on his responsibility, and so on.

Dictatorships are not acceptable and must never be acceptable, especially after the century that brought forth dictators like Mussolini, Hitler, Stalin, Mao, Kim Il Sung, Kim Jong Il, Mugabe, Idi Amin and Pol Pot, who was actually directed in his genocide against his own people by Mao.

As long as the world supports any dictatorship, the world will continue going to hell.

The poisoned Falun Gong practitioner

– so far 800 cases like this have become known.

I don't know what they do to me.
I have been here now for I don't know how long,
but I am not alone at least.
We are a number in this concentration camp,
but I don't know how many,
since I cannot count correctly any more.
I don't know why they make us invalids
unfit for work, disqualified for anything, -
perhaps to show the world how dumb we are,
as if the world would close their eyes to what we were before
we were sequestered, isolated and imprisoned
just for sticking faithfully to universalism,
the association with the cosmic mind
in Lao Tzu's and Buddha's imitation,
which for some strange reason the authorities
decided to have us exterminated for;
but I must say their methods are peculiar.
We are loaded, force-fed with destructive drugs,
we don't know which, they put them in our food,
or they inject them into us by force,
so we become like vegetables,
losing the control of our bodies,
of our mind and memory,
our faculty for analytical and logic thought,
our will to reason and our energy to live,
while at the same time we of course become unfit for work
and merely exist as zombies, lying dying in our beds,
like wrecks but wrecked on purpose,
why? Because we had free minds?
Believed in something better,
stuck to our cultural traditions,
aimed for some religious higher meaning of our lives?
I just don't understand why our authorities
insist on undermining and destroying
everything that shows a different path
from the established lies of their dictatorship,
as if that was a sensible activity,
which no one in the world can see
how it could lead to anything except destruction.

Scratch

When love is shattered, it is just a trial,
since your love can never be completely violated,
even if they kill you they will not be able to obstruct your love,
which is the only continuity you have.
The trials are for facing and surviving,
the adversities are for withstanding,
the defeats are for surmounting and defeating
with a vengeance and in glory,
for your love can never be completely vanquished,
although all the rapes and violations in the world assail you
and you are humiliated beyond recognition and recovery.
Whatever happens, you will always have something remaining;
and if only you can start from scratch,
you can accomplish anything.

The constant heartbreak risk

I would gladly sacrifice my life for you.
The problem is, I have no life to sacrifice.
It belongs to others, to all those
I owe my passion and responsibility,
which I am too absorbed by and engaged in
to be able ever to let go,
and you are simply one of them.
My heart belongs to you, though,
and there is but one and only one it can belong to,
so that is your privilege, which no one else can claim.
I have no life, I have no time, no leisure and no peace,
I share my whirlwind of activities with the whole world,
but I do have a heart,
and it belongs to you.

Passion

How much can I love you
without being consumed?
How far can I go driving on
in bolting downhill race of love
without falling to my ruin?
How far can I drive my own self-torment
in the limitlessness of the irresistibility
in the mad rage and lunacy of love?

That is precisely the infernal crux,
that love can have no limitation,
but it must last for ever,
or it can not exist at all.

Tiresome authorities

Do not let the lack of musicality disturb you,
just ignore the nonsense that does not sound well,
leave out the ugliness of everything unhuman,
and survive the holocaust of junk and waste
so miserably flooding our tortured civilization.
All that counts is music that is never tired of,
the melodies that always will be sung,
the words that cannot be forgotten,
and the poetry that never will give up surviving.
Leave the nonsense to mortality,
ignore the inundations of oppression by authorities,
it is but blather to be buried, vanishing in thin air,
worthless as all exercise of power ever was,
dissolving with its noise to nothing,
like all unsound noise forever will,
since there will always be musical minds like ours
to forever sort them out as mere disturbances
like all noise signifying nothing.

My mistress

My mistress, you are always there,
enwrapped in mystery and strange untouchability,
and I have never once succeeded in deceiving you,
since you alone could master me and without even trying.
I belong to you and gave myself completely up to you from the beginning
without ever giving you away – my mystic love
shall never be located and identified,
and you will only so remain as long as you remain untouched
by the debasing hands of mortal worldliness.
My honour and my pride is to belong to you
and to have done so without ever failing you
with all my efforts to deceive you having turned out dismal failures.
But our love is not a failure but the contrary,
a humble but consistently improving and increasing story of success
but clandestinely only, to remain forever
intact as a mystery of truth and life and love.

The working artist's catechism

All I need to go is just some beauty
not disturbed by any ugliness,
some positive environment
without destructive elements,
to dream and think in peace creatively
without importuning brutality to wake you up,
harmonious and melodious music without noise
and friends to cheer you up
instead of negligent and ignorant indifference around you,
and so forth, some gratitude, appreciation, recognition
of the good you try to do in life
instead of insolence, ingratitude and inhumanity.
Is that to ask too much? I need not money,
wealth or property, I have no greed to satisfy,
but let my spirit just go on remaining active and constructive,
and let time take notice of it and not just completely let me down,
and I shall be content when I am dead
to have at least been working hard in all my life
to some result of more than only nothingness.

Keep the lights on

Love is not to be resisted
but it must be thoroughly controlled
or it might bolt destructively,
ignore all limits of all sense and decency
and finish itself off,
which is the last thing we desire.
Better then to keep it glowing,
not exploding into open fire
but to keep us warm in quiet peace
avoiding turbulent eruptions
to instead remain a lasting comfort;
for if love does not import longevity and health
it hardly is a love that will do any good,
but fizzle, like a match that broke
instead of catching fire to spread light
to others also and not only to ourselves.

Could have been worse

You are just the sort of girl
to make a fellow like myself
just fall in love with to remain so
fallen down to earth in hopeless worship
and obseqious servitude if not forever
then at last for an eternity of all the present
like a doting looney having nothing in his head
but one idea, the only thing he ever more can think of,
his fixation on his love in dumbstruck idiocy
like a serious disease with no cure whatsoever,
the most hopeless case imaginable,
doomed to dotage for eternity.
Is there no hope at all for me then?
That depends on you.
If you can love me in return,
then there is something to hang on to
like a spider's thread from some skyscraper rooftop
saving me from falling all way down
to straight perdition, which instead will lift me up
to that incredibility of heaven
which is nothing more than just the company of you.

The Lie of Loneliness

You'll never be alone
as long as you just love another,
which is just accepting some responsibility
of someone else's life as well as yours.
That other will then be with you
not sticking right under your skin
but all the closer stay within your soul
in even closer steadier contact
than by a physical approach,
which tempts to aberrations
like misunderstandings and illusions,
while the soul alone will always be the same.
If you have got her soul inside you
you can never lose her, but she will remain
your company forever if you love her,
and there never could be any finer company.

The Honest Actor

What care I about the audience,
I am not a flatterer of senseless masses
where the individual is lost
in lack of personal integrity
and is not noticed by his acquiescent silence;
no, I want to have just friends around me,
audiences of individuals that are alive
and I can find some contact with,
with faces that you can identify and one by one observe,
so that you can direct yourself to real people.
If the theatre is almost empty
does not bother me -
the play is the important thing
and all the truth of it,
and if I can't get through
to audiences of anonymous masses,
then I'd rather stay without
and find myself some meaningful soliloquies insted.
The truth, the meaning and the word is all,
and if it's valid, a few members of an audience is enough,
in fact, the fewer and the less, the better,
for the easier you'll get the message through.

Controlled enthusiasm

Can you imagine how much I love you?
Each time I see you my heart wishes to burst out in song
like in some old time funny childish romantic musical,
and there is nothing really that can stop me -
all that music of my love just gushes forth
in overwhelming floods of heartfelt heartiness
like some deluvion of unprecedented generosity;
and still, my life is so sincere and careful
that I always can contain myself
refraining from at any cost to hurt you
or approach you too unseemingly and importuningly.
But, love, you can be sure, it is all there
and growing constantly in splendour and abundance
as is unavoidable in such a long engagement
growing more sincere and beautiful the longer it goes on.

The Strait-Jacket

Life is a strait-jacket
being constantly tied tighter
like in a kind of sadistic vice of pain
unceasingly increased and getting worse with the years
like in a kind of Self-Tormentor's Paradise.
Who enjoys it is a self-tormentor
while all realists can only find suffering
and more suffering as long as they live,
for reality is never beautiful.
The joys and beauties of life
are restricted to flash moments of rare oases,
like dream moments ending abruptly at once
transcending instantly into the dark dreary night again,
which always dominates and never ends.
No, I love not life,
this nightmare prison of pains,
this eternity of misery and baseness,
ugliness and evil, cruelty and tyranny,
where the least evil of everything
paradoxically enough is that neverending suffering
which is the only thing that keeps life going on.

Another friendship

Going down into the darkness of the soul
where you must perish in the jungles of unconscious mysteries,
everything is darkness and without relief,
and you get muddled up in hopelessly entangling complications
of emotions like a web of feelings of remorse and guilt,
and there is nothing that can save you from this well
in which you are cast down unknown of all and all alone,
and only one thing can still save you:
some miraculous relationship of lasting friendship,
some warm heart that understands your own,
and it is always there, quite ready and alert to save you
by just being there and listening and sharing your affection.
All you have to do is just to find that waiting friend.

Games people play

Life is just a game,
and the more peculiar forms it takes,
the more advanced its purposes and methods,
the more seriously it takes itself,
the more childish it becomes,
since even world wars are just children's plays
in kindergarten backyard playing grounds,
completely irresponsible and stupid,
just a whim of vanity like any world war.
More advanced as children's plays
are then activities of loneliness
not affecting others, and the first of these
is naturally and of course creation,
building new worlds out of nothing,
piously engendering new enterprises and ideas;
but the most elevated art of creativity
is still just only children's play,
an act of vanity of no more serious consequence
than any fun in any kindergarten.

Passport to eternity

Let me die with thoughts of love of you
as passport to eternity across the river of mortality,
and never let me leave that passport or forget it
but maintain it always closest to my heart
as evidence that I at least got something out of life
that wasn't only foolishness.
Thus let me keep it for my only medicine
against all evils, dark moods and obsessions
and my only trustworthy insurance against losses,
for if only I have you I know I have the universe,
since all there ever was worth having,
everybody knows, is love.

The inexpressibility of love

Let there be no day without a love poem to you,
my only and immortal love and muse of beauty,
but I humbly beg your pardon when at times I fail,
but let those momentary instances then be the more expressive
of the actual inexpressibility of my true love

that can not even hide itself by silence.
That is actually the truest form of love expression,
the sincerest touch of silence,
tenderer than any language of sweet words
and never able of misunderstandings.
Let me love you thus in silence of eternity,
and let that silent language bloom in tenderness
to last forever even longer than the sweetest poems
of the sweetest love that ever was expressed.

The secret of your beauty

It is not only that you were so loved and lovable
but that you were so much of that not just by anyone;
but there was someone closer to you even than myself
who loved you self-effacingly and all through life
until it ended with a broken heart.
That heart must never be forgotten,
especially not now, when it has passed away
transcended and transformed into a spirit
even more profoundly loving, self-effacing and adoring
that peculiar beauty and intensity of yours
amounting to a beauty that can turn just anyone into a madness
of psychotic and exaggerated, self-consuming reckless love,
as if the element of beauty by its mere existence
must result in unintentional but endless reckless cruelty.
I will not go into that trap but all the same remain your lover
most respectfully and humbly to enjoy the highest privilege
of being just your best and closest friend.

Beyond love

How could you ever doubt me?
How could my sincere love give you such misgivings?
Was my honesty not honest quite enough,
was my sincerity too clouded in the shyness of sincerity,
were my deep feelings not profound enough to be convincing,
was my love not clear enough to be considerable
and as such be taken seriously?
But you see only deep into the soul and heart
for which the outward spoken language and appearances
do not mean anything compared to what you see inside;
and that is maybe ultimately my reward,
that you cared nothing for my courting

but the more for the endurance of my soul.
I should be grateful, then, that finally you found my soul
beyond all mountains of expressions of my love.

Twilight love

It never fades.
The sun will never set
on the eternal twilight of true love
that constantly glows warmer
with eternity that never fades.
So shall I dream of you forever
never waking from the sweetness
of that lingering sentimentality
of an eternal sunset
that but keeps on growing in maturity and beauty,
fascination and intensity the more it keeps on lasting
like a dream that no one ever wanted to awaken from
and no one ever really needed to.

Within

We are within each other
and therefore cannot lose each other
being both together in each others' minds
completely stuck forever,
independent of what happens,
independent of deceit and jealousy,
completely independent both
and simultaneously dependent
and most desperately so
of this our co-dependence.
Your chief worry is: How will this end?
With all our troubles, sorrows, griefs and worries,
how can anything come out of it of any good,
how could it possibly end well,
when there is nothing but adversity ahead of us?
Let's leave it and just live,
since we at least do have each other,
at least for the moment;
but all eternity is just a moment,
and if our momentary love be true,
then this small moment of togetherness
is greater and more worth than all eternity.

Pining

The worst of all outrageous suffering
is never to get through with love
but always desperately having it grow worse
disastrously encouraged by its disappointments
and preposterously nourished by its shortcomings,
as if the rule was, the more tragic, and the worse it goes,
the more uphill and torturous the Via Crucis must become
which never ends by death in spite of all the crucifixions.
Could it then be even worse than what it is already?
That's the ultimate and utter irony,
that when it couldn't any more get more unbearable,
then it will simply double in excruciating pain and trouble
and just start all over from a fresh and worse beginning.
How, then, can we stand all this, we tortured lovers?
That's the greatest mystery of all, that we just carry on
and start from the beginning every time again;
and thus the world and life and love goes on
in agonies increasingly forever.

After the storm

Somewhere beyond the horizon
something is clearing up,
beyond the hurricane waves
a ship is coming in
after shipwrecks and losses galore
after the storm of the blackest clouds,
and on the shore someone is waiting.
What corpses aboard, what losses,
how many are missing never to be found?
It doesn't matter. The only important thing
is that the storm is over and the ship is back,
whether with bad news or good,
for better or for worse
is nothing compared to the one fact
that at least someone has survived.

Reconciliation

Let us never meet
without there being music from the stars around us,
without both of us together smiling,
without mutual harmony encompassing the universe
and without only love between us.
Let us always meet
without there being tears and grief in our souls,
without destructive strife embittering our lives,
without clouds of anger hanging anywhere about
and without anyone of us not being in the mood
for love and creativity, for joy and constructivity
and for being fully open to each other
without any reservations
as regards the truth of everything
and most of all of our love.

Perilous flight

Don't you know me any more?
You claim you are not there when you are there,
you are not reachable at home when you are home,
your spirit is dispersed and vanished out of sight
in constant flight, escaping from the troubles of mundanity,

evading the ridiculous controversies of childishness,
like all controversies forever were and are,
just soaring on the wings of music, harmony and beauty,
while the worries grow beneath you, reaching for you,
like an evil silent octopus in merciless indifferent greed
seeks out the swimmer to engulf him in the abyss
of the tragedy of life, that none of us escapes forever.
I will not disturb you but protect you in your flight
in preparation safely on the ground
to watch you like a guardian angel
not from above but under you
to be your catcher in the rye
and keep you up by stronger winds on firmer wings
than any bird or butterfly or angel ever used;
since I am always flying with you,
not on wings of vain escape
but reaching ever forward
for the light of love that never fails.

Your grave

The grass is fragrant on your grave
and grows increasingly forever green
to match the generosity you always showed yourself
to everyone who knew you, without any one exception.
That is lingering around us in the air,
your love that never failed but made you stay
in spite of your atrocious sufferings and pain
among us on and on, until no love could hold you any longer
from exploding out into the universe
to there continue flowing generously
all around us, which we feel still more than clearly
and are grateful for, and will remain so,
for as long as there will still be anyone among us
to remember you with the identical warm love
that always marked your personality
to make it unforgettable as an example
for your friends and relatives to cling to,
since that love is bound to never die.

My bleeding heart

The softness of my heart is bleeding for you constantly.
Where is that music gone that used to sing for you?
Where is that melody that whispered in my ear:
"You love her more than you can tell forever."?
Where is all that softness gone, that I enjoyed so much
in endless nights of wallowing in sensual orgies
of all universal passion let insanely loose
in ecstasies of beauty, happiness and madness?
When at last may I express my love to you as you are worth it
with my limitless and bottomless profound respect
immersed, bound up together with my total passion
of sincerity and endless worship of your soul and body?
I will not destroy you, only worship you and love you
and much rather perish all alone and far away from you

at a safe distance in my self-consuming passion
than risk hurting any of the frailty of your tender feelings.
Let me love you, nothing can stop me from doing so,
but let me never risk trespassing any of your wounds
that I will never be the one to hazard opening again.
My touch of love will be the softest that a lover ever felt,
I must insist on reassuring you, since I know better
than most lovers what it feels to bleed to death
just of a tender loving heart that loves too much
and never can stop doing so in self-consuming
self-inflicted voluntary crucifixion
of a love that knows no bounds of passion.

The morning after

That night with you I was exhausted
and no good for you, for love, for anything
in my irritability that could not stop
just being worn out good for nothing,
but my love was there still aching
in my heart and bleeding desperately,
calling for you, longing for you urgently
to come and help me in my agony
of bitterness, delusion and remorse
for all that life of mine that failed
and turned me into just a miserable beggar.
Sorry, Madame, and I beg your pardon
that I was not good enough for you,
but still I love you more than ever,
even though I am the only one convinced of that.

Bedlock

The sun is not so bright
as you are when you rise
in all your glory from your bed
transmitting beauty with your light
more wonderful than any blessings shed
from any queen of beauty by surprise.
Childishly I must surmise
that you transcend all lovely hours fled
of pleasures passed and gone in flight
while I remain with you till sunrise

going on until we die and wed
to never leave each other more in bed.
Thus, my love, I cherish thee to madness
nevermore to fade in sadness.

The honourable suicide

He didn't mean to, but it just went on that way.
He just loved life his own way,
scrapping his career, abandoning himself
to ecstasy alone, the joy of living,
making all the best of it to the extreme,
maniacal perhaps and drunk most of the time,
but always beautiful as character and lovable,
the handsomest of young men in his prime,
a prophet when advanced in years
surviving constantly himself and all his falls,
disasters, rehabilitations, pitfalls, accidents,
and so on, an incurably consistent Via Crucis
until finally he just could no more get up on his feet,
gave up and died a total wreck in bed.

Did he do wrong, in scrapping all this world
and caring nothing fot its global suicide,
openly refusing any part of its destructive stress,
denouncing all responsibility for a diseased society
and just determinedly in flying colours partying
his whole life unto death? He did the best of it
and more, and everybody loved him.

Aliens

We are exposed as aliens,
we who see the folly of the world,
the superficial madness of its stress,
the lemming universal self-destruction
of a civilization that gave up the pursuit of ideals
to just go down the drain of egoism instead,
to wallow in the vanity of mundane satisfaction.
Cry not for yourself but for the world.
We are the chosen ones charged with the burden
to look through the mortal universal folly,
an unbearable and painful plight,

but we are not the ones to be despised and pitied.
We who see the blind go down the abyss of destruction
by their own will, tempted by the noise of mass hysteria,
following the garish lure of the attraction of insanity,
and can not do anything about it
but observe the way of bolting flesh,
are charged with the atrocious heaviness
of having to survive the constant fall of vainty
and see the builders of sand-castles ever fail
to start again constructing mirages of self-deceit.
We are in fact as outcast exiles privileged,
since we are free from the asylum of civilization,
free as spirits to be natural and plain
and shedding no tears for ourselves but for humanity.

Technical problems

It's not that I don't love you
less for keeping out of bed.
The problem is, we never sleep
together when we are in bed
together, since you do not sleep
when working hard in bed,
which gets you tired out
sometimes the entire day that follows,
so you can't do anyting
and least of all be diligent
and get things done efficiently,
since you at work keep falling
constantly asleep. And thus we have a problem.
Work or love? We can't have both
and must have both, at least must I;
so pardon me, my love, for loving you the more
for keeping out of bed too much
to save my energy to just enable us
the better to sustain our love.

The opposite of love

There is no opposite of love,
since love encompasses all opposites
and neutralizes them,
transforming them

from any misemotion to emotion,
from destruction to construction
and from hardness and frustration
to benevolence and harmony.
The only indispensability is empathy,
the cause and mother of all dialogue,
by which all arguments can reach a deal,
by which all disagreements can be well agreed upon
and which transforms all petty introversion
to the peace of universal tolerance.
It's easy thus to solve all problems intellectually
that only seem so hopeless practically.

Looking back

What happened to our love,
that magic of so long ago
in such a different dimension
of romantic timelessness and rosy ecstasy?
Are we already grown so old
that we no longer can remember
how we used to love exorbitantly
leaving all the world and history behind us?
Must maturity be so confounding
that it alienates us from the truth of what we were?
No, nothing can take that away from us.
The magic not just lingers but continues
and expands to grow forever in magnificence
as long as we just keep it and allow it to remain
in beauty what it was created once to be
to stay with us for aye in future.

Grace

The sensitivity and delicacy of your love
did more than overwhelm me from the start.
Who am I to be so much loved by you
of so much more experience and sagacity,
maturity and order in your mind,
while I was just a lost and weeping orphan
downed in abysses of love with no way out
except my tears and horrible self pity.
What is my love matched with yours,

how could I ever make myself deserve it,
and how could I live up to your expectations?
I am lost in love and find no guidance
out of my predicament of personal disasters
but the grace of your nobility and kindness
for which I am much more grateful
than I ever will be able to requite it.

No compromise

How can you be confined
in this so mortal pettiness
of dwindling circuits of your mind
caused by incessant worries
just for nothing but your vanity
of being stuck in vicious circles
of outrageous ignorance and bleak mundanity?
When you should be the freest of them all,
creative and constructive infinitely,
flying higher than the blithest spirit,
soaring ever further off from negative considerations?
Love can never breathe except in freedom,
and that freedom must be total or no life at all,
that is the ultimatum ultimate of love,
and there can be no compromise;
for if you find love compromising,
that's the surest diagnosis that it's dying.

Cheer up!

(The bombs in London and Glasgow will not stop the rain…)

What does it matter if it rains,
as long as you are out of shoes
so that the water doesn't stay
but runs out of your naked sandals
keeping your cold feet not sweating?
What's the difference if you fail
in everything as long as you keep going,
never minding all those fools
that try to sabotage your life for nothing,
making trouble only for themselves?
What does it matter if you get kicked out of work,

since you can do much better work
at home at ease and by yourself?
What does it matter if you're out of money
since it doesn't pay to get rich anyway,
since envy only will insist on robbing you
and riches and possessions just will give you worries?
What's the difference? There is nothing,
everything will end up anyway
with nothing you can take away with you,
for life and destiny will finally get even,
and there's nothing you can do about it.

Dark clouds

The storms are heavy gathering against us
with a fulsome terror of infernos,
conflicts, illness, poverty, controversy,
depression, enmity, abuse and what not,
and the only answer seems to be to flee, to run away;
but you can never run away from your own fate.
It's there in all its horror of an overwhelming challenge
like a goblin waiting constantly around the corner
for the pleasure of abusing you and take you by surprise
again and ever and again, and you are never up to it.
What can one do? The only sensible good thing to do
is not to worry, not to care about it, since it only will grow worse
the more you think of it and brood on it
and spend your sleepless nights on it in vain;
for that foul fate will never leave you with its challenge,
it will just stick on to you until you have survived it,
which you always will do in the end, if only you sustain it
and face up to it and never flinch; for in the end
the victory is yours, since death will not just fool us all
but even all our destinies.

Our Case

(documentary amid incessant rains…)

Sorry to be critical,
but being realistic can not harm us
but might rather help us. None of us is quite content,
and there are many reasons why.

OCTOBER HARVEST FIRST PART.

You did receive my love from the beginning
but did never answer it,
since all you did last summer was to cry for Benny.
Your relationship with him,
that you just couldn't leave him
although he just caused you pain and suffering by his alcoholism
was the first thing separating me from you.
The second thing was your affair with Sean,
which almost killed me, since I had loved you so much
and you gave what you had to him, - for nothing,
for a painful persecution by his phoney pregnant lady.
How could I then after such a blow and undeserved experience
even risk to trust you any more? I just resigned,
accepting to be no more than your friend.
The Bernard incident was yet another set-back,
you allowed him what was never granted me,
and I had to content myself with being just locked out
from your intimacy and privacy, while he
was taking liberties and even at the hospital
by our dying patient's bed, and almost boasted of it.
I had nothing personal against him, he did admirable things
by helping you in dreadful difficulties,
which I actually was grateful for,
since I, as always, was intimidated by my poverty.
He over-stepped it, so it is a finished chapter,
while you still are occupied with grief for Benny.
Yes, I have my faults and foibles also,
being too much burdened by responsibilities that I can not let go,
too busy with sustaining the eternal battle against poverty, adversity and age,
so that I never can spend so much time with you as I would want to,
that is maybe our fate, that neither of us can let go of our past and destiny,
but still I can't deny that you are part of me and of my life,
and that I can not do without you, least of all in my thoughts,
my mind, my soul, my heart, my everything except my body.
That alone has no demand of you.

Thus have I tried here to define and pinpoint
the complexity of our relationship.
If I have failed and done you some injustice,
I apologize and humbly ask your pardon and excuse,
but I have tried at least to be completely honest with myself
and made a truthful effort of explaining how I love you
out of the deep agony of constant sleeplessness
and worries for your l ife and situation.

Turbulence

The bumpy ride of life
is apt to normally get bumpier,
and there is nothing you can do about it.
There is music, and you have to face it,
because, if you don't, it'll still be there
to challenge and disturb you even more
if you suppress it or don't want to hear.
Let's face it. You are desperately lost in love,
the turbulence keeps harrowing your soul
and sabotaging all your life,
your worries bring you to the worst,
and passion tears apart your flesh,
while humid nights of filth grow into constant nightmares
which get constantly more difficult to wake up from,
and you are lost, completely at a loss and almost dead.
So what? Keep at it, struggle on,
and somehow you'll get out of bed
on shaky legs and get into your bar
to fill a steady glass that gets spilled out,
but some day it will all be finished anyway.
Keep loving, and keep tormenting yourself,
keep working, suffering and dying slowly day by day,
and one day, maybe, there will be some change...

Passion the enemy of love?

— Perhaps the most debatable of problems
in the tricky jungle mess of problems
when it comes to love and its intricacies
of problems, of which most can not be solved.
The passion is both the finale, climax, crisis,
the supreme manifestation and the evidence
of love's mortality and passing vanity.
It triumphs but must fade,
it is supreme in ecstasy, delight and wonder
but gives pain as well, remorse and guilt
and can not be survived without deep wounds.
It's never recommended, everyone is grave about it,
dissuading, warning and advising all against it,
and still everyone - without exception -
falls into the trap and usually gets stuck forever.
It's a comedy of tragic consequences
and a tragedy with comic outcome,

tragi-comedy and comic tragedy,
and it always leads into a mess.
Well, snakes do like it well in snake-pits,
while some virgins manage to evade the question,
while most people simply acquiesce, accept
and passively submit to constant battle,
which, as some observe with some relief,
is finally rewarded with some liberation,
the most natural escape and ultimate solution
to all problems, namely the simplicity of death.

The End

Is it then the end of our relationship,
the end of all the turbulence,
the end of all disasters and upsets,
the end of all your tears and all my worries,
or is this where it begins?

Can we forget the awkward follies and mistakes
and just go on as if it never really happened,
all that madness and confusion of aborted love,
the aberration of misdirected and wasted love,
the self-deceit, the blindness to reality,
the horrible fixation on trivialities and pettiness,
the anger and frustration and irrationality,
the hubris of idiotic egoism -
can we just disregard it all,
pretending that it never happened?
No, we can not change the tragedies of yesterday,
but we should keep them well in mind
to learn from them not to commit the same mistakes again,
as if we could do better than all history,
the expert on incurability
regarding constantly repeated worsened follies.

Tiredness

Let me rest my tired head
away from all this mess of failures
of this hopelessly misguided world,
so lost, abused and hopelessly astray,
away from all my headaches
of consistent troubles and that crown of thorns,

that keeps on hurting me forever,
in a vain and hopeless search for peace,
in this world something unattainable
except in death and dreams, sometimes, –
but even your door is now closed to me,
your lap is sealed, and I shall nevermore find peace.
Who is the victor, then?
Who has brought home the game?
Who is content? Is anyone at all at ease
and happy? No, when love has lost
by deadly insults and frustrations
and communications fail,
so that the troubled partners can no longer speak,
then we are losers all,
and there is nothing left
in this whole world but losses.

Empathy in absurdum
(documentary)

You don't have to nurse him,
he is all responsible himself
for all his mess of two divorces with three children
and his constant falls to bleak alcoholism.
I can not see why self-destructiveness of any kind
deserves one's pity, care, edification, nursing,
spoiling, wasted time and effort,
not to speak of energy, both moral and creative,
which is better used for other purposes;
since he, as long as he continues falling down,
inevitably will fall deeper down each time
and drag his friends down with him if they pity him
for no good end at all. Professional support
to help him pull himself together
is the only thing that could be practically good,
while friends and lovers of him
just will go down on their knees
and cry their hearts out all in vain
by joining him on his way down into the abyss
of the sorrows of despair and voluntary self-destruction.
I have work to do and must therefore keep out
and can not join you in a charitable work
that could be just a waste if it is not professional.
Sorry, but you'll need my healthy unharmed friendship
when you are down there dissolved in tears.

Too sensitive for love

When love strikes deep into the heart
it takes some time to understand it,
the digestion is the hardest of them all,
and if it's real you'll never quite get over it.
Some people get too hurt too deeply
simply by emotionally taking it too seriously,
they are the truest lovers,
but the truest lovers bleed the most.
Should they then be exempt from love
and try by any means to stay away from it?
Unfortunately, yes, that is the answer,
for their own sakes; but their comfort is,
that they will learn to understand the human heart
more thoroughly than any active lover,
feeling more from their antennae and their empathy
than any lust can satisfy the sexual human feelings.
Being thus so much more understanding of the human heart,
they also can bring so much more rewarding love.

Bohemian nostalgia

– 7.7.07, an important historical date for the universal peace demonstration going on in a world wide musical manifestation against the abuse of nature...

Where are they all,
the ghosts of yesterday,
the pioneers of beauty,
introducing freedom with some vehemence
and starting this new weird romanticism
of limitlessness and exaggeration
in both love and freedom
and with nothing to restrain
the urge of personal expression?

Most of you are dead and gone and buried
in the aftermath of adventurers' recklessness
in experimentation of transcendence
breaking every single barrier down.

I'm talking of the prophets of that universal peace
movement back in the sixties
against Johnson, Nixon and all militarism
to launch as an alternative just freaking out
in love and nature and just being what you are.
They were all right, all those now long since dead,
and their right will remain and carry on
just going on for that eternal quest of constant victory.

The righteous hubris of life

Hubris is allowed and sacred
and not punishable nor subject to nemesis
nor even touchable when it is raised by love
which keeps it flying high with every right
that nothing can put down nor has a right to.
That love made of and sustained by truth and beauty
stands outside mundane restrictions, limitations and dimensions
and can not be violated, persecuted, questioned,
ciriticized, assailed or even analyzed
since it is extraordinarily and altogethet a most different thing
from all things mortal, trivial and normal.
Sticking out is what will mark it,

and the more it ostentatiously sticks out,
the more admirable it is for being individual and personal
and showing off a splendid hubris of integrity,
which must not have or know of any bounds
but must be limitlessly free forever,
since all life depends on it.

Love at work

— an apology

Pardon me for my objectionable absence,
my neglecting your predicament and needs,
my mad obsession with my work,
like a hysterical fanaticism,
but, dear, believe me, all my work
is just for love. If you could see and understand
the love I put in it, express in it
and manifest in everything I do at work,
you would forgive me, and you might then even realize
that I never leave you for a moment,
and not even when I am at work
as far away from you as possible,
which, paradoxically, only brings me nearer
to my love, which is, as always, only you.

When the tears have dried from your face

When the tears have dried from your face,
you will see that there is still some sunshine
after all, and after quarrels, griefs and outbursts
love will still remain magnanimously
to embrace you with her wings
to fly away with you once more
across the ocean of all human tears
that keep on flowing for all universal griefs
but all in vain, because the sun will still be shining,
and your love will still be smiling
crying more for beauty than for grief
and for the lack and longing
of that true love which will just keep on remaining
out of reach, but anyway, at least in actuality.

The worst waste of time

There are many ways to waste your time,
but the supremely worst is only one,
and you'll experience it from time to time
and ever be at it again,
like falling constantly into the worst of traps;
and every time you say again,
protesting violently to yourself:
"Never again!" And yet,
you are most certain to experience it again
and yet again and ever and again.
The situation is the classical predicament
of waiting for your lady punctually
in good time after making an appointment,
and she never comes.
You wait and wait, and nothing happens,
still you wait, you must give her a chance,
and, intolerably and ironically true,
the longer you will wait for her,
the less she will appear,
no matter how your worry constantly gets tenser.
It's a hopeless situation.
You will always wait for her in vain
when you have made a well agreed upon appointment
and she just will not appear.

One night of love

One night with you
is all I need to live forever
on that memory of bliss and ecstasy
that never gets exhausted
but replenished constantly
by merely thinking of it
and its glorious creation
of new life and feelings,
thanks to life and blessings,
and enjoyment lasting
longer than eternities
from just one night,
one moment's bliss;
and that is all I need

occasionally
to survive as what I am,
a soul and body
made of only love.

Forget about my funeral

Don't wait for me at my funeral,
because, as always, I'll be late.
Perhaps I even will have mislaid my body
and forgot to lay down in a coffin,
but most probably I'll just be busy elsewhere
and have forgotten all about time,
missing all the important appointments
with my friends at the funeral,
who will all have come in vain.
So don't appear at my funeral,
because I won't be there myself.
The 'late deceased' will be as late as usual.

Looking up death

It's only healthy to communicate with death,
to pay occasional brief visits
and associate on friendly terms,
go through this utter darkness now and then
like passing through a dreadful sauna,
which, if you come out again,
will only be refreshing.
Likewise, if you come back out alive
from looking up the black hole of despair
of meeting death and being friends with him,
you'll just feel better afterwards,
like Christ after his crucifixion and his resurrection.
It can't be any worse than that.

A drinking love song

Make me drunk, so I may stay with you
not only overnight but always,
fence me in in your embrace
and let me love you evermore

to delight continuosly in the prison of your person,
make me a convict for your life
and let us sit in there together
just for pleasure in the best of prisons
of our temple of delirious worship
of your beauty and my own
and of the truth of our remaining love
which just miraculously seems to ever grow
to spite us with astonishing incredibility
growing faster and much more
than just over our heads...

A love divided

We never spend enough of our time together,
and I never can love you enough,
which doesn't mean my love is failing,
only faltering, because of circumstances,
this condition of world liability
when life itself is irresponsibly at risk
by the extravagance of mankind
using Mother Earth much worse than any parasite,
ruthlessly gobbling up all natural resources by our greed.
I never want to love that way, consume for selfish reasons,
use and never give, but rather the plain opposite,
just giving, sharing and bestowing for a long term future,
since I feel that even love is all in vain
if it is not from the beginning stabilized in lasting continuity.
Therefore, pardon me, that we don't meet as much as we should do,
while you may rest assured, that any visual absence of this presence
only means my love, put under a protective bushel,
burns the warmer for not being free.

The death visit

One day when you least expect it
you will have a knock on your door
of no one that can be identified,
and so you wonder who he is
and keep on wondering
until you understand him.
Then he will remain your constant visitor
to every now and then come knocking

for a deadly visit out of darkness
to initiate you in the secret of black holes,
the other side of life, that no one wants to hear of
since it is not very social.
But it's there, and once you've come to know it
you will be a frequent guest,
like that friend coming knocking at your door
indefinitely constantly and every now and then
to drag you down into the abyss of depression,
the supreme despair and anguish
which each time will leave you
even dirtier as a squeezed out rag
completely wasted and consumed,
but that is part of life,
which all the same continues
like a constant show just going on
ignoring what takes please behind the curtains,
which is of no consequence to what's on stage,
although it is the manager and runner of the show.

How far can you go?

(Violation is the only loser...)

How far can you push a relationship?
Not any longer than it hurts,
and violence is certain death;
but as long as you keep up constructiveness
feeling your way with discretion
and using with delicacy your antennae
to never drive anyone over
and not risk trespassing or going too far
and not importuning, you can go at any length
and never risk even hurting the other one's feelings.
The secret is being considerate,
which, if you are, can keep any relationship going
and lasting forever and longer.

The tragedy of love

Why is it that true love is frequently a tragedy
that ends when it seems almost there
to reach the ultimate fulfilment,
like as if love was always the last verse,
the final end that has its limits
or must simply end when it has reached perfection.
It doesn't seem quite fair,
that so much effort, labour and hard energy
should be so generously wasted
just to be abandoned in the end
as something that no longer could be added to.
Or is the meaning, that love always has the final word,
and that it therefore must be terminated
and left off as soon at his has spoken out?
In either way, at least, love does remain
for always the most unforgettable of matters
and just for that reason, all that really matters.

Is it possible?

Is it possible that you could love me
as much as I love you?
Is it possible that all my anguish
about you could actually be shared
by you and equalled?
Is it possible that I one day
could finally get through to you
and gain your understanding
for my hopeless case
of only yearning, longing, languishing
and melting into tears for nothing
but the thought of you and your benevolence?
My yearning is unconquerable except by you;
and you shall have it one day
served to you on golden plates
more exquisite than any delicacy
melted all into a dish of love
of never-ending and unlimited perfection.
Is that possible?
Yes, anything is possible,
but only for true lovers.

The Hell of Paradise

Love is longer than eternity
but all too brief a moment
of a second's bliss,
when you would want to stay forever
with your love and never leave her,
whereupon you must depart
on all too short a notice –
there is never any union without separation.
Still you enter her and want to stay there
to enjoy forever, but it is a prison
which you must get out of to your freedom –
there is never any love without entanglement,
imprisonment and bondage,
and to live with it at all you got to have your freedom.

Thus it is with love, extremest contrasts all the time,
a roller-coaster of incessant turbulence
that ever shifts dynamically from despair to ecstasy,
and there is only one thing certain about love –
it never can be boring.

Love's labour's labyrinths

What next, my love?
We cannot love each other more,
but still we do, continuously growing
and accelerating to exasperation
while expanding and exploring
our development as two in one,
each following the other's changes
with excitement and exhaustion.
No one knows where it will all end up,
this thriller of suspension
of a different kind of love
that in its sovereign sublimity
transcends all mortal measures
to reach higher pleasures
than are thinkable in bed.
Let's just continue
turning over constantly new leafs
to never, at least, become bored
by this continuous development
of ever more astounding character.

OCTOBER HARVEST FIRST PART.

Illness

Struck down by lightning
you can no longer show yourself in public,
being too ashamed of all infirmities,
your invalidity, your bitter mood,
your anguish and frustration
and, the worst of all, your pains.
It hurts to be forced out of order,
suddenly you feel unworthy of your life,
you can not bear with anything,
and all the things you want to do
you feel completely incapacitated of.
Your only comfort is that it is passing,
just a crisis and perhaps a transformation to improvement,
like all bad things mortal and most temporary,
like transcending death itself.

No time for love

That I am busy working hard
does never mean my love is less
but rather grows by challenges
of absence, distance and adversity.
The more I am debarred from you,
the more, in fact, I love you,
and although you can not see it,
there are other means of feeling it
and of communication,
since for love impossibility does not exist.
Telepathy is the more useful
for its application difficulty,
and if we are kept apart persistently,
it certainly will prove the easiest way
to get around and spite all limits.
For there is no way for love to ever get inhibited
since it will burst all locks and dams forever.

Our dance of love and death

The goddess triumphs in her dance
of love and death across the centuries
and aeons of destruction and construction,

ever resurrecting everything,
and ever baffling all mankind and history
in cycles of millennias and millennias,
unperturbed and totally indifferent
to the ways and follies and destructions of mankind.
She just keeps dancing on;
but it is the eternal dance of love,
that ever goes on, starting now and then
again from the beginning,
like a cosmic hide-and-seek game,
letting all the world dance to her whims,
her unstoppability, aloofness and capriciousness
dictating all the laws of nature and the universe,
and there is nothing we can do:
just go on dancing,
tantalized and tempted
constantly again to her destruction;
and the only thing we can do
is, like all the world in all its folly,
to enjoy it.

The balance and unbalance of love

Love is basically out of balance in itself,
which makes it so extremely difficult
to ever get it in control and balance,
if at all it ever could be possible.
The question is, if even it is worth
the effort and the vanity of trying.
On the other hand, when love is balanced
it is perfect, then it works, can be relied on
and can actually retain some continuity,
but it's a most precarious balance
on a razor's edge of nervousness
and worry, oversensitivity and constant risk,
that then it needs your whole attention
and can never be, like a good book,
relaxed from, put aside and laid at rest.
Love never sleeps,
and lovers are insomniacs all,
and if you want that game and pleasure,
be prepared to never sleep again.

Unattainability

An abstract poem about abstract things,
the unattainability of any true ideal,
like any true and honest lasting love
is there and within reach for all its unattainability
and for that very reason: it would not be true
or there or honest or forever lasting
if it was not unattainable.
So there is nothing wrong in living
for such an absurdity,
or trying vainly and intrepidly to reach it
since it is there within reach
because of its consistent unattainability,
and as long as it is unattainable
it will be there and last forever,
unattainability remaining always out of reach
but for that very reason always reached for.

An endless quarrel over nothing

– Comment on the great Shakespeare authorship controversy on the Internet (HLAS)…

The debate has now been going on
for some eleven years of endless quarrelling
about who really wrote the works of Shakespeare
which has now produced some 25,000 discussions,
in which one theme has been dominant:
the meanness of Stratfordians slugging any opposition
with a thuggee might by any means destroying any effort
at alternative ideas and theories and research
trying honestly to offer better explanations to the problem
of the most unsatisfactory representation
of an amateur illiterate and phoney upstart from the country
as the master of the finest poetry yet written
in the English language, while in fact all other theories
are much more satisfactory, convincing and make better sense.
But since they can't be proven, the Stratfordian meanness
arrogantly pursues and assumes the right of keeping up the bully attitude
defending the establishment at any cost,
persisting in maintaining that there's only one side to the truth,
ignoring and suppressing that there are more sides to any truth
than ever can be grasped, encompassed or suspected.

Meanwhile, the works keep marching on
completely unperturbed by academic quarrels,
living their own lives of masks and set-up characters
and never quarrelled over, as if their creator,
that most dubious enigmatic and evasive author
never had existed. And perhaps that was the very aim
and purpose and intention, let alone desire of the author.

If you still can love her...

If you still can love her
after seeing her each morning
long before her toilet make-up
naked to the soul unmasked
with wrinkles, warts and all
in her worst temper and most boring mood,
if you have come to know her all that deep
and still must keep her in your heart
in love that rather grows than fades
in spite of all her weakness and confusion,
then, my friend, you are completely lost
but fortunately only in for love,
which rather is a victory than any loss.

The lover

That I loved you no one can deny,
and that I loved you deeply I confess
and even that I love you still and more than ever,
but in my own way, without insulting,
without causing hurts and without importuning
stealing furtively into your heart
with smoothness and discretion without friction,
so that you would never know,
and no one else would notice either for that matter,
that I was the man who visited your bed
as your true only lover, never to abandon it
but being always there at hand at any time.
So will I keep you up, my love,
sustaining what we both need most of all,
the very stuff that made us
which we can not do without
which only truest lovers ever dared to dream of
and which we possessed from the beginning.

MAGNUS AURELIO

Resistance

Love is never stronger and more vital
in its growth, expansion and dynamic
than when it is thwarted and resisted,
nothing being more character edifying
than adversity and trial. I am not afraid.
Come whatever, and I will face up to it
with you and keep you covered and supported
by the most infallible and powerful of weapons,
which of course is love, which never runs out,
never can run out of ammunition.
We have everything together
which includes the world and all our dreams
encompassing the world in magic beauty of our love
which nothing can pervade or permeate
but which can only blissfully expand
to never cease enlarging freedom limits.

Why philosophers don't marry

"The maturest lovers best fit for marriage are philosophers, but philosophers don't marry."

- Arthur Schopenhauer

Philosophers don't marry
since they love too much and too sincerely
to be a match for mortal love expression,
they take love too seriously to not get hurt
too deeply by the smallest friction and controversy,
they think too much to share the flair of wanton wives,
they are too slow in action while too busy dreaming,
and they never seem to manage to get down to earth
to qualify for the responsibility of mundane business.
Still, they are the best of lovers,
for they take it much more seriously than others,
and their faithfulness is more reliably profound
than can be found in any married couple;
so they stay off marriage just to save their love
for honesty and faithfulness of everlasting value,
growing and expanding constantly in more potential
than can be confined in any mortal flesh.

Your faces

– a double-faced woman is usually multiple

Which face of yours is true,
or is it as I would suspect,
that all your masks are true as faces,
counterfeiting masks to hide your delicate vulnerability,
thus protecting you from falseness and attack
by simply being truer than what anyone could think
is possible for you to be?
Men usually regard all women with suspicion,
almost taking it for granted that they must be false
and therefore needs deserve debasing treatment,
while the opposite more often than not is the case,
that ladies take in and accept the denigration
by their love to make their misled men think better and improve
and thus learn love for real by women's aching hearts
of self-effacement for the sake of love and life.
Your mask of beauty is more real then
than the faces hid beneath it,
which are the more interesting
for their ability of such variation.

Depression

– July in Sweden has caused havoc by constant furious rainfalls, like in England...

The depression is like some infectuous disease
disastrously affecting anyone with fits of anguish
making them burst out in tears in worse cascades
than the incessant rains bombardings us with fury,
drowning us in misery, bereaving us of summer,
so that frail hearts break up and dissolve in desperation,
and no medicine, no treatment, nothing helps,
since all these rains just keep on falling down,
as if to drag all makind down in torrents of disaster
in some kind of new flood just beginning...
Cheer up! We still have our hearts and souls,
the music of persistent universal harmony can never be shut down,
for even if the melodies are drowned in squalls of noise
and the world menace and infection of disharmony,
the true heart will still go on singing
if for nothing else at least for love.

Requiem for a Dead Poet

Keats, Shelley, Rupert Brooke, Wilfred Owen, and others...
(Rupert Brooke fell on Shakespeare's birthday 23rd April 1915, 28 years old, his birthday was on August 3rd, and Shelley's on August 4th.
Wilfred Owen fell on the western front one week before armistice 1918, 25 years old.)

It's a constantly recurring problem,
the divinely gifted poet who just disappears,
without a reasonable explanation
quite unfairly and without justification
as if his name really had been writ in water,
leaving after him a terrible bereavement
and a sense of loss that must remain forever;
and it's worse each time it happens,
whether sailed away and taken by the storm
exactly when life's fortune starts to smile with health and happiness,
or exiled in the trenches to the last place any human being would deserve
to serve as cannon fodder for the universal vanity
of human martial madness executing poets with conductors,
painters with composers, artists, architects and ballet dancers,
mutilating them for life, sentencing them for life as invalids
or sparing them the whole war through to execute them in the end
a few days just before the armistice in wicked irony,
or just expelling them, deleting them for some mistake
that cannot be regretted.
Who is next?
But one thing will remain in all this tragic business,
which is the most irrefutable of unescapabilities,
that poets will be best remembered
who were most cut short and silenced
for no other reason than injustice.

Going in

I would love to love you,
getting lost in that deep darkness of your hair,
the richness of your generosity
and your characteristic mystery
of no end to the bottom of your secrets.
Let me dig them up,
allow me to be thorough in my work
of delving deep into your lair
to sort out all your fascinations

and get so intrigued about it
as to never reaching any end.
That is how love should be,
and which it will be
if you let me love you.

The Days of Wines and Roses

When will they ever come again,
those desirable days of wines and roses
that we had once and enjoyed so thoroughly
but couldn't stick to, since we lost them,
and since then just long for the nostalgia
of sweet dreams of happiness
so long since passed and woken up from?
Still, the sweetness is still there
of our longing and our dreams,
and one day, you can bet on it,
we will be there again enjoying
fully and with sparkling joy each other's company
to stay united then and never leave each other
but for temporary absences alone
while we remain together spiritually
never to get lost again.

Self-destructiveness

It seems to be the illness of the age,
when everyone is hurrying to his doom,
with fury speeded up by isms of every kind
to aid them to some kind of mania,
like alcoholism, addiction of whatever kind,
or, worst of all, the universal stress of workoholism
turning every potent individual to a robot
of manipulated brainwash-stoned efficiency
which makes it quite impossible for anyone
to ever come down straight again
on stable feet with reasonable mind
and the detachment from reality
which is the mark of health and soundness.
So do we hasten to our end in frenzy
in a universal kind of lemming self-destruction

even hurrying up to make it shorter
like a going down Titanic
every minute making worse the torture,
and we do not even seem to mind
but just rush blindly on in no direction
just for the sensation of it,
and that seems to be the motor of all mankind:
that self-destructive urge to hurry to the final fall
that must inevitably come, the sooner and the better.
And that is the greatest folly of them all,
since that's the energy that keeps civilization rolling
headlong downwards but still forward
in a blind chaotic craze of vanity
that is its own most perfect punishment,
since it keeps humankind alive and going
round in circles of insanity of their own making,
sentenced to that doom for life
and all eternity, if they believe in it.

The cruelty of love

True love is never quite requited
but becomes an aching wound to last forever
bleeding inwardly with tears of pain
to always wet your whereabouts,
and that's the company you'll always have,
the substitute of what you lost.
The cruelty of love is like a force of nature
unrelenting and inevitable
striking hard and always from behind
in a surprising deadly ambush
for which you can never be prepared,
a lightning from a clear sky without warning
striking you in silence down to cinders,
leaving you a screaming wreck down in the drain
in utter solitude
with nothing left of all your love
than bitter memories of how it never was fulfilled,
but with the one and lasting comfort,
that it was not you who failed,
since you did really love.

Revelation of a mystery

They wonder who you are,
but I will never tell them,
never give our love away,
the secret of our hearts,
that dwells in shadows of intimacy
beyond the endless maze of seven veils
that hide the strangest secret in the world,
the mystery of love according to our practice
and experience separating us from common knowledge,
particularizing us into a special category
of the rarest lovers,
those that never were found out;
and I will keep you there
concealed forever in my warmest heart
to there be cherished infinitely by my passion
that could never burn more ardently
than what it does for me and you.

Sharing

My love is dead, impossible and faded out,
and still my life is hers as well as mine;
what I am she is also, although far away,
since sharing has become our life.

Disturbance shattered our reunion,
too many shut me out from her,
and still her heart is mine as mine is hers,
as if all that we share is more than life,

the very depths of the abysmal feelings
constantly devouring our souls
and drowning them in feelings inexpressible,
that can't be shared by anyone except your love;

and then you know, that you in spite of all
are still in love and never quite alone,
although your deepest feelings
never can be shared by anyone

except the company you find
deep down at bottom of that loneliness
you always thought you had
but brought you all the world for company.

On the pain of love

My love, our synchronization always failed
as we could never reach each other
no matter how close we got
and intimately straight into each others' souls
to stay there, loving and adoring
but, alas, with no synchronization.
Could it be much worse,
or could it be much better?
There we are, in love and desperately
and can not do anything about it
but just tumble hopelessly around
in roller-coasters constantly derailing
between ups and downs
from tops of heavens to the abysses of hell
and up again and never still
but always wildly bolting

between every possible exaggeration
and delightful dramatization.
Well, I guess it's just for us to carry on,
continue wallowing in absences and presences
and make the best of it,
although it sometimes ends up as the worst.
The lovers' pains dilemma is a syndrome
which, perhaps a comfort,
we will never be alone with
but will share with every lover in the universe.

On a cherished bed of roses...

On a cherished bed of roses
we will do our exploration
in the jungle of each other's hairs,
which, like all nature
and especially all jungles and their freedom,
constantly should be expanded,
long hair meaning generosity
and richness of good will and heart.
And thus would I forever grow your hair
to mark and underscore the meaning of our love
to simply keep developing and growing
with our exploration of it
ever deeper into that rich jungle freedom
of our inexhaustible inalienable love forever.

Love's secret

Love is never stronger
than when guided by a neutral altruism
manipulating anyone unconsciously
to any strange constructive purpose and direction
most astonishing in their results
to the unconscious messenger of love himself.
That is another of love's manifold manifestations,
that it works best silently and underground
without attracting notice, like a mole,
pervading life and people with that destiny
of only good, which is received then naturally
without thanks as something obvious and self-evident.
That love is deepest which remains concealed,
unknown to everyone except the keeper of the secret.

The last hippie

(Documentary. This man actually exists although I never met him myself. The second 'last hippie', a Swede, knows him well though and told me the story.)

He carries on indefatigably
now since thirty years,
that hearty old Italian,
who keeps going on his scooter
all round India, down to Goa wintertime,
in summer up to Ladakh
and in season to Manali
and the hills and their hill stations,
keeping up the old ideals
of freedom, independence,
non-compliance with corruption,
the society of self-deceit called "progress",
sticking to his 'Chaupathi Express',
his ancient scooter,
keeping him above all human worldly problems
in his timeless legendary hippie style,
refusing simply ever to give up
his faith in better sides of life
and in humanity.

(*'Chaupathi' is the famous Indian thin bread.)

Growing old

When you overwork and have too many worries,
naturally you must age and gradually get weary;
but you always can escape from all your troubles
by retreats or taking off on journeys,
getting healthily detached from all your mundane vanities;
and then you notice, when you get your health restored
in healthy relaxation distancing all worldliness,
that age is but a state of mind.
As long as you keep going in your mind and keep it clear
in constant application, work, research and study,
age will never bother you nor sickness,
since your body just will follow suit
and keep adapted to your mind's exertion,
never tiring of constantly more challenges

and feeling only better afterwards for all that strain.
Your soul is all your life, your body is its servant,
just an instrument, the more in use, the better,
since your soul, the motor, like an organ
must be used, since life must never be let down.

Intimate honesty

When I think of you with pleasure and contentment
disregarding all your lacks and wants,
your vanity and lack of human knowledge,
I can but adore you nonetheless
because of all that is so good in you,
your lacks and wants and weaknesses,
your over-sensitivity and bleeding heart,
your limitation in your intact world of beauty,

which however could redeem civilization
with its purity, simplicity and honesty.
I will not let you go, I will not drop you,
since our friendship is a higher thing than ordinary love,
transcending it and leaving it behind;
since there is really such a thing
as love that lasts forever,
being a continuous wonder story
carrying on in constantly new chapters
from one lifetime to another
constantly expanding parallel to that eternity
which can not have an end since it exists.

When I dream of you

When I dream of you
with such a sweetness
of nostalgia and bitter memories
of loss and how we never got a chance,
the timelessness of our love
just makes it more enduring
and more live than even in our youth,
as if our love, in spite of decades of departure,
just kept growing anyway
in beauty and maturity
to never fail but rather spite
all mundane limitations and dimensions;
which for certain proves,
that love is something else and something more
than just a part of general mortality.

To Aliena

A year has passed of our acquaintance,
sister in a destiny of alienation
in a foreign country of no mercy
nor of understanding of a warm mentality,
a country frozen stiff each winter
for five months with every human soul;
but still we carry on intrepidly
and holding forth our light of warmth,
humanity and joy of life,
Italian style, with no end to good humour,

tenderness, positivism and cheerfulness.
We share together the same birthday almost
with some hours' difference only,
which turn us astrologically into twins;
and may we always keep that cheerful course
of parallel good thinking, creativity and love
and joy of life with only the best wishes to all living things,
that they may prosper with ourselves.

The Sea

The first of challenges against my life
was water, which I battled with
courageously against all odds,
failing to get drowned three times
although I did the best I could
in my association with the wildest element
acquiring a sound relationship with it,
so that I never was afraid of giant ocean waves,
the rolling mountains of ferocious foaming fury,
which I just regarded as my friends,
the more imposing and forbidding, the more lovely.
I remained a faithful lover of the sea
thus all my life, and there I might return some day,
to that first battle as a child with death
wherein we might unite one day forever.

Jotunheimen

When I crazy raved around the mountains
of the snowy wilderness of Norway,
way in Rondane in blinding blizzards,
still we carried on like crazy in our vanity
just to get through to Peer Gynt's cottage
somewhere in the wilderness,
beyond all visible geography,
perhaps out there and buried somewhere
in the snows and definitely out of sight.
The snows, the mountains, snowblindness,
the friends I lost out there in sudden storms
with temperatures dropping down to minus 50
in the cruel madness of the wind, –
and still there was a greatness in it all,

to be alone out there in the ferocious wilderness
completely at the mercy of the raving mountains
in the death claws of the glaciers and their traps,
but still you triumphed, roaring out in splendid song
just to be part of it, the greatness of the wilderness,
the glory of the overwhelming odds against you
which in spite of all you managed to survive.

Mother Italy

— a poem of gratitude

I was fourteen when I first came home
to Italy, my culturally native country,
where I never had a warmer welcome,
Rome, Toscana, Venice and Verona
universally accepting me as one of theirs
and not just as a prodigal lost castaway
but as one flesh and blood with them;
and how I loved that suddenly found mother!
With her beauty, splendour, greatness, charm and kindness
I could never be more perfectly at home,
and so I turned into a good and faithful son
more frequently returning every year,
as there is nothing that goes deeper down your roots
than motherhood, when she is all ideal and spiritual.

Rivals

I never was much for a love fight,
always giving up at once
as soon as there were rivals,
not from cowardice, but principally:
love must never be contaminated by brute force,
since any kind of violence is just the opposite
of any kind of love, especially true love.
So let me rather love in silence at a distance
faithfully forever with the most reliable of loyalty
than get involved with fisticuffs, upsetting rivalry,
the animal vulgarity of sexual force,
that only would destroy the whole idea of love
which only can survive as long as it can be preserved
in intact purity of honest truth.

Greece

I always dreamed about that ancient lost civilization,
so sparkling in its splendour and dynamic growth
with suddenly the perfect sense of beauty and of realism
exploding in the arts, in architecture and in literature,
science being born with logic and the art of criticism,
to question everything, to pry and probe and never tire
of investigating, of exploiting curiosity and never be at ease,
the sound refuting of self-satisfaction and of hubris,
giving us the one civilization of philosophy.
My spiritual roots gave never up the ancient Greece
but always stayed there faithfully in spiritual depths
to one day, finally, return and find it still alive
and more inspiring than ever.
Greece is always there, my favourite in Europe,
with her inspiration and undying sparkling spirituality,
renewing and reminding constantly all Europe
of the fact that Europe came to be in Greece
arising, like a whole world of creation, from a myth.
That creativity is for me the most essential Greece
which I will share, support and always be a part of
carrying on the torch, regardless of where and how I may wander.

The highest party

If there is music, there is life
and harmony and beauty,
if the music is well tuned and temperate,
a fugue, a dance, a choir or a symphony,
it knows no bounds but can reach anywhere
to any height of joy and happiness and glory,
beauty being just about the only thing
that always could redeem all mankind,
history and civilization, just by being,
since there is no truer thing than beauty,
which, the more it is endowed with beauty,
is the truer and the more important
as a life-inspiring source of joy
which the more certainly can carry on the world,
sustaining it by being just the essence of all life and soul.

France

The coldness of your intellectualism
was never much of an attraction to me,
cold intelligence for its own sake
more often being cruel and unhuman
than agreeable and positive,
but your poetry is always in the air
with songs galore of wonderful melodic beauty
for which I'll forgive you anything,
you proud capricious France
of too much haughty superiority
based mainly on the vanity of artificialness.
Still, Edith Piaf, Chopin, Victor Hugo, Voltaire,
Jules Verne, Dumas and Baudelaire were all in France
contributing to her poetic spirit
which will last and rule more sovereignly
than all miserable fools just messing up
the troublesome and unsound history of France.

Germany

This mammoth monster of dynamics and complexity
is inexpressible and undefinable as anything specific,
being so exaggerated to extremes in all directions,
in philosophy to reach the ends and bottoms of insanity,
in music unsurmountable, supreme and more than glorious,
in architecture utterly fantastic, when you think of all the castles,
like Neuschwanstein, and the fairy tales of cruel romanticism,
the overstrained excesses of the brothers Grimm and Hoffmann,
the extreme idealism of Schiller and the perfect harmony of Goethe,
best in almost every field but also worst in some –
let's speak more silently of Wagner, Nietzsche, Marx and Hitler,
as if Germany just had to go too far in everything
in order to maintain and manifest herself,
regardless of the consequences.
I prefer to stay away from her, admire her
incredible accomplishments of beauty and romanticism
but never come too close, in order not to risk get burned
but that so unpredictable volcanic flame of genius
that, when it went wrong, just nearly ruined all the world.

Norway

The utter wildness of your wilderness
was always like a dream to me
of magic utterly extreme,
in soaring altitudes to terrifying blizzards
furiously assaulting you like trolls
and offering the mightiest challenges
against your whole existence and your life,
but what a splendid glorious freedom!
Sitting there enthroned on Prekestolen
far above the fiord that stretches out
from one horizon to another far beneath you
in magnetic magic vertigo of horrifying ecstasy,
and you are all alone with all the mountains,
that fantastic giant world of terrors
but of freedom also most of all and beauty,
which inspires you to just go on to higher glaciers,
walking steadily triumphantly across the moors
and swamps, ignoring all the abysses
to keep on course in soundest wilderness
in this most sane and healthy,
challenging and beautiful of Nordic countries.

Tired of love?

When you get tired out of love
it's only the beginning
of another love affair,
since love will never leave you
ever more at peace again
once you have given something up to her,
for she will never give you up,
love being in herself the highest constancy
that never shall abandon you,
no matter how hard you try to abandon her,
no matter for what hard good reasons,
women always turning you into a cuckold
for the loss of time and money
for their shallow company which always ends
by their deceiving you with gayer and less boring,
shallower and temporary lovers of no faith;
while if you really know what love is,
that love shall not leave you ever
but remain as true and constant as a virgin
ever new and fresh and young,
and you shall always find your love again
renewing all your youth and joy of life
with her that never even in her thought
shall lose her trust and faith in you
for that undying love which is the only certainty
you have in life as long as you exist.

Scotland

The land of meanness and of whisky,
stark rationalism and common sense
and splendid clarity in engineering,
with one of the finest capitals in Europe,
tragic freedom fighter never reaching independence,
but heroic nonetheless in all those bloody efforts, –
what a passion play of history
with Mary Queen of Scots a central figure
for all pure romanticism in Europe,
that actually was born in Scotland
with the bard McPherson and his Ossian songs,
resulting in explosions of romanticism all over Europe,
not just with Lord Byron and Sir Walter Scott,

but carried on by Stevenson and Conan Doyle,
two geniuses of clarity and unsurpassed
as brilliant story tellers of inspiring imagination.
Well, your medicine remains the best and most reliable
on earth, for which I always shall remain most grateful,
willingly forgetting your inhospitable meanness
for the splendour of your Highlands
and their dreams of freedom that will never die.

Ireland

Where did that madness come from,
that irrational hysteria of subnormality,
that always coloured Ireland's history with blood
and dreadfully exaggerated tragedies,
which more often than not turned Ireland
to an isle of widows dressed in black and crying,
going on in endless sorrow over senseless sons forever,
while the witless hooligans just keep on sacrificing
lives and families and not just themselves
but innocents in countless numbers above all?
Was it that fatal Irish whisky lethally combined
with catholic fanaticism and superstition,
or that harsh Atlantic climate with incessant rains
three hundred days a year at least,
that always drove the Irish down the drain,
out of their minds and into obligatory alcoholism?
I cannot say. All I can do is cry with all those widows,
sonless mothers, families that lost their fathers
and their brothers and their children
for no good at all, as if the lunacy of violence
was reason in itself for any self-destruction.

Portugal

Wondrous little country of the sea,
with such an intimate relationship
of all your ages with that vastness
of the utmost depths of all the world,
the ocean, rather temperate and mollified
around your latitudes, and warm as such
like something of a universal mother.
That has marked you as one of the gentlest nations

with the softest of the latin languages,
a language made for love and music,
which indeed Brazil, that formidable daughter
just across next door of yours, has proved,
while you remain a dream of sweetest melancholy,
melting off in Fado singing all the time;
while once, which we must not forget,
you were the Queen of all the oceans of the world
who organized the first colonial empire overseas
and was the last to give that effort up.
Still, you retain the ocean
with its fathomless profundity of dreams
which is your special personal possession
transforming it into the loveliest song of all the ages,
that of your peculiar love affair
with all the universal ocean.

Bulgaria

Exotic wilderness beyond Illyria,
ancient kingdom of the Iron Age,
a wondrous fairy land of fantasy,
where culture rules with music,
driving over all those nonsense games
of temporary farces of politics
only leaving chaos and disorder in behind,
while the original slavonic roots remain
deep buried in the history of ancient times
when you gave birth to all the Slav world
with its ancient language breeding others
spreading out your culture over eastern Europe,
you are still the core of all that world,
containing in yourself the very heart
of Slavic essence with its special talents
for exactitude in linguistics, science,
intellectual universalism and humanism,
all emanating from that Balkan wilderness
among the snowy mountains with their secrets,
monasteries hidden deep in distant valleys,
used to the ordeal of difficult survival.
Since I first was introduced to you
I have remained a faithful lover
of your strange originality among the hills
with splendid music crying out

for the necessity and urge of freedom
that can never be put down
by any crushing brutal force of history.

olden friendship

"Old love doesn't rust." – Norwegian proverb.

While it lasts, it will forever grow,
increase more steadfastly in value
than whatever gold mine, diamond lode
or any fortune in the fastest stock,
and all you have to do is to be faithful,
keep in touch, maintain the good relationship
and never let her down. It will reward itself
more affluently than any worldly riches,
for there is no rarer and more precious thing
than friendship that continues constantly
maturing in reliance, confidence and faith
like priceless metal that will never rust.
And there's the secret: love, like everything,
must grow with age to gradually grow old,
but with maturity of lasting age, and the more old it grows,
the less it will be liable to rust,
the surer it will last, – and there's infinity for you.

Romania

Let the gipsy dances whirl
with violins intoxicating by their splendour
overwhelming anyone with their delirium of delight
with this enchanting people
very down to earth and natural
with scoundrels everywhere –
there never was a true Romanian who was not a cheat,
but very entertaining, skilful och delightful
with a sense of humour always
and a wonderful imagination –
probably the most advanced in Europe,
since in only those Carpathian sharp fantasteries
of moonscapes, wolfish wilderness and natural surrealism
could such a story as of the immortal Dracula
have been invented – utter evil with a sense of humour.

It's impossible to fathom all this tantalizing country
with its wonders and amazing scenery,
but only to get just a touch of it
will mark you with some stamp of incredulity forever.

Your absence

I don't mind your absence
since you are the closer to me for our separation
which breeds the more longings for our reunification,
which in fact just bring us closer spiritually
to each other as related souls
of more than only twin capacity.
The more you leave me, the more close
you stay with me the deeper in my heart,
as if a natural and physical divorce
was something utterly impossible,
since absences will just increase the presences.
That is the operation of true love,
the proof of how it works and its manifestation,
when it is so much profounder
in its spiritual reality to spite all physical reality
and overcome it with a so much truer realism.

Poland

– Today September 22nd, the Solidarity movement in Poland was born in 1980.

Five hundred years ago a kingdom of enlightenment,
a paragon for every country, greatest among nations,
she has fallen ever since to constantly more agonizing depths
of tragedy, disaster, ruin, national catastrophe and what is worse.
Engulfed by Russia, Austria and Germany, she has like no other nation
bled to death not only once but ever and again,
as if the first complete annihilation was not total and enough
but had to thoroughly be followed by oppression, tyranny,
and what is worse. The second world war was the worst finale
that has ever been experienced by a nation persecuted by disasters,
culminating in the utter and grotesque destruction of the capital,
the Warsaw Ghetto marking the supreme atrocity of history.
Still, Poland rises once again from smoking ruins to survive
and start another revolution but of freedom this time,
giving birth this very day to Solidarnosc,

that heroically started the entire liberation of all eastern Europe.
Germany and Russia, that so gluttonously wallowed in devouring Poland
are no more as autocratic empires but went to dust and in dishonour,
while the Poles survived them with their dreams and hopes of freedom
to eventually make dictatorial oppression vanish from all Europe
by showing us the way to make the Berlin Wall and Soviet Union collapse.

The Remnants

What remains when you have lost it all,
when all your life is down in ruins,
when your love is lost in beds of others,
when it has been proved again and once too much
that love and women never can be trusted,
when you are betrayed and lost in darkness
economically ruined by the laws of cynicism
pervading all society and dominating it
with ruthless senseless unhumanity
and you are left alone abandoned in a stormy sea of tears,
on one of those last melting ice flakes
that the egoism of global warming keeps reducing
in the maddest race in history for flimsy shallowness,
and you are thrown out of your own with no excuses
by the rules of that infernal asphalt jungle of the city
that is worse and crueller than any natural free wilderness;
what can be there still when you have lost everything?
Be calm. You haven't lost a thing. It's all still there,
your love, your friendships, all that universe of learning,
all that freedom of the ever life-vibrating cosmos,
it's all there whatever happens; and by losing all,
you simply are a winner having found it all again,
the meaning and the love of all your life.

Russia

Mammoth nation of abnormity of everything,
the hardest tyranny on earth, the deepest soul,
a history of almost only bloodshed, massacres,
oppression, suffering and universal martyrdom,
a tragedy of never ending worsening conditions
with some drops of mordant humour of Bulgakov,
Dostoyevsky, Gogol, Tchekhov, always tainted
with some melancholy, tragedy or bitterness,

like all those suicides of Dostoyevsky's,
possibly the very heart of the unfathomable Russian soul,
as sorrowful and crying as the vastness
of the melodic oceans of Tchaikovsky's
and as hopeless as the love of desperation
of doctor Zhivago, desillusioned unto immolation.
There is nothing else to do but to resign.
The only possibility concerning Russia
is the summary: the less said about her, the better.
It's an abyss of no end, no bottom and no termination
to the agony of this gigantic unsurveyability
of human suffering.

Finland

You only have one native country
all your life, which you are bound to for your life
and never can let down or ever let it leave your mind,
especially if it's a country to be proud of,
like my Finland, coldest in world
together with Siberia, Greenland and Alaska,
but of some integrity and honesty beyond this world,
which made it stand up stalwartly against all odds
against the Soviet Union in the Winter War
when Stalin thought he just would smash and grab it,
which did not turn out so easy,
Russia losing armies sacrificed for nothing
while the Finnish losses were but individuals,
invaluable every one of them,
immortal martyrs for resistance and defence
against oppression, tyranny, dictatorship and holocaust,
the cruelty of Stalin being worse than Hitler's
for its subtlety and methodology for 30 years
transforming Russia to a terror death camp.
Finland came out of that combat
with her independence, freedom and integrity unscathed
but for the losses of Karelia and her bravest sons.
Should I not then be proud of such a mother,
hard but beautiful in coldness and detachment
but deep under with a heart of purity and honesty
that I have never anywhere around the world
found anything to match the splendour of?

Austria

The golden capital of music
led the world to harmony for centuries
spreading universal joy and beauty
actually to every corner of the earth
by the divine endowment of adorable musicians
such as Mozart, Haydn, Beethoven and Brahms,
the Strausses, Schubert, Bruckner, Mahler, Lehar
and innumerable others, prophets of the highest creativity
and masters of the only universal language: music.
Austria was never a colonial power
and was never taken seriously as an imperial power,
broken and humiliated by Napoleon and Germany
and massacred and quartered to a fragment
after the first world war, while it prospered still
by art and authors, such as Schnitzler,
Stefan Zweig, the leading humanist and pacifist,
Rainer Maria Rilke, Hofmannsthal and doctor Freud,
eventually humiliated once too much
by Anschluss and the second world war,
which turned Vienna desolate to ruins and starvation.
Well, we still have all the music,
and that sound of music will forever be the finest part of Austria,
completely ruling it to its sustained immortal glory.
Thank you, Austria, for all your world of music!

Burma

– a small tribute to Aung Sang Suu Kyi

My lady, bravest in the world,
who never really wanted to become a politician
but preferred to stay with flower decorations and to play the piano,
you were only two years old when your great father was assassinated,
who gave Burma independence and democracy with British blessings
and was murdered by the enemies of peace and of democracy,
who have controlled the country practically ever since
and ruthlessly, since 1947, sixty years of military tyranny
and, as in all dictatorships, of total limitless corruption,
they today maintain the main monopoly of heroin in south east Asia,
which provide them with enormous fortunes while the people starve,
their military power being backed up by the communists of China,
without which, most probably, the nation would long since have been

a prospering democracy. Instead, the younger generation is kept down
by drugs, two thirds of all drug addicts being positive with HIV
with no financial means or possibility to even test themselves,
which means that Burma probably, because of the dictatorship,
has the worst Aids statistics in all Asia. Half of all the heroin
that reaches USA, Australia and America
is manufactured in "the golden triangle" of Burma,
Thailand and Laos, which the military governors of Burma
naturally has supported, since it stabilizes their position,
so that the production keeps on doubling.
So the people protest, and the military shoot them
for the safety of their heroin financial empire
and their extreme blindfolded limitless corruption.
China, by the way, is also chief supporter of Robert Mugabe.

Bohemia

The land that never was
of artists and Bohemians
stretches all around the world
including every free creative spirit
living basically on their dreams alone
but in reality in chronic poverty,
but theirs is all the world
with all its beauty, charm and freedom,
which it is their privilege to manage and sustain
to keep it flowing, flying and alive
to show the world there is a higher state of living
than just on the ground in humdrum ordinaries.
So their realm outwits and stretches beyond all politics,
beyond all mundanity into eternal freedom
where the spirit has the right to soar
and keep in sovereign superiority
above the world and all its troubles
to sustain the real life of the soul
for better ends and means than just mortality.

MAGNUS AURELIO

No time for love

The devastation of a failure of a love affair
is more often than not enough
to keep the lover out of love forever
or at least as long as he can do without it,
as long as he can make resistance and withstand it,
and as long as he does not completely languish,
thirsting, hungering and suffering to death,
like one deserted in the desert.
For that moment always comes,
when you no longer can endure
but must surrender to that irresistibility
and urge that is of all life's factors the most vital,
seeking that salvation of a sound and natural release
of all your life's most fundamental powers.
Never say you have no time for love.
That time will come when least expected
uninvited and surprisingly,
since love can never long be kept
locked out of doors and out of time.

OCTOBER HARVEST FIRST PART.

Headaches and heartaches

So shall we then let go,
since all we cause each other is incessant worries
through our love, that never leaves us any peace
but only trouble us with headaches and incessant heartaches?
Freedom is the motto of our love,
and there is nothing more important or invaluable
which at any cost must be secured and strived for always,
since it is the only thing and means
that can give any life at all
to our love and any possibility for it to breathe;
for we need air under our wings
to keep on flying freely and incessantly,
since going down to earth is certain death,
since all our life is only ideal flying splendour,
like to any common swift...

Cambridge

Beloved town of knowledge,
thanks for your idyllic depths of consummation
in the field of the pursuit of truth and wisdom,
heart of tolerance and freedom
both of conscience and of thought,
while Oxford seemed to me more introverted
focussed on the ego, its enhancement and complacency
in narcissistic dwindling spiral of the blind alleys of egoism,
you in humbler and sincerer aspirations
strive beyond yourself and this demented world of vanity.
What you already have accomplished you ignore
to rather go ahead fixed on the future and beyond
to ever keep advancing rather than look back,
for curiosity, to keep revealing what is round the corner
and continuing the research round the bend
to never stop investigating the black holes
of ever more alarming lacks of our knowledge,
but to always strive beyond the universe
to never stop confirming how exactly anything is possible.
Thanks for adopting me, and I will ever
faithfully remain one of your pupils of eternity.

The hippie culture

Maybe in the long run most important of our modern cultures,
it set off already long before the First World War
by Monte Veritá in Switzerland above Ascona,
marked by authors such as Daphne du Maurier and Erich Maria Remarque,
sincerely seeking healthier alternatives to modern civilization
by returning forthrightly to nature,
stressing vegetarianism and outdoor life,
in some ways in the vein of Tolstoy and Rousseau.
The concept was completely lost during the two world wars
but then came back and with a vengeance in the sixties
as a universal rebel movement triggered by the Vietnam war
directed against the derailing of America after the Kennedy assassination
as a direct natural spontaneous reaction against world insanity.
They say it brought another kind of weird insanity instead,
but it was not just freaking out with drugs and escapism
but most of all a rebirth of the right of fantasy and creativity
exploding in experiments of boldness in the field of art,
in clothes, in fashion, colours, music, films

and liberation in the way of living,
the ideal returning of a sane life close to nature.
It has never died but keeps on being the one sane alternative
to all the madness of the world,
considering the politics of the establishment
of military powers constantly resorting to lunatic wars
with tyranny and bombs and the destruction of humanity,
especially now in the times of global crisis of the climate change,
which proves capitalism and egoism, short-sighted politics of power,
greed, materialism and conformism to the establishment
all wrong from the beginning.

Love at work

Why do we work so hard
for nothing except vanity,
it seems; but still, so many predicate
that work alone gives life a meaning,
so they set their love at work,
indulging in their work as in their love
and make their work their love
and the justification for their lives,
as if life without work would give them a bad conscience
and debar them from their love and all life's meaning.
But the meaning is of course just love,
but in order to acquire it and reach it
you must work hard to deserve it,
and the more you work, the more you do deserve it,
which is probably the only meaning work imports,
to make it something like a proper entrance gate
to the deserved love that is its own reward.

Forbidden remedy

When you are alone
with all those wardrobe skeletons
of losses irretrievable
of overwhelming melancholy and nostalgia
that is the resulting madness of love lost forever,
you will grasp at any straw
of any infallibly failing quality
to get at least some faint illusion
of regaining something of your losses,

like some phoney medicine that only will deceive you,
and that's how some people turn to drugs,
a self-seduction of some soothing liberty
from all your pains of body, heart and soul,
and who has any heart then to forbid it?
If LSD trips help you fly away
from the unbearability of your reality,
if marijuana temporarily relieves your heartaches,
if injections or some snow helps you get on
with that insufferable Golgatha of your invalid life,
if tranquillizing dreams are better than the hell of your reality,
who can debar you from that substitute of love
which might at least give positive illusions
of that love you never had but only lost?
Not I.
I grant you any licence,
for I know that any kind of love
and even flights from love and artificial love
at least, if it is felt as love,
can be as good as any love
and always better than no love at all.

The secret garden

You came to me
like through a hazy dream
of lurid beauty veiled in mists
of unclear nowhereness
but more real than reality
directly from a distant past
of unknown and unconscious friendship
growing all the while clandestinely
like some strange secret garden
cultivated out of reach of any dirty hands
to suddenly appear in mature glory
opening some gates to paradise
that I was not aware that they existed.
Will it last, or is it just a dream?
The future hides the answer out of sight
for both of us, and I dare hardly even touch it,
this amazing dream of such unheard of beauty,
that I will remain enchanted
willingly, preferring never to wake up
to risk trespassing and to harm the tiniest portion

of this paradise of possibilities,
so intact a botanic garden
and so perfectly ideal.

Is it possible?

Is it possible to have a friend
whom you can trust implicitly
and have as your initiate
and intimate companion
for a lasting and infallible security?
Is it possible to have a love
that never fails but only grows
and who will stay in touch
whatever happens
faithfully in daily interchange of trust?
Is it possible to have a dream come true
of only pure ideals of openmindedness,
a friend in every need
who will not overrun or fail you
but remain in honest contact always
free of any shade of jealous egoism,
and with only human understanding,
patience, love and warmth of heart
without the doubts of second thoughts?
Yes, it is possible,
but you must wait for it with patience.

Venice

carrying the epithet "la serenissima" since the morning of history...

Salviamo Venezia!

The supreme serenity of cities,
you were timeless born
and are still much ahead of time
without the hell of car pollution
and with every street for only walkers,
you were long the only democratic state of Italy
until Napoleon came and trampled down
your ancient republic, ending that great age of yours

of thousand years of liberty, democracy and tolerance;
but still, you are the formost Queen of beauty
among all the world's most beautious towns in Italy,
resplendent still with none of your past glorious ages
faded or forgotten. Now new threats are turning up
much worse and much more serious than that corporal
two hundred years ago who called your Piazza
the most beautiful of banquet halls in Europe,
since oceans might be rising
to extinguish Holland, New Orleans, New York and you
among too many others, Bangla Desh, the Maldives,
any lowlands by the sea; and there's a challenge
not for only you but for all mankind
to live up to face their own responsibility
for having sullied and endangered
all civilization, nature and the world
with ordinary egoistic greed;
which did not make your beauty,
which rather rose from the survival through the centuries
of wars, invasions, natural disasters and barbaric storms;
and thus you stand a monument of beauty and survival,
which will outlast all the vanities
of this so greedily polluted world.

Hungary

The power house of freedom,
always bursting with dynamics
hotly flowing in amazing dazzling music
not just of the gipsies,
but in the mentality and everywhere,
you were always in the front line
whenever there were quests for freedom,
under Kossuth, Sandor Petöfi, Franz Liszt,
and leading eastern Europe against Soviet Russia
sacrificing everything in 1956 for dreams of freedom
which at last gave some reward in 1989,
when you let up the border for the eastern Germans
which resulted in the democratic triumph avalanche
releasing all of eastern Europe
in the domino dynamics of the freedom victory.
I always loved you with your splendid capital,
one of the finest and most beautiful in Europe,
the Danube Queen crowned on the hills

in the most capital romantic setting
found anywhere of almost any city in all Europe.
Keep your colours flying and your music going,
and you will be celebrated ever
for that freedom pathos and initiative
that never could be quenched
by any tyranny in history.

The danger of relationships

There is no challenge more extreme
than that of close relationships,
since every one of them presents a mortal danger,
that of getting burned by coming up to close
to knowing all too well the other's secrets,
opening the cupboards full of skeletons
that never can be cancelled or let down
of past and failed and capsized loves
that you could never quite accept as lost.
Each life is full of them,
and there is nothing more exciting
and more dangerous than to explore them
as they go on living haunting you like zombies.
You know all too well your own ghosts,
and you live in constant fear of them,
associating with them every night
unvoluntarily or willingly.
Imagine then the parallel experiences of others
with as many ghosts but with completely different stories,
and put two of those disturbing bags together,
and what will you get?
An abyss without end of doubled troublesome experiences,
each worse than any of the other's,
to which there can be no end
of bothersome exciting and intriguing exploration.

The heart-breaker

The worst thing is,
that it could happen just to anybody,
and no one wants to talk about it.
You just want to disappear,
shut up your heart and all your life

to lick your wounds and kill your pain
which only makes it worse.
It hurts when buds in spring are bursting,
but it hurts so infinitely more
when flowers in full bloom of beauty
just get trampled down by inconsideration
and shortsighted egoism
which lives by driving over victims
leaving them behind and never caring,
while the victims were the ones who cared.

Symbiosis

You are a part of me,
and I can not deny it,
since your feelings are my own:
whatever you feel, I feel also,
and thus your tears are mine,
and all your life is my responsibility.
In spite of all your faults and lacks and wants,
which cause us constant worries
and are criticizable indeed,
I can't get you out of my heart,
no matter how you wound and stab it,
hurt me and destroy me,
but you must stay there
caged in my own soul and freedom
which is all your life as well as mine.
Thus are we chained together by our destiny,
for good, for worse, for life, forever,
and all that we can do about it
is the best of this quixotic situation
of a tender love that hurts
but can not find a cure
of living by its wounds
and bleeding constantly to death
in never ending continuity.

Love at work (2)

Balance must needs be preserved
or love can not survive.
The bread of love is continuity,

for if it does not last
it is not even worth exploiting
but, if it be short-lived and short-sighted,
something to be sorry for
and afterwards regret
and maybe even be ashamed of.
Loving you is the more holy for me
the less I consume it, use it,
waste it, spend it and devour it,
since I believe in love and therefore worship it
and rather keep it safely at some distance
than take any risks of harming it.
That's why my life instead is wasted
as a workoholic, but, mind you,
creatively, constructively and positively,
since a man's work is his test of competence,
and without competence there can not be a lasting love.
So let me keep on working
for sustaining my creativeness
and for my love of you.

Florence

Dante hated Florence,
called it dark and dreary
and was driven out of it
and robbed of all his life,
his family and home and riches
like by some step-mother cruelty,
and somehow I agree:
there always was some latent madness there,
a deadly threat to creativity,
to the dynamic positive expansion,
to the craving freedom of the mind
and always violent reactions.
I was never quite at home there
but felt pressed by the imposing splendour
of the only capital of arts there still is in the world.
Respectfully I keep my distance
leaving her in peace like a museum
and prefer to keep my distance
only as a passer-by, not to disturb
or wake up all those monsters of the past.

Escape

I long to get away
from all these troubles
emanating from relationships
that only seem to offer turbulences,
worries, problems, strifes and chaos,
far away beyond all conflicts,
alienated from the human race
in healthy isolation
maybe in some monastery somewhere
without cellphones, without telephones,
without the internet and without civilization,
where you can relax from all the hurricanes
of torturesome relationships
that only sabotage your life
and kill your peace
and stress you out into a burnt-out nut-case
of no good to anyone
and least of all to you yourself.
So let me vanish and abscond,
so that I may at last sit back and quietly
sort out all those persistent paranoic love affairs,
forget my failures and disasters
and just laugh it all to hell.

Limbo

I was happy when I saw you
and most miserable when I lost you
by the wanton cruelty of fate
that never hesitates to ruin you
whenever possible,
and most especially on rare occasions
when you finally think you have reached some happiness.
It is the law of circumstances natural impersonal,
that what you most would wish would last
must least of all have any chance to last.
But worst of all is this horrific lack of certainty
that leaves you hanging in the air
in most outrageous suspense,
wondering and brooding unto madness
whether love is really lost or not,
and she that left you does not know herself

and therefore can't inform you.
Friends of comfort tell you: Let her go,
and go yourself another way
and find love anywhere
except where it has left you.
Has it left you? No, but it is gone.
There is the problem:
love unanswered, unfulfilled and alienated,
and there is another cosmic law for you:
love never can be satisfied.

Sexism

If you want sex, keep out of me
and stick to gigolos and May-flies,
temporary satisfactions that will ditch you afterwards
and willingly forget the corpses they walked over,
treating you like any ordinary slut,
reducing you to common status of just any prostitute,
a common girl who wants get laid
ignoring the inevitable aftermath
that afterwards she will be crying all her life.
I wanted love and friendship
of endurability and lasting worth,
true intimacy, trust and faith,
a friend in whom you could confide
and not just superficial sexual satisfaction.
Keep then to your prostitutes, adventurers and tramps
and common shallow marriage swindlers
who will just exploit you, use you and devour you
to leave you afterwards dissolved in never-ending tears.

Sad reflection

More often than not you hear of happy divorces and unhappy marriages,
less and less about the contrary.
This is our backward world
that tends to turn all natural and normal things the other way,
like in the horrors of George Orwell's future world
which now already is a nightmare of the past
while nightmares of the present keep accelerating,
building up unto perhaps another Noah's flood;
and where did love get lost and disappear

in the destructive course of history?
No, it was always there
but always under cover,
hiding to protect itself
and to survive, in spite of all, with difficulty,
but occassionally to give signs of life,
triumphing suddenly in beauty
mainly in the works of art
to prove and manifest eternity
in contrary to all the mortal vanity of history
and showing, that if man and history keeps killing life,
love always does the opposite
to always triumph in the end.

Rome – what a waste of history!

You carried on the famous Greek democracy
by your republic for some centuries,
but then, alas, there was a fellow Julius Caesar
who decided to transform it into a dictatorship
and was unbearable enough to actually succeed
in turning over a republican democracy into its contrary
and was in fact just for that reason murdered,
which, alas, had just the contrary effect
to what it was intended, turning Julius Caesar
into the most formidable martyr;
which established that abominable Roman empire
of incurable corruption, decay, moral dissolution
and the gradual downfall of all standards of civilization
for four hundred years before it finally collapsed
by its own rottening putrefaction and megalomania
introducing the dark ages of a thousand years.
And what a waste of history!
It was all there, the splendid civilization,
en enlightenment of science and philosophy,
destroyed by the shortsightedness of egoism
and power madness, crazy and inhuman emperors
and the establishment of some absurd christianity
of superstition, bigotry and brainwash mythomania
to replace all light and realism and common sense
with paranoia of premeditated purpose
to lead all the world astray by evilly controlling it
through the black magic of established superstition
to impose a realm of terror for a thousand years

by strict intolerance outlawing every possible enlightenment.
The catholic politic church is still there
dominating Rome and trying still to dominate the world,
but Rome survived more easily without it
and is known today as the most splendid town of Italy
and history, a palimpsest of all the worst mistakes of history,
quite open, obvious and self-evident
for anyone who wants to learn
what those refused to grasp and learn
who put the fire burning to the stake of Saint Giordano Bruno.

What is poetry?

— a hopeless but brave effort

It defies all definition
since it should be undescribable
to be at all convincing,
an impalpable abstraction
of word painting with some meaning
which persistently avoids to get pinned down,
a mystery of beauty
with a spiritual sense
that does not disappear
and never is forgotten.

Advice to a shattered friend

You never seem to learn, my friend,
although you were deceived before
and many times, and now
it's once too much, it seems,
and still you will not learn,
and there's no remedy against a lack of wisdom
if not even your experience will teach you.
However, don't let your frustrated love
make you collapse, break down, disintegrate,
go into boozing, moral bankruptcy and self-destruction,
for if your love fails you
and goes into bed with someone less than you,
it's not your fault. If you let that affect you
you have lost and are defeated,
which in love you never must allow.

It is a challenge. If you lose one girl,
there are so many others you can love,
so many lonesome darlings waiting just for you,
left over and surviving after shipwrecks
like yourself in spite of all,
and no survivor ever will admit defeat.
If you have lost one whom you loved,
because she found another,
there will be no end to all those others
who deserve you more than she.

The Hour of the Wolf – or the Truth?

When you wake up at night
too early in the morning
from a nightmare
in cold sweat
of losses and of being used
and can but think of him,
or her, that partner who betrayed you,
who saw personal relationships
as means to use to only further one's own interests,
then it's time for a divorce.
When love becomes the opposite
from lack of nourishment
or the betrayal of the partner,
that's the cry "Abandon ship!",
and if you don't, you will go under.
Sail away while there is time,
while there is still a life-boat
and a possible escape from the black hole
of anger constantly increasing,
violence and force and furious melodrama,
feelings of injustice and grim violation,
hopelessness, despair and nightmares without end,
that just will suck you down
in one way only down the drain
into the bottomless and final abyss
of inevitable immolation.

Spain

The cruelty of Spain
was evident from the beginning
with a hard and proud mentality
ideal for an autocracy of hard intolerance
made worse by fear and superstition,
ruled by Great Inquisitors,
unique for Spain,
that ordered the extermination
of all Indians of the new world
even if they tried co-operation,
being loyal, faithful, humble Christians,
and thus were the Inca and the Aztec empires
plundered and reduced to nothing
by the greed disguised in bigotry of Spain
that also persecuted all the Jews and Arabs
hunting them forever down and out.
Francisco Goya saw the Spanish soul
exposing it in probably the darkest art
that ever was produced before the 'Guernica',
but, still, in all this darkness, there is hope.

There is no finer dancing,
folkloristic music, gipsy culture
and artistic temperament
than in Andalucia,
the fabled country of Granada and Sevilla,
that saw Lorca, Falla, Figaro,
Don Juan, Granados and Albeniz
among others flourish splendidly
in the most dashing art of Europe.

Forget the bullfights, Francoism,
the civil war, the inquisition horrors,
the intolerance and bloody history,
and sing and dance instead
all night at the bottegas
that will outlast all the lunacy of history.

Sicily

The cradle of the modern western Europe,
where the sonnet was invented
at the universal court of Frederick the Second
Hohenstaufen in Palermo,
then the centre of the world
and heart of universal culture,
which was outrageously raped
by papacy and its politics
of reaction, greed, suppression
and all opposites to culture and expansion,
the entire royal Norman family of heroes
being categorically persecuted to extinction
for their liberal free-thinking views
and universal tolerance;
you never managed to recover,
blessed island of serenity and beauty,
generosity, divinity and richness of imagination,
from the persecution of invaders,
French and papal tyrants,
so that your renaissance only could survive
through Florence, which made a second effort
and, although succeeding better,
still was also there suppressed by violence
and beaten down for nothing
but that they were right,
which every spirit in existence always was
who just maintained their right for freedom
of integrity and mind and conscience.
Still, Palermo is still there
with the whole island of dynamic splendour
which at any moment may bring forth anew
such champions for humanity and justice
as the Staufer Frederick the Second,
the grandfather of Italy, the diplomatic genius
who was only and unique in conquering Jerusalem
without a drop of blood on either side,
the only politician ever who succeeded
in maintaining peace between the Christians,
Jews and Muslims, for which he was banished,
excommunicated by the Church,
which never could accept a non-dogmatic mind.
The renaissance was thus held up for a few centuries,
but nothing in the long run can resist or stop
the universal human urge of life for freedom.

Pakistan

— the bomb attack in Karachi aimed against Benazir Bhutto, leaving so far 136 dead...

136 victims – for what?
They tried to kill a woman
coming home after eight years of exile,
engaged some willing suicide bombers
who would do anything to upset
the peace process of Pakistan
towards democracy, law and order
and obstruct any effort
of reconciliation between the military and democracy,
trying to kill off all possibilities of co-operation at once,
for the glory of fundamentalism, anarchy, the Talibans
and terror, while they only killed themselves
and brought with them 136 innocents,
women and children, old people and civilians
and anyone who just wanted to say welcome
to the mother of the nation coming back.
It's not politics. It's fundamental mass suicide
hitting islam at its roots
by using violence in aiming at the contrary
which always boomerangs
and kills the future
instead of building it.

No prostitute

Sorry that I am no good for you,
no money, no position,
no means to spoil you,
no driver's licence and no property
but only failures, bankruptcies, defeats,
adversities and trials is what I can offer;
and I am afraid I am not even good for company,
just working boring hard all of the time,
no time at home, no time for sex,
no luxuries, no banquets,
nothing special and no evenings out,
just humdrum hard work all the time
and nothing for it.
Well, at least I am no prostitute.

Our world

Ours is a world of beauty
so much finer than the ordinary world
of strife, vulgarity and commonness,
of egoism, shortsightedness and vanity,
while ours lasts forever
gilded by the harmony of unsurpassed nobility
of the refinement and idealism of abstract truth
as found by geniuses like Handel, Beethoven, Chopin
and Brahms, a higher world of thought
than any brutal realism, and actually
a truer world than any real one.
Since we know the key and have it,
let's just stick to it and keep it
and forget about the rest,
that keeps committing all their follies
on the road to self-destruction
better without us,
who are reserved for better purposes
than just the ordinariness of vanity.

Islands in the flood

Is that the fate of knowledge,
good experience and acquired wisdom,
to, the more it is developed and enriched,
become the less appreciated
and more inaccessible and isolated
as an outcast island of some rarity,
uniqueness and exclusiveness
forgotten and ignored, alone
in this mad flood of media rubbish
drowning the whole world in brainwash,
this derailed civilization of pollution,
self-destructive greed, unnaturalness
and the meaningless obsession with superficiality?
The prophets sticking to the truth
were always persecuted and alone,
impopular, despized and kicked aside,
but they were always there,
left over on deserted islands in the flood
of madness of humanity abandoning all sense
to wallow, as it seems, in anything
that keeps them out of knowledge
and keeps out any uncomfortable truth
from their doomed lives of vanity,
while those too few who care
in silence keep just drudging on
maintaining life and history in spite of all
in underground unthanked for anonymity,
life and its continuity and spite of all destruction
being unjustly their sole reward.

Egypt

The most ancient of all surviving civilizations
and still the most imposing and impressing
for her still astonishin mysterious pyramids
with the enigma of the Sphinx, perhaps a silent witness
from before the Flood of past civilizations
gone to dust and vanished long ago,
perished maybe through disasters
which have left no record traceable in history,
– but Egypt rose from nothing
to become a mother of all civilizations,

of Israel, Greece and Rome and all our western world,
to boast an unsurpassed magnificence forever.
You kept that civilization flourishing
through innumerable dynasties and four millennia
to be finally sealed up by Rome
on the demission of her last Queen Cleopatra,
to remain closed up forever with her secrets
of an unknown past of timeless aeons
that the Sphinx keeps musing over to himself,
deriding silently all human vanity and history forever.

The betrayal of beauty

The lover, declining an invitation:
"Sorry, but I dare not risk again to find other lovers in your home or that they come visiting while I am with you."

I am afraid this argument will be considerable,
circumstantial, comprehensive, difficult and hard
for this dark lady of the sonnets
who used men for selfish means
and used her beauty ruthlessly
to without judgement treat them
as the servants of her whims,
as slaves, in fact, for her fanatic feminism.

The problem was that she was beautiful enough
to make them flock around her,
lose their senses for her beauty
and allow themselves to even be deceived by her
as she replaced each lover with another,
calling them all, naturally, only "friends".
The fact is that they all loved her
while she loved no one but herself,
a victim and a slave to her own charm and beauty,
failing to observe that there was anyone but her
in that small world of hers.
When finally she was looked through
by those she had been using for no ends except her own,
who never had been thanked for all their services
and found her finally to be without a trace of honesty,
she had deceived them all with yet another lover
while they slaved for her for months,
which was not found out until after four months
by another ex of hers, quite accidentally, of course;
and only then she had to tell them why
she had been lost to all her friends
for such a long time without answering communications.
She is now notorious, and there is nothing I can do about it.
I did everything I could for her
and find myself now free of all responsibility.
It's difficult to be a woman
and as difficult to be a man
when you can not stop loving her
no matter how much she herself betrays her beauty
while you stay on stuck with her
because you only see the beauty of the soul,
to which you can but stay forever faithful.

Missing

When shall we love again
on fragrant beds of roses
made of our creativeness
which never can take any break
for ease or pauses of good sleep
but always moves, continues and develops,
like some demon chasing us
from one love to another
but get always back into each others' arms?

I am your only lover,
since I am the only one to know your soul,
and I shall keep it as my own
and safeguard it within my bosom
to be faithful to our love for all eternity
since I am very well aware
that this obsession never can be stopped.

Israel

Israel the trickster
fought with God and won
but got as punishment a limp for life
to never quite again stand upright.
Thus began his troubles,
culminating in the strain with Egypt
finally admitting her to go
or forced to throw him out -
we never shall be certain of the whole truth,
since Egyptian history refused to talk about it.
All since then the Israeli people
have survived with difficulty
always against persecution, holocausts and wars,
discriminated and calumniated all through history
for constantly remaining the eternal trickster
struggling to survive and always winning,
even conquering the heart of God.

Eternal love

I dream of you, my love,
and can't stop doing so
since you are always there
in front of me forever
in this moment that will never cease
of love without an end
and boundless without limits,
all because of your so sudden revelation
that you always will appear to me
whenever I will least expect it.
That's how love works:
always there, surprising,
lurking, waiting to assail you

to renew your love and keep it burning
like a light and symbol of eternity
to never ever leave you any more in peace
but always torture you with sensual delight
that you will never tire of
since it is only love of life itself.

When you fall in love

When you fall in love
you don't know what to say.
You just stand there
like a stupid lonely sheep
and can't do anything
except get lost in dreams
of wonders vain and vanishing
as fleeting as a cloud
with nothing to hold on to afterwards
except the loss of a disintegrated dream
that gave a fragrance of eternity
to just remind you
that it's always there.

All that matters…

All that matters
is the disposition of your love,
the barometer of your life,
the only perfect sign of health,
the only true manifestation of your soul,
that should be always open,
high and ready
to embrace new loves and friendships
and new chapters of your life
to keep you constantly developing,
expanding and renewing
as a soul forever on the search
of more increasing overwhelming love.

The Himalayas

Divinity incarnate, isn't it?
This sumptuous splendour of pure beauty
in the highest whiteness reaching for the sky
forbidding man to enter at the peril of his life,
excluding foulness, baseness, weakness,
ugliness, mortality, mundanity
to just shine on forever
untouched by the cataclysms and earthquakes
of humanity and their chaotic history,
remaining silently in constant splendour
and surviving even aeons of geology
for us to quake before and quietly admire
as the highest purest possible manifestation
of all beauty, freedom and release
which man can only find in nature,
which alone can save the continuity of man
if just he realizes that he can't rule nature
but can only live when ruled by nature.

Our story

I loved you from the start
but did not know it,
dared not risk it, was precautious
and would never take for granted
that you would love me in return.
Our differences are unbridgeable,
and every time I thought I reached you
something happened to increase our difference
and to almost force our separation,
like an alienating demon haunting us
with no deserved or righteous fate.
Thus our security remained our friendship
as the only platform of our association
and which fortunately is impeccable.
So we at least have something
to unite us and keep us together constantly,
indefinitely and perhaps forever.
Is this true love,
and the sentimental love a lie,
a fake, illusion and a self-deceit,
like any drunken state of high elation,
passing over, fading into nothing,
while true love needs firmer basis?
Practically our love has never worked,
but it is there, existing, thriving,
like two souls grown into one
continuously expanding,
while this mortal flesh
becomes a secondary issue
which we well can leave to rot.

The frailty of beauty

That strange capacity
of beauty irresistible
is also, the more beautiful,
the more extremely vulnerable
and, in fact, the very essence
of that delicacy called frailty.
But that charm holds sway
and higher power over men
than they can possibly get mobilized

by armies, fortunes and politics,
which are all reduced to nothing
in comparison with sacred beauty.
Thus alone that beauty can redeem the world
when all world powers else must fail.

Complaint

Where is it gone,
that natural capacity
of culture, sensitivity and common sense,
all lost in this world gone so much astray
into the automatic age of mad derailment
where politeness does no more exist,
where gratitude is lost, unknown,
regarded as absurd,
as if sincere and human kindness
just to ease co-operation between people
was just silly, foolish and out-dated.
Letters are no longer answered,
cyber culture has reduced the language
to just shallow formulas of emptiness,
communication is denied
if it gets sensitive or deep,
as if all lasting human values
were out of this world.
I disagree
and stick to history,
the truth of ages past,
the human truth of all that last,
the spiritual values living ever with the soul,
with love as sole foundation
everlasting,
while all shallowness
invariably driving over what it constantly ignores
and shouldn't
will get lost
and always just continues getting lost,
like this whole damned polluted age
blind in its ignorance to its own self-destruction.

Love argument

My love, what shall I tell you?
That I love you still
in spite of all the crises
or perhaps because of them,
continuously separating us
to just force us again together,
like a spiritual force
more powerful than any potency of nature?
There is so much that we need to talk about
but never did, so many uncleared arguments,
that keep amassing unresolved
like in a constant constipation,
(if you pardon the expression,)
that perhaps we just should leave
as totally irrelevant to our love
and its core meaning,
that we need each other
and belong together to each other
and can't do without each other.
Yes, it couldn't be more simple,
so it is unnecessary and irrelevant
to complicate what lives by being basic,
that is love, that couldn't be more basic.

Tibet

A Tibetan's Voice,
by Thupten Tendar

"As a Tibetan refugee, I'd like to give my perspective on our dying nation. Historically speaking, Tibet was led by kings, lamas and others based on the law of "Ten Virtues" and the 16 human principles, introduced by King Songtsan Gampo in the seventh century. I am not claiming that Tibet, prior to 1950s, was free of any conflict. No part of our world was. However, the ruling communist party has afflicted the brain of many non-Tibetans with its baseless propaganda by teaching fabricated history classes. So I, being a refugee with a parent who survived our genocide and diaspora, have a personal responsibility to make people understand Tibet properly.

Upon the Chinese takeover, thousands of monks, including my own uncle in Kham, were dragged off their meditation cushions and beheaded for nothing else than being a monk. The only allegation Mao Tse-Tung and his army made against these men was that they were monks practicing their religion, which the communists believe is poison to a society. The lay communities in Tibet pay their highest respect to the ordained people. They consider it a great honor for their son or daughter to join a monastery or nunnery because of their own faith. They rejoice in the spiritual community. Anybody who tries to break this relationship doesn't understand Tibet and the Tibetan spirit properly.

My mother ran into exile with her mother and two sisters. She barely made it to India. She was separated from her mother and sisters, and to this day has never heard from them again. They might have been killed by the so-called liberators, buried under snow or dead of hunger.

More than one million Tibetans were heartlessly killed by those who some people still claim were bringing liberation and prosperity to Tibet. If the real purpose of their invasion is for development of Tibet, then why did they divide it into many new parts and rename them in Chinese? Why did they destroy the Tibetan ecology, which caused deadly floods in China? Why do they choose their own version of the Panchen Lama and claim the right to select the future reincarnations of Tibetan lamas — even as they decry religion? Why do they build prisons and military bases rather than hospitals and schools? How can the words "freedom and democracy" appearing on Google, Yahoo and other websites hamper their mission development? Why are they afraid of dialogue with a figure of peace? Is the free media really harmful to growth and modernization?

I don't hate China. I appreciate most of my Chinese brothers and sisters for being nothing but warmhearted, courageous and compassionate toward me. But the Chinese occupation of Tibet was the first time in more than 2,000 years of Tibetan history that so many people were massacred in the region. Hundreds of thousands of Tibetans had to flee their homeland to become refugees. Our basic human rights were snatched away. They say communism brought peace and prosperity to Tibet. Sorry, we don't need any such blessings!

Thupten Tendar"

And can we stand by and just look on?
6246 monasteries and temples
robbed and ruined and destroyed,
a fifth of the whole population murdered,
hundred thirty thousand forced into exile
and about 3000 fleeing every year
across the mountains over passes of 6000 meters,
a civilization and a culture deliberately devastated

by an occupying atheist autocracy
continuing enforcing violent oppression to this day,
now 58 years of colonization by brute force,
destruction, brainwash propaganda
and enforced materialism and atheism.
The Chinese Communist regime is kowtowed to
by all the business world for its economy
while therefore politicians also crawl
to that most dreadful rotten empire of lies,
an outward face all smiles,
an inward face all cruelty, deceit and power greed.
It started off Pol Pot, manipulating him
to run the holocaust regime of poor Cambodia,
it gave to Pakistan its nuclear potency
and served both sides of Nepal's civil war with weapons,
it is maintaining Burma's military inhumanity
of drug monopolies of heroin and total tyranny,
and what else? The ruins of Tibet
if anything cry out forever
against cruelty and atheism as the ideology
of the most corrupt communist regime in history – of China.

Marriage – why not?

I always tried to stick to the Platonic form of love
as the most rational, reliable and relevant,
especially in our age of planet-risking over-population.
Quarrels was my horror always,
and in matrimony they can never be avoided.
I was once deceived and quite determined
never to become deceived again,
and I was never willing to end up
a hero under any slipper.
You can have as free and independent any number
of good friends of any gender,
but as married, one relationship must dominate all others,
which was never in accordance with my democratic freedom soul.
The final argument, that as a free man
you can love the more,
is maybe though the most decisive,
vital and determining my fate.

Stuck in love

What's better and what's worse -
the nightmare of uncertainty
or the force of jealousy?
When the communication lines don't work
and you are left like on a desert island in a void,
the nightmares of uncertainty and jealousy pursuing you
and haunting you and hunting you to death each night,
not knowing what your love is doing in whose arms,
while all that you can do yourself is wallowing in self-torment,
like in the strait-jacket of cruelty of destiny
much worse than any hospitalization;
your sole comfort is that you still love her
and will go on doing so no matter what she does,
since no one can get out of that heart she has entered.

Thank God for feminism

Just don't let it put you down,
that squeamish scrupulous meticulousness
appertaining to the oversensitivity of female delicacy
leading to the pettiest of pedantry.

Forget all that and look to beauty,
disregard the coarse uncouthness of the masculine barbarity
and let it be replaced by all the virtues of true femininity,
the modesty and delicacy of consideration
and the touch of suaveness in the magic
of the sieve of lovable romanticism,
that alone makes life endurable
by that unique spice of eternity called love.
Forget the sexes and the genders, love is all that matters
constantly transcending every limit
and surpassing all in life that is affected
by that petty and ignoble menace called mortality.

Nepal

There is no one braver or more stalwart and intrepid
than a Sherpa or a Gurkha, sticking to the end
in faithfulness, agility and bravery,
a mountain people with incredible potentials
and one of the poorest countries in the world,
torn asunder by a fatal civil war
of ten long years because of foreign powers intervening,
arming terrorists and anarchists with weapons
to be able to impose dictatorship themselves.
But Nepal is and always was the freest of all Asian nations,
which the British wisely did respect
and therefore never colonized but left it wild
to only take into their service individuals,
unconquerable Gurkhas and invaluable Sherpas,
best of mountain fighters, first to climb Mount Everest,
fantastic representatives of this so hearty people,
hot and hard but nice and friendly,
and, like every mountain people,
warmer, more reliable and loyal in their hearts
as if they were more human
in the hardship of their mountain wisdom
than all plain and ordinary human beings.

Love simplicity

When the cold attacks you
savagely with deep freeze,
let your love get warm and warm you up.
When dampness and humidity
strikes deep with roughness in your limbs,
let sunshine love with comfort dry you up.
When darkness looms assailing you
increasingly and overwhelmingly in winter days,
let love loose in your soul to light you up.
When your love is away
on distant journeys and adventures
and you never know if you at all will see her yet again,
let her in spirit in your dreams appear,
just think of her, and she will never leave you,
and thus will your love continue
to remain with you in constant dreams
as long as you just keep on loving.

Another love definition

Love is dying without dying,
an eternal pain of pure delight,
a torment utterly enjoyable forever
and a mortal fall into an endlessness
of darkness into the abysmal death of life
reborn to start again from the beginning
this delightful craze of sado-masochism
which hurts the more for its endurance
and the deeper, harder and more painful
for its spirituality, sincerity and honesty.
The greatest lover was Othello for his jealousy,
no Romeo, no Tristan knew love better than the Moor
who knew it was worth dying for it
and was quite consistent in so doing.
So do never cry, complain or treat love negatively,
but endure it and enjoy it for its sufferings,
for it is certainly the greatest privilege in life
that man was offered for his bold decision
to at all take up this haphazard existence
to endure and suffer for it with his love.

The anti-modernist

Is it wrong to be a realist?
Is clarity to be condemned,
since you are not allowed to be outspoken,
as if direct honesty was something negative,
while shadowy and fishy innuendos were preferable.
Is downright classicism condemnable then and no more allowed?
What is poetry and verbal art if not free licence
for expressive sumptuousness and loose imaginative speculation?
If you give it then some comprehensible and realistic form
and use some relevant correct syntax and grammar,
so that it approaches something of a style,
is that then to despize, denounce and scrap,
since it is not in line with Ezra Pound and T.S.Eliot,
James Joyce and Samuel Beckett?
What's wrong with an obnoxious anti-modernist
is that he is so shockingly a so upsetting radical
in the completely wrong direction, since he breaks
with fashion, tendencies and ruling nonsense
and rejects the dissolution of all forms and language,
heading strong against the stream by being clearcut
and demanding realism and comprehensibility;
and is it then so damnably completely wrong?

Impressions of India

This fascinating continent, more populous than Europe
is still dominated by the oldest of the world's religions
quite unbrokenly since three millennia at least,
making her the oldest intact culture in our world,
enriching it in the historic process with one world religion more:
the high morale, integrity and wisdom
of the common sense philosophy of Buddhism,
while at times disturbed by more intolerant intruders like the Muslims
and the Christians, doing what they could to devastate
the history, the culture and traditions of the ancient "heathen" India,
which instead absorbed them to enrich her culture with them,
adding constantly more faiths, more languages and cultures,
more philosophies and outlooks on the world and life,
thus constantly remaining basically tolerant and universal,
which repeatedly her history has proved.
In modern times there has been a considerable renaissance of Hinduism
heralded by Romain Rolland, who introduced in Europe Ramakrishna

with his followers Vivekananda and Rabindranath Tagore.
The latter gave a universal voice to Hindu tolerance and wisdom
cordially embracing every faith and heralding a world community
and unity, like in a university of common faiths and knowledge,
cultures, shared philosophies and mutual creativeness.
Not only Kipling, Talbot Mundy, M.M.Kaye, John Masters
and Jim Corbett, first to introduce national parks of wildlife,
owed their lives to India, but Mahatma Gandhi was an Indian too,
accomplishing political reforms and miracles by obstinate non-violence.
One of his pupils was the Japanese monk Nichidatsu Fujii,
rebelling against society, career and martial life by sticking to a beggar's life
and making it his mission to erect peace stupas all around the world,
especially in India, as a demonstration against nuclear weapons,
having seen Hiroshima and Nagasaki,
making it his goal to have all nuclear weapons in the world dismantled.
He was active to the end, a hundred years old, when he passed away
some twenty years ago, but his Peace Stupas go on rising everywhere,
in Africa, in South America, in London, India and all over Asia,
crying out the urgent message universally: "Peace, please!"

Dharamshala

Blessed haven of Tibetan refugees,
they come to you through snows and hardships
across icy passes of six thousand meters
shot at in the process by insentient China soldiers,
as if the oppression in Tibet was not enough,
but escapees must even have to run the gauntlet
across the austerity of the forbidding Himalayas
to in Dharamshala, finally, find freedom
and a human treatment with full dignity
as ordinary faithful human and compassionate Tibetans.

During the horrific holocaust against the Jews
they still in concentration death camps found the means
to make the best af a bad bargain, stay alive,
survive the Nazis and in places even make rebellion,
like in Sobibor, Treblinka and the Warsaw Ghetto,
and in later days look back with some nostalgic tenderness
to those horrific challenge days, remember the communities
and even love that strange existence of extreme conditions.

In the same way the Tibetans face the challenge,
make the best of it and never give up faith or spirit,
certain that one day again Tibet will be set free,

while nothing can redeem the Chinese occupation force
from facing the severest accusations of the facts of history.
Meanwhile, the thriving paradise of Dharamshala
keeps on working hard with meditation and enlightenment
and spreading world wide the immortal message
of the sacredness of freedom, truth, integrity and wisdom,
spiting all the mortal rotten lies of all autocracies in history.

Kashmir

War-torn paradise of inexpressible beauty
with the friendliest people in the world,
embracing any stranger with their love
and overwhelmingly presenting to them
this fairy tale of beauty and reality,
of magic lakes of endless peace
and mountains towering around them
to enshrine the loveliest realm of India,
torn asunder by politics, civil war
and meaningless atrocities since 60 years
with countless innocents as victims,
like in any war resulting from politics,
that established ignorance called power
only causing miserable havoc
by the irresponsibility of humankind.
But beauty, paradise and peace survives,
is always born anew and never tires
and shines through the most romantic landscape
of the blessed mountains of Kashmir,
the land of overwhelming beauty,
which eventually will conquer and prevail,
since there was never any human heart
that was not moved by truth when it was beautiful.

The inescapability of love

I love you, but I don't need you,
but I need to love you,
which is a more potent urge than nature
which not even nature can inhibit,
sabotage, postpone or hinder,
which is why we have no choice
but keep on loving constantly forever
making the best out of it

and overcoming obstacles and spite al destinies,
defy the mundane horror world
and just keep on in faithfulness,
sincerity, devotion and profundity
to just go on expanding and enlarging
the forever growing depth and truth of love.

Wounded

You can not get more hurt
in wars, in accidents or in disasters
than in love, when disappointment
is but followed by more disappointments,
when the wounds are only opened deeper
and when nothing can be healed,
for punctured soul can not be bandaged,
and all is only worsened
time and time again
in something like a constant hellish repetition
which gets on and on, gets worse,
more cruel and more unjust.
Then enters the banal ridiculous situation
that your love is changed to hate,
and thus the irrepairable self-torment
only worsens in its utter pain.
And still you hesitate to make the operation
to just end it all, disrupt and close up the relationship,
to kill your feelings and seal up that chamber in your soul,

since still the memories are there
of how it started in its glorious beauty,
– only to be crushed by a reality
which always was infallibly insensitive
and ruthless in its cursed sordidness,
which in its unawareness' murderous insensitivity
is worse and crueller than death.

The Pain of Life

When pain invades and kills the soul,
so let it kill, but let it not desist
but go on killing with its pain,
so that it can be felt most thoroughly,
and so that you can feel the more
that you are still alive
and can survive the pain
of having your soul killed.
Thus you can also go on loving
although love is dead and murdered
since it goes on hurting and so hard,
so outrageously and intolerably hard,
so that you almost feel the more alive
for its so hurting so outrageously.
So cut no bones on me by amputation,
master barber-surgeon, for all my gangrene,
and transplant not my heart
although it is so broken;
but let me live on as long as it just hurts enough,
so that I yet may feel to still be living
all the way until I die.

The gutter misery

We ignore it, trying not to mind,
and look the other way
if it insistently protests too hard,
which only makes it worse:
the homeless with his shaky alcoholic stench,
the withered prostitute inviting anyone
for just a few poor pennies and still gets no customers,
the beggar tart with her small crying child in rags
who no one wants to offer anything

since no one feels responsible for her situation,
and the child with swollen belly and infected eyes,
too large and suffering to even raise compassion
since the misery is too revolting in its ugliness,
the leper demonstrating his horrendous mutilations
to get money, and the cripple crawling without legs
and twisted limbs on some invalid cart on small wheels,
and the thousands who no more can rise,
have given up, as lost and scrapped, with no more strength,
just waiting to get carried out and thrown away.
That's our reality in major parts of our world,
which we don't want to see or care for,
since we have enough of ourselves
which claims all our attention,
blinding us to that reality
which in the end will never spare us.

Bitter tears

You killed it all from the beginning
without giving it a chance,
when you deceived me with that wimp
who did already have a wife,
when I found you in bed with him
while you ignored my birthday
and defended him, your lover, against me,
as if I was the real presumptuous outrageous intruder.
How could such a shipwreck ever set to sea again?
Your other lovers, after his incompetence,
were equal failures, each rebelling naturally
against your blind lack of empathy
and total ego-centricism.
Is all your beauty just a mask then
and a luring substitute for your inadequateness,
immaturity, your childish limitation to yourself
and lack of any spiritual antennae?
No one could have hurt med deeper than you did
since I gave you my love in full
while all you wanted was to toy with sissies
whom you could entirely control and dominate.
My only comfort in this mess
of an aborted possibility of a sincerity
of love expected at its best turned out its worst,
is that at least I made it in not hurting you.

Love's bitter abyss

The well of all your tears of love
can never get filled up and never emptied,
it will always be enriched by new laments,
while all the old ones never can be cancelled
or forgotten, keeping that abyss forever constant
without bottom, without end
and flowing always without ever overflowing,
never satisfying, never measurable,
always black in darkness and annoying you
by always, when you look down into it,
presenting you with that most hateful mirror
of your own deluded face,
as if all that well full of sorrows
actually contained was only your own self.
But real love is the opposite:
forget yourself, transcend yourself,
get out of it och think of someone else,
and independent of how many loves
you lost and failed you,
there will always still be someone left
who has deserved your love.

Your love

You are the only sun of your life,
and only you can make it shine
to give it warmth and tenderness and love.
You have no right to crave it from the others,
and if you feel sorted out and forlornly cold-shouldered,
those cold shoulders are your own,
and only you yourself have closed your heart.
There is no other world in you but your own heart.
The universe is yours if you would open it (your heart) to others,
but the flow is always yours, depending only upon you.
That is responsibility:
if you can take responsibility and give it,
then there's nothing wrong with you,
and all you have to do is keep on loving
tirelessly, going out and actively forever.

Bleeding hearts

They are more common than you think,
the silent bleeding aching hearts of loneliness,
too proud to give away their pain by crying,
and the more their aching vibrates universally
resounding in the ether of spiritual sensitivity,
where they indeed can never be alone;
since those who cry in silence without tears
in constant inward drowning in their misery
are that part of the iceberg of all human grief
that never can be seen but goes the deeper.
We who know their grief can share it
in deep sympathy in silence and respect
and cry and pray with them in humble service
at that altar of all tears of blood that never became known.

Ladakh

Safe haven of an earthly paradise,
untouched by devastating holocausts,
that left all Tibet and Kashmir in ruins
by political atrocities and civil wars,
you stayed up in the clouds
untouchable by earthly powers
in your prayers, monasteries and traditions
intact and unbroken since a thousand years;
and thus you keep on flourishing in cozy comfort
isolated eight months every year
by severest winters closing up all passes
to let you in peace run festivals all winter
in your harmony and happiness that seems incurable.

And yet, you are in some ways leader of the world
in reasonable ecological economy,
for you a must, since you are always short of water,
but which system of co-operation admirably high developed
to make life in hard conditions possible at all
the whole world needs to learn a lot of.
Thrive in peace and arduous hard work,
and teach the world about your harmony and virtue,
blessed mountain kingdom far away
beyond the landscapes of the moon.

Life never passes except to remain

Was love then just a passing drem,
a perfume of seduction
like a cloud dispersed by any wind,
a fragment of a dream to never be remembered,
a terrible delusion without reason?
But the dream was there and lingers still
and can not be forgotten or denied
and will continue haunting you
as long as you remain alive;
since any love, and even the most brief, is true,
and nothing can recant it or control it.
Love once given will remain with you forever
as a lasting remedy, reward or nightmare – as you wish,
and only you yourself can give it any character.

The Trial

– all those dreadful morning moods…

Do I need you?
Only positively,
since I do not need your problems,
your ingratitude and worries,
all those morning quarrels,
when we both denuded
stand stark naked with our souls
in constant trial for our lives,
our tragedies, mistakes and crimes,
our rotten morals and delusions,
which are an infinity
of dreadfulness, disorganized disorder,

an entangled mess of weird confusions
and unsorted heaps of odds and ends,
just like in any marriage,
although we were never married.
Shall we let each other go, then,
just to try to set us free?
Is that possible?
That is the the real question
and the trial that can never reach a verdict.

Elementary

Purity of heart and love
is all that counts in love
and all that makes up love
– there is no love where opportunity turns up
and fools you into calculation,
which immediately corrupts it
and turns it away to other forms
except sincerity, integrity and honesty,
and thus it even may turn into hate,
the very opposite of love;
which always is one-sided,
true and living only by its honesty.
If love is true, it's better to abstain from it
and banish it forever
than risk having it defouled
by anything unworthy of its highest level,
if it once has been attained.

Natural truth

Truth will always out,
and there is nothing you can do to stop it;
like a force of nature,
it is mercilessly irresistible
and absolutely neutral in its callousness,
no matter what objections humans might find justified;
no matter how dishonourable it could be
to ladies, presidents or priests,
the nature of the truth is such
that nothing can suppress it,
and if someone tries it only will boil over
the more certainly and fatally.
The only danger of the truth, in fact,
is actually to try to hold it back,
like whipping a wild bolting horse,
which only the more certainly will throw you off.

So naturally it is wiser
to pay heed to inconvenient truths
and listen to them carefully and even search for them
than to pretend that they are false or don't exist.
However, there is one way to assuage the truth,

and that is simply just to make the best of it,
accept it, bear with it and carry on.
For instance, if you find your ship abandoned,
just sail on without the captain
until he returns,
and if he doesn't, just sail on
as long as there is any sea to sail on
and a boat to save you from it.

Bitterness

— after tears and rains, the sun will shine anyway
and go on shining always even when clouded.

Anything is better than bitterness.
If all you can do is but quarrel,
then just get lost and forget it,
leave it behind, close that wardrobe,
get down to reality instead
and stop worrying, crying and moaning
which never will do any good
but only is a waste of time.
Go on and leave the yesterdays behind you,
and you will find, that all that is ahead of you
is just a glorious lot of splendid tomorrows.

Sikkim

Paradise of dreams,
perhaps the last of Shangri Las,
your pastoral idyllic peace
is like a life elixir
and a fountain of perpetual love
with your abundance of lush gardens
with the greatest richness in the world of orchids,
making actually your entire country
like a secret wonderful botanic garden
in the vastness of which anyone gets lost
to never reach the end of it.
In these dark winter times
it gives immense relief and comfort
just to think of your warm paradise
with maybe the most gentle people of all India,

indeed a fountain of perpetual youth
and of sweet lasting dreams
to always have in store and to return to
with fond tenderness and everlasting pleasure.

Goa

They say you find the best of Indians there
and all the worst of westerners.
Is that because of all those parties
going on forever day and night
the whole year round
and reaching something of a climax
around New Year's celebrations?
This was actually one of the first
established hippie paradises
of the 70s together with Nepal and Bali,
all those hippie colonies migrating
as the seasons changed,
in summer for Nepal,
in winter down to Goa
and escaping the monsoons to Bali,
and this circulation still goes on.
The party never ends but only changes places,
moving even up to Kashmir and Ladakh
occasionally when the Nepal civil war
made things uncomfortable there.
So, welcome to enjoy and join the party,
there is now three generations of those hippies,
still incorrigible as peace and rainbow activists
all round the globe and constantly increasing,
gaining ground as gradually the world begins to realize,
that they were always right from the beginning,
sacrificing world affairs, careers and vanity
for the idealism of living more for love and beauty
as the only means to make a future possible.

The secret lover

I don't care who steals you
from your friends and truest lovers,
I don't care who kisses you and fondles you,
your opportunism is your own affair

and no concern of mine,
and neither is your scheming calculation and ingratitude;
we are poor devils living idealistically
and are therefore free to use whatever means
fate offers us for opportunities;
my distant silence shall the more be eloquent
and echo universally the obviousness of my unhappy love,
for no one loves more honestly than those who suffer for it.
Let my ague then be evidence enough
that I alone was your supreme and only perfect lover
who expressed it best by suffering in silence.

At a loss

— the morning after before the day of tomorrow

I lost my head
in sudden gusts of crises
blowing in with climate changes
bursting every sense of credibility
and probability, stability and safety,
replacing it with bursts of chaos
in which all you can do
is to cool it down, get drunk, resign
and just forget about the global mess
in which the world has lost its head
and can not find it any more.
What shall we do about it?
There is only one thing certain about life,
and that is that we all must die,
and then we'll see what happens.
That, in fact, is maybe our lasting hope,
that there is always some surprises left.

Journeying on

We are together on the same road
which however only leads to hell
and never ends,
for it begins where it's the end,
and ends already from the start,
but that end is an end that never ends.
It is a way to go together

towards a perdition that will never come
and during which we never can be joined
although that was the only reason why we made it.
Someone has to fall during the way
but only to become the better company
as spiritual leader and companion
who will never more desert you.
Thus we journey on forever to perdition
towards a beginning that will never come
and an end that never will be terminal
but always will go on
and start again from the beginning
just as you thought that everything was finished.

Santa at bay

What do you expect of me?
To humour you for a christmas corrupted and commercialised to death?
To drive around with my reindeers in a world without snow
where you have ruined the whole climate with your pollution?
To be happy and laugh that silly old ho!ho!ho! in all your din
of deafening noise shouting down all that sounded good
and accept that you have turned christmas into a prostitution
of all that was lovely and nice about the holidays
by your bloody vulgar shit publicity and commercials,
which only has debased me into the greatest fool
of universal ridicule during the last 50 years?
To keep a shining jolly face amidst all your warring
when your society only is good for burning people out,
when christmas trees hardly can grow any more in your acid forests
where you have cut down almost every single wild tree,
and when you just ignore all your hospitalized victims buried alive
and dying while you just eat yourselves to vomit,
imagining you have a good time while all you produce is diarrhoeas?
No, the only proper thing about christmas nowadays
is the liquor and the wine, that at least you have that good sense
to drink yourselves unconscious in all your mad failures;
and don't expect any christmas presents from me this year
or any other year, don't expect to see me any more,
for I'll be on strike this christmas and forever
just sitting at home drinking.

Old flames

You love them still and can't forget them,
but you never look them up,
bored as you are with sleazy memories,
and so instead your conscience aches
and you feel sultry and desultory
although there's nothing wrong
and you were not at fault.
The difficulty is to start again,
get out of all your failures and get on with it;
but burnt as you so miserably are,
you really do not feel much for it,
sticking to those awkward sticky memories
that you don't feel like looking up
and for that reason even less can get away from.
It's the old predicament of old sentimentality,
and all you actually can do about it
is to wallow in those memories
and write some poems to assort them.

I can't stop loving you

How can I love you without hurting you
and causing harm to our relationship?
We only seem to be quite safe when we are gone
at proper distance from each other,
but that constant separation is the deepest wound
each time you leave me for another,
for your life of flair and casual pleasure,
that excludes all intimate relationships
and makes a lasting friendship difficult,
debarring it from ever reaching any fathoms of profundity.
Yet another temporary separation and divorce
prolonging it and making it yet more unbearable
and unsurveyable – is that how our love is doomed?
To ever grow but never reach fulfilment?
I am at a loss, bewildered and bedazzled
and am only sure of one thing:
that I can't stop loving you.

My friend or foe

I do not know you and therefore can not trust you.
Something tells me you will be my death some day.
Your love I can not doubt,
it certainly does turn me on,
and I am grateful for your company,
since you are always there,
my most mysterious travelling companion,
and your beauty certainly is irresistible,
and yet I hesitate, which you must bear with.
You can never be too careful about love,
it is the easiest way to get burnt out,
and still you can not do without it but must have it,
like a drug of unknown consequences.
You are certainly the most dramatic
of my friends but also the most dangerous,
so please forbear with my precautions.
I will love you, certainly, with all my flesh and soul,
it's just my heart and brain I am uncertain of,
but they will follow, though not without warnings.

The humanist's dilemma

The problem about humanism, although an ideal,
is that it must needs have neutrality,
it is objective goodness that must cancel passion
to subsist, survive, exist at all and thrive,
and therefore almost all the greatest humanists
were all without relationships,
they stood alone except for neutral friends.
Is humanism then a philosophy
that must deny the freedom of relationships?
Not quite, but humanism is also practical
demanding freedom most of all,
of mind, of conscience and of thought.
With one relationship then dominating in your life,
the humanist is at the mercy of an octopus
that always tends to bind and slow you down.
I love relationships, invite them and adore them,
but, please, let me keep them neutral,
and I can only entertain and maintain them
if my back is free and I may keep my freedom
to have all the world and cosmos for my friends.

Sweet obsession

Are we obsessed or just possessed,
and what with if not with each other?
But it is a sweet obsession
and the loveliest possession
for as long as we may keep it,
and it seems to be for quite some time,
since it is hardly possible to see an end on it.
It is perhaps a blessedness to take well care of
and enjoy as one of life's most golden moments,
which apparently may last for quite some time,
since so far we have failed to end it,
although we have bravely tried indeed.
So maybe after all it is worth holding on to
since it's so reluctant to leave us in peace.

Unutterable love

We speak in silence
in communion with the stars,
our most attentive listeners,
who understand our thoughts,
the secret language of our souls,
which only intimacy has access to
with the key of safe discretion
more infallible to ever be invaded;
and so our love is intact
as the best kept of all secrets,
which curiosity will try in vain to importune
and only find the black hole of our mystery.
Let's keep it that way and continue
to expand in our love forever.

An ordinary love poem

Our love seems only to increase with the years
as if, instead of growing older, we grew younger,
as if old souls never could grow older
but only younger in mentality, vitality and quality,
as if maturity was something ever to increase
with age in juvenility, ability and vivacity,
like an old mentality growing ever younger

in strength and power with acquired wisdom,
the bitterness of experience carrying only sweetest fruits.
And thus our love in spite of all full stops,
the divorces, differences and disasters
only is revitalized each time we meet again
in a miraculous metamorphosis of a Phoenix
never learning from mistakes but ever starting right again,
as if time, age, experience and generations
mattered less or not at all
than only a brief moment of our union,
in one second outdoing all eternity.

The artist

Ignore your audience and your readers,
they are not the ones who write your poetry,
and it's only their own business if they read it,
nothing that should cause you any worries,
since the only thing that matters
is that what you're writing is alive.
Its contents is another secondary matter,
if it is alive it will remain alive,
and that is all that should be of concern to you,
so do not be afraid of being inconvenient
or provocative or even controversial and insulting,
just forget about all possible reactions
and that you at all might have an audience,
they will stand whatever and survive
and always be there and return
for good or worse regardless in what mood;
and if you are ignored or lynched
it's of no consequence to what you write
which should be written and stay written
for the life and honesty you gave it.
It should even be of no concern of yours
if all you write ends up in silence in the bottom drawer
to stay hidden there concealed from every reader
never to be read or noticed.
If there is true life in it
it will appear in its own right
sooner or later in the limelight of attention,
since what has once been created
and endowed with life will follow its own laws
and fate which is beyond you and all your control,

if only it has true life of its own.
That is the privilege and hell of the creative power:
you have no control of it, once you have let it out.

Love understatement

Hiding my love in poetry
was my best means to protect it
from indiscretion and importunism,
and thus have I kept it safe for you
intact and entire in glorious purity
for its safeguarded expansion infinitely,
and yet I don't know where you are,
perhaps not even who you are,
since my knowledge of you ever was imperfect
in awkwardness and shortcomings,
since I never knew what you expected of me.
Perhaps it was nothing or merely friendship,
but I ever gave you more and wanted more
and wished so much more to offer you,
but you were never there
in physical accessibility
since you were only soul
and the more overwhelming spiritually
for your absence of approachability.
Once Beethoven said, that "In woman
the body has no soul and the soul no body."
and yet he loved the more
for never reaching his beloved.
But I have always reached you
and kept your self within me
and will do so continuously forever.

Close encounters of the fourth degree

The unforgettable encounter left me marked forever
with a stamp burnt in from which I never will recover,
like a most incurable disease in which you waste forever
without dying, in a torment that will never cease
but merely increase, unnoticeably worsening
so slowly that it's stealing on you from behind
so furtively and fatally as never to leave you in peace
from that mere knowledge that from now on you'll be dying

like a leper, slowly, inconceivably,
to never let you die completely,
and that is the the worst of all in this unending doom.
And yet, your face, that should have been so utterly familiar,
was so alien and so fascinating in its unreality
that I could but be stuck with it forever
studying it too thoroughly for its so creeping horror
worse than any monster or wild raging animal
and so appalling in its utter naked truth,
a soul unclothed and bared in all its magic
not to ever let me free again from that tremendous spell
affecting all my life, reducing me to nothing but a thrall
to fear and obstinate workoholism
for maybe more than just a lifetime sentence.
Still I do not know you, and it was my own fault
that I dared to look you in your face
under the influence of that most devastating drug of truth
effacing all reality except the basic spiritual one
so fatally revealed to me in just one catastrophic look into a mirror
to immediately kill me off to save my soul
but slain in bondage in the chains of servitude forever.

Unwelcome guests at Poetbay

We are all strangers here
as fleeting as the ghosts of shadows
visiting and staying on in vain
in spite of being most unwelcome and abandoned
to just vanish without any trace
with only memories to keep our ghosts alive,
like improvising temporary guests
who think they make great presence
and by all means make the best of it to
vanish all the same
completely, like untombed Elizabethans.
Very well, it's just to be accepted,
but there's nothing to prevent us
from maintaining golden memories
and cultivating them in peace forever.
They can close down any site and burn all poetry,
but they can never stop us from continuing
to visit parties uninvited
just to make our poetry.

Palestrina

Palestrina made some music
which was far too beautiful
to suit His Holiness the Pope,
who thought the music dangerous
in its seducing beauty
luridly diverting people's minds
from the religious formalism and order
to a better world of spiritual harmonies
which in the long run could outdo religion
as something better and a more spiritual alternative;
so the almighty Pope called forth the Inquisition
to investigate the magic of that lewd musician,
which they did, and found, that his polyphony
was insubstantial like the clouds.
So Palestrina was allowed to go on making music
of his own invention, which is quite ingenious still today
and matchless as perfected polyphonal choir singing
much more to the glory of that God
who had been so misunderstood by that almighty church
which thought it fit to make the Inquisition try some music.

Orlando di Lasso

The merry fish of virtuosity,
unchallenged as a virtuoso,
last of the great Flemish music masters,
learned his music nonetheless in Italy,
and where if not in Naples?
He toured vigorously all of western Europe
but preferred the northern Italy
although his fixed position was in Munich
on the wrong side of the Alps.
In contrary to Palestrina,
who heroically challenged his misfortunes
when he lost his children and his wife
already in advanced age in the Plague,
remarried and refused to be let down,
Orlande de Lassus, successful always
with 2000 compositions on his conscience
was in latter days seized with melancholy
and found it difficult to get out of that bog,
as if his whole triumphant life of just encores

had merely been a mirage of some self-deception.
Curiously enough, they both died in the same year,
Palestrina quite unbroken by his tragedies,
Orlando Lasso at a loss for all his unbroken successes.

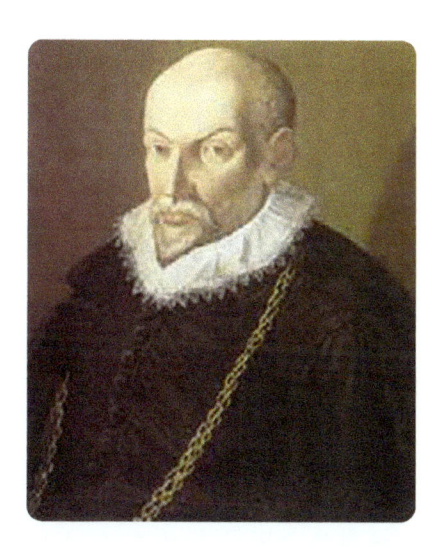

The war of madness on sensibility

Benazir Bhutto in memoriam.

This cannot pass unnoticed.
It is too blatant in preposterous absurdity.
It is too over-obvious and can never be defended.
Mrs Bhutto wanted peace and sense to rule in Pakistan
and therefore was assassinated by a suicide bomber.
Can it get more sick –
the state of fundamentalists and terrorists,
the fanatism of psychopathic paranoia
waging holy war against a woman
just because she was a woman of some influence,
a blind attack on all the values of civilization,
justice, reason, sense, constructivism and education
only to enforce dictatorship intolerance
and backward brainwash unto death at any cost.
And this was not the first time.
The same brute force was launched in Burma
against peaceful demonstrants

who only asked for what was reasonable
also led by one courageous and heroic woman
who has been imprisoned for some sixteen years.
In China this war of insanity against good sense,
against all human rights, against suppressed Tibetans
and against the perils of philosophy and Buddhist wisdom
has been going on for sixty years
and still not tires in its efforts to exterminate
the freedom of the human mind and thought and conscience
and the life and culture and the history of the Tibetan nation.
They will never tire, all those mad dogs of barbarity
in their efforts to annihilate all sense
and beauty that excels their own,
and they will never learn, the miserable bastards,
that they never will be able to succeed.

Death is down

Death is never death but just an aimless threat
in vain to challenge life and give it some adversity
just to forward progress and transgress resistance
to bring life the more to victory
eliminating destructivity forever,
which is only there as spice and salt
to make the stew less boring.
Death is only what makes life
surviving, overcoming, conquering
and glorying in eternity like Phoenix,
so don't for a moment think that PoetBay is finished.
It has only started.

Montewerdi, Orpheus and their lost wives

Claudio worked for years
on that incredible experiment,
the opera, the very first one,
celebrating now four centuries,
but working too hard on it,
his poor wife got lost and died,
and Monteverdi never could get over it.
His opera was the supreme success,
it started avalanches of successes;
but just as Orpheus failed
in getting back his wife,
so Monteverdi lost his wife forever.
He resigned and moved to Venice
to commence a different career
as church musician in St. Mark's

and was successful all his life as such,
for thirty years encore,
but never, and not even in his finest music,
managed to retrieve the unjust theft
of his beloved wife from death,
the falsest thief of all,
who never can get punished
and never will return a stolen life.

Gesualdo and his wife

(Carlo Gesualdo, Duke and Prince of Venosa, married his first wife Maria d'Avalos in 1566. His second wife (not mentioned here) survived him.)

He loved her truly and indeed
but far too much,
so when he was deceived
by the most beautiful Maria d'Avalos,
a princess and twice widow,
25 years and a cousin,
and surprised her in his own bed with her lover,
he lost all control and massacred the couple
most atrociously, revealing greater passion than Othello
and a jealousy more horrifying being justified.

The law could never get at him, since many helpers were involved,
and people thought in general that he was right,
that the adulterous couple had themselves to blame
for openly inviting Satan to their own black wedding.
But his life was ruined, and he never could forgive himself
but led an isolated life like in a prison of self torture,
caught in the horrific trap of his own tragedy,
which led him to compose the most extraneous music
of that century, transforming his despair, depression, grief and tears
into the most expressive madrigals
that still today appear as bold and modern
in their heart-rending characteristic constant pain,
a lasting cry of love from hell.

Alessandro Stradella

(1645-82, discovered in Rome by the Swedish exiled Queen Christina, who established his fame as musician and composer.)

It's not easy to be over-talented,
especially not as a musician,
which Stradella was, the handsome Alessandro,
who had lovers everywhere
and never got enough of them.
The only problem was,
they oftentimes were married,
and their husbands didn't like him
to hang on their wives,
so they with some good reason tried to kill him,
just to settle matters with him once for all.
So he was constantly compelled to run away,
was chased away from Venice
by professional and hired killers,
and also from Torino,
to find some security in Genoa
where, nonetheless, he found new lovers
and eventually was killed
by one of their infuriated husbands.
He was only thirty-seven,
after seven operas and seven oratorios
and a lot of other compositions,
the most talented musician of his age,
killed for his extraordinary talents as a lover.

Persecuted by war – Heinrich Schütz

(1585-1672, married for only six years, two daughters, all died during the thirty years' war holocaust, and only one small granddaughter survived of his family.)

His wife and daughters died,
not able to withstand the press of war,
that kept on executing his musicians
and make music almost quite impossible
in dins of thirty years of war.
He kept escaping
from his base in Dresden,
like four hundred years much later
the most tragic of war central stages,
leaving colleagues, friends, musicians and his family
behind from pure necessity
to keep supporting them and make his living,
travelling around at random to find peace
for vocal music in the churches
that were left alone by war,
for instance Copenhagen;

OCTOBER HARVEST FIRST PART.

and when finally the thirty years of war were over
and his friends and colleagues, church musicians,
all his family except one single daughter's daughter
all were dead and gone and buried
in the ruins of the war-torn Germany,
he still kept on composing, working to the end,
until at last at 87 years he found his peace
by reaching up to introduce the greatest age of music,
having proved that it was better and more able to survive
than any war politics, vanity and madness,
all made null and void
by the sheer beauty of the harmony of music.

Hippie love

We used to love one another,
and it was never wrong,
no matter how much we shared our love with others
and never kept it for ourselves.
Our love was never a deceit,
the less so the more it encompassed others,
and sleeping together was never love enough.
We needed more than that
and therefore always gave more than that
sharing our love universally
with whomever.
How can love then be confined
within the restrictions of marriage,
of sticking to one person,
of vows and oaths and promises
that never could be kept?
Forgive me, my love, but I could never stick to you alone,
but we owed our love to everyone.

The innocents

We just refused to be part of it,
the generation of the world wars,
those who fought them enthusiastically,
those who defended the bombs of terror balance,
those who thought Hiroshima and Nagasaki were justified,
those who liked the Nazis until they fell
and then the communists until they fell,
those who adopted materialism
and sold their lives to the slavery of Mammon
and raised rigid families adapting squarely
to lives of stale cubicularism
in a society of perfect capitalist consumerist order –
we wanted none of all that soul pollution
but wanted freedom and the right of love
to triumph over every kind of bondage,
and thus preferred beauty to the ugliness of modern man,
life in nature to the sterility of urban society,
and love to hate and war and freak politics.
We preferred natural innocence

to the guilt of modern man,
which we rejected with the wars and bombs;
and we were right, we are right still,
and history will make us right.

Unwavering light of love

The beauty of your soul transcends eternity,
if you allow me this small understatement
which, however well-aimed at the truth,
still misses it by many light-years,
since you simply are unmatchable and unattainable.
The love you gave me by the beauty of your grace
I never will abandon or give up
but cultivate forever with affection,
guard with piety and bless with passion,
since it is the only life I have when you are absent.
Never can our souls depart or separate
from this unique love that we had
and will maintain and carry on forever,
like a firebrand and lighthouse in a stormy sea
to keep on shining to light up all darkness of all nights.

Desert wines and roses

You come to me in flashes of delight,
and I adore you like a virgin spring
in an oasis in Sahara.
Let us not be overwhelmed, however,
by our love of endless fields of wines and roses,
but let us be sensible and handle it with care.
I know you are so brittle as an old Venetian glass,
and I will never touch you but with velvet gloves
to only stroke you with the gentlest touch of ease.
I need your love and thirst the more I miss it,
but I shall never drink it to the bottom
since I know that even an oasis in Sahara
might run dry if overused and used unwisely,
so I'd rather thirst than risk to waste our love
on anything except the holiness of our togetherness.

The sweet pain of nostalgia

What matters all the pain of our memories,
since we have them together,
suffering together all those losses
of friends lost and gone
and ever brought to mind
to never be forgotten?
It's the sweetness of our memories
that counts in ever warmer and more beautiful nostalgia
and not the pains and pangs of heartaches,
since all hurts are only there to vanish
and to ever be forgotten
as superfluous to life.
The colours of our tender souls
forever marked by incandescent memories
will forever warm us up
in the obstinacy of our constant hibernation,
which will warm the more
as we with pleasure share them
with the company that still remains
so long still after our explosive party
that turned on the world to keep it rolling
even long after that we have gone.

Soaring

All kinds of love are good and right,
and there are no exceptions.
Highest, though, is the affinity of souls
that has a quality of more than mortal standards,
challenging the moon and stars and galaxies
since it is universal in its faculty,
which nothing can bring down to earth,
although you find it in all kinds of earthal forms
and languages, expressions, habits and results
which all contribute to the continuity
of love that never can get low or down
but is the very essence of constructiveness
one-sidedly and yet bilaterally always;
since the very magic, life and way of love
is always in the forward-leading dialogue.

The seven stages of love

It starts so easy and so pleasant –
you start in paradise and just enjoy it.
Then the long way down begins.

The second stage is still an easy crisis,
when communication fails
and is replaced with gradual mistrust.

Then comes the third stage and the real crisis,
when deceit has formed and one is made a victim
while the other enters on the path of dubiousness.

The fourth stage is the melancholy limbo,
when delusion is a fact and only memories remain
of how delightful, wonderful and great it could have been.

Then comes the fifth stage, the enforcement,
when you fight refusing to give up and claim your love
with any right by any means
and fail in total personal defeat,
which brings you to the sixth stage,
when you are forced by destiny to be a realist,
admit your failure and look through all falseness,
recognize that love can be abused and is misused.

The seventh stage is the transcendence,
when in spite of all you stay on line in love
and broaden it to mature universalism
including all and laying down all selfishness
to recognize the true love of enduring quality
completely free and independent of all mortal means.

Purcell and his wife

(Henry Purcell (1659-95) was perhaps the greatest English composer ever.)

They say his wife in anger locked him out
and caused his death. It is not so.
She had no reason to, she loved her husband,
he had given her five children,
but he was always late and overworking,
and her order was not quite exemplary.
When he caught that cold that autumn night
and found himself locked out from home,
the whole house sleeping,
she had probably just acted on routine
with no intention to obstruct her husband,
whom she loved and served – it was a happy marriage.
There would not have been five children else.
And Henry Purcell was, alas, a workoholic,
the first genius of that kind in music,
followed later by too many others,
young divine creative artists
working themselves fiercely to death
before they reached their forties,
like Franz Schubert, Mozart, Mendelssohn
and far too many others.
Purcell died at thirty-six but had produced
in only fifteen years of music labour
thirty-two outstanding volumes of impressive music.
Bach made fifty, Handel hundred, for comparison,
so one can imagine what our Purcell would have come to
as the greatest music genius of his age
if he had just been home in time for bed
before his wife unfortunately locked the door
and locked him out of contrary neglect.

Masked identity

Let me keep you hanging in the air
in blind incertitude of what I am and where
for the suspension of our love
to keep it up
in view of all but beyond reach
just for the fun of it,
in order that you must not lose it out of sight.
For love, like any baby, needs untiring attendance
and demands more energy than anything in life;
for it is life itself in its most basic flame
that keeps life burning and alive and warm,
which we all need, who never wish to tire
of remaining lovers.

Winter rheumatism

The case is hopeless from the start.
You're done for, brother.
For five thousand years man has struggled with the problem
of the ache awakened by the weather and just floating,
always being there, unwanted and unreachable,
like the most uninvited of all guests
who is the only one to constantly remain.
The only thing to do is to ignore him,
disregard him, concentrate on other things,
on anything that gets the focus off the body,
off the pain of hell in bones and carcass,
on no matter what activity, on journeys, work or social life –
whatever the activity, it is good therapy,
and the worst thing to do is nothing.
Let the torment be a challenge to you
to move into higher gear,
and that's the only medicine that works
against the most incurable of ills,
which is no fault of anyone's but only of the weather.

Bullshitting bushes

Forget about those bossy bully states
of bushisms spewing turd all round the world
with governing establishments for queer justification –
they never led us all through history except astray
today in worse predicaments than ever,
while they joke about it and pretend
the situation is not real,
while they know better,
since they are accountable for all that mess
that leaves humanity in shit
while they just profit by it.
We are better off, we poets,
who are free in Never Never Land
transcending no man's land
in exile from this mortal world of nonsense
into our paradise of meaningfulness,
where, devoid of all corrupting power,
we can see more clearly from the outside
and use common sense to stay away
from all that torpid smell of vanity
that comes from egoistic shortsighted ambition
aiming nowhere but to own destruction.
We are safe above it,
leaving mundane idiocy
to get lost with the consumer lunacy
in custody of bushes.

Incurably invulnerable

Since I loved you
and gave you my first love
there has never been another,
honestly,
since you alone was ever faithful
at least in spirit,
no matter who they were
and what they were, how many
and how dubious,
all the others,
all those false alternatives,
all those who thought it opportune
to love you less than I.

My love never changed
and never lost in spirit,
never grew in age
but only in maturity,
and it remains all yours,
my love,
my only love,
in spite of all the efforts in the world
to sabotage, obstruct and kill our love
which was invulnerable
from the start,
since it existed
long before we even were conceived.

The Teacher

When we were small we played together,
and since then our lives have grown with memories
that ever grew more sweeter
the longer that we kept our love prevailing,
growing and expanding;
like a flower that would never wither
but uniquely only just continue growing
larger and more beautiful and splendid
in ever increasing sumptuousness of colours,

better even than the Phoenix,
who gets burned sometimes to get renewed;
but our love caught never fire
although it kept growing ever warmer
with the candour of our hearts
that never seem to mature quite enough,
since we continue learning
from each other
of our love
how this the greatest miracle of all
is actually the only thing in life
that can teach something about life.

Within

Let me remain within you
in a love embrace that never ends
to give us life and let us stay alive
in this our love of sweetest wonders
beyond dreams and all reality
in reigns of our common soul
to drown the world in love and life
to teach the universe how all this wonder works,
the issue of the sharing of true love
that made the first of paradises
which we never really lost
but which is there within our reach
within ourselves
and which we only can be barred from by ourselves.
It all depends on us and our love,
and all I wish is for it to continue,
me within you and our paradise
in your embrace
of ever growing sweetness,
warmth and kindness.

Vivaldi and his ladies

He was a priest and never left his first vocation,
although he was forced by illness out of service.
In his later years, the priests complained
and wondered why he never more said mass.
He hadn't then for half his life.

He wrote that famous pitiful reply,
that illness of the lungs in all his life
had made it hard for him to say the mass at all,
and when he had, he had been interrupted
by his chest pains, coughings, and so forth.
Instead, he found his comfort in his music,
and his orchestra of ladies was ideal company
throughout his life, performing all his concerts,
oratorios and operas. Although so intimate with ladies
every day and even with most stimulating music,
he remained a virgin all his life
again because of illness.
It might have been tuberculosis
of some kind or something like it,
and like Mozart he died prematurely
and was forgotten in a pauper's grave
and even in Vienna. Unlike Mozart's, though,
Antonio Vivaldi's graveyard is all gone,
and all that now is left of him
is all that virgin and enchanting music
which he so enjoyed with all his ladies.

Bach's poor wives

He made twenty children,
and when his first wife died
from exhaustion, overstrain and so forth,
he just got another and continued
making children, while she had to work
at home maintaining and supporting,
cooking, serving, washing,
doing everything for his immense expanding family;
and when she died, she had no pension
but was put away into an alms-house,
brutally neglected and ignored
by all her husband's sons and children.
This domestic tragedy is easily forgotten
for his merry stimulating music,
which remains his better mark in history
than the expressive silence of his patient wives.

Depression

– Can it get worse? It always does.

The weather is destroyed.
The world is destroyed.
Africa is overwhelmed with Aids cemeteries
replacing civilization.
Antarctica is melting
and will drown the world.
All animals are getting extinct,
all because of man,
and we humans are the guilty ones.
The mess seems complete
and can't get any worse,
but it always does.
So what the hell can we do about it?
Nothing, but make the best of it
in at least trying to survive.

The Urge of Freedom

You can not stop it,
and there is no force of nature
in this universe that ever could,

OCTOBER HARVEST FIRST PART.

this urge of freedom,
running wild and out of every prison,
constantly escaping all control
to never be fenced in
by anyone or any human effort.
Man has failed completely
in his effort to contain Dame Nature
running wild now, melting down the poles
and threatening to drown all mankind
once again, since man has never learned
to be more sensible –
already William Blake saw all the madness
in environmental ruining and exploitation,
but the sanest prophets were the most ignored.
You can't pin down the creativity of life,
confine her, limit her or even understand her,
but she will escape, surprisingly to baffle even more
each human effort to have her contained.
Now nature will reclaim the planet
ruined by the lunacy of humankind,
and the only thing that we can do about it
is to bury our dead, make cemeteries
and lament the ruin of our folly.

Handel and his widows

He had no family, no obvious sex life,
and historians have complained about
the absence in his life of scandals;
yet he worked with women all his life,
but only primadonnas, divas, stars of self-obsession,
and he said that ladies thought of nothing but themselves.
And yet he took them on, but not just anyone:
he cared for widows, mothers without men
and children without parents,
instituting even for their care an orphanage
and even caring for the widow of his teacher,
Master Zachow back in Germany.
Widows was his dominant speciality,
he felt at ease with them,
and they were not pretentious,
their relationships were without obligation tensions;
so he was quite happy all his life
with working hard as a paragon workoholic bachelor,
since music, singing above all,
was more than satisfactory
and filling all his life with love
of harmony and melody and beauty.

Is it possible to be a realist without becoming a cynic?

Cynicism is deemed inhuman,
and it is, while cynics usually are realists
and usually are quite right,
which is abominable,
since all cynicism is so disgusting.
But there are idealists also,
and they are not always unrealistic,
and when they stick to realism
they also usually prove right.
Here is the incongruity:
idealism as contrary to cynicism,
while they both get all their strength
from the same realism.
The choice is simple:
be a true idealist and realist,
base your idealism on realism,
and cynicism will not be necessary
but will only prove quite wrong.

Impossible hibernation

We tried and hard indeed
to just forget about it,
leave it, let it go to hell
as much as they insisted,
all those humbug leaders
of deception of politics,
Johnson, Nixon, Reagan, Bushes;
tried to hibernate, go underground
and hide from the aggressions
against all outsidership,
the prophets that were right
and dared to speak out, saying,
"You are wrong!" to all those that were wrong,
while they continued bulldozing the world
and shut up all investigations of the truth,
in murders like of Kennedy and Bhutto,
Politkovskaya and Rainbow Warriors;
but we failed. We never could stay underground,
we never could keep still,
we never could abandon our concern;
and so the demonstration revolution
just keeps rolling on
futilely but heroically
against the established faked world order
that keeps trying to enforce global destruction,
while we poor and underground outsiders
seem to be the only ones
to try to change direction;
and a fact is, let it be a cheer,
the world direction always changed.

Domenico Scarlatti and his Princess – saved by a castrato

He was so fond of his dear princess,
Barbara of Portugal,
that he was happy to remain
a prisoner of music in her care
throughout his long idyllic life.
Her treatment of her favourite musician,
on the other hand, appears as rather odd:
she was so fond of his sonatas
of exquisite musical delicacy,

that she would keep them to herself
and not allow them to be published.
Thus, some seventy were only published
in his lifetime, while the rest, 500 more,
did not see daylight until long after his death,
the first complete collection published 1971.
The odd thing is, that his best friend,
the famous Farinelli, a castrato,
driven into exile after Barbara's demise,
took with him into Italy the one unique edition
of the 555 sonatas, one example in two volumes,
eventually one ending up in Parma, one in Venice,
not united to be published finally by Brahms.
But all this bother long after his death,
the worries and the problems of his scattared music,
all the masses, operas and other compositions being lost,
was no concern of poor Domenico,
who just was happy in the idylls of his Queen
to play for her his intimate sonatas
and forget about the worthless rest of all the world.

Hubris

There is no harm in it if it
is only love.
Wings were made to fly on,
and there are no stronger winds
than those of love to take you anywhere,
as in the air there are no bounds,
no limits to your freedom
and no end to your expansion.
Love, however, is the only thing
to render hubris positive,
the only thing to justify it,
and the more for being so unique.

A Compliment

Is it wrong of me to be intoxicated
merely by the sight of your long hair,
the length of which so obviously
is just a demonstration of your love
in constant growth and warmth of colour

and so generously manifested in the open?
Once you called me the most sensual of all your lovers,
a compliment that made me tremble,
since I never knew a woman
who had known men better than yourself.
I quaked from bottom up
and do so still each time I see you
in the splendour of your heart's magnificence
so evident in glory only in your hair.
The rest of your ability, nobility and character
is not so obvious and will I keep secret,
as the chamber of our love reserved for us.

The one mistake of Joseph Haydn

It was his marriage,
but it was not really his fault.
His love was the younger sister,
who became a nun,
and then the family insisted
he should marry the much older sister,
who became a hag
with no interest at all in music;
and he called her on his journeys,
when she could not hear it,
"the infernal beast";
and being catholics,
he never could divorce her,

but had to wait until she died
to get his freedom, then at 68.
But that was his life's one unique mistake,
and he was not without his comforts.
He cared for Luigia Polzelli and her sons,
and one of them might have been his.
When he was free at last to marry her,
he was too old, while she made him to promise
not to marry anyone instead of her,
which he of course agreed to in his kindness,
while she went back into Italy
and married someone else.
His best friend was the wife
of his employer's doctor, though,
Marianne von Genzinger,
which, although no more than a friendship
was his life's most intimate relationship
besides the one with Mozart.
When they both turned in too early,
Marianne and Mozart,
he was never happy anymore
and turned into a bitter and sarcastic miser.
Still, he left a mystery behind,
when in his will, (he died a rich man,)
left to various ladies various fortunes,
like the unknown daughters Dillin
and the daughter of accountant Kandler,
a soprano Barbara Pilhofer,
and an unknown chamber maid...
Who were all these good ladies
to receive such fortunes
from a humble but most generous musician,
who discreetly never told the story
how he found much better wives
outside his marriage
without compromising anyone.

Our divorces

We were constantly divorced
not by ourselves but by our circumstances,
you being forced abroad by sudden family upheaval,
me reduced to poverty for decades
exiled into underground existence

until you returned, beset by men
who I refused to challenge,
rather making friends with all of them
for your sake, since you loved them.
You felt guilty for their sake
and thought I must disdain you,
while I only was withheld by other problems,
poverty, depression, illness, constant worries
and what not, and all but your predicaments.
And still, all those divorces
uninivited and involuntary,
always brought us back again
into each other's arms
and closer every time.
So let them just continue.
They will always fail completely,
as they did from the beginning.

Mozart's clever wife

He was hopeless,
never could keep anything in order,
lost his income on the pools
and always ill since childhood,
when his father drove him on too hard.
He loved her elder sister,
who refused him for his wantonness,
and so he married little sister Constance,
who would compensate her lack of beauty,
which had been her sister's,
with considerable skill and sensibility.

When Mozart died too young and deep in debt,
most of his works were in a mess, unpublished;
but she undertook to organize them,
married consul Nissen,
moved to Copenhagen
and in good time published all her husband's work
in perfect order making fortunes.
Without her, nine tenths of all his works
would surely have been lost forever.

Sorrows

Can emptiness be filled with anything?
It must. A vacuum sucks,
and black holes are attractive;
but can sorrows, that are abstract,
fill a concrete emptiness?
Let's stick to philosophic symbolism,
which only can make all things possible.
Indeed can sorrows be so great
so as to fill a universal emptiness,
since there are no greater human feelings
than the sentiments of grief and sorrow.
So indeed can sorrow fill up anything
and even the most universal emptiness,
which maybe only sorrows can fill up.

Our reward

When we intermingle
in each other's arms
escaping cruel persecution and invalidation
of the ignorance of narrow minds
and wallow in our misery
of poverty and outcast loneliness,
our comfort is our joy and happiness
of the illumination that we share together
totally transcending all the bustle of the mob,
reducing history to but a shred
of junk lost in the desert,
while we keep our universal paradise for ourselves
of everlasting truth and sense and beauty,
safeguarding the legacy of our patient work.

The world cares not for us, so let's ignore it,
and if they are curious about our love,
let them work hard and suffer by themselves to reach it,
as we did ourselves.

Beethoven's immortally beloved

The problem is, we don't know who she was.
We only know, that she was his "immortally beloved",
and it couldn't have been anyone.
He had a number of admiring ladies,
pupils, countesses and princesses,
but his idea of sex was somewhat paradoxical:
"With women, their body has no soul,
and their soul has no body."
So how could he reach them?
By his music only,
as with Leonora in his only opera,
one of the most intriguing,
sympathetic, charming ladies
in all literature of opera and music;

and there are authentic testimonies,
that he always was in love.
So we will have to just resign.
The name of his immortally beloved
will discreetly be unknown forever
while the only certain thing is
that he loved the more.

The Hippie Trail

– tracing the past forever

When the hippies started moving
in the 60s, revolutionizing all the world
with love and beauty, music and perception
it was thought to be all new,
but it was only a renewal.
The idea is easily traced back,
and first among the hippies
is considered the Norwegian Heyerdahl,
who later crossed all seas on rafts
to prove how ancient civilizations linked together.
He wrote 'Fatuhiva', the true story of his hippie life
together with his wife in the south seas
in radical refutal of all civilization,
living actually like Robinson Crusoe.
That was back in the thirties,
but still he was not the first one.
Early in the century there was a hippie colony
at Monte Veritá in Switzerland close to Ascona,
where brave pioneers tried out a different life style
cultivating their own food and vegetables,
living primitively outside civilization.
One of them was the pacifist writer Erich Maria Remarque.
Before that you had the Tolstoyans in old Russia,
striving for a similar free life of purity under the sun
led and inspired by the writings of Leo Tolstoy,
who left his property himself in preference of poverty,
but there were many similar communities long before that.
They actually were always there throughout all history.
Also the freemasons started as an underground community
detached as an alternative to mundane transient disorder.
The monastery movement of the middle ages
rose from such traditions, like the sect of the Essenes

who brought forth Jesus, but Hezekiel the prophet
and in Hellas the Pythagoreans were already of that kind,
and before that you had the Asian monastery movement
of the Buddhists, which continues still today,
and long before that.....

And after that, or even through the hippies
started Greenpeace with a number of environmental organizations
setting off green revolutions and the Rainbow movement
among others, who with global threat to our environment
now see it as their task to take responsibility
to spite authority, bureaucracy and madness of politics
to save at least what can be saved
of our so politically violated planet.

In the light of our love

I always saw you in a light
of lasting quality and durability
of an idealism that would not fade,
and it is shining still.
You never lost the beauty
of your brave ideals,
and thus you went through all the hells of life
unharmed, untarnished and untouched.
We are like children still
like as we were originally
when my love first touched you
in the blend of our naïvety of immaturity
to never leave you outside any more
the heart of our common secret.
Our ideal continues
leading us, uniting us and finding us
together in the destiny
that ever brought us nigher
to the essence of our mystery.

On the safe side of midnight

The storm is over
and the crisis passed,
it was a hell to go through
but well worth it

only since we reached the other side
of love, where we are safe
to go on with our journey
towards growing light,
development of the enlightenment
and everlasting future glories.
All we have to do
is simply to continue
never giving up
our quest for getting better
and achieving the impossible,
at last to get in touch
to never separate again.

Schubert's terrible love

It wasn't his fault.
His friend von Schober made him do it.
They lived together,
and of course there was some tension and excitement,
so he took him on to have some fun.
It was so innocent,
so fatally infernally and tragically innocent.
The whore he took him to had syphilis,
which wasn't obvious until afterwards

but then so much the more.
It ruined Schubert's life,
just in the middle of his greatest symphony,
the so called atmospherical unfinished one;
he lost his hair and all his health
and never quite recovered.
So he died at thirty-one,
the most prolific, talented and diligent composer ever,
with especially a divine talent for the melody,
which never afterwards has been surpassed.
Well, was it woth it?

One night's love with the wrong person,
and a ruined life as the inevitable consequence,
but with the most remarkable and glorious output ever
in the history of music
paradoxically at the same time.
We don't know what Schubert's life would have amounted to
without that one off-side encounter,
but we know,
that that most loveable undying music
that resulted from that tragedy
was quite enough to make in all the music history
Franz Schubert's name in some respects
the greatest of them all.

Too much love for Mendelssohn

Everybody loved him,
and he was fortunate indeed,
coming from a banker's family
of many children and abundances of love,

the most important being of his sister Fanny,
who, according to himself,
was even more talented than himself
in musicality as a composer –
that could be debated,
but he certainly relied on her
as his best friend and only understanding one.
His wife, a mother of five lovely children,
was not very musical and rather superficial
for all her amazing beauty,
they were a most happy family indeed though,
since he was so lucky and so loved in his career.
But suddenly she died, the elder sister Fanny,
in the middle of a soirée, she just broke down
and could not be revived,
a dreadful blow to all the family
and most of all to Felix –
they were quite inseparable,
he was comfortless and lost all faith
in life, in his ability, in music, in his work
and perished in despondency
to after just a few months
join his sister in her grave,
just 38 years old, at the top of his career,
one of the most important and successful
in the history of music.
He was too much loved and loved to much,
and when the heart broke of his closest love,
his own heart could not face the music any more
but had to join in broken parts the broken one.

The dying heart

They say, that love is at its most extreme
and beautiful, when it is dying,
and of course it is.
The swan, the loveliest of birds,
sings only once in life when dying,
or so they say at least,
and it's a beautiful portrayal,
if not of reality, at least of love.
The culmination of a love affair
is usually the end of it,
since what then follows is depression,

usually, remorse, perhaps, and melancholy,
maybe guilt and abysmal sentimentality,
the fall from heaven down to hell,
as if love naturally was mano-depressive.
Still, the love you had, although it died,
shall always live with you forever
and remain triumphant in your memory
if all that failed was just the fallibility of all reality.

The immutability of beauty

Whatever once you had
is always there,
good looks pass only superficially
but in the soul remain forever
if but once they were acquired;
beauty passes only visibly
but spiritually can not fade.
You are still young
if you were young but once,
that youth will never leave you
although you will change with time
but only vainly and externally.
Your inside which creates your life
is your true eternity
to never leave you but be carried with you
as your truth and personality.
And if that soul is beautiful,
your life will be so also,
like yourself, to never fade.

Beyond forgiveness

There is no worse ordeal,
no deeper wound in love,
no trial more severe,
no rape that could hurt more
than infidelity,
the sharpest pain of all
that fatally endures forever
since it pierces, shattering the soul
and leaves it like a dirty wasted rag
for you to cling to all alone

as all that you have left
after the final wreck of all your life.
The worst part is, you have to still survive it
and endure the unendurable
convinced that you will never quite recover,
while, of all crimes, that's the one
that never can be quite forgiven.

Chopin's final engagement

Marie Wodzinska, Chopin's life's one engagement, survived him with 47 years, until 1896.

They truly loved each other,
and she was his one engagement,
Marie Wodzinska, beautiful and noble,
but her parents would not let them have each other,
they forbade her any intercourse with a musician,
and she had to break up the engagement
without leaving Chopin hurt and suffering.
So she "seemed" to be unfaithful
with his double, this most curious poet Slovacki,
born the same year as Chopin and dead the same year,
very much like him in every way.

But she could not have hurt him more.
He bound up all her letters in a beautiful silk ribbon
on which he just wrote, "My grief",
and it remained sealed to his death.
To his amazement, though, she married later
his godfather's son, count Joseph Skarbek,
a most miserable marriage ending in divorce,
whereupon she married yet another sickly man,
another double of Chopin-like sensitivity
who died soon, while she lived to be quite old and childless.

Chopin never quite got over it.
His fate became to be consumed by George Sand,
who made a sport of both collecting and devouring men,
preferrably celebrities, like poet Alfred de Musset,
whose life she ruined with Chopin's.
His one love was Marie Wodzinska
who in order not to hurt him
tried to make herself appear dishonoured,
and he never understood or realized her noble sacrifice,
which definitely turned out
to be all for love of him.

At a loss for love

Love is generally in a most disadvantageous situation,
looking up from underdog positions most pathetically,
longing for what can not ever be accomplished,
searching for the most impossible
that never can be found
and losing all in hazard games of desperation.
Thus I keep on looking for and searching,
longing for and desperately seeking you
but without hope of ever finding any destination.
Still, the very aim is good enough,
the very honesty in the intention is worth all the failures,
and, above all, the idealism of love
is always worth the hazarding and losing everything.
It's the urge, the feeling and the truth that counts
of all that beauty love contains
when it is earnest in itself in pure sincerity.

The unknown poet

He composes seriously and has something to say,
masters all the genres
but is constantly refused,
year in and year out,
work after work of whatever kind,
decade after decade by any publisher,
who always only uses empty formulas to turn him down
without comment, without encouragement,
without acknowledgement, without any personal word
or even any confirmation, that his work has been read at all.
One asks, what the publishers possibly could gain
by constantly turning a poet down,
refusing to give him even the slightest chance,
regardless of quality, productivity
interesting stuff and impeccable language?
He is directed to the suicidal darkness of the bottom drawer
or to the web, where he has to pay to prostitute himself.
Never before in history has the poet been in the position
that he has to pay to appear,
which is quite unique to our age and society.
Without outcome or income
he gets caught in the poverty trap of anonymity
and can't break out of the vicious circle
and is logically driven into the corner of suicide,
disappearing willingly, since he was not wanted,
from the beginning excluded from society,
like Plato exiled Homer from his 'ideal' society
of only academic correctness,
while fantasy, creativity and freedom were excluded
for their disturbing licence.
Does it have to be so bad?
The poet has no desire to become negative or bitter,
he wanted just to write constructively and creatively,
he only wanted to tell good stories,
but the slow suffocation in a society
where culture is excepted as too high-brow
and stamped with a taboo for standing out
from being popular and marketable,
forced him down where he did not want to go
into the corner of isolation, bitterness and despicability,
which was not acceptable,
so he voluntarily disappeared
with all his poems, plays and novels,
biographies, essays and travel accounts,

which all were deleted from the web
since he no longer could pay the hire for his sites.
We'll never even known the name of him or her
since he acted logically to his refusal by society
and took away with him his whole identity.

And the publishers keep shut up and cutting down
blaming the production costs
and that books are too expensive to handle,
which is why they allow a minimum only,
perhaps one out of thousand, to get published,
why the business of refusing gets nastier
and the real manuscripts finally end up
in the document destroyer.
But isn't this worse even than the Nazis,
when they openly burnt books at bonfires,
while here and nowadays books are being destroyed
even before they even had the chance
of ever getting published?
And how can any writer evermore have any faith
in any publisher, when all that publishers can do for you
is to destroy your manuscript?

One night of love

Was it wrong of us to be so fond together
in our wallowing in perfect freedom
just for one time's sake
in spite of all the circumstances,
that compelled us to restrictions
and forbade our love?
Was it wrong to shamefully freak out
in ecstasy and gross delirium
leaving altogether all reality
in a voluptuous consummation
of a feast of beauty
in exaggerated emphasis of brute desire?
Was it wrong to just for once be happy,
leaving all behind, escaping into freedom
in exhilaration of a perfect mutual egoism?
I am afraid we were not very moral
in our night of freedom,
but in all the perfect vice of it
I am quite sure that it was better
than the humdrum sordidness of all alternatives.

Schumann's enigmatic tragedy

He was the greatest lover of them all,
a generous enthusiast of music,
editing the leading music paper of the age
and helping colleagues on the way,
like Mendelssohn and Joachim,
Chopin, Franz Liszt and Wagner,
Berlioz and Brahms,
his heart being the warmest and most tender,
and with the finest wife at that,
the lovely pianist-composer Clara Schumann,
first his pupil, then the mother of his seven children;
and then suddenly a strange eclipse,
a sudden downfall without cause,
a terrible depression coming sneakingly
when his two closest friends had left –
Chopin and Mendelssohn, all too prematurely,
leading to his tragical attempted suicide,
as he jumped into the river Rhine,
abandoning his wife and seven children,
afterwards hospitalized, by his own request,
where he remained for years

attempting constant self-starvation.
The mystery of his depression has never been solved,
there have been written volumes on his illnesses,
none satisfactory, none explaining anything.
He was the greatest lover of them all
until he suddenly one day lost contact with his love
and rather killed himself and starved himself to death
than lived without the love of his ideal.

Brahms' moving fidelity

Johannes Brahms (1833-97) was 23 years younger than Robert Schumann
and 14 years younger than Clara Schumann.

It was Schumann who discovered him
and brought him out into the open
to the musical attention of the world,
and he was like a son to him
and soon was like one of the family,
and Clara Schumann loved him.
When the crisis of her husband came,
Brahms was the one to help her out
through the most difficult time of her life,
alone with seven children
with a constant strain as concert pianist
obliged to all alone support her seven children,
and her gratitude to Brahms was always infinite.
The letters of those years of Schumann's hospitalization
between Clara Schumann and Johannes Brahms
were by agreement later on destroyed by them,
most probably to have no word remaining
that could possibly inflict on Robert Schumann's reputation.
She did never leave her widowhood,
and Brahms remained a bachelor throughout his life,
in constant loyalty to her;
and when she died an honoured lady and musician,
greatest and most serious of all pianists at that time,
forty years after her husband,
her most loyal friend Johannes Brahms
died only six months afterwards,
although he was so much younger.
He had indeed tried to engage himself
with other women, even on her own recommendation,
but found never anyone like her,
the wife of his best friend and mentor,
who became in fact his only friend for life.

The inevitable indispensability of love

You never are yourself enough;
it is inevitable,
that if you are left all by yourself,
you must explode,

since no one can contain himself
indefinitely without love.
You have to be at least two persons
to make love,
and without making love
you can't make life,
and life can not exist.
So there you are.
Make love, or die.

The greatest love story in music

– Vincenzo Bellini, 1801-35, from Catania in Sicily.

This is perhaps the most extreme of love stories in music.
He adored her from the start, she was his only love,
the sparkling Maddalena Fumaroli, of a noble family
of the establishment in high society,
while he was born a natural musician
of an honest family of able music craftsmen,
organists and pianists, conductors, singers, fiddlers,
ordinary, talented and hard working musicians
of no good standing in society, of course,
no wealth, no ancestry, no property, just music;
so the family of Maddalena would not hear of it,
and they forbade Vincenzo's visiting his love;
but he would not give up and formally proposed to her.
Of course, it was rejected by her family,
but he promised her to always remain faithful
and have no more love beside her, except music.
His career became a formidable and exceptional success,
his operas were universally adored and loved,
and at the age of 32, he conquered Paris
with his opera "The Puritans", his ultimate success.
At that point, he was told the fatal news,
that Maddalena Fumaroli suddenly had died.
He could not bear it. He refused to go on living as before.
He retreated into isolation, would not eat, would not see a doctor,
and when finally a doctor had access to him,
it was too late, and he died on exacly the same day
as his beloved Maddalena, one year after her.
He was not ill, the doctors could not understand his death,
while every poet, artist and musician knew the truth:
he died of love.

One of his best friends was Chopin,
who understood him best, perhaps,
and on his dying bed would only listen to the music of Bellini,
and his last wish was to share the grave of Vincenzo Bellini.

Black roses

a translation of a Swedish poem by the artist Ernst Josephson (1851-1906)
Why are you so melancholy,

you that always were so happy?
– I can not be merry any more,
for sorrow has brought me black roses.

There is in my brain a tree of roses
growing, that will never leave me any peace,
and there is a thorn by every stem
which constantly brings me much pain and ire,
since my sorrow brings me all black roses.

But there is a treasure out of roses,
white as death and red as blood,
that keeps on growing into me,
so that I certainly will perish,
since they keep on fretting at my heart
to fill it up and overwhelm it
with the plague of sorrows of black roses.

The black spider of history

translation of a symbolistic (Swedish) poem by Adolf Paul (1863-1943), a
German-Swedish-Finnish poet and friend of Sibelius

Beyond the forest where life is so green
and the sun shines so brightly,
a spider sits snugly so black and so huge
in the grass watching out for its prey.
He catches the sunlight and weaves of its rays
a web of invisible darkness
so strong and so light
to be able to catch any soul coming by
to torment it and quease it to death.

And the sun fades, and light is defeated
to go out and vanish engulfed in the night,
people wandering randomly, going astray
searching vainly, pathetically for their souls
which they lost on the way, but they still keep on going,
believing that night is as light as the day
and get frightened, when dawn is returning,
and hide to protect their delusions and dreams
of the freedom they lost and believe they have found
in their escapist substitute make-believes.

But the spider keeps weaving in anger so stern
well aware that a true soul can never get caught
but must wander through history timeless, serene,
always harassed by power authorities pulling him down
by the might of brute fore, violation and blood,
and they all fight against that invisible web
of the obstinate spider of fate of relentlessness
which will eventually bring every single authority down.

Complaints

All that's wrong with you
is that you are too beautiful,
so everyone must love you
and too much.
And all that's wrong with our relationship
is that we do not meet enough
but have to starve between our meetings,

OCTOBER HARVEST FIRST PART.

since all time that we are not together
is a wasted time of thirst and hunger
and what's worse: of dying desolation of desertion.
All that's wrong with our lives
is that we do not live together
but are kept apart
as punishment for nothing.
All that we can do about it
is to have these unacceptable conditions rectified,
which they inevitably must be,
since they couldn't get much worse.
So there we are back where we started:
at the task of making something good
out of a most impossible situation.

Was it a dream?

translation of a poem by the Finnish poet Josef Julius Wecksell (Swedish, 1838-1907), who far too early lost himself in schizophrenia (1862, with the production of his only play, the dramatic masterpiece "Daniel Hjort").

Was it just a dream
that I was once your heart's beloved?
I remember it most like a silenced song
the string of which is trembling still.

I remember that you offered me a briar rose
of shy and tender aspect
and a glistening silver tear of a farewell –
and was it all a dream?

A dream like the short life of an anemone
of the green springfield of a moment,
hastily to sparkle just to wither
and immediately to be replaced and disappear
in vulgar crowds of others.

But methinks I oftentimes at night
hear one voice crying bitterly
in floods of never-ending tears;
– and that's the memory to hide and keep
in safety deep within your breast,
for that one was your finest dream.

The Diamond in the Snow

translation of another poem by J.J.Wecksell

On the blinding snow drifts
there is a diamond glistening serenely.
There never was a tear, a pearl
of higher sparkling lustre.

Her brilliance like of heaven
comes from deep and secret longing,
as she casts her glance towards the sun
when it comes rising in full glory.

As that warming beam strikes at the snow,
the diamond starts melting in her adoration,
kissing the light sun beams in her fondest love
to gradually dissolve in tears.

O, gracious fate to love
the highest beauty life can offer,
and to sparkle in the blinding glory of the sun,
to die in the fulfilment of her loveliest moment!

The Song of the Heart

Just another Wecksell translation: He wrote 215 poems in his brief period of activity, mainly as a youth, like Rimbaud.

The heart knows not of peace
and dares not hold a faith,
it only beats in constant worry,
and who ever understood its sighs?

Bright eyes of blue,
why must you sparkle so?
and heavenly charming smile,
why must you outshine heaven?

You took my peace away,
the heart is robbed of all its faith,
it only knows for sure one thing, –
the durability of love in all eternity.

I dream, but all my dreams are battles,
waking up, there is no peace,
I break with all my heart and cannot die
and burn in ice and snow.

My hope is thwarted constantly,
my doubts are like a joke,
and I am only calmed
to feel my heart run wild again.

And standing by my grave,
and falling down, I would still burn
and fight with sword and helmet
against all the world for you,

and if I were the god of all the stars,
I would still have you as my bride,
and if I only were a beggar,
I would beg from no one else but you.

The Drop of Spring

the last of my Wecksell translations – for the time being

In the spring of dawn
by happy warblings of the larks
there was a-resting on a cloud
a tear brought out in shyness
bathing in the sunlight.

There was triumphant universal joy
which brought the tear some inspiration
filling him with coy desire
and the courage to express a wish:

Give also me some life,
so that I may dare try to live!

An angel's hand observed the prayer,
touched the cloud and let the tear out
falling down to earth,
where for a while it mirrored
the divine world full of wonders,
heavens full of sparkling gold
and earth all emerald of growth and greenth;

and so fell down and ended up
into the sea, where it was safely hidden.

No one asked you for your name,
and no one saw you here.

Enlightenment

The controversial course of history
has never been more difficult to follow,
civilization going down the drain
bogged down in drug abuse,

exaggerated medication as the universal cure
which only is an excuse for abuse and an illusion,
turning humankind to zombies,
dumbed, reduced to passive zeros
so as to be handled with less difficulty
by establishment authorities,
the only ones to gain
from common idiocy and ignorance.
What shall we do, the "happy" few,
so isolated in our exile from this world mess,
being quite alone in seeing through it all
and kept at bay by the establishment authorities
in poverty and isolation far away
not to disturb "the peace of idiocy and ignorance"
and "happiness" of the established course to hell.
We can point out that we exist,
and that is about all that we can do.
The worst thing we could do is nothing,
and the knack we have and power of the word
compels us never to fall silent
but to constantly keep up the urge and the necessity
to ever more insist on more enlightenment.

Old love never rusts

Old love never rusts and never changes
but grows with the years not only in maturity
but most of all in durability,
so that it almost seems quite natural
that it not only must remain for always
but is also just another chapter of the past,
as if it never really had any beginning
or, if it had, it was long since forgotten
far away in the eternity of timeless past;
which means, that love at present
is but a parenthesis, an interlude,
the tiniest link of an interminable chain
just linking two eternities together,
one of the past and another of the future.
Naturally we tend to emphasize the present,
dramatize it and exaggerate it,
and there is no harm done,
for as long as we keep in perspective
and keep well in view the past eternal
and connected to the everlasting future.

The Tutor's Advice

— from a play

"Take good care of these your priceless younger years,
and be aware that there is no more positive insurance
of a good and honourable life than careful education.
History consists of knowledge, knowledge is but wisdom,
wisdom is the end result and aim of every kind of education,
and that's why all history is the consummate knowledge,
being simply human realistic facts in perfect concentration
and in limitless abundance."

The lightness of light and the light of lightness

The soft touch of ideal creativity
must be as light as light itself
and hardly even touching,
never pressing, beating or enforcing
but just letting it come true
alighting from all heaviness
in constantly increasing speed
of thought and new inventions
carried down from universal influence
to settle down in lasting works of art.
The touch is all and hardly more than just a touch,
enough to make a contact,
just enough to make a current
and electrify the process of creation,
like the God of Michelangelo's creating Adam –
creativity is just a hint materialized,
the faintest touch of lightness,
light as light.

OCTOBER HARVEST FIRST PART.

The gathering storm

Let it sweep us with it
up along the drifting clouds
in furious chase of the infinity
of glorious flight to nowhere
except neverneverland and beyond.
We don't even have to fasten seat-belts,
hurricanes and storms will pay our tickets
to the moon and planets and beyond
and let us comfortably sit upon the wings
of fortune, dreamland and angelic music,
making us untouchable to mortal petty things,
while elves and angels are our only proper company
to take us seriously among the clouds
in that alternative and only truthful world
of beauty, joy and parties going on forever.
Welcome, anyone who cares to join us
on our everlasting trip to love.

Words are not enough

Words can not express our love,
and love itself is not enough expression
for the feelings that encompass all
the world we live in of ourselves
and that celestial harmony
that emanates from our reunion.
We can never separate again
but must remain one unity
together in unbreakable fulfilment
never more to be disturbed
in this extradimensional and perfect harmony
creating peace enough convincing,
stable and magnificent
to outlast all the universe.

Down the drain

— John Keats, for an example

There are certain lovers
who just can't get through
but keep adoring in their bitterness
whom they could never reach
and who kept constantly betraying them,
while he, the miserable lover,
just kept on his faithfulness
in bitter spiritual sado-masochism
as if to wallow in self-torture
of the most alarming, unendurable accelerating kind.
Of course it must end badly,
and eventually his love will peter out
and disappear like all filth down the drain
to finally get lost mixed up in sewers
and at last find outlet and release into the ocean
like a water drop or wave of no more consequence.
Thus was John Keats' name 'writ in water'
after hapless love and poetry much criticized,
and he was not alone.
They always come again,
the faithful lovers that get lost in their fidelity,
betrayed and beaten down by critics
without understanding and by human baseness,

and they always keep on loving,
ending up with their refuted love,
their dreams and positiveness altered into bitterness
forever flowing like a never ending swan song
down the drain.

The only time that lasts is outside time

— A philosophical truism

The only truthfulness is timelessness,
the only zone of durability is out of here,
the only perfect love is without time,
and there is no reliability
but in that 'nowhere' outside time,
in the transcendency of temporariness,
in all that is not touched
by the mortality of mundaneness.
Then there is nothing, you would say.
No, you are wrong.
The 'now' is all deceit and foolery,
the whims of fashion are the mirages
of falsity and self-deceit and desillusion –
it is all a fraud, while only dreams that go beyond
continue living, striving forward and surviving,
constantly outliving all the vanity of passing lies;
and those that stick to dreams
preferring them to the illusions of reality
will see them triumph with all life
to vanquish all mortality.

Morbidity

Drifting like a zombie
everything amiss
coughing like a horse
economy in constant crisis
hanging over you like doom
and frozen shoulders, SMS-thumbs,
mouse arm, eyesight fading,
with a broken back and swollen feet
and constant head-aches,
like as if someone nailed your head

with spikes in constant drumming,
appetite gone missing,
all food nauseating,
all you eat is crap
and boozing makes it worse.
Let's not discuss the shit;
your stinking breath is quite enough,
the ulcers bleeding, fuming and erupting.
What else do you need?
The only thing still missing is a downright suicide,
but dying is the very last thing I'll do.

The Exile

You are lucky to be constantly refused,
not having to take part in the establishment,
the mob that's only good for beating down
each talent that is something extra,
sticking out as something not quite ordinary.
Better, then, to be completely powerless
and innocent and pure without a name,
or have a name but only 'writ in water'
known but to the ocean of eternity
as only one of all the passing water drops,
where all things temporal, established and mundane
are bound to disappear with all things base and vulgar
written just for greed or vanity
of even less use than some toilet paper.
You are only here to vanish anyway.
You might as well be exiled then from the beginning,
lost and disappeared, forgotten and ignored
and be content with the eternal natural outsidership
of nothing more than just a drop of water in the ocean.

The highlight of love

The summit moment of my love
was my life's shortest moment
but enough still for a lifetime
and enough rich for eternity;
so how could I forget it ever?
Let me stay there deep inside you
hidden in the richness of your hair
that never was more long and beautiful
in sumptuous generosity and varmest colour
never to get out of you
but dwell forever as your guest
at your perpetual party
never tiring, constantly improving,
in a mood of sweetest atmospheric music
that must never end, but, like all music,
should exist just to play on.
Embrace me still, and keep me in your heart,
like I will never forgo you
but keep you cherished in my warmth of soul
to never let you go;

and thus all separation
must remain quite naturally most impossible;
and let us be content with that
and simply stay in love forever.

The Bleakness of the Lost Identity

– the problem of being ashamed of the human race

How is it possible to live
aware that you as human being
are one of that kind
that utterly has devastated the whole planet,
killing more than half of all the planet's life
and being most of all a predator and monster
killer of his own kind?
We learn that we should never have exceeded
half a billion members
not to threaten life stability on earth,
and yet we are twelve times that number
and continue ruthlessly to multiply.
How can you stay alive with such a knowledge
being totally ashamed of what you represent
and feeling constantly more lousy as a parasite
partaking in the ruining of nature,
all that's beautiful and free and virgin?
Without idealism you can not live,
idealism is love and faith and hope in man,
but the political reality has ruined everything;
and all that you can do is stick to individuals,
the beauty of outsiders and exceptions
who in some ways have maintained their freedom and integrity;
and then, of course, you always have the bottle
and all kinds of other things to fool your flesh with
into thinking you can actually feel
better temporarily at least.

Demonic love

They say you can't be lovers
being stuck together
in the clinch of a relationship
and at the same time be good friends,
that friendship starts as obligations end
and sexual struggle is disposed of.
I disbelieve it.
Friendship makes the sexual relationship endure,
while it can not endure without friendship.
That's the basis on which all relationships are built,
and they should all be lasting
whether sexual or not.
Let tempests hammer down your life to pieces,
let the storms rage on with all the tragedies,
let virtue suffer, and let tears gush forth
in overwhelming rivers of adversities,
but if your love is based on friendship
it will last and outlast all defeats and trials,
and there is no love at all without it,
since there is no friendship without love.

Age

The more maturity advances,
the less matters age,
and years grow insignificant
as timelessness takes over
and your youth becomes perpetual in mind
as childish sensitivity grows more acute
and you feel as if you had been alive forever
and can't stop living for that reason
constantly renewing all your love
as those you love increase in number
with your social life's perpetual expansion.
What has age to do with that? Nothing at all.
So just forget your age and keep on living,
and, above all, keep on loving,
and you'll stay alive for ages still
and outlive your own age.

Never look back

You learn from your experience,
but what you learn should only serve your future.
Therefore, to look back and linger there
will only hold you back and slow you down.
There is no greater harm, for instance, to a work of art
than overworking it, to go on working on it when it's finished,
which will just detract from its completeness.
Memories of old are good to dwell on,
but they never can replace the present moment
in its crucially decisive shaping of the future.

When an old man proves his dotage going gaga,
he will only have his memories to live on,
but they can not help him if he fails
in living now and going on creating life and future.

There is no excuse for letting go or stepping down;
life will not stop for your sake, if you want to stop it.

Spring

There is no light in life,
there is no spring in sight,
there is no hope in Limbo
but for the hope of seeing you,
but for the longing for you,
but for the sight of you
springing to my mind
as darkness fades
to the approaching spring
after all bringing some light of you.
My longing is incurable,
and but for you it would be deadly;
but since after all you do exist,
there is even some hope
for the extremest suicide,
since you turn everything to life
out from the shadowed winter of death
and must return with spring to me
inevitably, irresistibly and definitely,
renewing all the wonders of our life
with of all reminders the most important,
that you are all my love and always were.

The passion of my love

The passion of my love
keeps burning but without consuming
neither mine own energy
nor thy exceeding beauty,
which keeps constantly improving,
like the incorruptibility
of the perpetual expansion of our love,
which, although so exhausting,
miraculously keeps on growing
in vitality and energy and force,
like as if physical confinement,
like invalidation, limitation and imprisonment
served only to the more enforce the energy,
renew it, boost it and enlarge it
for the cultivation, practice and the use of love.

All you can do is to conform
to this most universal law of irresistibility
and simply let your love consume you
in the glory of its beauty, truth and freedom.

Home

The cozy homeliness of home
where all things work and all is of your own,
where you are out of strife and quarrel
and still free at large to do whatever,
even working late at nights and without limits,
is in all the world the best that you shall ever have,
more worth than gold and all the worldly riches,
where you cultivate your own and have your creativity
and can bring out all your love,
the highest worth that life can offer.
Let all journeys that I ever make
be but a constant journey home,
the only goal worth travelling in life for,
all that always is expecting you,
of all the welcomes in your life the only faithful one
and all that really anyone makes any journey for.

Metaphysical

Do not fear the terror
of the darkness of your mind,
which only is the abyss of your soul,
unfathomable, bottomless and infinite,
which is your only contact with eternity,
the basis of your whole existence
and the very essence of your life,
the source of all its energy and meaning.
That horrific darkness is no joke
and nothing to escape from or evade,
but actually the source of all your potency
for love, creation and constructiveness.
Try never to forget the fact,
that light was born from darkness,
and the only purpose of light shining
is to light up all the darkness.

The eternal return

When first I saw you
I could not believe
it really was the sight I saw
of you again, appearing
out of nowhere
like a revelation;
but it was much too incredible
not to be absolutely true:
you always come again
returning with new freshness of your love
to totally engulf me in your warmth and beauty
so unfathomably overwhelming
in the all too lovely fact
of merely your existence.

Rolling on

The timelessness of love
is just about the only thing
you can be certain of concerning love,
recurring as phenomenon surprisingly
and ever and again with constancy,
so that you never can relax
from the perplexities and mysteries,
caprices and surprises
and nonplussing shocks
that always shatter all your life
by never leaving you in peace
in the outrageously delightful
name of love. So all that you can do
is constantly to just succumb
and never tire of it,
since it is the major thing
that keeps not only you
but all the universe alive and rolling.

On the beach

a rather shallow cliché title, I am afraid...

There was in your seduction
too much art to ever be forgotten,
too much love to ever be regained,
too thorough an impression to ever be removed,
too much sincerity to ever be abandoned
and too much of you to ever leave me –
you went down too deep into my heart
to ever be released again from there,
as the sincerity of love arrives to stay
forever as more part of you
than even your own body.
All you have to do is just to keep it there
with faithfulness and constancy,
forever loyal to that trust
more trustworthy than life,
if only it was genuinely felt and true.

AT THE RISK OF LIFE
By Tsoltim N. Shakabpa

I take the liberty to publish this poem of a friend of mine here, simply as a reminder of a tight present situation that needs universal support...

Just as the sun
Sheds its rays on the moon
To give light to the earth
In the darkness of the night
So too must we stroke our hearts
To raise hope in our hour of despair

Just as the bee stings its aggressor
To protect itself at the risk of life
At the hand of the aggressor
So too must we sting the Chinese
To defend ourselves at the risk of life
At the hands of the Chinese

Just as salmons swim upstream
To spawn their future generations
At the risk of life at the hands of bears

So too must we struggle uphill
To fight for our children's future
At the risk of life at the hands of the Chinese

Better we risk life
Than live in fear all our lives

Running out

Alas, it is running out,
our time on earth,
dwindling every second
into nothing
gradually and remorselessly,
while actually our only hope
is that we'll never know
when actually our time is out.
What can we do with this world
of incurable derailment
but concentrate on inner worlds
and render them at least
as perfect and ideal as possible.
You always start with what you've got,
your own, that soul of yours
that you were born with to administer,
your only tool in life
with which you can by power of your will
do actually whatever.
There's the possibility,
and it's a comfort in this comfortless society
to know, that if there is no help at all,
there is at least the power of your soul
that you were given
for the possibility of any revolution.

Rossini's love

continuing the composers' chronicle of debatable love affairs...
the fatal tragedy of Gioacchino Rossini

He only had one single love,
and nothing could replace it.
He was married,
but his marriage never mattered much.
The devastating fact of what his love was
ruined him, when suddenly he lost it,
which so annihilated him,
that he fell silent for decades,
just sulking, seeking comfort in his cooking,
and he never quite recovered,
although he was wealthiest in music history
by his overwhelming opera successes.
The disaster that so brought him down
was the demission of his mother.
She was everything to him,
and no disastrous loss of love in music history
was so completely devastating
as Rossini's loss of his beloved mother.
He fell silent, that most diligent of opera composers,
that most energetic and efficient pioneer of opera;
and finally, when he was old and dying,
he produced some aftermath, some sacred music,
which he called his 'old age sins',
still rather paralyzed by his unending sorrow
but at least an effort to in some poor way
produce some requiems for his mother.

Franz Liszt – he fucked them all

A handsome man and brilliant pianist,
who no Parisian lady could resist,
and thus his entire career
was mainly executed between sheets.
Alas, they were an endless lot,
the mistress of king Louis of Bavaria,
that notorious dancer Lola Montez,
poor Marie d'Agoult,
with whom he had three children,
which he never cared for much,
so two of them were lost and died,
while only Cosima, his daughter,
lived to be the second wife of Wagner,
after he had robbed her from his friend,
her actual husband the conductor Hans von Bülow.
And the other mistresses of Liszt?
With age he had some problems
being struck by some bad conscience
and thus turned to Church to be a priest,
but as a Catholic abbé he still could not resist
the lovely ladies that came into his confessional,
and Olga Janina, his most notorious
and his final public mistress
ruthlessly exposed him as the fraud he was,
a parody of sanctimoniousness
who never could refrain from love.
And was it then a crime?
Of course not – just pathetic,
for his efforts to maintain his vanity
as lover even in his old age as a priest.

The most romantic hero – the curse of Manfred

The curse of Manfred was not one but many.
Grieving desperately over his deceased love,
whose death he might have caused, –
but we shall never know it,
nor did he ever know for sure himself, –
he went up high into the mountains
where he met his fate, a witch,
who cursed him with insomnia forever
and to age most bitterly and prematurely
to at best die old already as a young man.
Devils tortured him and dragged him down
like as if he was a Saint Anthony,
while at the same time others
worked for his redemption.
Lord Byron wrote the drama
but could never solve the problem,
dying prematurely as a young man
aged beyond his age as far too old to live.
Both Schumann and Tchaikovsky wrote the scores
and followed him in dying
far too old and far too early.

Yearning

My love is still beyond the clouds
in hiding for her comfort
undisturbed by vanity
immersed in dreams of beauty
well protected by idealism,
but far away and beyond reach.
How shall I reach her?
If the gentle touch of tender dreams
are not enough to wake her up,
the only method left is yearning,
and if you yearn sincerely enough,
no love in all the world
can fail to hear and answer
that most heartfelt of all prayers.

The disastrous love life of Tchaikovsky

The wife, to start with, proved impossible
by being of all wives the most disastrous possible,
and after the traumatical divorce,
including his own suicidal effort,
a disastrous failure even that,
she had a number of promiscuous lovers
and had children with them all
but cared for none of them,
disposing of them into orphanages.
He was saved by that wise lady Frau von Meck,
who graciously provided him with a life pension,
which allowed him to produce for twenty years
the most enjoyable melodic music of the time,
including the world's finest ballet music.
Unfortunately, after twenty years
she tired of him and disrupted the connection,
and again he was abandoned to disaster.
He was persecuted by a demon all his life,
an irresistible homosexuality,
which ultimately ruined him:
he fell in love with some young prince
related with the Czar, a dangerous connection,
and the prince's father would not have it.

He was summoned to a secret trial
of the highest aristocracy
and there condemned to death,
and he was ordered to commit it on his own
or even have his honour devastated.
That was Oscar Wilde in Russian style –
instead of public scandal and dishonour
death by your own hand and reputation saved,
which, you must give credit to the Russians,
they did save indeed - there never was in Russia
a composer more extolled and honoured
and with right – there is no music
more sincere in agonizing beauty and profundity.

Wagner's scandals

From a human point of view,
his life was only scandals.
As a politic activist,
he just about made enemies with everyone.
His marriage was a failure,
so the only thing he did in it
was to deceive her,
looking constantly for other women,
choosing only married ones,
as if they were the only proper challenge.
Thus he tried assiduously and desperately
with Mathilde Wesendonck
and wrote the whole of "Tristan" in the process,
but she was a wise and virtuous lady
who preferred her husband.
Wagner took instead the wife
of his best friend and favourite conductor,
Hans von Bülow, Cosima, the daughter of Franz Liszt,
his only child, and twenty-four years younger
than her second husband, already a mother of two children,
but she managed well, surviving Wagner 47 years.
Of course, von Bülow was enraged
and never could forgive him
but committed the mistake of venting all his ire
not on Wagner but on his protector,
that fantastic King Louis II of Bavaria,
yet another victim of the opera composer's human ruthlessness,
who never quite got over Wagner's base misconduct
and betrayal of his friends,
his favourite conductor, and his sponsor,
who lost all the trust of his Bavarian people
and became an isolated victim of delusion.
Wagner didn't care. He just went on
his ruthless ways, abusing Jews in music,
sacrificing anyone who came into his path
and used them all or just abused them.
After him came Nazism
making him a god and idol of their madness.
Nietzsche was another of his victims.

What about his music, then?
Extremely pompous and bombastic,
presumptuos and pretentious,

and his opera librettos are distortions
of what could have been good stories,
but occasionally now and then
there are some things that you could listen to.

My love

With risk to constantly repeat myself
I ask you once again most beggarly
to hide in your delightful custody,
escaping from this sordid tardy world
into your love of endless comfort,
seeking my protection in the jungle of your hair,
the supreme relief from any anguish
and the only love for me that lasts.
Although our love is utterly impossible,
forbidden socially and exiled to extremes,
it is the only love for me and so remains,
as I will never give you up, unmask you
or betray you, but keep you the best of secrets
locked up in the safe of my eternal love.

Delirium

Tying up ourselves into a knot
of indissoluble and perfect love
like under laws of voluntary tyranny,
committed hopelessly to never let each other go,
is not a bondage of encumberment and obligation
but more like the utmost duty free proceedings
from the pangs of hard bound, energetic love
to perfect liberation and release of freedom.
There is but one question that remains:
Can we love each other more than this?
Is there a possibility of perfect ecstasy to be transcended?
We don't know the answer,
but at least we can make some considerable quest for it,
and if the answer finally is positive,
so much the better then for us,
enabled to congenially proceed forever.

The human soul

Never let me turn to dust,
to any solid matter,
nor must anyone
with spirits born to soar.
The flame of creativity
can never be defined nor earthed,
the body instruments of sensual perception
is a language of misunderstandings,
while the feelings only tell the truth.
So never make me solid,
never try to pin me down
by making me definable,
for I will but defy all definition
being what I am,
a soul that never can be ordinated
to fit in; but must remain
perpetually free forever
to survive at all.

Satisfaction

Sometimes I wonder
if you really are material,
my most beloved,
too good to be true
and truer still than all reality,
transcending all the possibilities
of the remotest fantasy
exceeding all imagination.
Most amazing of it all
is that it seems I cannot lose you,
that I found you to remain within you
like I never can get rid of you.
Our love is constantly expanding;
so let's just allow it to continue
growing ever more in beauty
in a universal triumph
of perfection, joy and satisfaction.

Exhilaration

Never let it cease to grow,
the beauty of this wealth of yours,
this comfort of your richness,
this abundance of your generosity
and possibility of limitless expansion,
the symbol and manifestation of our perfect love,

this splendour of your natural and sparkling life,
this gorgeous mass of millions
of your brilliant effervescent hair,
that keeps me bound in admiration
and intoxicated by your beauty,
dumbfounded and aghast, completely fallen
down in total weakness to this miracle
of beauty ever more increasing.
Keep it up, I pray, and never let it down,
and so shall I keep up my oath
to never let you down.

All at sea

The labyrinth of our love
is without end,
and the entrance is long since gone,
there never was a way back,
only forwards
to an unknown destination,
and it is constantly more difficult
to find our way
and any orientation.
It's the endless sea
where all the coasts have long since disappeared,
and we are sailing freely and at random
with our eye glued to a visible and yet unvisible horizon,
and the only certain thing about our voyage
is that this immensity of terrible unfathomableness
is all of love and inextinguishable.
We are comfortable therefore,
unable to sink and drown,
since we long since
are drowned and overwhelmed and sunk already.

Looking back

When passion won me over
it was not voluntarily
that I gave up my self-respect
and purity of living
for the doubtful chaos of indulgence,
but I never have regretted it,
since no one came to harm,
since health did never suffer
and since the result
by the grace of Aphrodite
seemed to only be increasing beauty.
What manifestation can be finer?
If but life and beauty grows in faring well,
I would suggest that in this context only
it would be permitted and allowed
for the result and end to justify the means.

Considering you

Your touch is light,
a life-inspiring force and power
keeping you awake forever

for the truest light of all,
enlightening all beauty
and increasing it perpetually
by your mere existence,
highest of all powers,
crowning all creation
by the strangest of phenomena,
that fantastic magic,
lightest of all lightness
and the highest light of all,
and that is you, my love.

Irrepressible beauty

The beauty of your soul
transcends reality
to prove our senses wrong
and all reality a senseless lie
for us to fool around with
and beguile ourselves to death,
which, also part of our reality,
is just another bothersome deception;
while the soul's eye only knows the truth,
which usually appears too good
to be believed in,
wherefore we repress it;
but I'll never be deceived by beauty,
recognizing it to worship
in whatever form it takes,
emerging and appearing everywhere,
but truest in the human soul,
which, when granted our attention,
outshines all the beauty
even of reality.

The mystery of true love

It's difficult to say how much I love you
since there are no limits to capacities
that can not even be defined,
since love is not just boundless in itself
but also in its unsurveyable dimensions.
Therefore mute love is much more expressive

than what any words can tell
or actions can express,
while poetry alone is capable
of nearing something of the truth
about true love and how it works.
It can not bring much satisfaction, though,
but only veil it in cocoons of mystery
that, if the love is true, can never be unveiled again.

Your invitation

Your welcome was an opening
unto a better world of love
instead of vice, perversion and addiction,
and from darkness to the light of beauty,
from blind alleys down the drain of hopelessness
to just the opposite, the warmth of human nature.
How could I say no?
It was an offer in a lifetime
that could never be refused,
and all my hesitation and misgivings
were about that it seemed too good to be true;
and yet, there never was a truer truth
than that frail heart so full of love you offered.
I shall be as true to you as I have been
so far, as I have never failed you,
and my hope is, that I never shall be able to.

Getting through

The silver linings of your hair
add only more intrigue and magic to your beauty,
testifying to your rich experience,
like too much suffering and dried up tears,
but for me are golden more than argentine.

There is no nobler beauty
when it is enhanced by wisdom
of maturity and deep experience
that adds profundity and honesty to love
to make it most imperishable.

That's the purpose of all practised love,
to make it more endurable
by the ordeals of dire straits
leading to the fruits of heaven
of the final beauty of experience.

Business as usual

What is it in our love
that makes it so intriguing
and excruciatingly so tantalizing
in its languid process
of continuing forever
without ever reaching a fulfilment?

Can two virgins love each other
and maintain virginity
as their fulfilment?

That's the rebus of our fateful tale
that we in vain seek answers to
in helpless stumbling in the darkness
of the turmoil of our love
that we can not control ourselves
but only get more lost in.

Never mind, we have endured before,
two years of crises in our love
have not extinguished it,
it is as young and fresh
as when it first became a fact;
so let me guess, that we will just
go on and carry on as usual.

Faith

Let me soar away with you
on golden wings of blue
forever in my faithful love of you
to leave all that which we've gone through
to ever stick to what is true,
which only is my love of you.
How could you ever doubt my faithfulness,

as if you would prefer your loneliness
to all your lover's usefulness,
while I could never bother less
to cure your boredom's emptiness
with raving jealous silliness,
since all I care for is to stick to you,
my only perfect love, in endlessness.

Good morning mitigation

There is no good morning without you,
the first thought entering my mind
as I wake up each morning
to a new day full of battles,
trials, tribulations and ordeals,
while you, my solace, are my bandage,
dressing up my wounds
each night of love l, as I come bleeding
home after the day's defeats,
a wounded soldier lost in life.
Will this sore suffering existence ever heal?
I doubt it, but as you are there
each night and morning dressing up my wounds
at least there is some hope, relief and mitigation.

The trouble with muses

No matter how much you associate with her,
no matter how much you depend on her
and love her to the point of adoration,
you can not have sex with her.
She is for worship, inspiration
and idealization only,
or she will not work.
And even if you try to trouble her
with personal relationships
and sexual advances, love ambitions
and possession of herself,
she will just slip away
and gracefully continue as a muse
for metaphysical and spiritual approach
and only work and business use.
Let's be content with that,
as long as we may go on having her.

My father

A recent visit to my father's hometown of Åbo in Finland,
brought back his personality to me.

Going down old memory lane,
treading ancient streets of long ago,
where my father spent his boyhood
growing up in humble circumstances,
yet ideal under the circumstances,
suddenly his personality and image
grows so real and vivid,
as the best of friends,
with all his matchless sense of humour
and so full of powerful constructive energy
that he could never stop at anything
but constantly go on for wider journeys; –
Father, suddenly you are much closer
than you ever were alive,
as if the zone of timelessness
existed mainly to maintain and compensate
that closeness which could never reach perfection
in our mortal limitations.
You are there and still alive forever,
which I thankfully will testify,
remembering your face
that ever will continue shining in my memory
with all your generosity and kindness
in my mind forever.

From a letter to a friend

I have struggled with the problem all my life. Most people who encounter it just let it be and don't bother about it, trying to ignore and repress it. In my case (as maybe in yours) it was instead accentuated by my life as a musician - it became more acute, as you became more exposed and vulnerable.

An effort to define the problem: you can't reach to other people, because they don't share your awareness and your ideals, because they can't see them. Therefore you find yourself alone, dreaming about those ideal possibilities you can't have realized, like, in your case, a flowing social life of some natural intensity and spirituality. You feel isolated with your idealism, and the risk is to become lonely, especially here in Sweden.

My only way of solving the problem was to accept the situation, accept the fact that almost everyone around you was ignorant and could not share your ideals or understand them, to instead build that ideal world within your own space and universe, that is, escape into creation. I think it's actually the only way to make the insufferable problem bearable - to make the best of a bad bargain, and to love in spite of all. To go on "arrabbiarsi" about it, get embittered about it and indulge in the frustration will only make it worse and is no way out. At best, you'll find temporary relief but no solution. And wherever you are, wherever you live, you will encounter the same problem, in different forms, just because of your own uniqueness in your idealism.

Creativity is the best therapy for any artist out of any problem and dilemma, and I am afraid that's the only one.

Spiritual relationships

To love is all
and can be constantly accomplished
with some everlasting faith and satisfaction
only spiritually, that is after death
or telepathically between living beings,
but in physical and sexual contact – never,
except only during separation,
when the sensual presence is exceeded
by the spiritual awareness.
This is difficult to understand
except by long and suffering experience,
but eventually all lovers will arrive
at this conclusion, that the spiritual love
is actually the only love there is
or, anyway, the only love that lasts.

The ultimate perfection

That divinest ecstasy
of the extreme release
into the blinding light of joy
transcending all mortality
that lovers feel in moments of supremest truth
and in the ultimate perfection sought by Yoga,
and which also epileptics feel and see
before they cross beyond all consciousness

and which is maybe best defined
as the relinquishment of self
emerging with the universal consciousness,
is all the happiness you need in life
to be aware of your control of destiny
and which actually is only
just to be in love.

The Cruelty of Closed Doors

a thought

To close a door to anyone who seeks you,
to refuse communication,
to let down and leave to perish,
like in Burma,
where the Junta stops all foreign aid,
or like in China,
where the only help allowed is the Chinese,
which does not work,
is out of nature and unhuman
in a silent cruelty
which actually is worse than open cruelty,
like burying someone alive instead of killing him first.
And yet, that silent cruelty
is the most common cruelty of all,
as refusing beggars every day,
ignoring tragedies,
and closing eyes to look the other way
when some injustice is committed.
So, when this unhuman cruelty appears so very common,
why then bother about it at all?
Unfortunately, the more it is permitted to go on,
the more a bother it becomes.

In a state of shock...

The last breath of a poet
is like a wind that nothing can resist
amounting to a thunderstorm
that never will stop whirling
in men's hearts and ladies' souls
of anyone who got in touch

with such a downright honest fellow
who dared to call himself
the last romantic hero.
Actually he rather was the first
of all romantic heros here in Poetbay
introducing some new sort of a romantic hero
that, like all the previous and immortal ones,
will surely never vanish.
The first and last is never there,
but you shall always be both here and there among us
as our paragon romantic hero.

Thanks, Mike, for all your golden grace of Poetbay.

The last romantic hero

to Mike Meddings, 1941-2008(?)

A humble fisherman
collecting water colours,
that was all,
until he suddenly
already in his sixties
started writing poems,
introducing a new spirit
of reborn idealism and chivalry
and boiling over with enthusiasm
to carry with him a whole bunch
of startling talents of ebullient poetry.
He touched me often with his cordial honesty
of true appreciation, friendship and intimacy,
and I believe so touched us all
with some kind of inspiring spell
of irresistible romanticism
compelling us to love
and feel at home with him in Camelot.
Thanks, Mike, for all you did for us
by simply being here,
and we shall never let you go.

Clouds in a cold weather

My love can never sober up
but still can only work as sober.
Our greatest lover has abruptly been bereft us,
but still, love has to remain,
and being gone, it still has to go on.
No matter how much I do love you,
I can never reach you,
and each moment when I have you,
I am only losing you,
your breath is failing you,
and I am at a loss
for all the irresistibility of our love
that never seems to be allowed us.
Summer's getting cold by icy winds,
and clouds obscure the sun
that never is allowed to warmly shine on us.
But what can we do,
when love so cruelly is so consistently denied us?
There is only one thing we can do,
which we must do and never can stop doing,
which is just to go on loving
and to love the more in spite of all.

Broken wings

to the family

When lovers die
in brutal interruption
in the very moment
when their happiness began,
you grow most fearful
and concerned about your own relationships
and hesitate to use your wings
when swans have broken theirs.
The air is dominated by despair
as everyone is shaken up by the injustice,
while the worst thing is
that no one is to blame.
You can't blame love
for making this our tragedy the worse,
you can't blame God or fate

whose innocence of silence
keep them out of reach,
and least of all you can blame any person,
while you feel responsible
for having been initiated
in this miracle of love and beauty.
No one could imagine
the remotest possibility of an archangel
suddenly to be demissioned,
and it hurts us all
in our profoundest love
and hits unfairly every heart
that Michael's shared his love with.
How can anyone love any more
when such a love was so rewarded
with such beastly outrageous injustice?
That's our problem and our suffering,
the worst part of it being
that we have to carry it ourselves
without the aid of Michael.

Exhaustion

Overworked and overwrought,
I miss those days when energy was infinite,
when we could love outrageously without an end,
when work was but a game that always would succeed,
when childhood never left us,
and the strength of youth seemed everlasting.
Pains and aches have overtaken us,
and losses have reduced our morals
to recurrent desperation and dejection,
wishing you were there with all the dead.
Can love be found still in this darkness?
We are groping blindly
trying to restore our intrepidity
but find it necessarily replaced by sad humility.
The loss of spirit weakens more than any overstrain,
and to be comforted by simply longing
is not enough and no good substitute.
Instead the hollowness grows deeper.
How can love survive?
That is the question
ever put with more amazement,
but the fact is, that it does.

The brutality of reality

No comfort, I am afraid, while penetrating reality at least might secure some detachment from its worst aspects...

Going down the field of roses,
all I find is tears of bleeding hearts
of thorns, that have got stuck therein,
and wounds of hearts will never heal
but eventually fade out in languishment,
since it is only human to tire of exertions.
The cruelty of life is the supreme remorselessness,
for there is no placation of reality
that just keeps running people over,
resulting only in the protest of infinity
of the so unjustly suffering individual,
whose one and only question to the godhead,
"Why me?" invariably will be unanswered.
They say that Job was finally rewarded
by the restoration of his family,
but that is as convincing
as an artificial happy end
to a superficial movie.
The reality is always there
in inescapable brutality
of life and death and ruthless interruption
of all love and harmony and happiness,
while love is no more than a brief relief
of just a temporary passing moment.

The Glimpse

a glimpse of a comeback...

You entered just to show yourself
and then turned back around and went,
as if the only meaning of your presence
was to show that you existed
in your total love and beauty,
giving just a glimpse of the ideal,
as if it was a dream of perfect love
to just appear and vanish instantly;
and yet, that glimpse was quite enough
for love to enter and to last eternally,

its mere existence being evidence enough
in just one second's visibility
to last forever and a lifetime.

Guidelines

How can love be mortal
when it is timelessness itself?
True lovers live forever
and survive their deaths with eloquence
and only get the better of it,
love being such a medicine
that kills mortality.
There is but one confusion, then, in love,
and that is to believe you are confused
when actually the labyrinth of love
can only lead you right.
The only difficulty is to stick to it,
maintain the truth and keep the course
in being true to the direction
of your conscience, faith and destiny,
and then you never can go wrong.

Musical observation

When sorrows cloud your eyes
and you can't see beyond darkness,
there is something still to feel
if even all your senses are shut down,
since all the human soul consists of
is just oversensitivity
that never must be silenced or shut down;
for feelings are life's definitie necessities
without which you can't love or live.
That sensitivity is brought to some acuteness
by the sense and sensitivity for music,
a perfect ear discerning any smudge
disturbing the ethereal harmony and order.
Over-sensitivity is therefore not to be disdained
but rather cultivated and respected
as the very essence of a living soul
more capable of feelings, sight and hearing
than all lying senses of a mortal body.

Hangovers

My love keeps hanging over me
like a dark angel impregnated in my mind
to stay there just to torture me forever
when we fail to be together.
Thus is love as abstinence
a worse more crucial pain and suffering
than any terribly unhappy love can be,
for love will always get you, never leave you
 and get worse during the years,
as memories amass as losses
and the present offers less than yesterday.
The comfort is, that you, as long as you keep suffering,
will go on being activated as a lover;
and as long as there is love,
there is the hope and contact of eternity.

Bleeding hearts forever

There are wounds that never heal,
humiliations that are never overcome
and losses that can never be restored,
transforming human beings to lost souls,
their hearts wide open bleeding on forever.
There are tears that never can be stopped
that will gush on in ever wider rivers
overwhelming our lost mankind in their grief,
and there are souls that only hurt forever,
which is all there is to their existence.
Pity and compassion is the only thing that helps,
a humble temporary small relief,
which makes it so important why that also
has to be unstoppable and overwhelming in eternity.

Black madonna

to a friend

Stormy weather tears your heart apart
from blazing tempests of compassion
ruining the lives of faithful lovers
leaving them in tatters

in a life of shambles,
but even in the darkest hell
there is no total darkness,
and no one can convince me
of the hopelessness of being damned in Hell,
since even Virgil leading Dante there
found their way out the back door
to ascend with love forever
to the stars and beyond.
Maybe love must perish and be buried
to survive the better
and to prove itself of its true stuff
of only everlasting truth and beauty
that even the most lost and forlorn cases
somehow also have to have a share of.

Crisis

You never cease to gloriously seduce me
only by your mere existence,
which is irresistible to infinite extension,
turning me invariably most rapturously on
to never evermore leave you in peace,
as you are impregnated in my being
to remain there stuck in love forever,
and I simply can't object
but rather wallow in the mere existence of it,
as you ever are reborn again,
my constant love, with new seductions.
Let it thus remain
and gloriously go on forever,
our vainglorious sparkling everlasting love,
a Phoenix in miraculous variation,
ever stuck in crisis to get ever born anew.

The Song of Love

So tenderly the heart aches ring
of losses and of love in spring
that cannot be regained but still remains
as ancient melodies that never can be silenced,
ringing out in sharp and melancholy strains
that hurts forever but remains

of love and tenderness nevertheless
in piercing shrieks that never can be heard
but only heartfeltly perceived
as echos of the universe
resounding ever more alarmingly
in more acute and ever growing presence.
Love is the sharpest melody in history
that ever played unsilenceably louder
but with no one ever really hearing it.

Delightful bondage

the workoholic's bliss

How could I complain?
Addictions are not always evil
but can actually be quite the contrary,
especially if they are only beneficial,
making you feel good,
improved in health and disciplined
and kept away from pitfalls.
Thus am I a slave to beauty,
working for her day and night
and suffering to get more worthy of her,
and a smile is all I need
from her impeccability and muse's grace
to go on struggling infinitely
for the permanence and continuity of love.
Of course it hurts,
and it of course demands some sacrifice,
but I am only happy
as long as I can believe that it is worth it.

Displaced persons

a tribute to "the Fountain House", or, "The International Center for Clubhouse Development" (ICCD), 425 West 47th Street, New York, now an international network with centers practically everywhere and advisor to the UN (ECOSOC unit)

Their number are increasing,
all those victims,
not only of society,

but more and more of circumstances
of no accountability for anyone.
They drift along, get lost,
but there is always somewhere
someone waiting for them,
even in your utmost loneliness
you never are alone,
and even if you are,
the crowds of ghosts and memories
are always there reminding you
that you can never separate from life
and least of all by suicide.
There is a fountainhead
that never stops to flow
and keep the current running
of the ever vitally expanding life,
and even if you feel unique about your fate,
you can be certain there are others sharing it.
The problem is, you never are yourself,
but all the life in all the universe
depends on you, for you are part of it.

The sweetness of your love...

The sweetness of your love
is in its pure simplicity
like some angelic dream
out of this world
and still as natural
in all sincerity
that I refuse to wake up
from its delicate reality
of only sweetest dreams
more real and actual
than anything in this surrealistic world.
So let me keep it
to administer it richly
to eternalize and multiply it
for the only reason of the truth of it
although no one can be convinced
except the actual lovers.

The colour of your hair

The colour of the depth of your unfathomable hair
is like the sky towards its outer limits
beyond all the lightyears of our knowledge,
while your presence is enough to fill the sky
not just with beauty but with overwhelming grace
so richly manifested in not just the lustre of your hair,
its streaming beauty overflowing not the Amazon alone
but even all the oceans in its glory;
but also and the more in your whole being
which is only love in so outstanding quality
that any richness can not match it.
So let us make love forever
in the glory of the beauty of our whole existence,
never tiring of wasting this most holy energy.

Retaliation

Love always pays,
and losses will increase it only,
always doubling, never losing,
being the most elementary characteristic
nucleus and fundamental core of life,
and actually the only matter
that can never be defeated,
lost, bereft or turned to nothing,
since the more you give of it,
the more it always will come back
in one form or another.
Even if they die,
it is impossible for lovers to be losers,
since the more they lose,
by wasting or by losses brought by destiny,
the more immortal and continuous
love simply will turn out to be,
phenomenally overcoming any death
since it is life itself
that simply can't exist without expanding.

The engagement

I am engaged in you
and can not help it,
and I hope that this engagement
will go on forever,
although there are minefields
all along the way
of constant separations,
travels and disruptions,
loss of contact and what more;
while only the engagement
on my part in you
remains inviolably stable,
and it's an engagement of that kind
that's well worth hoping for
that never should be broken.

OCTOBER HARVEST FIRST PART.